Adventurer

THE LIFE AND TIMES OF
GIACOMO CASANOVA

Leo Damrosch

Yale UNIVERSITY PRESS

New Haven and London

Published with assistance from the Annie Burr Lewis Fund
and the Louis Stern Memorial Fund.

Yale University Press books may be purchased in quantity for educational,
business, or promotional use. For information, please e-mail
sales.press@yale.edu (U.S. office) or sales@yaleup.co.uk (U.K. office).

Set in Adobe Garamond type by Integrated Publishing Solutions.
Printed in the United Kingdom.

Library of Congress Control Number: 2021949604
ISBN 978-0-300-24828-9 (hardcover : alk. paper)

A catalogue record for this book is available from the British Library.

This paper meets the requirements of ANSI/NISO Z39.48-1992
(Permanence of Paper).

10 9 8 7 6 5 4 3 2 1

MIX
Paper from
responsible sources
FSC
www.fsc.org   FSC® C013056

Contents

Acknowledgments

I owe special thanks to three people above all. Tina Bennett became my agent twenty years ago when I had never published anything for general readers; with each of the six books that ensued she has inspired and encouraged me, and sustained me with her rock-solid support. Jennifer Banks, my editor at Yale University Press, for this and three previous books, has an ideal combination of intelligence, imagination, and wisdom, helping each of them to find its best form, and afterward presiding over a superb production team. And my wife, Joyce Van Dyke, brings a fellow writer's insight to everything I write. Her advice has been essential in developing each project, she has improved every page and every chapter with a keen critical eye, and her perspective as a playwright has been invaluable in creating narrative energy and flow.

Finally, this book is appearing at a cultural moment when the story of a notorious seducer needs to be addressed frankly and critically. For helping to conceptualize and ponder the issues involved, I am deeply grateful to these gifted advisers.

The Challenge of Casanova

Everyone knows that Casanova was a seducer. He belongs to that rare company of mortals whose personal names have floated free from history, and we know what a Casanova is even if we know nothing about the man who bore that name. He was Giacomo Casanova, a gifted and complicated Venetian who lived from 1725 to 1798, and his story is a fascinating one. But although he was more than his myth, the myth is grounded in truth. His career as a seducer, already notorious in his own time, is often disturbing and sometimes very dark. It challenges any reader today, and still more it challenges a biographer. Casanova aspired to a life of freedom from restraints—but freedom at whose expense?

There have been a number of biographies of Casanova, but the time is overdue for a biography of a different kind. He was the first to tell his own story, in a massive autobiography entitled *Histoire de Ma Vie*. Fluent in French, he wrote in that language since unlike Italian it was understood throughout Europe. The word *histoire* can mean "story" as well as "history," and a story it certainly is. Previous biographers have tended to retell it as he told it, adopting his own point of view with only occasional queries. Some have betrayed a vicarious investment in his tales of seduction, just as many readers clearly have; it's interesting that men with great political power, such as Winston Churchill and François Mitterrand, have been especially warm admirers of Casanova.

In fiction such a character might be a charming rogue, but in real life Casanova's behavior was often far from charming, and this is evident even when all we have to go on is his own narrative. In 2006 Judith Summers published a book entitled *Casanova's Women: The Great Seducer and the Women He Loved*. In describing a dozen of his relationships over the years, she emphasizes his interest in the individuality of his partners: "Just as Casanova the lover once kissed their dewy skin with breathless abandon, Casanova the writer breathes life into their shadows." But at one point she calls him, almost in passing, "a seducer who, if he was operating today, might well be in prison for breach of promise, incest, fraud, pedophilia, grievous bodily harm, and rape." That shocking catalogue is entirely true, and will be addressed frankly throughout this book.[1]

Proud of being a bad boy, Casanova was self-serving in every aspect of his life, not just the sexual, but the erotic encounters in the *Histoire* vary greatly. Sometimes his behavior was abusive in ways that are not just disturbing today, but would have seemed disturbing to many people in his own day. At other times he convincingly describes experiences of deep mutual enjoyment.

Casanova did value his partners' individuality, and he genuinely wanted to share mutual pleasure with them. But the balance of power was always unequal, and every one of his relationships was short-lived—sometimes only a single encounter, and never lasting more than a couple of months. Not until very late in life did he live with a woman for more than a brief time. And although he occasionally considered marriage, or claims he did, he made sure that it never happened.

With only two or three of his many partners—and he names over a hundred—was Casanova really what most people consider "in love." What he calls "love" usually began with excited infatuation, and sometimes it developed into passion, but it always burned out fast. The psychoanalyst Lydia Flem claims, "There is not a trace of misogyny in Casanova; in the great book of life, women are his masters." But if his technique of seduction sometimes gave women a feeling of power, that feeling never lasted.[2]

To hear him tell it, desire was always mutual and relationships always ended amicably. But even in his own telling, it's obvious that some women got involved with him against their better judgment, and were regretful or bitter afterward. Even if relationships did end amicably, what would that mean? Casanova saw it as evidence of his generosity of spirit, but it can also be seen as invincible narcissism. The critic François Roustang provides an insight that goes much deeper than Casanova's rationalizations: "He is incapable of making the women he deceives suffer—not so much for their sakes as for his own, because he cannot stand the thought that they might no longer love him. Each breakup must result in happiness for the other, so that he can preserve all of his self-esteem and lightheartedness." But as another writer says dryly, "He was always in love with his prey."[3]

In reality, Casanova's treatment of women was manipulative. He had power over them, he knew it, and he enjoyed exploiting it. He hardly ever acknowledges the power imbalance between women and men, but once in an essay he does mention "our despotism" over women. That seems to mean the social and legal power over women that "we"—the male sex—take for granted.[4]

Women in the eighteenth century were subjected to social and legal constraints that Casanova never was. Some with whom he got involved were adventurers like himself, traveling opportunistically under assumed names and enjoying their independence. But most were in no position to move on freely, as he always did, after an affair came to an end. They were girls still living with their families, or wives who were willing to risk a brief holiday from marriage. Since respectable marriages were arranged by families for financial considerations, with little regard for the desires of the spouses, the numerous wives with whom Casanova slept may have found him romantically as well as erotically exciting. He says they did, and there is probably some truth to that. But when he moved on they couldn't, and didn't.

There were prostitutes, too, sometimes in upscale brothels, sometimes encountered casually. Like most men, Casanova didn't reflect about why they were reduced to supporting themselves in that way; he simply took their existence for granted. Many were orphans with no other means of survival, and some were girls whose impoverished parents had literally sold them into prostitution. He also had a number of encounters with girls whose parents, lacking other sources of income, were openly pimping them out, though he usually paid them with "presents" rather than cash.

Regardless of social class, all women had to fear pregnancy at a time when there was hardly any birth control. Condoms existed but were crude and unpleasant, and Casanova seldom used them. According to researchers, the only other method in Europe at the time was coitus interruptus, which was far from infallible. Casanova sometimes practiced that, but not often, since he regarded it as inadequate enjoyment. In either case, a woman had to trust the man; birth control was up to him. And if it failed, she bore the consequences.[5]

Abortion doesn't enter into Casanova's story, and in fact he was opposed to it, since he knew that the herbal concoctions used to provoke it were frighteningly dangerous. But he did get a number of women pregnant, and because his relationships were short-lived, he hardly ever knew about it unless he ran into them years later. Several times he met a son or daughter he never knew he had, but only once did he form any sort of relationship with the child. On one occasion, in Paris, he did know that he had gotten a young girl pregnant, and he arranged to have the infant consigned to a foundling home. That was quite common at the time, but by no means free from ethical blame. Rousseau did it as a young man, and struggled in vain to explain himself when the story became public years later.

We do have one remarkable work by Casanova—but only one—that expresses progressive views about sexuality. In his late forties he spent some time in Bologna, where a pair of anatomy professors claimed to have proved that feminine thought originates in the uterus, and is therefore irrational and literally hysterical ("uterus" is *hystera* in Greek). Casanova published a response in Italian with the Latin title *Lana Caprina*. That comes from Horace, his favorite classical poet, and means "goat's wool"—something pointless or valueless. He argued, just as Mary Wollstonecraft would argue two decades later in *Vindication of the Rights of Woman*, that any differences between the sexes are due entirely to education and social conditioning. And after all, "Why incriminate the uterus in women any more than the sperm in men?"[6]

In this argument, Casanova was responding to a contemporary medical controversy. Historians have traced a transition from a "one-sex" to a "two-sex" model for understanding gender. During the Renaissance it was believed that men and women had very much the same sexual feelings, and that their sexual organs were variants of a single kind. By the end of the eighteenth century, however, writers insisted on a radical difference between the active male and the passive female, with two different kinds of bodies rather than one. The two-sex model seems to have been taken over from medical theory as a reaction against political theories of equality. It was seized upon as evidence that women were intrinsically unequal, and it led to the Victorian ideal of asexual "womanhood."[7]

But Casanova's position was simultaneously progressive and old-fashioned. In the older view women had been regarded as actively sexual beings. That was acknowledged in Renaissance medical writing: it was believed that the female orgasm was essential to conception. Casanova didn't want conception, but he did want his partners to experience the same pleasure that he did. In that respect, at least, he held an egalitarian view of sex. But only in that respect. Most men were embedded—he might have said trapped—in conventional obligations and expectations. Women were still less free.

The mutually gratifying encounters helped him to write eloquently about sexual experience in a way that was unique in his own time and has rarely been equaled. Eighteenth-century pornography is explicit, but conventional and repetitive, and its female characters are nothing more than fantasy objects. Some serious authors—Henry Fielding, for instance—probably could have described the kinds of experiences that Casanova evokes, but since they were writing for publication they had to confine themselves to tactful hints.

Even private writing from the time falls far short of Casanova's subtlety. When James Boswell's diary was discovered in the twentieth century and published as *London Journal 1762–1763,* it created a sensation by its frankly recorded sexual encounters, but most are perfunctory episodes with prostitutes. When Boswell does try to bring a sexual relationship to life, he is reduced to a stream of clichés—"sweet delirium," "snowy arms," "amorous dalliance," "luscious feast," "godlike vigour," "supreme rapture." Casanova constantly found effective language to recreate each new shared experience.[8]

Recently a team of Canadian psychologists collaborated on an exploration of the meaning of "great sex." The characteristics of truly satisfying sex that they identify are ones that we see described again and again in Casanova's writing. These include being fully present in the moment, exceptional communication, risk-taking, exploration, a feeling of union or even identity between partners, and an experience of transcendence. Casanova testifies joyously to this fullness of experience.[9]

The authors of the study quote an informant as saying, "The room could be on fire and I probably wouldn't even notice." In one of Casanova's early encounters, he and a married woman finish making love in a garden just moments before her mother and husband arrive. Later on he asks her what she would have done if they had been caught in the act. "Nothing," she replies. "Don't you understand that in those divine moments, one is nothing but in love? Can you believe you weren't possessing me entirely?"[10]

Casanova often uses religious language to describe those "divine moments" of transcendence. As one writer says, his aim is not to defile the sacred but "to render voluptuousness sacred."[11]

Still, the divine moments were only occasional, and there were many more of the other kind. Laurence Bergreen declares in his biography of Casanova, "Each love affair was, for him, a meeting of the mind and spirit, a glimpse of eternity and ecstasy." That's highly romanticized, not to say sanitized. Most of the encounters with women were opportunistic, and some were disturbingly exploitative. Casanova himself is frank about that.[12]

Although the *Histoire de Ma Vie* is full of stories of seductions, it is also about many things besides erotic encounters, and the breadth of experience that it recreates is invigorating. At various times Casanova was a university student, an apprentice priest, a naval officer, a theater violinist, an entrepreneur, a professional gambler, a practitioner of magic, a novelist, a spy, and a con man. He was also a voracious reader, and often spent time in libraries; a commentator speaks of "his almost carnal relationship with books." He saw himself as a rational intellectual, but like many of his contemporaries he had a strong interest in magic and the occult, and he took them more seriously than he wanted to admit. And he was a lover of fine cooking; over two hundred meals, often shared with lovers, are affectionately recalled in what has been described as his "gastrosexual journeying."[13]

Above all he was an adventurer, a type that was well known—indeed notorious—in eighteenth-century Europe. More than fifty "adventurers" of his time can still be identified by name, moving freely through society and exploiting it to their advantage, sometimes by ethical means and often not. They all knew each other, sometimes preying on each other and sometimes collaborating; in this book we will encounter a number of them repeatedly.

Adventurers were a true subculture, which overlapped with other subcultures that were important in Casanova's story but have not been adequately explored by previous biographers. He was a lifelong gambler, for example, and that was not just a recreation; it was a way of life. The Ridotto or casino in Venice played an important role in the public life of the city, and throughout Europe people gambled for money in private houses on social occasions. As a gambler, Casanova's mastery of card games gave him access to an aristocratic milieu that might otherwise have excluded him.

And his interest in magic is very much of his time; the occult was still taken seriously by many intelligent and educated people. We will hear often in this story about alchemy, Cabbala, and Rosicrucianism—the symbolic and mythical thinking that opposed the programmatic rationalism of Enlightenment thought. For Casanova it had real worldly advantages; his persuasive self-presentation as a magus won him some of his greatest social and financial successes, as well as some disasters.

In addition Casanova thought of himself as a libertine, in a countercultural tradition that asserted freedom of thought against restrictions of every kind, intellectual as well as moral. For a libertine, prohibitions against sexual transgression violated the instinctual promptings of "nature." Casanova often expressed that view. But once the old rules had been rejected, it was no longer obvious what limits there would be against vicious transgressiveness. The Marquis de Sade claimed to be simply following nature.

Casanova was strongly interested in contemporary thought, and prided himself on being a thinker in the style of the Enlightenment. The eighteenth century is often remembered as the Age of Reason, but that's true only of some of its theories. The Enlightenment was a movement rather than a unified program, and Casanova took some things from it but not others. Unlike the French philosophes, whose political theories were strongly reformist, his thinking was in many ways profoundly conservative. Even though he flouted conventional mores in his behavior, he thought of them as intrinsic to society. He admired aristocracy, did his best throughout his life to impersonate an aristocrat, and was appalled when the French Revolution swept away the Ancien Régime.

In the same way, Casanova supported established religion because it stabilized the social order, even though he privately disbelieved most of its doctrines. He briefly launched a career in the Catholic Church, yet he never showed the slightest indication of spirituality, and he relished the Church's institutional worldliness. Some of his most inventive sexual adventures were staged in churches.

As for the book in which Casanova recreated his experiences, the title he chose—*Histoire de Ma Vie*—was most unusual. The normal word was "memoirs," which meant recollections, often miscellaneous and with no story line. The word "autobiography" didn't exist until it was invented in the following century to satisfy a newly perceived need. His contemporary, Jean-Jacques Rousseau, wrote one of the first books of this new kind, published a decade before Casanova began his *Histoire*. Rousseau called his book *Confessions,* borrowing his title from Saint Augustine; but Casanova had no interest in confessing, much less in demanding, as Rousseau did, that readers grant him absolution. He thought of his life as a compelling story even as he was living it, and in the *Histoire de Ma Vie* he reshapes it as an engrossing narrative.

Though Casanova's attempts at plays and a novel were unsuccessful, he drew skillfully on literary techniques in the *Histoire*. At its best it has the narrative energy of a novel and the vivid scenes and dialogue of a drama. When it was first published three decades after his death, a reviewer said that no popular novel of adventure could offer "more diversified incidents, more novelistic invention, more surprising accidents of fortune, or liaisons richer in interest and entertainment, than you find in this truthful compendium of Casanova's."[14]

In getting to know Casanova through the *Histoire,* we also get to know an entire world that he knew intimately—one writer calls it *l'immenso cosmo casanoviano,* the vast cosmos of his life. Another describes "his perpetual tour of Europe," during which he covered something like 40,000 miles all told, on foot, in carriages, and occasionally in ships. In the single year 1760, he spent time in an almost incredible total of twenty-six cities. At various times he made extensive stays in France, England, Poland, Russia, Spain, and Constantinople. He revisited many places repeatedly over the years, and a map showing all of his travels would be an indecipherable mass of crisscrossing lines.[15]

This restlessness has been aptly called his *nomadismo,* and a friend in later life, the Prince de Ligne, compared him to the Wandering Jew. Of course that allusion was probably meant to carry an ironic charge. The Wandering Jew of legend taunted Christ on the way to the Crucifixion, and as punishment was condemned to walk the earth ceaselessly until the Second Coming. Casanova often hit the road not by choice, but because he had gotten into trouble and was forced or even commanded to leave town.[16]

"It is thanks to Casanova," the novelist and playwright Stefan Zweig wrote, "that we know so much of the daily life of the eighteenth century—of its balls, theaters, coffee houses, festivals, inns, dining halls, brothels, hunting parties, monasteries, nunneries, and fortresses. Thanks to him we know how people traveled, fed, gamed, danced, lived, loved, amused themselves; we know their manners and customs, their ways of speech. Superadded to this abundance of facts, to this wealth of practical details, we have a tumultuous assembly of human personalities, enough to fill twenty novels and to supply ten generations of novelists."[17]

Casanova was a brilliant storyteller, and there is recorded testimony from contemporaries that he held them spellbound with his vivid narratives. But that raises a fundamental challenge for biography. To what extent is the *Histoire de Ma Vie* a trustworthy autobiography, and to what extent is it really a series of tall tales? A recent commentator observes that estimating the proportion of fiction to fact is especially challenging "when the author was an acknowledged gambler, escaped criminal, practitioner of black magic, perpetual exile, and occasional spy."[18]

We do know that the *Histoire* was based on voluminous notes taken over the years, in notebooks that Casanova playfully called his *capitulaires.* The word (from ecclesiastical tradition) means a document divided into "chapters," and he thought of his life in just that way. After a memorable experience or conversation, he would often write down an extended account immediately afterward, and these records swelled to impressive proportions. When possible he deposited them in safe places, and at other times they traveled with him in his luggage; a customs inspector in Barcelona was startled to find that his trunk was two-thirds filled with notebooks. For many years he had no thought of eventual publication; his motive must have been much like Boswell's in his own journal: "In this way I shall preserve many things that would otherwise be lost in oblivion."[19]

Unfortunately Casanova seems to have thrown the notebooks away after using them for the *Histoire*. Still, it's important to know that they existed. His story is filled with so many details that if he had been relying on memory alone, it would be hard to put any trust in them.

But as for the perspective he brings to his story, that's another matter altogether. The *Histoire* would never have existed if he had not felt frustrated and angry during his final decade, exiled successively from most of the countries of Europe, and working reluctantly as a nobleman's librarian in Bohemia. His relief from depression was in recreating the past, which he did for many hours each day. "By recalling the pleasures I've had," he says, "I renew them, and I laugh at the pains I've endured but feel no longer." While he was working on the manuscript he told a friend, "Though I'm old I'm not wise, and I would give an arm and a leg to wake up tomorrow at the fine age of twenty-five."[20]

The *Histoire de Ma Vie* is an enormous book, filling over three thousand pages in modern editions. Yet long though it is, the story breaks off abruptly at the year 1774, when Casanova still had twenty-four years to live. By that time he was turning fifty and his life was becoming futile and repetitive. In a real sense, when he was no longer young and charismatic, he was no longer Casanova.

Was he recreating the past, though, or inventing it? It's remarkable, given his posthumous notoriety, that during his lifetime very little was recorded about him in any detail. Researchers have located some police reports in various cities where he got into trouble, but those are specialized documents that throw light on specific misdeeds but don't tell us much about the man himself.

In addition to the paucity of external evidence, a further problem is that Casanova has little interest in exploring his own motivations, or in detecting ones that might be less than flattering. He was aware that much in the *Histoire* would seem disgraceful to readers, but he told a friend, "I tell all, I don't spare myself, yet as a man of honor I can't call my memoirs confessions, for I repent of nothing." The *Histoire,* as has been well said, is "an autobiography of pleasure, written for pleasure, in order to give pleasure." It has also been called "Casanova's hymn to life." But that was how he chose to remember his earlier life, at a time when he was forbidden to return to his native Venice, or to most of the other cities and countries he had once enjoyed.[21]

Some philosophes, most notably Rousseau, sought freedom and a natural life by dropping out of society. Casanova was the opposite. He achieved his kind of freedom by exploiting society from within, living like a parasite inside it, or like a virus against which it had no adequate immune system. That lifestyle succeeded for quite a while, but not indefinitely. He wrote the *Histoire* to recreate past pleasures because there were no more pleasures in the present, and never would be any in the future.

That didn't mean that the pleasures had been unreal at the time, however, and Casanova celebrates what they felt like in the moment. In this he was taking a different view from the usual Enlightenment ideal, famously expressed by Thomas Jefferson as the pursuit of happiness. The word "pursuit" is often thought to mean an unfinished quest, but Jefferson and his contemporaries understood it as a continuous engagement, as in the expression "the pursuit of medicine." Casanova believed strongly that although pleasure brings happiness, it can never be continuous. Just because it is intense, it can't last long and always burns out. But that doesn't mean it isn't precious.[22]

Over the years, Casanova became increasingly weary and defeated. Biographers have given little attention to his final quarter-century, since he broke off his narrative just when that began, but enough letters and other materials survive to show what it was like, and I have made full use of those. In the end he was worn down by what psychologists call the hedonic treadmill, a pursuit of pleasure for its own sake that is exhausting and ultimately hollow. Yet his account of that pursuit, as recreated in the *Histoire,* is filled with life. It was a superb artistic achievement to recreate the joyful eagerness of his youth without allowing his final tragic mood to darken it. In this biography, my own goal has been to evoke that life in all its fullness—its dark side as well as its bright—and to do justice to the energy, intelligence, and charm of an extraordinary character.

A NOTE ON THE MANUSCRIPT AND EDITIONS

The original manuscript of the *Histoire de Ma Vie* fills 3,682 big folio pages, the size of a modern atlas. It has had a remarkable history. After Casanova's death it was acquired by the Brockhaus publishing firm in Leipzig, but was never made available for outsiders to view. Brockhaus eventually commissioned a French professor at Dresden, Jean Laforgue, to prepare the first published text in 1826, twenty-eight years after the author's death. By then Casanova was so nearly forgotten that some readers believed he never existed; Stendhal was suggested as possibly the author of the *Histoire*. Stendhal did indeed love it, and the German historian Friedrich Wilhelm Barthold wrote in 1846, "The *Memoirs* of Casanova are not only the most complete and detailed picture of the customs and conditions of a society in the century preceding the French Revolution, but are as well a mirror of the life of the State and its various divisions—in short, the innermost secrets of the life of an era."[23]

Without acknowledging it, however, Laforgue rewrote extensively to regularize Casanova's idiosyncratic French, and he also omitted completely a lot of material that was considered indecent or otherwise inappropriate. Over the years writers and scholars often tried to get a look at the original manuscript, but always in vain. "The gods themselves," Zweig said, "would struggle in vain against Brockhaus."[24]

In 1943, after fierce Allied bombing, the manuscript was carried by bicycle through the ruins of Leipzig to the only bank that was still standing, and deposited in its vault. When the war ended, Winston Churchill, who had enjoyed the expurgated edition and wanted the original text preserved, arranged to have an army truck transport it to Wiesbaden where the Brockhaus firm had been reestablished (today it's in Munich). In 1960 Brockhaus at last published an unexpurgated edition that for half a century was standard, and was the basis for an excellent English translation by Willard R. Trask.[25]

Finally, in 2010, the Bibliothèque Nationale in Paris obtained the actual manuscript, at a cost of $9.6 million. It turned out to contain a great deal that was new. Many words and longer passages that Casanova deleted are still legible, since he generally crossed them out with a single line; others are so heavily scribbled over that they're impossible to decipher. There are also alternative drafts of some chapters, as well as afterthoughts that he pasted in—sometimes using red sealing wax—on separate pieces of paper.

As a recent writer says, "The erasures, the corrections and additions, the altogether personal spelling and script of the author, the visible spots of ink, water, coffee, oil, and sealing wax—all provoke emotion, since they give flesh to an author who has already become a myth."[26]

Two distinguished editorial teams have used the manuscript to publish superb three-volume editions of the *Histoire* and supplementary texts, in Gallimard's Bibliothèque de la Pléiade in 2013–2015 and in Laffont's Bouquins collection in 2013–2018. I am the first biographer who has had the good fortune to be able to use these editions, and my book would be far poorer without them. Laurence Bergreen, in *Casanova: The World of a Seductive Genius* (2016), does mention hastening to Paris to "examine" the manuscript at the Bibliothèque Nationale as soon as it arrived there, but there is no evidence in his book that he actually drew upon either the manuscript or the new editions. He claims also that in translating from the *Histoire* "I returned to the urtext for a more accurate rendering," implying that he worked from the new editions or even from the original manuscript, but in fact his quotations are taken word for word from Willard Trask's 1966 translation.[27]

In addition to the *Histoire* itself, the two new editions include hundreds of pages of Casanova's unpublished essays and other writings, many of them never available in print before. There are also valuable appendices, such as a comprehensive table for converting eighteenth-century currencies into modern equivalents, which I have used frequently.

I have made my own translations from these essays, and also from the *Histoire.* After half a century the style of Trask's translation has become somewhat dated, and I've tried to capture Casanova's narrative energy and his conversational freshness. In addition, I have made extensive use of modern biographies and commentaries in French and Italian for which there are no published versions in English, and which biographers have ignored. Some titles will suggest their range and depth: *Casanova Mémorialiste; Casanova en Mouvement: Des Attraits de la Raison aux Plaisirs de la Croyance; Casanova: Un Voyage Libertin; Casanova: La Passion de la Liberté; Une Insolente Liberté: Les Aventures de Casanova; Casanova dans l'Europe des Aventuriers; Casanova: Un Franc-Maçon en Europe au XVIIIe Siècle; L'Uomo Che Inventò Se Stesso: Vita e Commedia di Giacomo Casanova; Il Demone di Casanova; Casanova: L'Ultimo Mistero.*

For readers who might like to look at the complete manuscript of the *Histoire,* it is easily accessible online: https://gallica.bnf.fr/ark:/12148/btv1b6000810t/f11.item.

A selection of the most interesting pages is also reproduced in *Casanova: La Passion de la Liberté.* For anyone who knows French, to read even a bit of the *Histoire* in Casanova's handwriting gives a potent sense of contact with the man himself.

The first page of the manuscript is reproduced here in color (plate 1) to give the full effect of the yellowed paper. *Je commence par déclarer à mon lecteur que*

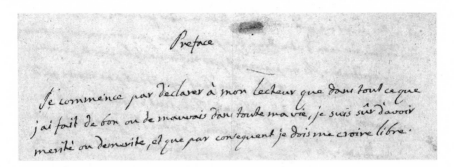

1. First Sentence of the *Histoire*

dans tout ce que j'ai fait de bon ou de mauvais dans toute ma vie, je suis sûr d'avoir mérité ou démerité, et que par conséquent je dois me croire libre—"I begin by declaring to my reader that in everything I've done, good or bad, in my life, I'm sure that I've gained either merit or disapproval, and I must therefore believe myself to be free." That's oddly expressed, and it's hard to be sure what it means. Is he saying that since he has already been judged, he is beyond judgment now? Is he saying that we have no right to judge?

The epigraph from Cicero, *Nequicquam sapit qui sibi non sapit,* means "no one is wise who is not wise for himself." That's ambiguous too. It might mean that experience of life has made Casanova wise. It could also mean that his story reveals, all too tellingly, that he never did achieve wisdom.

A closeup of the first sentence shows that even in illness and old age, Casanova wrote in an elegant script.

CHAPTER I

City of Masks and Mirrors

Giacomo Casanova was the child of a love match between two actors. His father, with the grand name of Gaetano Giuseppe Giacomo Casanova, had left his family in Parma, moved to Venice, and joined a company of actors at the San Samuele theater. There he fell in love with a young actress named Giovanna Farussi, "Zanetta" in the Veneziano dialect. On stage she was known as La Burinella, after the island of Burano where her parents came from.

Zanetta's father Girolamo, a hardworking shoemaker, regarded actors as "abominable personages" and tried to block the match, but the young couple got a license and were married by a bishop on February 17, 1724, as a church register confirms. Zanetta's mother Marzia filled the air with her cries when she found out, and Zanetta's father "died of grief" soon afterward. Thirteen months later, on April 2, 1725, their first son was born and they named him Giacomo Girolamo Casanova, after his grandfathers. If that was a bid to propitiate the Casanova grandfather back in Parma, it failed. Gaetano was twenty-eight and Zanetta was seventeen.[1]

In the *Histoire,* incidentally, Casanova says that he was born just nine months after the marriage, and he evidently chose that number deliberately. As we will see later, there were rumors about his possible illegitimacy, and if he wasn't sure about the dates, he might have suspected that Zanetta was already pregnant when she married Gaetano.

The family lived on the Calle della Commedia in the San Marco sestiere, a narrow street of modest houses behind the theater. The street still exists, but efforts to identify the house itself have failed. The San Samuele neighborhood was notoriously disreputable, as some anonymous verses testified:

> *Contrada piccolo, grande bordel,*
> *Senza ponti, cattive campane,*
> *Omini becchi et donne putane—*

> Little district, big bordello,
> Lacking bridges, with dreadful bells,
> The men all cuckolds and the women whores.

Becchi is "goats"—the cuckold's horns.[2]

Before long siblings began to arrive. First came Francesco Giuseppe in 1727, two years after Giacomo, and from 1730 to 1734 Giovanni Battista, Faustina Maddalena, Maria Maddalena, and Gaetano Alvise. Giacomo was always fond of Francesco and they would sometimes live together in later years, when Francesco was on his way to becoming a famous painter. Giovanni also became a painter, but Giacomo never had much use for him, and Gaetano he utterly despised. Faustina died in childhood, and he has nothing to say about Maria Maddalena except that they enjoyed their occasional meetings in later years, when she was living in Dresden (it was to her son-in-law Carlo Angiolini that he bequeathed his unpublished memoirs). Whatever the siblings' relationship was like when they were young, it doesn't appear to have been close, and in later life they were almost never together.

It was common for troupes of Italian actors to work abroad, and when Giacomo was not yet two, his parents joined a troupe in London, leaving him behind in his grandmother Marzia's care. In London the Prince of Wales got to know Zanetta, and was sometimes rumored to be Francesco's real father. There's no evidence at all for that, and no sign that he did anything for Zanetta after becoming King George II the following year. There were also rumors, which Giacomo seems to have believed, that his own biological father was in fact the San Samuele theater owner Michele Grimani. We will return to that belief later in our story.

During Giacomo's childhood Zanetta had further engagements abroad, and when he was ten she left Venice permanently, moving first to Warsaw and eventually to Dresden. She took Giovanni and Maria Maddalena with her, but not the other boys.

It's very possible that Giacomo felt abandoned by a mother whom he re-

membered as *belle comme le jour,* "beautiful as the day," and some have spec-
ulated that his lifelong pursuit of women was an endless attempt to recover
lost intimacy. However, his own account of the parting doesn't suggest much
grief at separation from the mother who had largely ignored him all along.
"She took with her my brother Giovanni, who was eight, and who wept in
despair at leaving. That made me suspect some stupidity in his character, since
there was nothing at all tragic in this departure." Giacomo adds with obvious
resentment, "He was the only one who owed his entire fortune to our mother."
That was true.

What we do know is that he loved his maternal grandmother Marzia,
"whose *bien-aimé* I was," her beloved. She was the only grandparent he ever
knew, and it was she who raised him, extricating him—as we will see—from
childhood difficulties whenever they arose. The psychoanalyst Lydia Flem suggests persuasively that he gained from Marzia "the disarming confidence of a
small child who was once loved unconditionally."[3]

In the *Histoire* Casanova makes the extraordinary claim that he remembers nothing whatsoever until the age of eight years and four months. "Before
that time, if it's true that *vivere cogitare est* [to live is to think], I wasn't alive—I
vegetated." Cicero had said it long before Descartes did. It may be that Casanova simply didn't believe that early childhood was interesting. Rousseau—
whose *Confessions* we know he read—was the first autobiographer to give more
than a couple of pages to his first years. But Casanova may also have repressed
or deleted memories that seemed inconvenient or irrelevant.

In the *Histoire* he mentions one incident that involved Francesco, when
he was nine and his brother was seven, "which will give the reader an idea of
the way my character developed." Their father wasn't much of a success as an
actor, and supported the family instead by working with optical instruments.
In the days before mechanization, skilled manual labor was in wide demand;
the seventeenth-century philosopher Spinoza ground lenses for telescopes and
microscopes (and probably died from the effects of glass particles in his lungs).

One day Giacomo was captivated by a faceted crystal ball that reflected its
surroundings in multiple images. Enchanted, he slipped it into his pocket.
Francesco was there as well, and when their father realized that the ball was
missing, he promised to thrash whichever boy had taken it. While they were
searching the room Giacomo deftly transferred it to his brother's pocket, and
it was the innocent Francesco who got the beating. "Three or four years later
I was stupid enough to boast to him about that trick. He never forgave me."
Perhaps he prized the story because it demonstrates that even at that early date,

he was showing gifts as a trickster. He reproaches himself not for having done it, but for admitting to Francesco that he had.

If we know little about Casanova's early life, we know a great deal about the city and culture he was born into. He has been rightly called "a human compound of the attractions and corruptions of the Venice he knew and whose symbol he may claim to be." Getting to know eighteenth-century Venice, with its music and theater and gambling and masks and role-playing, will be important for understanding Casanova.[4]

He thought of his life as a drama, as the title of a recent study suggests: *The Man Who Invented Himself: The Life and Commedia of Giacomo Casanova.* As with French *comédie,* a commedia can be any kind of drama, not just comic, and it was certainly as a drama that Casanova lived and understood his life. This writer says, "With its plot twists, tears, rebirths, defeats, love affairs, and cross-dressing, it gives us not only the portrait of a man, but also the panorama of an era."[5]

In every way Venice struck visitors as unique, as indeed it still does. The city could be reached only by water, rising spectacularly from the sea, with no need for the defensive walls and gates that were common elsewhere in Europe (color plate 2). In the foreground is the island of Giudecca, or more properly a chain of islands joined by bridges, with the great church of San Giorgio Maggiore to their right. In Venice proper there were 145 canals, crossed by 312 stone bridges and 117 wooden ones, connecting what began as separate islets in the lagoon. Many of the campi, the public squares, were originally grassy fields. The names of several districts recall their origin: the Rialto was Rio Alto, "high shore."

The city was and is a labyrinth, daunting for strangers, as when Launcelot Gobbo gives directions to Shylock's house: "Turn up on your right hand at the next turning, but at the next turning of all on your left; marry, at the very next turning, turn of no hand, but turn down indirectly to the Jew's house."[6]

Venice was an emporium swarming with people from all over the Mediterranean. Casanova took that for granted and never bothered to talk about it in the *Histoire,* but he recalled that when he was in Marseille some years later, "I believed I was back in Venice. . . . I seemed to see everywhere the freedom of my native country in the mélange of nations and the various costumes. Mingling together were Greeks, Turks, Africans, pirates or at least men who looked like they were, Jews, monks, and charlatans. From time to time I saw Englishmen, who either didn't say anything or spoke in low voices among themselves without looking at anyone."[7]

2. Temporary Bridge over the Giudecca Canal

More even than elsewhere in Italy, there were frequent celebrations and feast days. Over forty of them happened on fixed dates throughout the year, commemorating the anniversaries of saints, famous naval victories, and other notable occasions. The magnificent baroque church of Santa Maria della Salute, at the entrance to the Grand Canal, was an expression of thanksgiving for the city's deliverance from plague in 1630, an event that was commemorated every November 21 with a temporary floating bridge across the canal to the San Marco side. Still more magnificent was the festival of Il Redentore, the Redeemer, in memory of an earlier plague in 1576 that killed 50,000 people, one of whom was the painter Titian. To this day, every third weekend of July, a floating bridge more than a thousand feet in length is installed to span the wide Giudecca Canal so that people can walk across the water to the church of Il Redentore. In the evening the canal fills up with pleasure boats and there is a spectacular fireworks display. If Casanova could see the modern celebration he would feel right at home.

The local people spoke Veneziano, not so much a dialect as a romance language in its own right, still used today. "I love the language," Byron wrote, "that soft bastard Italian, which melts like kisses from a female mouth." One Venetian word that is now understood everywhere is *ciao,* which comes from *schiavo*—literally "I am your slave," or more politely, "at your service."[8]

Venetian culture was profoundly theatrical. Everyday life was performative, and actual plays (mostly comic) were hugely popular. Although both of Giacomo's parents were actors, apart from occasional amateur theatricals he never acted himself. Still, it's fair to say that his entire life was a theatrical improvisation.

Zanetta was a star, talented as well as beautiful, and took on leading romantic roles, but no record survives of what her performances were like. Giacomo never says anything about that, or even if he saw her act, though presumably he did. She was said, however, to be the favorite actress of Carlo Goldoni, the greatest Italian playwright of the century and a prolific writer of plays for San Samuele and other theaters. In his memoir Goldoni mentions Zanetta in passing as *molto graziosa e abile,* "very pretty and very able."[9]

Casanova knew Goldoni, then and later, but is unenthusiastic about him in his own memoir. The one mention of him comes in a conversation Casanova had with Voltaire in 1760. They were discussing Italian literature and Voltaire asked what he thought of Goldoni. Casanova's reply was positive, yet curiously qualified: "He is our Molière. He calls himself a lawyer, but he's one only by training. He's a good comedy writer, and that's all. I am his friend, as all Venice knows. In society he doesn't shine; he's insipid, and soft as a marshmallow." Goldoni was clearly not Casanova's type, but he never wanted to be. In his own memoir he says, "My mother brought me into the world with little pain, and this increased her love for me. My first appearance was not, as usual, announced by cries, and this gentleness seemed then an indication of the pacific character which from that day forward I have ever preserved."[10]

Goldoni's conception of theater, inspired by French models, was actually counter to what Venetians loved best. He wrote out complete scripts and expected the actors to memorize their parts; that Zanetta performed hers well suggests verbal skills and intelligence. But the genius of Venetian theater was improvisation, in the tradition known as commedia dell' arte. It was regularly performed in the dozen established theaters, but its roots were in street improvisation in which mask-wearing actors took traditional roles and competed with inventive riffs on the gossip of the day. There were no scripts, just brief outlines of scenes and situations that would be posted backstage. It was essential that actors be quick-witted, and also skilled at playing off each other's sallies, which made it a true ensemble genre. It required years of experience, effective teamwork, and skills that ranged from music and dance to acrobatic display. Numerous professional troupes gained fame all over Italy.

The roots of commedia have been traced all the way back to ancient Rome. Stock characters wore traditional leather masks, such as a black one for Arlecchino or Harlequin. (It's not certain what the black mask meant; in Roman times it may have represented an African slave.). The stock character known as the Dottore wore a birdlike beak; in the Middle Ages those had actually been used by doctors in times of plague, containing herbs through which they would inhale and supposedly gain protection. Other characters included the pompous merchant Pantaloon, the humpbacked Punchinello who became the English Punch, and the buffoonish Zanni, the Venetian equivalent of Giovanni, which gives us our word "zany." Female characters were a minority and were confined to *inamorata* types and servant girls.

Most popular of all was the nimble, mischievous Arlecchino; he was athletically agile and a clever trickster, which wouldn't be a bad description of Casanova himself. As shown in this pair of porcelain figurines (color plate 3) he and Arlecchina wore outfits with vividly colored patches to suggest a chameleonic nature. He usually carried a *battachio,* a magic wand that he would wave to signal each change of scene. Its hinged halves made a loud clap when banged together—the origin of the word "slapstick."[11]

The wearing of masks placed a special demand on performers, who had to express emotion with voice and body language. All of the best actors were gifted mimes, and that too went back to ancient times. Cicero said admiringly of one performer that "his very body was laughing."[12]

Foreign visitors were enchanted by the inventive freshness of these performances, and by the clever way current gossip and events were woven into the stylized character relationships. Goethe, for instance, loved the sunny freedom of Venice, and he especially enjoyed commedia.

> During the daytime, squares, canals, gondolas, and palazzi are full of life as the buyer and the seller, the beggar and the boatman, the housewife and the lawyer offer something for sale, sing and gamble, shout and swear. In the evening the same people go to the theater to behold their actual life, presented with greater economy as make-believe interwoven with various stories and removed from reality by masks, yet in its characters and manners the life they know. They are delighted, like children, shouting, clapping, and generally making a din.

When the audience appreciated a performance the applause was unrestrained. They would cry out in Veneziano, *Benedetto el pare che l'ha fatto! Ah! cara, me buto zozo!*—"Blessed be the father who begot you! Ah, dear one, I throw myself at your feet!"[13]

Like the best comedy of every kind, commedia dell' arte was much more than just farce. In the next century George Sand's son Maurice published an illustrated study of it, and she herself wrote, "In essence it is quite serious and, one might say, even sad, like every satire which lays bare the spiritual poverty of mankind."[14]

All of this resonates deeply with Casanova's temperament, and with his experience of life. He was an instinctive improvisor, in words as well as actions, and he loved a challenge. On one occasion which we will encounter later on, a young woman he didn't know hailed him at an inn in Ferrara as her cousin, introduced him to her fiancé's parents, and claimed that he was a great musician, which he wasn't. With no idea what it was all about—it turned out to be a scam of hers, and he loved scams—he picked up the clues she tossed him and pulled off the impersonation with complete success.

In spite of the enormous popularity of commedia, Goldoni, whose hero was indeed Molière, was determined to bring dramatic structure to Venetian comedy. He felt that commedia dell' arte gave actors too much license to make things up as they went along, and to rely on memorized phrases and gags. He also thought that mime was not enough. "Whether he be wooing, or ranting, or clowning," he wrote, "the actor always has the same leather face. He may gesticulate and change his tone as often as he will, but he can never communicate by the expression of his face the passions that rend his soul." A historian agrees. "Taking off the mask meant that characters could emerge as individuals, to grow, to change, to feel love or pain or disgrace."[15]

Responding to a Venetian demand for endless novelty, Goldoni turned out an astonishing number of plays, over two hundred in all, often completing one in a single week. Not surprisingly, the result is uneven, and he never approached the elegance and depth of Molière's classic comedies. Still, they were highly popular, especially since he made liberal use of his native Veneziano. A rival playwright, however, Carlo Gozzi, championed the traditional improvised commedia, and in 1761 Goldoni gave up and moved permanently to Paris. By then it had been years since Zanetta was a member of his company.

The Venetian theaters themselves were impressive, even spectacular. A picture of San Samuele (color plate 4) shows its deep projecting stage that permitted some actors to play in the foreground while others were active behind them. Candlelight was multiplied by mirrors, and there was a tall candle-holder in front of each of the boxes along the sides. The boxes were expensive and were often purchased for an entire season; the floor below could be fitted with various kinds of cheap seats. San Samuele no longer exists. It was torn down in the nineteenth century, and the site is now occupied by an elementary school.

In addition to plays, operas were popular in eighteenth-century Venice, and so was music of all kinds, performed in concerts and also sung spontaneously in public. A French visitor heard a shoemaker and blacksmith burst into an aria in the Piazza San Marco, joined immediately by others, and they sang superbly in several parts.[16]

The English musicologist Charles Burney recalled that the very first music he heard in Venice was performed by street musicians, two violins and a cello accompanying a female voice. The singing was admirable, the violinists "played difficult passages very neatly," and the cello was likewise excellent. Music was indeed a constant presence. "If two of the common people walk together arm in arm, they seem to converse in song; if there is company on the water in a gondola, it is the same. A mere melody, unaccompanied with a second part, is not to be heard in this city; all the ballads in the streets are sung in duo. Luckily for me, this night a barge, in which there was an excellent band of music consisting of violins, flutes, horns, basses, and a kettle-drum, with a pretty good tenor voice, was on the Great Canal, and stopped very near the house where I lodged. It was a piece of gallantry, at the expense of an *inamorato* to serenade his mistress."[17]

For Casanova, as for many Venetians, real music had to be vocal. Instruments were just for accompaniment, and expressive *bel canto* singing was indeed the glory of music in Venice. Jean-Jacques Rousseau spent a year there as a young man and was profoundly impressed. Years later he published a *Dictionary of Music* in which he included a nostalgic description of the celebrated barcarolles: "A type of song in the Venetian dialect that the gondoliers in Venice sing. Although the airs are made for the people, and are often composed by the gondoliers themselves, they are so melodious and charming that there's not a musician in the whole of Italy who doesn't pride himself on knowing and singing them." Rousseau added that many gondoliers had Tasso's epic poem *Jerusalem Delivered* by heart and would sing alternate stanzas from boat to boat across the lagoon on summer nights. Goethe, too, heard them and wrote, "The sound of their voices far away was extraordinary, a lament without sadness, and I was moved to tears."[18]

More formal music was widely available, notably at a uniquely Venetian institution, the four Ospedali, hostels for orphan girls who had no other means of support (there was no equivalent institution for boys). The very existence of the Ospedali was remarkable, since in most places in Europe there was almost no provision for orphans. Elsewhere in Europe if they were lucky they became household servants, but many ended up on the streets as beggars or prostitutes. A historian comments, "Men are willing to pay more for sexual access than for almost any other form of female labor."[19]

The Ospedali housed hundreds of residents, most of whom were trained as seamstresses, but those with musical talent were selected in girlhood to become virtually professional musicians. Elsewhere in Europe it would have been unusual, or even unheard of, for an accomplished ensemble to be entirely female. Quite a few performers who were trained there became celebrated stars.

Some Ospedali specialized in choral music, others in instrumental. For years Vivaldi was the music master at the Ospedale della Pietà, and his compositions reflect the resources there. Bassoons were little used in Venice at the time, but he wrote no fewer than thirty-nine bassoon concerti, undoubtedly with a particular performer in mind. Rousseau heard the singers at the rival Ospedale dei Mendicanti and said, "I had had no idea of anything so voluptuous and also so moving as this music."[20]

Religion too was theatrical, and church services were a sensory feast. As a native of dourly Calvinist Geneva, Rousseau was transported by the total effect: "Brilliant illumination, paintings by a skillful hand, perfumes destined for the gods whose divine voluptuousness delights human nostrils before ascending to the heavens; and thou, ravishing music!" The word "gods" suggests the paganism that Rome had shrewdly coopted. Calvinism denounced incense and religious art, and its church music was limited to simple psalm tunes that an entire congregation would sing in unison.[21]

For most people, indeed, religion was recreational rather than solemn. Still, conventions had to be observed. An eighteenth-century visitor told a story: when the consecrated host was elevated in the church of San Marco, the whole congregation knelt down but an Englishman remained standing. A Venetian senator told him he had to kneel, and he replied, "Sir, I don't hold with transubstantiation"—the doctrine, abhorred by Protestants, that the consecrated bread and wine become the literal body and blood of Christ. *Ne anche io,* the senator replied, *però ginocchione, o fuor di chiesa*—"Neither do I, but either you kneel or else you get out of this church."[22]

In the streets and piazzas there were shows of all kinds, including puppe-

3. Clara the Rhinoceros

teers, magicians, and mountebanks selling nostrums. In 1751 a special attraction was a rhinoceros named Clara, shown here in a print made from a painting by Pietro Longhi. Her keeper is displaying a rhinoceros horn, while an assortment of Carnival-goers look on, some masked and some not.

Venice itself was like a stage set, with its center at the magnificent church of San Marco and the adjacent Ducal Palace from which the city was governed. Like the palazzi along the canals, these structures dazzled visitors with riches plundered in the past. In the thirteenth century, at the time of the Fourth Crusade, hundreds of marble slabs from the East had been shipped home and used to cover the exterior of San Marco.

Flanking the Ducal Palace is an arcade of columns, all beautiful and all different, that were pillaged from ancient buildings all over the East. The twin granite columns on the Molo, the waterfront, came from Syria, and the bronze creature on one of them was originally a chimera from China, combining serpent, goat, and lion. Wings were added later to turn it into the iconic lion of St. Mark. The other column is crowned by a statue of St. Theodore, the city's

4. The Winged Lion

original patron until the ninth century when the remains of St. Mark were smuggled from Alexandria in Egypt, hidden under a cargo of pork to discourage Muslim inspectors from finding them. According to legend St. Theodore killed a dragon; the beast he's standing on here, however, is a crocodile (it's the right-hand column shown in figure 27, page 195 below).

Not until the nineteenth century did the church of San Marco become a cathedral. In Casanova's time the actual cathedral of Venice was located in the northern Castello district, and San Marco was simply the private chapel of the head of state known as the doge. Except on certain feast days ordinary people were not permitted inside. As a chapel, though, it was extraordinary. "No monarch on earth," Casanova said, "could boast of having its equal."[23]

In a solemn ceremony on Ascension Day known as the *Sposalissi del Mare*, the doge was rowed out into the lagoon on an immense galley called the Bucintoro, whose name implied "covered with gold," *oro.* There the doge would cast a golden ring into the water, proclaiming *Desponsamum te Mare, in signum veri perpetuique dominii*—"We wed thee, O Sea, as a sign of true and perpetual dominion."

5. The Bucintoro

Galleys played an important role in the powerful Venetian navy, but the unwieldy Bucintoro was entirely ceremonial in purpose, and an Ascension Day with strong winds caused alarm since it might well capsize. Casanova commented that if that ever happened "it would make the whole of Europe laugh, saying that the doge of Venice had finally consummated the marriage."[24]

The greatest celebration of all was Carnival, when masked revelers thronged the streets and canals during a two-week period that culminated in Martedì Grasso, Mardi Gras. Foreigners had the mistaken impression that Carnival lasted for fully half of every year, but that was because they assumed that masks always meant revelry. In fact they were worn on ordinary occasions from October through March and again for two weeks after Ascension Day, which usually fell in May. Strangely, there's no clear explanation why they weren't used in summer. Perhaps the scalding Venetian heat was reason enough.

People wore masks in church, in cafés, at the theater, and in public generally. Servants wore them on the way to the market, lawyers wore them in court, and mothers even put them on their babies. The mask was sometimes called a *masca* and sometimes *larva,* from an ancient word for souls of the dead that return to haunt the living. (On the same analogy, entomologists used it to describe the life cycle of insects.) As shown in a picture (color plate 5) the complete costume included a robe called a *domino* and a closely fitting hood, the *bautta*.

The significance of masks is that they facilitated freedom, not to say license. A historian says, "More than a disguise, the mask was an incognito. It was secrecy, anonymity, secure impunity; it was licensed folly." Masking also permitted members of the upper class to associate freely with people whom they would normally have kept at a distance. It was considered a serious social offense to say you recognized someone in spite of his or her mask.[25]

The major industry of Venice was pleasure, and that was profoundly significant in Casanova's development. Visitors (mostly men) came from all over Europe to take part in Carnival, and for them the city was like an eighteenth-century Las Vegas. A Frenchman exclaimed, "The people are not satisfied with ordinary libertinism; they improve and refine all their pleasures, and plunge into them up to the neck." Prostitution was ubiquitous, so openly that foreigners were astonished. Local prostitutes were supplemented by others from out of town.[26]

Voltaire trenchantly criticized their exploitation. When Candide visits Venice he encounters Paquette, a former servant girl who had been seduced by the philosopher Pangloss and is now a streetwalker. "If you could imagine," she says, "what it's like to have to caress, with the same enthusiasm, an elderly merchant, a lawyer, a monk, a gondolier and an abbé; to be exposed to every insult and affront; to be reduced often to borrowing a petticoat so as to have it lifted by some disgusting man; to be robbed by one man of what you earned with another, or have it extorted from you by officers of the law; to have nothing to look forward to but a hideous old age, the poor house, and the refuse-heap—then you would agree that I am one of the unhappiest creatures alive."[27]

There was a wide difference, however, between streetwalkers and higher-class "courtesans" who might be shared as mistresses by one or more men; they had social standing and were treated with respect. Casanova would encounter a number of those, in Paris as well as Venice.

The commercial heart of the city of pleasure was gambling at cards, for which foreigners served as eager victims, whether at the officially sanctioned Ridotto in its palazzo near San Marco, or in more obscure venues that were called *casini* (*casa* is "house," and *casino* just means "little house"). Elsewhere in Europe gambling was a recreation, tolerated in some places and prohibited in others. In Venice it was an official institution and a major source of income for the state, and women as well as men were encouraged to gamble.[28]

At the Ridotto the participants wore masks, but the bankers, who were always noblemen, kept their faces uncovered so there could be no doubt about who they were. A painting by Francesco Guardi shows the *sala grande* (color plate 6) with the banker making a payout at the far left. Another banker would have presided over each of nine other gaming rooms, and there were rooms for refreshment as well.

During Carnival the Ridotto was open day and night, and to prevent disruptions strict silence was enforced. A historian says, "Guardi and Longhi have immortalized the strange atmosphere there: masked figures from all social conditions pressing around dozens of gaming tables, to the sole sound of the clinking of heaps of zecchini and stifled whispers." Zecchini (the English called them sequins) were coins worth 115 modern Euros apiece. In 1774 the Ridotto was shut down because it had been the ruin of many once-wealthy families, but that just drove all gambling underground into the casini, after which the word "casino" acquired its modern meaning.[29]

A notorious French card sharp named Ange Goudar, who spent some time in Venice, wrote a detailed manual on how to cheat at cards. Card sharps were known as "Greeks," and his "history" of these Greeks, with detailed deceptions for every possible game, was subtitled *Ceux Qui Corrigent la Fortune au Jeu*—"those who correct fortune by gambling." Benjamin Franklin collected his Poor Richard aphorisms as *The Way to Wealth,* preaching hard work and self-discipline. Goudar taught that the way to "correct fortune" was not laborious accumulation, but encouraging Lady Luck to correct any errors she might have made. The card sharps prided themselves, in an expression of Goldoni's, on plucking the quail without making it squawk—*pelar la quaglia, e non la far gridare.*[30]

A painting by Caravaggio from an earlier era (color plate 7) illustrates this theme with psychological depth. At the left, a naïve youth is concentrating earnestly on the next card to play in the game of primero, a forerunner of poker. His equally young opponent is cautiously withdrawing a concealed card from behind his back, meanwhile gazing up earnestly at his teacher, who stares down at the oblivious victim's cards. His gloves have gaps at the fingertips, the better to identify marked cards, but on this occasion he won't be using them. All three are expensively dressed; card sharps presented themselves as social equals of their victims. There's also an ominous clue: the apprentice has a dagger at his belt in case of need. Caravaggio painted this picture in Rome, where a cardinal not only purchased it but became his patron.

Throughout his life Casanova spent endless hours gambling; his excellent memory and skill at rapid numerical calculation were invaluable assets. At the Ridotto he lost more than he won because the rules ensured that the house would come out ahead, but people also played cards for money on social occasions where skill was rewarded and where cheating was far easier to pull off. In the *Histoire* Casanova claims that he never stooped to that, but his disclaimers are unconvincing. He does admit that in Naples in 1770, low on funds, he joined forces with none other than Ange Goudar himself.

The biographer Ian Kelly observes that Casanova had a couple of favorite expressions in French, *faire semblant* and *jouer*. With both he was exploiting double or even triple meanings. *Faire semblant* means to pretend, but also to make something seem real even when it's not. And *jouer* means to play, as children do, but also to play-act; in England actors were still called players. It can also mean to gamble, as Italian *giocare* likewise does. In French the word for "game" is *jeu;* the croupier says, "*Les jeux sont faits,*" "the bets are made," when the roulette wheel starts to spin. To place a bet, in Casanova's French, was *ponter,* a word that pervades the *Histoire;* the English said "punt." For him gambling was as normal as breathing.[31]

Casanova lived for the thrill of risk-taking that gambling supplied. "What he wants," Stefan Zweig says, "is perpetual tension, the unceasing alternation of red and black, of spades and diamonds. Only in these perpetual ups and downs does he find contentment for his nerves." In a classic study of games and play, the sociologist Roger Caillois emphasizes that even when money changes hands in a game, "it creates no wealth or goods," and that was what appealed to Casanova. "It seemed to me," he says in the *Histoire,* "that money won in gambling had cost me nothing." Still more important, like all forms of play and unlike everyday life, gambling occupied a privileged space observing fixed rules. As Caillois says, "The game's domain is a restricted, closed, protected universe: a pure space."[32]

Thomas Kavanagh, in an engrossing analysis of Casanova's strategies and skills, makes a further important point. People of fashion gambled constantly, not just in public venues but at private dinner parties. With Casanova's social charm as well as mastery of the favored games, of which there were many, gambling would be his entrée into the privileged world of the aristocracy everywhere in Europe. "Without gambling," Kavanagh says, "Casanova could never have become Casanova."[33]

Theater and music and masks and gambling were central to life in Venice, but they were never the whole of life. The city-state, with extensive holdings on the mainland known as the Veneto (in purple at the top of a map of eighteenth-century Italy, color plate 8), had grown rich through dominating Mediterranean trade. Although commerce had dwindled over the years, it was still lucrative, and the state maintained an impressive navy to protect it. In a view by Guardi, the Bacino, the "basin" (color plate 9) teems with activity, from sea-going commercial vessels to the ubiquitous gondolas. In the distance a naval galley is anchored in front of the ornate Ducal Palace, with the dome of the church of San Marco rising beyond it, and the great campanile to the left. Venice was often referred to as "La Serenissima," alluding to its preference for peaceful commerce rather than military conquest.

It was in Venice in the fourteenth century that the transition from barter to money first took place in Europe. Stable values were established for the myriad European coinages—there were at least thirty—so that they could be accepted anywhere. The money-changers close to the Rialto Bridge originally sat on benches, the *bancheri,* that gave rise to our word "bank." As their operations expanded they accepted deposits, on the strength of which they handled exchanges between customers, issued loans, and funded investments, none of which required actual coins any more. The *giro* system was the circulation of credit throughout the economy, and the archway where the benches used to be is still called the Sotoportego del Banco Giro. In addition, the Venetian money-changers invented double-entry bookkeeping, in which credits and debits must be shown to balance every day, making fraud much easier to detect.[34]

Although Venice was far from a democracy, it had always been a republic—one of the very few in Europe—ever since its foundation when the Roman empire was collapsing and settlers took refuge on islands in the lagoon. There was no king and no ranks of nobility—no dukes, counts, or marquis—but a hereditary aristocracy did control political power. Only men from the oldest noble families, recorded in a document known as the Golden Book, were eligible to hold office. Other families were later granted noble status, but without that privilege. In England a peer could marry a commoner, but in Venice anyone who did so was automatically expelled from the nobility. "The outcome of these iron rules," a historian says, "was to make a closed circle of the patriciate," with no possibility of reenergizing it through marriage between classes.[35]

Each member of the noble class bore the title *Nobile Homo* or *Nobile Donna,*

6. Guardi, *The Rialto Bridge*

commonly abbreviated as N. H. and N. D. There were a lot of them: about 3,500 individuals belonging to 300 families, roughly 2 percent of the total population. To keep fortunes intact, there was a custom of strictly limiting inheritance. One son would be designated the heir, and his brothers would be expected to remain unmarried (illegitimate children had no legal rights). In the eighteenth century, fully two-thirds of Venetian nobles remained bachelors. There was also a large underclass of truly indigent nobles known as *barnabotti* since they clustered around the parish of San Barnabà. Many survived on poor relief. Noble daughters were often placed in convents so that only one sister would get a big dowry. Two out of three Venetian noblewomen never married.[36]

To prevent autocracy from developing, as it did in most Italian states, there were stringent safeguards against the abuse of power by any individual or group. To keep elections honest they were elaborately complicated, with a new drawing of lots at each of several stages to ensure randomness. Also, the terms of office were brief.

The head of government was the doge. The name came from the Latin *dux* or leader, as did "duke" (hence the Ducal Palace), but unlike dukes elsewhere he was an elected official with a fixed term, not a hereditary ruler. From the election of the first doge in 726 to the deposition of the last by the French in

1797, there were 119 of them. He was in fact a figurehead, making no decisions without the consent of several groups of advisers. A French visitor called him "a mere figure of a prince, an animated statue. The doge is the image or representative of the republic, whose pleasure it is to reflect its glory upon him." The only gifts he was allowed to receive were "rose-water, flowers, sweet-smelling herbs, and balsam—than which," Jan Morris remarks, "it is difficult to conceive a more milk-sop selection." To emphasize his dependent status, in formal processions he was followed by a man holding a broad-bladed sword. That was to recall the fate of the doge Marino Falier, who attempted a coup in 1355 and was beheaded.[37]

Venice had a legal code, but it was never made public until 1678, and even then a proviso was added: "Written law is to be interpreted in the light of custom, which may modify and even override it." It was common for suspects to be arrested without charges and condemned without trial. There was a grim saying, "The Ten send you to the torture chamber, the Three to your grave." The Three were a committee of Inquisitors—not to be confused with the religious Inquisition, which played no role in Venice—who were chosen from the larger elective Council of Ten to take up cases in total secrecy.[38]

A French ambassador, François-Joachim de Pierre de Bernis, with whom Casanova would develop a relationship, vividly described the subtle repression. "In the Piazza San Marco during Mardi Gras I've seen more than forty thousand people assembled; no one loses so much as a handkerchief, even though there are no bailiffs or police to control the crowd. Order rules in Venice because of the certain knowledge that the government is informed about everything, and the Inquisitors will have anyone killed without ceremony who disturbs the public order. The fear of secret executions impresses people even more than the fear of public torture."[39]

Mary McCarthy suggests, however, that by contrast with the high-handed rulers of other Italian city-states, the Venetian Inquisitors were "positively benign, like Platonic Guardians. Unlike the modern police state, to which it is often compared, Venice feared power and surrounded it with checks and deterrents. Its real desire was for business as usual."[40]

The authorities employed spies to report suspicious behavior, and informers were encouraged to write out accusations and deposit them in *bocce dei leone,* "lion's mouth" apertures set into walls throughout the city. After Napoleon conquered Venice he got rid of most of them (he had the Bucintoro destroyed too), but a few still survive, including this one at the Ducal Palace, though it's a human face, not a lion's. The inscription in Veneziano calls for

DENONTIE SECRETE
CONTRO CHI OCCVLTERĀ
GRATIE ET OFFICII,
Õ COLLVDERÃ PER
NASCONDER LA VERA
RENDITA D ESSI

7. A Mail Slot for Informers

"secret denunciations against anyone who will conceal favors and services, or will collude to hide the true revenue from them"—i.e., from the State.

Montesquieu, in his classic *Spirit of the Laws,* understood the implications clearly. "A hidden magistracy is needed because the crimes it punishes, always deep-seated, are formed in secrecy and silence. The inquisition of this magistracy has to be general because its aim is not to check known evils but to curb unknown ones." Secrecy was supposed to protect informers from reprisals, but that's not to say that the system was benign. Montesquieu added, "A stone mouth is open for every informer; you might say it is the mouth of tyranny."[41]

It wasn't just surveillance, either; it could amount to deliberate entrapment. When Goldoni was briefly trying to find work as a lawyer, "a fair, round, plump woman of about thirty" told him that she followed court cases closely and specialized in connecting lawyers with defendants who would pay well to get acquittal. She gave some examples, such as laundering a marriage contract that needed to have its date altered to make it binding. Goldoni replied indignantly that he was an honorable man and had no wish to get involved in that. "Our conversation has been not without mystery," the woman told him; "bear it in mind, and take care never to mention it. Adieu, sir; be always prudent and always honorable, and you will find your account in it." He stood astonished as she walked away, but afterward learned that she was a spy who had been sent to try to incriminate him.[42]

The time would come when spies for the Inquisitors would file detailed reports on Giacomo Casanova. He would be under suspicion for multiple reasons: he was heard to speak skeptically about religion, he dabbled in forbidden magical practices, and he used those practices to con rich patricians into giving him money. Worst of all, he lived flagrantly above his proper station in life and ignored warnings. He needed to be stopped.

CHAPTER 2

Awakenings

The first episode that Casanova says he remembers from his childhood was one of great symbolic significance to him: it involved mystery, secrecy, and magical healing.

When he was eight years old he was afflicted with copious nosebleeds that no one knew how to stop. Doctors were of no help, and in desperation his grandmother Marzia took him to the island of Murano, half an hour away by gondola, which was and still is the center of Venetian glassmaking.

On Murano they entered a hovel where they were received by an old woman with a black cat in her arms and half a dozen more around her. *C'était une sorcière*—"she was a witch." After being paid a silver ducat, a considerable sum for the impoverished Marzia, the *sorcière* put the boy through a symbolic return to the womb. "Opening a chest, she locked me inside, telling me not to be afraid. That would have been the way to *make* me afraid, if I had had any spirit, but I was stupefied. I kept still, holding my handkerchief to my bloody nose, indifferent to the racket I heard going on outside; it was all the same to me. I heard laughing and weeping by turns, cries, singing, and rapping on the chest."[1]

When they took the boy out, the bleeding had stopped. Fragrant plants were burned, his face and neck were rubbed with ointment, he was made to swallow some pleasant sweets, and then he was free to go. There was a warning, however. So long as he maintained absolute secrecy, his cure would succeed; but if he ever told anyone what had happened, he would die. The injunction was important, since witchcraft was considered satanic by the Church. If detected, the old woman would have been prosecuted.

Uncanny as the experience was, the sequel was still more so. The witch told him that when he was in bed that night a lovely woman would appear, and his future happiness would again depend on absolute secrecy. Sure enough, when he awakened after several hours of sleep,

> I saw, or believed I saw, a dazzling lady descend from the chimney in a big hooped skirt, dressed in magnificent fabrics and wearing a crown covered with sparkling gems. She approached with slow steps and a majestic air, and sat down gently on my bed. She took some little boxes out of her pocket, which she emptied on my head while murmuring some words. After talking to me at length, of which I understood nothing, she kissed me and departed the same way she came, and I fell back asleep.

In the morning Marzia repeated the command of secrecy, and—so he claims, at least—the nosebleeds ceased.

As Casanova acknowledges in hindsight, the apparition might have simply been a vivid dream, provoked by the old witch's prediction. Alternatively, it might have been a calculated masquerade. The costume and crown were theatrical, and his mother could have enlisted an actress colleague to play the role. Perhaps the mysterious lady seemed like an idealized substitute for Zanetta, who took little apparent interest in her oldest child. It was Marzia who was the maternal one.

In any case, the boy may well have been helped by the placebo effect. In pondering this experience he concludes, with real insight, that even if magic isn't real, belief in magic can be. "Remedies for the greatest maladies aren't always found in medicine. Every day some phenomenon demonstrates our ignorance. That's why I believe there's nothing more rare than a learned person whose mind is completely free from superstition. There have never been any witches in the world, but their power has existed, in the hands of those who know how to make people believe they are witches."

All his life Casanova would be fascinated by the ability of imagination to make the unreal seem real, and his interest in magic was never as cynical as he claims it was in the *Histoire*. It was awakened, indeed, during this episode. Angelo Mainardi links it to the alleged amnesia concerning his first eight years: "It's an initiation, a rite de passage, from a first childhood that he forgot or erased completely to an adolescence that would be astonishing for rapid learning and precocity of experience." What happened before that time is, as another writer says, a "black hole." It's as if his real life didn't begin until this moment.[2]

The solemn warning never to reveal what happened was important, too: "It was what caused me to remember the vision, and by placing it under a seal, I lodged it in the most secret recess of my awakening memory."

Just at this time, his father Gaetano experienced an agonizing abscess in his ear, which must have been an infection of some kind, and died within a week at the age of thirty-six. He left a widow who was still just twenty-six, with five small children and a sixth on the way. On his deathbed he appealed to Michele and Alvise Grimani, the owner of the San Samuele theater and his brother, to act as guardians, and they agreed.

It has been suggested that Giacomo may have felt an oedipal resentment of the father who possessed his beautiful but distant mother. In that case, a psychoanalyst would say that he unconsciously wanted Gaetano to die. It's certainly true that in the *Histoire* he doesn't express any grief at the loss.

It's not clear that Giacomo ever had much of a relationship with either parent, as contrasted with his affectionate grandmother. It's probably with some bitterness that he says, "My malady [the nosebleeds] made me gloomy and not in the least amusing. Everyone felt sorry for me and left me in peace; they believed my existence would be brief. My father and mother never spoke to me at all."

At some point in later life Giacomo began to suspect that his real father was not Gaetano Casanova but Michele Grimani. It's not clear how fully he believed that, or what evidence he thought there was. In his late fifties he got in a quarrel with a nobleman who mentioned the rumor in print, and in publishing an angry response Casanova accepted it as probable, but that proves nothing. What we do know is that he wished he had been born an aristocrat and enjoyed imagining that he actually was one, even if illegitimate—a sort of prince in disguise.

The one thing Zanetta would never do was tie herself down by another marriage. "Beautiful and young though she was," Casanova says, "she refused her hand to all who offered themselves."

Giacomo was turning nine by now. It was time to think about his education, and also about his still uncertain health. Even though the hemorrhages had ceased, they had induced a dull and feeble demeanor very different from his later vitality. Someone who knew him as a child told him later that he used to go around with his mouth always open. A famous doctor was consulted, and advised that the trouble was "thickness of blood" that was due to the thick air of Venice. He suggested that there would be more salubrious air in the mainland Veneto territory, known to Venetians as *terraferma,* and it was decided that the boy should be sent to a boarding house in Padua on the mainland, twenty-five miles away.

Giacomo traveled there on the Brenta River with his mother and two other adults, Alvise Grimani and a poet named Giorgio Baffo, who had been "a great friend of my father's," in a sort of horse-drawn houseboat known as a *burchiello.* A painting by Tiepolo (color plate 10) shows a burchiello being poled backward in the shallow lagoon while a sailor waits at the steering oar to the right. Some passengers relaxing at their ease can be seen within.

Casanova almost never describes his physical surroundings, but we have John Ruskin's account of the river: "The Brenta flows slowly, but strongly; a muddy volume of yellowish-gray water that neither hastens nor slackens, but glides heavily between its monotonous banks, with here and there a short, babbling eddy twisted for an instant into its opaque surface, and vanishing, as if something had been dragged into it and gone down."[3]

During the leisurely journey there was an episode of acute embarrassment that Giacomo remembered as formative. Waking at daybreak, the boy saw trees passing above a window in the ceiling, but he couldn't see the shore. "'Ah, dear mother!' I cried, 'what is that? The trees are moving!' They laughed, but my mother, giving a sigh, told me in a pitying tone, 'It's the boat that's moving, not the trees. Get dressed.'" That is the only thing Zanetta ever said that Casanova quotes in the *Histoire,* and it was anything but complimentary. Yet he claims that his embarrassment produced a startling breakthrough of insight.

> All at once I grasped the reason for the phenomenon, going forward with my dawning reason which was not in the least prejudiced. "Then it must be," I replied, "that the sun doesn't move either, and it's we who roll from east to west." My good mother exclaimed at my stupidity. Signor Grimani deplored my imbecility, and I was overcome with consternation, hurt and ready to cry. The person who came to my rescue was Signor Baffo. He rushed to me, embraced me tenderly, and said, "You're quite right, my child. The sun does not move. Take courage, always reason logically, and let people laugh."

Is it conceivable that Giacomo really came up with this? Possibly he was recalling some adult's previous attempt to explain the Copernican system to him, perhaps using balls to represent the earth and sun. Rousseau mentions in the *Confessions* that his own father did just that.

What matters, in any case, is the revelation about himself that the adult Casanova thought he had received. Without Baffo's intervention a nascent mental faculty would have been stifled. "To it alone," he says in the *Histoire*, "I owe the happiness I enjoy when I find myself face to face with myself." He was discovering a gift for independent thinking, resistant to dogmas of all kinds.

The timing is significant, too. He had just been wrenched from his childhood home; it may well have felt like eviction. He had left behind the grandmother who adored him, had received a humiliating public rebuke from his mother and his guardian, and was facing a new life when he felt far from ready for it. The little exchange on the burchiello was a revelation that in these new circumstances he was also discovering who he really was, rather than what people might expect him to be.

The plan was for Giacomo to study with a tutor in Padua, but meanwhile he had to get used to a shocking life in the house of an elderly Slavonian woman who took in boys, gave them room and board in Dickensian squalor, and undertook to have them educated. In the *Histoire* he doesn't mention her name, but he describes her with loathing as built like a soldier, with yellowish skin, bushy eyebrows, long hairs on her chin, and "hideous breasts, wrinkled and half uncovered, that hung halfway down her body." To a lonely and bewildered boy who had just turned nine, torn suddenly from his home, she seemed like an ogress.

They paid the woman six zecchini, which were supposed to last for six months, and she complained that it wasn't nearly enough; that was getting off to a bad start. The account of the move to Padua ends bitterly. "I was kissed, they ordered me to obey her orders always, and they left me there. It was thus that they got rid of me—*ce fut ainsi qu'on se débarrassa de moi.*" Casanova employs the impersonal *on* rather than *ils*—"one," not "they"—and Zanetta does seem to have treated him impersonally. Surely the theory about Paduan air was a rationalization, too. For whatever reason, she and the Grimanis did want to get rid of him.

After his domestic life in Venice, young Giacomo felt ill-used by the landlady and her insolent servants. His cherished silver spoon was confiscated and replaced with a wooden one, and the other boys bullied him, which he perhaps had never experienced before. The room he shared with them was filthy, infested by fleas, lice, bedbugs, and rats that terrified him by jumping up on his bed. All his life he would experience revulsion at rats. He was also half-starved and increasingly emaciated. He describes his hunger as "canine."

Fortunately, the tutoring turned out to be a liberation. He began to take lessons from a twenty-five-year-old priest named Antonio Gozzi, who had a kind disposition. Gozzi became aware of the boy's distress, and wrote to Alvise Grimani and Baffo about it; there was no use writing to Marzia since she couldn't read or write. Grimani replied that Giacomo had better learn to behave himself, but Baffo told Marzia and she hastened to Padua to intervene. "At her appearance I threw myself on her neck, unable to restrain my tears which she soon accompanied with her own. She sat down and took me between her knees." Without hesitation she arranged for him to leave the ogress and live with Gozzi. "My joy was inexpressible."

It was becoming apparent that Giacomo was exceptionally bright, and he made rapid progress in Latin, which would prove to be an invaluable acquisition in later life. His linguistic ability prompted still another symbolic scene. Gozzi took him to Venice to visit his family, Zanetta having returned temporarily from performing abroad, and Baffo invited them to dinner. One of the guests was a visiting Englishman who asked teasingly whether the boy's Latin was good enough to translate a riddle:

> *Discite grammatici cur mascula nomina cunnus,*
> *Et cur femineum mentula nomen habet—*

"Say, grammarians, why does the cunt have a masculine name, and why is the prick feminine?" This particular anomaly of gender does indeed exist in Latin, and in the romance languages that descend from it.

Casanova never got over his exultation when he produced not a mere translation, but a witty reply: *Disce quod a domino nomina servus habet*—"Say that it's because the slave takes the name of his master." Is it likely that a novice Latinist would come up with this line, or for that matter, that a pre-adolescent boy would be capable of conceiving the idea? The explanation he gives is that he had covertly read an obscene book entitled *De Arcanis Amoris et Veneris*. If he actually did read it, his Latin must indeed have been good. And was he already aware that Baffo was notorious for obscene verses? In the *Histoire* he calls Baffo "a sublime genius, a poet in the most lubricious of all genres."

At any rate, what he highlights in telling this story is a dawning awareness that he might aspire someday to "the glory that comes from literature." Skill with language would indeed be crucial to his success in the world, and so would quickness of mind. Surely, however, the deepest significance of the incident is a precocious intuition of the power of sex. Throughout his life he would try to convince women that it was they who held the real power, and that far from seeking to dominate them, he surrendered to them.

If Giacomo was to receive a formal education, what future might that lead to? Though his mother was an actress and Michele Grimani owned a theater, there seems to have been no thought of encouraging him in that direction, perhaps because—as Gaetano Casanova had found—only star actors could count on regular employment. For a bright boy with verbal skills, the church was a logical choice. The church was wealthy, and it could promise a secure career for an accomplished preacher. Also, Latin was its official language, and he was already acquitting himself well in that regard.

Alvise Grimani was an abate, equivalent to the French abbé, and that was what Giacomo would soon become. The term is not well understood today. It's related to the English "abbot," the head of a monastery, but meant something entirely different. There were four preliminary "minor orders" for an aspirant to the priesthood. After attaining the ranks of acolyte, exorcist, lector, and porter, their holder was entitled to use the title of abate. An abate was distinguished externally by a black robe and tonsured haircut. At some point later on he might be ordained a deacon and then a priest, but many abbés and abates didn't go that far and never intended to. Noblemen, in France as well as Italy, often acquired the title as a result of being given income from a monastic bequest, even if they led totally worldly lives. Commoners likewise sought the title, because it conferred a certain social status even when no income was involved.

Mozart's librettist Lorenzo da Ponte, twenty-five years younger than Casanova, began life in a similar career path. He was born Emanuele Conegliano in the Jewish ghetto of a small town in the Veneto, and when his family converted to Catholicism he took the name of the dignitary who baptized him, Monsignor Lorenzo da Ponte. After brief study in a seminary he received minor orders and could use the title of abate. "Taking minor orders," his biographer says, "meant little more than the monkish garb and a promise not to duel or dance. They were seen as not very different from lay [i.e., nonclerical] boys." Another writer says that even today in Rome, "one still runs into these *petits abbés* with plump cheeks." Da Ponte was later ordained to the priesthood, as was Antonio Vivaldi, but neither of them ever showed the slightest interest in religion as a vocation.[4]

In November of 1737, still living with Gozzi, Casanova was enrolled at the distinguished University of Padua (founded in 1222, three years before Oxford and the Sorbonne). At that time, incidentally, there was no university in Venice; the Ca' Foscari University that flourishes there today dates from 1868.

He was twelve and a half years old, a normal age for matriculation at European universities in those days. There he took courses for two years, concentrating in law, though he says that he felt an "invincible aversion" to it and would have preferred medicine. As for other subjects, he mentioned in an essay long afterward that a pedantic professor made him study the Ptolemaic system "and menaced me with the damnation of my soul if I believed that the earth moves." He added, "it was only after emerging from the slavery of Padua that I came to know many truths." Galileo himself had once taught there, but that was before he was compelled to disavow his ideas.[5]

Casanova was reading and thinking a lot. Late in life he told a friend that from an early age, his greatest passion had been "to learn the reason for everything, and especially what they didn't want you to know." Though he always claimed to be a good Catholic, that was for prudential reasons, and his innate skepticism was already apparent. So was an inclination to test the rules, and to transgress them whenever he could.[6]

In particular he got interested in the scandalous philosophy of materialism, which held that matter is the fundamental reality and that all processes, including human thinking, can be explained by it. When someone in later life told him that the Copernican system was merely a hypothesis, he retorted, "It must be the system of God, because it's the system of nature, and Holy Scripture is not the book from which Christians can learn physics."[7]

In the *Histoire,* what Casanova describes about the university is not his studies, but an exciting new freedom. "I made every possible bad acquaintance among the best-known students. The most famous were libertines, gamblers, frequenters of places of ill repute, drunkards, *débauchés,* ruiners of virtuous girls, violent, false, and incapable of the slightest feeling of virtue." It was during this period "that I began to know the world by studying the harsh book of experience." Theories of morals, he says, are no better than the index to that book, even though learning from experience means paying heavily for one's mistakes.

Part of learning from experience was gambling, which resulted in Giacomo getting deeply into debt. He sent to his grandmother for help; Marzia arrived and took him back with her to Venice. That was in October of 1739, after just two years at the university. He was not quite fifteen. It was the end of his formal education, but he wasn't missing much, since Latin and church law represented a narrow field of learning. That would have been true at most universities in Europe. Intellectuals whose names we know today were all essentially self-taught in modern ideas.

Giacomo and his younger brother Francesco were now established on their own in an apartment in the Calle della Commedia, presumably paid for by the Grimanis. Marzia's house, on the Calle delle Muneghe one street away, had room only for herself and young Gaetano. Faustina had died two years previously, at the age of five.

Giovanni Tosello, the priest at the nearby church of San Samuele, took an immediate interest in Giacomo and set about grooming him for an ecclesiastical career. The first step was to present him to the bishop of Venice, who conferred on him "by special grace" the minor orders that made him an abate. The bishop also gave him a tonsure. The ugly haircut was bad enough, but what followed was worse. Father Tosello complained that Casanova was behaving like a peacock, which indeed he would do for the rest of his life, carefully curling and perfuming his remaining hair. Remonstrating did no good, so early one morning, with Marzia's approval, the priest tiptoed into his room "and pitilessly cut off all my hair in front from ear to ear." Giacomo adds indignantly in the *Histoire,* "My brother Francesco was in the next room, saw it all, and did nothing to stop it."

Still, being an abate carried worldly benefits. When people heard that he was a Padua graduate "it attracted the silent observation of my equals in status and age, the compliments of fathers of families, and the caresses of old women. Many who weren't old wanted to pass for old, so that they could decently give me kisses."

That was invigorating, and so was the unexpected friendship of a seventy-six-year-old senator named Alvise Gasparo Malipiero, who was living in retirement in his Palazzo Malipiero on the Grand Canal, genial but crippled by gout. "He was handsome, a gourmet, and fond of wine; he had a sharp wit, great knowledge of the world, the eloquence of the Venetians, and the wisdom that belongs to a senator who entered retirement only after passing forty years in governing the Republic, and who didn't cease from paying court to the fair sex until he had had twenty mistresses, acknowledging with disappointment that he could no longer be pleasing to any."

Just beyond the palazzo was the church of San Samuele, and in this picture the Calle della Commedia—whose name was later changed to the Calle

PALAZZO MALIPIERO
a S. Samuele Sopra Canal Grande

Luca Carlevarijs del. et sc.

8. The Palazzo Malipiero

Malipiero—was beyond the alleyway between the palazzo and the church. Father Tosello knew Malipiero well, and made the introduction to help his young protégé get on in life.

Malipiero took an immediate liking to the youth, who in turn was fascinated by the distinguished patrician. Until then the only members of the nobility whom he'd gotten to know were Baffo and the Grimani brothers, whose patronage was dutiful but unemotional, whereas Malipiero was the first of a number who would be charmed by the young man's originality and wit. Malipiero was unmarried, though famous for affairs with women over the years, following the convention of keeping the family fortune intact for an elder brother. Giacomo never actually moved in at his palazzo, but he spent much of his time there and was soon being treated almost as a surrogate son.

Something he absorbed from his new mentor was a social skill that would serve him well, "to make people laugh without laughing myself. I learned that from Signor Malipiero, my first master. 'To make people weep,' he told me, 'you must weep, but you mustn't laugh when you want to make them laugh.'" Wit would indeed carry him far in life, but not in the direction the Grimanis and Gozzi thought they had mapped out. During his final years a friend confirmed that he had taken Malipiero's lesson to heart: "He doesn't laugh much, but he makes other people laugh."[8]

Malipiero announced that since it was his right to choose the preacher at San Samuele for the day after Christmas, he would name Casanova, despite the fact that he wasn't yet a priest. The boy abate—one writer calls him by the diminutive *abatino*—chose to preach from a text by Horace, which raised some eyebrows since that was a pagan poet, but he adapted it to denounce the wickedness of human beings, "which had brought about the failure of the plan conceived by divine wisdom to redeem them." He spoke with such eloquence that he was fervently applauded. "I was destined to become the greatest preacher of the century, since no one had ever performed so well at the age of fifteen." The pious Marzia wept with joy at the thought that her grandson was becoming an apostle.[9]

There were other rewards too. When a collection was taken up, it contained a number of love notes, which members of the congregation must have written during the service. It has been observed that in eighteenth-century Venice "it was never far from the pulpit to the boudoir." In an article entitled "abbé" in his *Philosophical Dictionary,* Voltaire quoted a popular song: "'Where are you going, Monsieur Abbé? You'll break your neck, going without a candle.' 'So? It's to visit the girls—you understand what I mean.'"[10]

Three months later, this brilliant debut had a sequel when Casanova was invited to preach again. It was a shaming anticlimax. Preachers were expected to deliver their sermons from memory, but Casanova hurried to the church after a convivial meal, "with a full stomach and a disordered head," and realized that he couldn't remember a single word. When he began desperately babbling, people tittered and walked out. The nightmare ended when he abruptly fell down. "I've never known whether I pretended that weakness made me fall, or whether I fell in earnest. All I know is that I let myself fall on the pulpit floor, banging my head against its side and wishing it would split open." This second sermon was his last.

It was usual in those days for university students to complete their formal instruction and then return at a later date to present a thesis and receive a degree. Casanova went to Padua to do so, and successfully defended a not especially controversial thesis arguing that Jews should be permitted to open new synagogues. He now had a doctoral degree in both civil and ecclesiastical law, which he often mentioned proudly in later years.

Meanwhile, he was getting advanced instruction in modern ideas that weren't taught at Padua. Malipiero and his friends acquainted him with the

Epicureanism of the freethinking French priest and mathematician Pierre Gassendi, a philosophy that was attractive not simply as abstract theory but as a relaxed and tolerant way of living. Malipiero also furnished Casanova with "a lesson I've never forgotten," which he would invoke often in the *Histoire*. That was the ancient Stoic maxim *sequere deum,* "follow the god." The "god" was not the same thing as the Christian deity, but a kind of inner voice. "'This,' he told me, 'was the *daemon* of Socrates *saepe revocans raro impellans* [often restraining, rarely impelling], and from that derived the *fata viam inveniunt* [the fates will find the path] of those same Stoics." The quotation (*invenient* in modern editions) comes from the *Aeneid.*[11]

Throughout his life Casanova would sense the influence of this *daemon* or *daimon* (he also calls it a *génie*), which was essentially amoral, not a guiding and reproving conscience. It hardly ever showed him what he ought to do, he said, but it did often make him draw back from something unwise. That was an ideal philosophy for a born improvisor like Casanova. It wasn't rigid fatalism, since he usually (not always) felt that he had free will, but it implied something deeper than random whim. At crucial turning points in his life, it was this daemon that he would thank for fortunate outcomes.[12]

CHAPTER 3

An Erotic Education

Confident though Casanova became with women, he didn't begin that way. The first experience he narrates was with his tutor Gozzi's sister Elisabetta, who lived with them and whom everyone called Bettina. Casanova says she was thirteen at the time, though she was probably older. He generally remembered his partners as younger than they were (though women later on may well have misrepresented their age). He was ten when it began. That story fills two dozen pages in the small-print Pléiade edition of the *Histoire*—much more space than his two years at the university.

Bettina had a habit of sitting on the boy's bed to wash his face and chest—though why she was allowed to do that isn't clear—kissing him and calling him *son cher enfant,* her dear child. When he turned eleven these attentions began to interest him in a new way, though he was too shy to kiss her back until she teased him into doing it. On one occasion, after combing his luxuriant hair, she started to wash his legs, preparatory to pulling on some stockings she had knitted for him. As he recalls, "She carried her zeal for cleanliness too far, and her curiosity provoked a voluptuous pleasure in me that didn't cease until she saw that it could increase no further. Calming down, I felt guilty, and I thought I should ask her pardon. Bettina wasn't expecting that, and after reflecting a bit, she told me in an indulgent manner that the fault was hers, and it wouldn't happen again."[1]

In his naiveté he was bewildered and shocked. "She left me to my reflections, which were cruel. It seemed to me that I had dishonored her, betrayed her family's trust, violated the laws of hospitality, and committed the greatest of crimes, which I could make up for only by marriage, if indeed she could accept for a husband an impudent fellow who was unworthy of her."

The way Casanova presents these early memories is highly literary. At one point Bettina proposed to disguise him as a girl and go together to a ball. After he refused, he found a note on his bed: "Either go to the ball with me dressed as a girl, or I'll show you a sight that will make you cry." To this he replied, likewise in writing, returning her letter as well:

I will not go to the ball, for I'm determined to avoid any occasion of being alone with you. As for the unhappy sight you threaten me with, I believe you have enough sense to keep your word, but I beg you to spare my heart, since I love you as if you were my sister. I forgive you, dear Bettina, and I wish to forget everything. Here is a letter which you should be delighted to have again in your own hands. You can see what a risk you took by leaving it on my bed. My restoring it should convince you of my friendship.

How likely is it that Casanova could write so elegantly at such a young age, or remember it in such detail half a century afterward? On the other hand, he tells us that Bettina was an avid reader of romance novels, and maybe they really did talk to each other like that.

Anyway, there was a complicating factor. A fellow boarder named Candiani was making a determined play for Bettina, and probably receiving encouragement. He was fifteen, and much better placed to gratify her if that was what she was after.

At one point Casanova believed that Bettina had invited him to sneak into her room for the night, but he waited in vain for hours outside her locked door while snow was falling, like a lovelorn inamorato in romance. In the morning it was Candiani who emerged, gave him a kick in the belly, and left him groveling in the snow. "Deceived, humiliated, and mistreated, an object of contempt to the happy and triumphant Candiani, I spent three hours hatching the blackest projects for vengeance." He thought of telling Gozzi what was going on. He thought of poisoning both Candiani and Bettina.

But immediately there was a new twist in the plot. Fearing that her affair with Candiani would become known, the next morning Bettina fell into violent convulsions. Casanova suspected that these were feigned, but her mother and her brother the priest were convinced it was demonic possession, and they summoned two exorcists, one after the other. That gave Bettina an opportunity to utter appalling language that supposedly came from the devils within her. It amused Casanova that she kept up the convulsions much longer than necessary because the second exorcist was young and extremely handsome— "his hair was blond, his eyes were blue, and he had the features of the Apollo Belvedere." In an account of the exorcism that he wrote years later he commented, "I've noted that people possessed by devils are almost always nubile girls with a lively temperament."[2]

There was a shocking sequel. Bettina contracted smallpox, which swelled her face horribly, and for a time her life was despaired of; she was given the last rites. Giacomo stayed at her bedside and contracted a mild case himself, which apparently left some small blemishes on his own face, though they weren't obvious. He managed to persuade her not to scratch at the pustules, anguishing though they were, by saying that it would ruin her beauty and make it impossible for her ever to marry.

When Bettina recovered she declared that she truly loved him and not Candiani. Still, he refrained from "plucking her flower," since he believed that she ought to be a virgin at marriage. Probably he was aware also that as a barely adolescent boy he was out of his depth. Bettina did get married soon afterward, but it was to a "vile shoemaker" who made her so miserable that she had to move back in with her brother.

The lesson he took from this early experience was that a girl could skillfully manipulate his feelings. Or rather, he says, that was the lesson he should have learned. "I went right on being the dupe of women until the age of sixty." But how had Bettina learned so much about the human heart? "By reading novels." Whether that's convincing or not, it's an example of Casanova's fascination with the power of imagination to create reality.

There must have been experiences with women while he was roistering at the university, but he says nothing about it. Perhaps he thought they were too ordinary to bother describing. The next encounter he relates was with a courtesan, whom he met during a social occasion at the Palazzo Malipiero. All his life he would be intimidated by courtesans. They were consorts of wealthy and powerful men, socially confident and essentially out of his league. A 1739 English mezzotint entitled *A Venetian Courtesan* gives a good impression of the type.

This one's name was Giulietta, and her beauty was the talk of the town. She was an aspiring singer but not very talented, and her lavish lifestyle was funded by a series of patrician lovers who passed her along from hand to hand.

9. A Venetian Courtesan

Now sixteen, Casanova was becoming a connoisseur of female looks, and he was highly opinionated. All his life he commented on the eloquence of women's eyes. He found Giulietta's especially compelling—"illuminated by that incredible iridescence that nature gives only, and occasionally, to youth, and that generally disappears at about the age of forty, after having worked miracles." Her hands and feet, however, were unacceptably big. He made Malipiero's guests laugh by saying so, and that got back to an indignant Giulietta. People warned him that she would find a way to take revenge.

Giulietta asked him to persuade Malipiero to let her stage a ball in a big room in the palazzo, and when she arrived there she exclaimed to Giacomo, "Quick, take me to your room; I've had an amusing idea, and it will make us laugh." Although he didn't live there, he did have the use of a room on the top floor, and they went up to it, where she proposed putting on his garments while he dressed in hers. Cross-dressing always interested Casanova, as did the prospect of helping her to adjust the clothes where they fitted too tightly. But every time he ventured to use his hands, she pushed him indignantly away. "Suddenly turning coquette, she got angry because I couldn't conceal the too visible effect of her charms, and she refused a relief that would have calmed me in an instant. I tried to give her a kiss, she didn't want it. I became impatient, and in spite of her, the splattering of my incontinence appeared on her shirt." Giulietta slapped his face violently, and when they went downstairs everyone could see the mark of her hand.

This was another lesson in what sexual attraction could do when it was used against him and not by him. It's important to emphasize also that—as always in the *Histoire*—he describes what happened frankly but not explicitly. After quoting this passage a biographer chooses to explain "the too visible effect of her charms" as "his quivering erection." Casanova says nothing about quivering. Still less does he indulge in rhetorical flights like this one on a different occasion: "He felt launched into the empyrean, gulping great drafts of immortality with her." He is never obscene, and he never writes purple prose.[3]

At about this time, Casanova had a very different experience with a naïve but highly receptive country girl. He had been invited to visit a country estate at Friuli on the mainland. Many Venetian nobles had such estates, as a source of income and as a pleasant retreat for a *villegiatura* or summer vacation, moving their households there to escape the remorseless heat of the Venetian summer.

The caretaker had a pretty daughter named Lucia who enchanted him from the start. "She was a very young girl, formed like town girls of seventeen although she was just fourteen. Her skin was fair, her eyes black, and her hair disheveled. She wore only a chemise, and a petticoat laced askew that showed half her naked leg. She looked at me as freely and serenely as if we had been old acquaintances, and asked if I was contented with my bed."

After Lucia's parents told him how pious and virtuous she was, well suited for marriage but too young for it at present, Casanova resolved not to be the one to sully that virtue. The resolution wasn't easy to keep, since Lucia developed a habit of jumping onto his bed and flirting, much as Bettina had done. "The companionship of this angel made me suffer the pains of hell. I was in a state of continuous temptation to deluge her face with kisses, as she would laughingly hold her face two inches from mine and say that she wanted to be my sister. One single kiss would have blown up the edifice I had constructed, for I felt as inflammable as straw."

Casanova lectured Lucia on the dire consequences that could follow from acting on their feelings, and he began to weep. "At the end of my sermon she wiped my tears away with the front of her chemise, not dreaming that this charitable action displayed to my sight two rocks that were made to shipwreck even the most expert of pilots." She confessed that every night she awakened from a dream that he was beside her, and she followed that by sneaking into his bed. She knew what she wanted, but he continued to resist, which was stimulating in itself. "What made us insatiable was abstinence, which she did everything in her power to make me renounce." He returned to Venice rejoicing in his heroism.

Some time later Casanova felt moved to reconnect with Lucia, but when he got to Friuli he found that she was gone. Weeping, her parents said that a month after he left, she had been seduced by the household courier, whom Casanova remembered as *un coquin célèbre,* a notorious rascal. After getting her pregnant the man mistreated her outrageously, and then they ran away together. Hearing this, Casanova "was so afflicted for these honest people that I buried myself in the woods to digest my grief." This reminiscence prompts Félicien Marceau to remark that Casanova almost never mentions any features of the natural world; his interest was exclusively in people. "Let us salute those trees. In his memoirs there are scarcely any others."[4]

This time the lesson Casanova believed he had learned was that his restraint with Lucia had been a big mistake, just as it was with Bettina. "*If* I had proceeded with her, then after I left she wouldn't have been in the overwhelming state that must have been the chief reason why she yielded to the rascal's desires. *If* she hadn't known me before him, her still pure soul would not have listened to him. I was in despair at finding myself the agent of the despicable seducer. I had been working for him." The moral was that self-denial is a terrible idea. He would seldom practice it again.

Twenty years later his thinking seemed to be confirmed when he unexpectedly encountered Lucia in Amsterdam. She had become a prostitute in a sordid dive, and they didn't even recognize each other at first. He was convinced that if he, rather than the rascally courier, had been the first one to sleep with her, she would somehow have gone on to a better life. That's far from obvious, though. Why would sleeping with Casanova, who was never going to remain with her, have led to a better outcome? Throughout the *Histoire* his recollections allow him to congratulate himself, without considering what it all meant to the other person.

A meeting with a pair of young sisters occasioned a deeper and more extended relationship, and Casanova ponders its implications at some length. He had gotten interested in a girl named Angela, Father Tosello's niece, who used to come to his house to take lessons in embroidery. She was affectionate toward Casanova, but firmly refused any sexual contact before marriage, which she hoped would indeed happen with him. He was only sixteen at this time, and she was probably younger. Of course, if he were to marry he would have to give up a career as a priest, and he wasn't prepared to do that.

Learning embroidery with Angela were sisters named Nanetta and Marta. They lived with an aunt who was anxious to obtain admittance to a home for needy widows that was under the control of Signor Malipiero, and that fact gave the girls an idea. They would invite Angela to spend the night with them, as she often did. If Casanova, meanwhile, would plead their aunt's cause with his patron, she would undoubtedly allow him to visit her house. At nightfall he should pretend to leave, wait until the aunt had gone back inside, slip back in, and go quietly upstairs to the girls' bedroom. Perhaps in that setting Angela could be persuaded to yield.

The plan worked perfectly. Angela did arrive, and soon the four of them were teasing each other merrily. Casanova had brought two bottles of strong wine from Cyprus, which made them tipsy. When their single candle burned out they were left in total darkness and began a game of blind man's buff, during which he groped for the girls without being sure which one was which. The next time he was there Angela failed to show up, but the sisters assured him that she really did love him. When he asked how they knew that, Marta revealed that whenever Angela spent a night in their bed, "she covers me with kisses, and calls me her dear abate." Laughing, Nanetta put her hand over her sister's mouth, which led Marta to add that "since I had plenty of intelligence, it was impossible I didn't know what two girls who are good friends do when they're in bed together."

This acknowledgment of female sexuality was arousing for Casanova, and indeed scenes like this were not uncommon in (male) eighteenth-century writing. In Rousseau's immensely popular novel *Julie, or the New Héloïse,* his hero relishes the sight of Julie's affection for her cousin Claire: "What ecstasy to see two such beauties tenderly embracing, the face of one resting on the other's breast. Nothing on earth can excite such voluptuous tenderness as your mutual caresses." Julie and Claire are perfectly innocent; Nanetta and Marta were relatively innocent, but eager to be less so.[5]

Casanova and the two sisters got into bed, and he wished them goodnight. He wasn't sure whether they fell asleep or were only pretending, but he intended to find out. With extreme caution he drew closer to the one who was nearest, curled up with her back to him. "As I advanced my enterprise with the tiniest of movements, she realized that her best course was to feign sleep and let me do it. Little by little I went on, little by little she uncurled, and little by little, with slow and marvelously natural movements, she got into the most favorable position she could without giving herself away." Eventually she couldn't help taking part more actively, and he was surprised to realize that she must have been a virgin until that moment.

That turned out to be Marta, and Nanetta was next, lying peacefully on her back. "I began by delighting her soul. I kept on until she affected a very natural movement, without which it would have been impossible for me to crown the endeavor, and she helped me to triumph. But in the moment of crisis she no longer had the strength to keep on pretending. She unmasked herself and clutched me tightly in her arms, pressing her mouth on mine."

In a study of Casanova's fascination with lesbianism, Chantal Thomas says of this encounter, "The fiction of somnambulist desires, of bodies that grope one another without realizing it, removes all seriousness from the erotic games *à trois*." It was also the first of a number of encounters in Casanova's life when he would find gender ambiguity inspiring.[6]

Innocent or not, this was Casanova's first revelation of a tactic that he would use frequently in years to come when he found himself with a pair of girls or women. After recounting one such episode that happened in Geneva twenty-three years later, he describes his tactics with unusual frankness.

> In my long career as a libertine, during which my unquenchable penchant for the fair sex made me employ every method of seduction, I turned the heads of some hundreds of women whose charms overwhelmed my reason; but what always served me best was that I took care that when I attacked novices whose morals or prejudices were an obstacle to success, it was only in the company of other women. I learned early that a girl is reluctant to let herself be seduced because of lack of courage, whereas when she is with a friend she yields more easily. The weakness of one causes the other's fall.[7]

That seems sufficiently cynical, but several points should be noted. One is that Casanova is talking about "novices." With more experienced women it was generally the case, or so he says, that they shared his feelings and there was no need for artful seduction. Another point is that even the novices, in his opinion, are secretly eager to surrender, and it's only lack of courage that inhibits them. He never had much respect for conventional "morals," let alone "prejudices." And finally, this quotation comes from a chapter whose manuscript original got lost, and it's therefore the version that was first printed by Jean Laforgue. Most of the manuscript did survive, from which we know that Laforgue constantly rewrote Casanova's text, often insinuating his own moral disapproval. It may well be that Casanova didn't actually write as cynically as this.

When he next visited during the daytime, the girls' aunt was there, full of gratitude for his intercession with Malipiero. As he was leaving Nanetta slipped him an envelope. In it was a piece of dough on which the house key had left an impression, so now he was able to provide himself with a duplicate and get in whenever he liked. "In this way I remained in tranquil possession of the two angels, with whom I spent the night at least twice every week."

Six years after this, when Casanova was twenty-one, he returned to Venice from a trip and found the angels' house empty. Their aunt had remarried and moved away; she didn't need the home for widows after all. By now both girls were married, Nanetta to a count who lived near Modena, and Marta to Christ. She had become a nun, and a couple of years after that she sent him a letter, "imploring me, in the name of Jesus Christ and the holy Virgin, not to appear in her sight. She told me that she had to pardon the crime I had committed by seducing her, since it was because of it that she was certain of her eternal salvation, having passed the whole of her life since then in repentance. She ended by assuring me that she would never cease praying to God for my conversion."[8]

Casanova was always a Catholic, but hardly a virtuous one, and she meant that his soul was in danger if he didn't renounce his wicked ways. What he would not acknowledge was that Marta's remorse must have been deeply felt. That would have meant admitting his own responsibility in causing it. Slyly, he picked up on her hint to suggest that she was actually grateful in a peculiar way. It was sinning with him that had inspired her to seek eternal salvation.

His constant claims of mutual satisfaction with his lovers are not just self-serving in an obvious way; they reflect a considered philosophy in which pleasure was an end in itself and permanent relationships were a trap. François

Roustang concludes, "He tries to construct a free man, in the sense of freedom from any obligations or constraints. Through laughter and libertinage, he seeks to corrode from deep within, without disturbing the surface, whatever impedes his obsessive quest for total license; hence his need to wear myriad masks, so that he will never see his own transgressions."[9]

One erotic encounter, however, put an abrupt end to Casanova's time at the Palazzo Malipiero. The old man had developed a passion for a seventeen-year-old girl named Teresa Imer, an aspiring singer who liked to show herself off at her window right opposite his bedroom. She was a daughter of Giuseppe Imer, manager of the San Samuele theater. Casanova was attracted to Teresa himself, but well aware that Malipiero considered her off limits. He must also have known that her father was widely believed to have been Zanetta Casanova's lover, but he makes no mention of that.

Teresa's mother brought the girl to visit Malipiero almost every day, but only after taking communion in the morning. Although she was flirty she would never permit a kiss, explaining that she didn't dare offend the God whom she had consumed at Holy Communion that very day, "who might still be in her stomach."

One day when Malipiero had gone for his nap, Casanova and Teresa found themselves sitting alone together. "The idea occurred to us, in the innocent gaiety of our nature, to compare the differences in our bodily formation. We had reached the most interesting stage of the investigation when a blow of a cane fell violently on my neck, followed by another, and there would have been still more if I hadn't escaped the storm by dashing out of the room." Soon afterward the housekeeper brought him the hat and coat he'd left behind, along with a stern warning never to show up there again.

To complete Casanova's erotic initiation, there was an encounter with a young bride. While on the mainland, he was invited to take part in a festive group that included a newly married couple, and he couldn't help observing that the husband paid more attention to the bride's pretty sister than he did to her. She noticed it too, and soon she was openly flirting with Casanova, while the husband apparently ignored her.

What followed a few days later, at least in Casanova's telling, reads like a fabliau right out of Boccaccio or Chaucer. He and the bride were the only passengers in a carriage returning from a visit to an outlying estate, and a sudden storm blew up. She trembled with fear at the thunderclaps, and when rain began to pour down he covered them both with his cloak.

Then the horses reared up, and the poor lady fell into convulsive spasms. She threw herself upon me, hugging me tight in her arms. I leaned forward to retrieve the cloak, which had fallen at our feet, and in doing so I picked up her skirts along with it. Just as she was about to pull them down, there was another bolt of lightning, and terror prevented her from moving. Wanting to cover her again with the cloak, I pulled her towards me; she positively fell on me, and I quickly placed her astride. Her posture could not have been more fortunate, and I lost no time, pretending to adjust my watch in my belt. She realized that if she didn't stop me right away, she wouldn't be able to defend herself, and she made an effort, but I told her that unless she feigned a swoon the postilion would turn around and see everything. Having said that, I let her call me impious as much as she liked, while I seized her by the buttocks and carried off the most complete victory that ever a skillful gladiator did.

Previously Casanova had been inexperienced and tentative; from this time on he would see himself as a resourceful seducer, prompt to exploit any opportunity.

He concludes the story with a little dialogue.

"You're a dreadful man and you've made me unhappy for the rest of my days. Now are you satisfied?"

"No."

"So what do you want?"

"A deluge of kisses."

"How miserable I am! All right, take them."

"Tell me you forgive me. Admit that I gave you pleasure."

"Yes—you can see that. I forgive you."

I wiped her dry, and when I asked her to do the same favor for me, I could see she was laughing.

"Tell me you love me," I said.

"No, because you're an atheist, and hell is awaiting you."

Kissing her hands, I told her that I must have cured her fear of thunder, but she must never tell anyone the secret of the cure. She said she was certain, at any rate, that no other woman had ever been cured by such a remedy. "In a thousand years," I replied, "it must have happened a million times."

After they parted "in great good humor," Casanova noticed that the postilion was laughing. "What are you laughing at?" "You know very well." "All right, here's a ducat. But be discreet."

This can't even be called a seduction, since seduction would imply planning. It was taking impromptu advantage of an opportunity, and of a woman. If they really parted in great good humor, then it would seem she wasn't sorry afterward, but we have only his word for that. Was annoyance with her husband reason enough to submit to Casanova? Why not slap him angrily, or cry out—what would it matter if the postilion knew? As it turns out, he did know. In effect he was complicit.

Even women commentators, Lydia Flem for instance, have tended to see the episode through Casanova's eyes: "He no longer sacrifices to love in a confused night spent groping between two pretty sisters. He asserts his triumphant virility in full daylight, with the grandiose power of the entire sky raging above him." But the young bride did, after all, try to resist. Maxime Rovere calls it *un viol,* a violation or rape. "The rape unites him with the world of men as they define themselves at that period: filled with their political and social power, they take their virility as a privilege to deceive during seduction, and also to resort to force if the occasion demands."[10]

As for the woman, to whom Casanova doesn't give a name, she vanishes from the story. Women who cross his path over the years often do.

By this time his erotic education had included encounters with the teasing Bettina, the innocent Lucia, the imperious Giulietta, the ménage à trois with Marta and Nanetta, and the playful experimentation with Teresa that got him banished from the Palazzo Malipiero. Tentative and insecure at first, he learned that with patience and tact he could encourage cautious companions to share pleasure with him. He also discovered that he could get his way—without hard feelings afterward, or so he claims—even when a woman was resistant. All of this happened while he was still in his teens.

CHAPTER 4

A Career in the Church

When Casanova was eighteen his life changed drastically. He lost his grandmother Marzia, who "couldn't leave me anything, since during her lifetime she had given me all that she had." He also lost the house on the Calle della Commedia in which he had grown up. Zanetta realized that she would probably never live in Venice again, and wrote to tell Giacomo that she had instructed Alvise Grimani not to renew the lease and to sell off all the furnishings. The children were to be put up in boarding houses.[1]

Giacomo bitterly resented this decision, and probably his siblings did too. The furniture can't have been worth much. Indignantly, he started carrying off some of it to sell himself, at which point Grimani had the doors sealed so he couldn't get in. Giacomo's resentment was now towering, but he seems not to have blamed Zanetta, whose request was simply being carried out. Instead he blamed Grimani and his consigliere or agent, Antonio Razzetta, who obtained a police order forbidding Giacomo ever to return to the house. He had no way of getting back at Grimani, but he would find a way to avenge himself on Razzetta. Perceived insults always filled him with rage.

This, at any rate, is how he tells the story in the *Histoire*, but knowingly or not, he badly scrambled the sequence of events. He claims there that his grandmother owned the house on the Calle della Commedia, which in fact was just rented by Zanetta, but at this point it was three years since Marzia had lived there. A document in the Venetian state archives tells what actually happened. In 1740 Marzia moved to a different house in the nearby Calle delle Muneghe or Monache, "the street of the nunnery," where she stayed thereafter on charity. The document is clear: "*Calle delle Monache, case no. 6 concesse gratis vita durante—Marzia Farussi no. 1.*" This means that Marzia would live free of charge in one of six houses that were given to deserving indigents, but at her death her family would have no rights in it.[2]

Casanova must have known all of this perfectly well, but he covers it up in the *Histoire,* no doubt to make Grimani look bad. As for the house he grew up in, Zanetta had allowed her children to continue living there for a while after she left Venice, but in 1743 she decided to stop paying the rent, and that was when Grimani had to find new lodgings for them.

Before long, however, a very different kind of message came from Zanetta. Working as an actress in Warsaw, she had become friends with Queen Maria Josepha, and also with a cultivated Franciscan monk named Bernardino de Bernardis. Bernardis was a native of Calabria, a region in the south of Italy that was part of the Kingdom of Naples, and he missed his homeland. It happened that Queen Maria's daughter had recently married the king of Naples, and Bernardis and Zanetta hatched a plan. Queen Maria had connections in Rome, and might well be able to get Bernardis appointed to a bishopric in Calabria. So they struck this deal: if Zanetta could arrange for him to get that appointment, he would repay her by taking Giacomo Casanova into his employment as a private secretary. That would be a normal arrangement for a bright young abate, who might afterward proceed to the priesthood and possibly become a bishop himself some day. Queen Maria had no objection to the plan and pulled the necessary strings in Rome. Bernardis got the appointment, and Giacomo got the job.

"Imagine my joy twenty or thirty years from now," Zanetta wrote to Giacomo, "when I see you a bishop at the very least!" Why not a cardinal, or even pope? He was appropriately grateful. Her letter, he says, together with a follow-up one in Latin from Bernardis, rendered him *fanatique,* connoting delirious enthusiasm.

But Bernardis would not take up his new position for six months. Casanova needed a place to live in the meantime, since Malipiero had kicked him out after the contretemps with Teresa Imer. That was found for him by Grimani at the seminary of San Cipriano on the island of Murano, near where the sorceress had once worked her art. Before he left the city he had time for just one more night with Marta and Nanetta, who "watered the bed with tears that mingled with mine."

In the *Histoire* Casanova remarks that lodging him in a seminary was a foolish plan, given his rebellious temperament, but that his guardian no doubt meant well. He adds, "I've never been able to decide if this abate Grimani was good because he was stupid, or if the stupidity was a result of his goodness. But his brothers were all just the same. The worst trick that Fortune can play on a young man with talent is to make him the dependent of a fool." Michele Grimani, who might possibly have been Casanova's biological father, was one of those stupid brothers.

Predictably, the seminary didn't work out well. Casanova already had a university degree, and didn't need the elementary instruction there. Still worse, he had to sleep in a big dormitory room—there were three rooms for three hundred seminarians—where there was constant surveillance by a monk, whose chief duty was to keep the youths out of each other's beds. Casanova and a handsome fifteen-year-old contrived to get together in the dark of night, though he claims they were just amusing themselves and not actually misbehaving. Inevitably the monk detected them, they were accused of sin, and thrashed while kneeling before the crucifix in the chapel. Alvise Grimani soon heard about this, and since the whole point of the seminary had been to keep Casanova out of trouble, promptly removed him.

This episode prompted a heavily underlined statement against repression in the *Histoire de Ma Vie,* though confined there to masturbation rather than homosexual encounters. Casanova especially criticized Samuel Auguste Tissot, the Swiss physician whose *L'Onanisme* was a widely influential diatribe against it:

> The authors of those rules were ignorant fools who understood neither nature nor morality. For its own preservation, nature demands this relief for a man who lacks the assistance of a woman, and morality is opposed by the axiom *nitimur in vetitum* [we desire what is forbidden]. Prohibition excites. What Tissot says may be partly right if a young man masturbates [*se manstupre,* "debauches himself by hand"] when nature doesn't call for it, but that will never happen to a schoolboy unless he's forbidden to do it. In that case he does it for the pleasure of disobeying, a pleasure natural to all men ever since Eve and Adam, who embrace it as often as they get an opportunity. Mothers superior in convents are wiser than men about this. They know from experience that no girl hasn't begun to masturbate by the age of seven, and they're sensible enough not to forbid this childish practice.

This is in line with the thinking of Enlightenment philosophes: what nature prompts is by definition natural, and should be allowed to take its course.

Grimani was determined to keep his troublesome ward out of the city, so this time Casanova was sent to the island fort of Sant'Andrea del Lido, just east of the city proper. There he was treated courteously but encountered a new misfortune. The fort was populated by several hundred Albanian soldiers, many of whom had their wives with them. Since they were mostly illiterate, they enlisted Casanova to write letters and petitions. One wife wanted help with a petition seeking promotion for her husband. She repaid Casanova by sleeping with him, but also by giving him his first case of venereal disease; there would be many more, almost certainly gonorrhea rather than syphilis. "When I was stupid enough to reproach the woman for such a base action, she replied laughingly that she simply gave me what she had, and it was up to me to be on guard."

There was time for further escapades, and Casanova narrates one at length, delighted with his own cleverness. This was to avenge himself on Grimani's agent Razzetta. The first step was to acquaint himself with Razzetta's whereabouts and habits. He got a gondolier to take him secretly at nightfall to Venice, where he made his way to Razzetta's neighborhood. There he got directions to the house from a waiter in a coffee house, and confirmed whose house it was by knocking on the door. He was told from within that Razzetta wasn't at home. Remarkably, the voice from inside was that of his sister Maria Maddalena, who had evidently returned from Dresden by this time; Grimani had lodged her with his agent, who had a daughter of his own. Shortly before midnight Razzetta turned up on his way home, and Casanova, who had been lurking by a bridge, now knew exactly where to attack him. He couldn't do it at that moment, however, since his guilt would be obvious.

The next day he arranged in advance for a nighttime gondola trip. He then pretended to sprain or even dislocate an ankle, and was carried to his room in the fort. A guard was supposed to be keeping an eye on him, but Casanova plied him with brandy and he soon nodded off. Casanova then went down surreptitiously to the waiting gondola, which took him to Venice. There he tracked down Razzetta near the Campo San Polo and gave him a ferocious beating with a stick. Razzetta ended up in a canal with a broken nose and missing teeth, while by midnight Casanova had returned to the fort and was back in bed. He put the finishing touches on his alibi by awakening the guard with piercing cries, claiming an attack of colic for which a doctor was quickly summoned.

10. Ancona

Razzetta afterward declared that he had recognized Casanova and demanded punishment, but everyone at the fort confirmed that he had never left his bed the entire time. This was the kind of exploit that he would most pride himself on: improvising a clever stratagem and getting revenge with impunity. In the *Histoire* he shows no sign of grasping that it might make him look bad to readers. Nor does he acknowledge that in abusing Razzetta he was really avenging himself on the Grimanis—not just Alvise, but Michele too.

At the end of the six-month waiting period, knowing that his new employer Bernardis was expecting him, Casanova had just time for one last farewell night with Marta and Nanetta. Looking back he remembered their relationship as his one experience of true innocence. "This love, which was my first, taught me almost nothing about worldly ways, for it was perfectly happy, uninterrupted by any trouble and untarnished by the least self-interest. . . . I departed with joy in my heart, and regretting nothing." It was an unusual kind of innocence, a naïve but erotically intense ménage à trois.

By now Bernardis was in Rome, receiving consecration as a bishop, and Casanova set out to join him. The year was 1743, and he was still just eighteen. The first stop was Chiozzia, a nearby port on the mainland, where he was to wait for a boat to carry him down the coast to Ancona. Due to the shallowness of the lagoon at Venice, large ships had to dock in Ancona, which was a very considerable port.

The reason to go to Ancona was that it was the closest place beyond Venetian territory that had a lazaretto, a large structure where arrivals from Venice were required to submit to quarantine, since plague was believed to reach that city from the East. Quarantine literally meant "forty days," but he was detained for somewhat less than that, twenty-eight days in all. It was a tedious wait all the same, apart from a frustrating encounter with a beautiful Greek slave whom he could only grope awkwardly through a hole in the floor, in a rather comic Pyramus and Thisbe situation.

After Casanova was released, he proceeded on foot to Rome, 130 miles to the southwest with the Apennines in between. In those days he didn't mind extended journeys on foot, though in later life he could usually afford carriages. In Rome he learned that Bernardis had already left for Calabria, but church officials provided him with funds and he journeyed onward to the town of Martirano where the new bishop had taken up his appointment. It lay far down the Italian boot, 160 miles south of Naples.

When he got there he was appalled. Calabria was rustic and impoverished. He and Bernardis were to live in a ramshackle house and serve a congregation of "animals" who spoke an unfamiliar dialect and were mostly illiterate. Accustomed to high living and stimulating conversations in Venice, Casanova had no interest in the countryside, and Calabria seemed like exile (in the 2011 census Martirano still had just six hundred inhabitants). "Even today," Félicien Marceau noted in the 1980s, "in little towns in the south of Italy one finds the bishop living in a big house, ancient, tumbledown, full of holes, and surrounded by sheds."[3]

After three days Casanova asked to be released from his commitment. He also made a preposterous suggestion to the bishop: "Give me your episcopal benediction and my discharge, and leave along with me; I assure you that we'll make our fortune together. Resign your bishopric to those who made such a bad present of it to you." Bernardis burst into laughter, but genially agreed to let him go. So much for the scheme his mother had cooked up with the Polish queen. He would have to depend now on his own resources, living by his wits.

It was hardly fair, incidentally, for Casanova to say in the *Histoire* that when Zanetta took his brother Giovanni with her to Dresden, he was the only one of her children whose fortune she made. Giovanni did become a well-known painter after studying art there, but in connecting Giacomo with Bernardis she had reason to believe that she was making his fortune too.

Leaving Martirano in June 1744, Casanova headed north to Naples, carrying a letter to a gentleman whom the bishop asked to supply him with the handsome sum of sixty ducats, as a sort of severance pay. There was also an embarrassment that still pained him half a century later. He always loved being looked at, preferably in fancy clothes, and a Neapolitan nobleman who befriended him paid a tailor to make him some. But a humble abate wouldn't normally own such finery, and the man's wife immediately guessed that he owed it to her husband's extravagance.

Recalling this with chagrin, Casanova comments, "There are situations in life that I've never been able to adapt myself to. In the most brilliant company, I get flustered if a single person gives me a sidelong glance. My good humor vanishes, and I become stupid. It's a fault." That insight seemed so significant that he underlined it in his manuscript.

There was a more pressing reason to leave Naples. The nobleman who paid for the clothes was named Don Antonio Casanova. Giacomo not only assured him that they must be related, but told some tall stories about their forebears in Spain. We know what this must have been like because he actually begins the *Histoire* with a romanticized genealogy for himself that goes all the way back to the fifteenth century, including a nobleman who eloped with a nun in Saragossa, and their grandson who died while voyaging with Christopher Columbus. There's plenty more of that, but almost certainly Casanova made every bit of it up.[4]

What he didn't anticipate was that Don Antonio Casanova would then insist that they go together to kiss the hand of the young Queen of Naples. The problem was that it was her mother, the Queen of Poland, who had arranged Giacomo's appointment in Martirano. It seemed likely that that story would come out, including the fact that Zanetta was an ordinary actress, a profession that was considered ignoble if not immoral. "Don Antonio would be scandalized, and my genealogy would be ridiculous." A modern commentator makes it explicit: "The son of actors, virtually a race of untouchables, was stuck at one of the lowest and dirtiest rungs of the social ladder." We remember the horror of Zanetta's father, only a cobbler himself, at the prospect of his daughter marrying an actor and going on stage.[5]

To avert exposure, Casanova took to the road once again, booking a place in a coach for Rome. Today the 140-mile journey takes two and a half hours by car; back then it required several days. What he remembered most vividly about this journey was what didn't happen. "Something incredible! During the whole day I never opened my mouth, listening with pleasure to the jargon of a Neapolitan and the fine speech of two sisters from Rome. It was the first time in my life that I had patience enough to pass five hours without talking, while vis-à-vis with two charming girls or women." His silence is significant.

When it was a question of sizing up new people, he knew how to keep quiet and pay close attention. Later on would be soon enough to deploy his conversational gifts.

At night the whole party shared a room at a post house, an inn where the carriage stopped for a change of horses. That was a common arrangement at a time when private rooms were uncommon and expensive, and Casanova got his hopes up. He was especially attracted to one of the sisters, Donna Lucrezia, who may have been in her late twenties. Her husband was the talkative Neapolitan, a lawyer on his way to Rome to argue a case before the ecclesiastical court. At the inn, the sisters shared a bed between the lawyer's bed and Casanova's. He persuaded himself that that after everyone was asleep Lucrezia might creep into his bed—"I was on fire for her"—but it was her husband's she went to. The next day, however, she indicated that the attraction was indeed mutual. "In the coach we spoke with our knees rather than our eyes."

The night after that, at another inn, produced bedroom farce. The sisters were again sharing a bed, and this time Casanova was sharing one with the lawyer. He prepared to make his move, but whenever he tried to get up the bed creaked loudly, and the lawyer reached out to make sure he was still there. Suddenly there was a racket downstairs and his companion hurried out to see what was going on (a quarrel among some soldiers, as it turned out). Casanova wasted no time, and threw himself upon the lady. That broke the slats of her bed, which collapsed in a heap just as her husband was returning. The lock on the door was jammed, which bought a little time, but when Casanova resumed his attack he realized that in the dark he was addressing the wrong sister. By the time he got to Lucrezia she implored him to leave, which he did.

Though no longer a bishop's secretary, Casanova was still an abate, and he resolved to see where that might take him. Introducing himself in Rome to church dignitaries as an aspirant to the priesthood, he quickly found patronage. He was carrying two letters of introduction from Bernardis, and he presented the first to a highly regarded monk, Father Georgi, who promised to give advice. There was one problem: "Do you speak French?" "Not one word." "That's too bad—you must learn it." French was the language of international diplomacy, and of aristocrats and intellectuals throughout Europe.

The other letter was addressed to no less a person than a cardinal, Francesco Acquaviva d'Aragona, the Spanish ambassador to the Vatican. Father Georgi was delighted at that. "I congratulate you, for he's the one man in Rome who can do more even than the pope." Casanova seldom bothers to

Veduta di Piazza di Spagna

11. Piranesi, *Veduta di Piazza di Spagna*

describe a man's appearance, but we know from the Président de Brosses, a Frenchman who was there at the same time, that Acquaviva was considered *le plus grand seigneur* in Rome, "tall, handsome, and witty."[6]

The cardinal received Casanova graciously, took him on as a private secretary, and gave him lodgings in the Palazzo di Spagna, just off the Piazza di Spagna that is depicted here by Piranesi. The picture shows the famous Spanish Steps, which were still very new, having been completed in the year of Casanova's birth.

The cardinal reiterated Father Georgi's advice: "It's important for you to apply yourself right away to learning French; it's indispensable." He assigned a personal mentor to the hopeful youth, a Portuguese abate named Gama de Silveira, with whom Casanova developed a close friendship. Gama set him up with a French teacher who lived directly across from the Palazzo.

After a while there was even an audience with Pope Benedict XIV, who laughed at Casanova's attempts to speak the Tuscan dialect, advising him to stick to Venetian. The pope cheerfully assented when Casanova asked permission to eat meat on Fridays and "read all the forbidden books." Pope Benedict struck De Brosses as "rather fat, with a robust temperament; his face was round and full, with a jovial air and the physiognomy of a good fellow, with a straight-forward nature, calm and easy-going, and a free tongue. His topics were indecent, but his morals were pure and his conduct very regular."[7]

Benedict's portrait, however (color plate 11), is a reminder that he was an altogether formidable individual, a potentate who possessed enormous power and knew it.

Remembering the encouragement Donna Lucrezia had shown during the journey, Casanova soon located her in Rome, but Gama warned him not to go too often to her house since that would provoke damaging gossip. After waiting for a few days he did pay a visit, and "after having passed just one hour I returned to the palazzo, igniting the air with my amorous sighs." He dealt with his unhappiness by writing a love poem which, since love was a conventional theme for poetry, he sent to the husband, anticipating that he would show it to Lucrezia as an example of fine writing without realizing that it was a covert avowal.

Soon afterward he joined the couple on an excursion in the country, and on their return he managed to share a carriage with Lucrezia, which produced another narrow escape.

> How much might we have said to each other, before giving ourselves to affection, if time hadn't been so precious! But knowing all too well that we had only half an hour, in one minute we became a single individual. At the height of happiness and intoxicated with satisfaction, I was surprised to hear Donna Lucrezia cry out, "Oh my God! How unfortunate we are!" She pushed me away and readjusted herself, the carriage halted, and a lackey opened the door. "What has happened?" I asked, making myself decent again. "We're home."

Lucrezia's husband appeared at the opposite door just as she was getting out, which gave Casanova a chance to buy a little more time. "Nothing can be put together again more quickly than a woman—but a man! If I had been on the other side of the carriage, things would have gone very badly with me."

A pattern was resuming that began back at Padua, when he seduced the young bride in a carriage during a thunderstorm. As he describes it, married women saw him as a welcome change from their marital relationships, which were likely to have been arranged between families rather than reflecting mutual desire. What especially excited him was the element of risk, seizing an opportunity when it suddenly offered itself. Throwing off caution seems to have been exciting for the women as well, if Casanova's stories are to be believed.

12. The Frascati Gardens

Not long afterward there was another excursion, to lovely gardens with ornamental fountains in Frascati, where Lucrezia confirmed that the passion was mutual. Stealing off by themselves, they could finally express their feelings. When she commented, "You know too much at your age," Casanova replied fervently, "Just a month ago I was still ignorant. You are the first woman who has introduced me to the mysteries of love." She replied, "Why am I not yours! You too are the first love of my soul, and will certainly be the last. Happy is she whom you will love after me! I'm not jealous, I only regret that she won't have a heart equal to mine."

At last they could snatch an opportunity to make love, though still with the spice of possible detection. "We were resting peacefully after the first brief combat, gazing at each other without saying a word, and with no thought of changing our position, when the divine Lucrezia looked off to her right. 'Oh!' she exclaimed. 'Didn't I tell you that our *génies* are watching over us? Look at this little daemon. Do you not see that lovely serpent, who seems to adore us with fiery scales and raised head?'"

What she was talking about was a snake that appeared among the plantings like an encouraging visitant from the pagan past, utterly different from the serpent of temptation in that other garden in the Book of Genesis. A com-

mentator has an interesting thought: "This creature with changing colors—
is it not a symbol of Casanova himself, skilled at taking on the most varied
forms, supple and slippery like the serpent?"[8]

The creature slithered away, and they took that as a warning to make
themselves presentable before Lucrezia's husband and mother showed up.
When he got a chance, Casanova asked Lucrezia what she would have done if
they had been caught in the act. "Nothing. Don't you understand that in those
divine moments, one is nothing but in love? Can you believe you weren't
possessing me entirely?"

There was still time in Rome for repeated erotic episodes. "Standing face
to face, serious, looking only into each other's eyes, we unlaced and unbut-
toned with palpitating hearts. . . . At the end of two hours, enchanted with
each other, gazing at each other most tenderly, we both said the same words:
Amour, je te remercie—"Love, I thank you" (it would have been in Italian, of
course). Lucrezia added, "Without you, my dear friend, I might have died
without ever experiencing love. For my husband I've never felt anything but
the accommodation one is expected to show."

Casanova was indeed in love, more overwhelmingly than he had ever been
with the playful young angels. In one of his unpublished manuscripts he
comments, "A man who loves nothing has an empty heart, but he cannot feel
his misfortune because his emptiness is invisible, and what surrounds it is
himself. He won't be aware that the emptiness exists until it yearns to be filled
up. That happens when he falls in love." All his life he would seek not just sex,
but this intoxicating fullness of being. Of course that was most possible at the
beginning of a new affair, which is why he could never stop moving on from
each relationship to the next one.[9]

It's possible that the story of what happened at Frascati got around. A
marchesa who was flirting with Casanova asked how he liked the gardens
there, and he replied that he had never seen anything so beautiful. "But the
company you were with was even more beautiful," she said, "and your vis-à-
vis was most *galant*." A *vis-à-vis*—they were speaking Italian, but she used the
French term—was a carriage in which passengers sat face to face.

The affair with Lucrezia fulfilled a pattern that would continue to dominate Casanova's relations with women. François Roustang puts it well: "She
is just 'passing through' in three respects. She is married, and thus belongs to
another man and has neither any intention nor any possibility of leaving him.
Her stay in Rome is guaranteed to be brief, since her husband is only there on
business. And the lovers are forced to meet for their trysts in carriages, in post

houses, and on promenades in the country. She embodies brevity, haste, fur-
tive happiness, and the banishment of any tragic element."[10]

There was one more thrilling encounter, during an excursion to Tivoli.
After a long day of sightseeing the party retired to bed in a villa where they
were staying, and Casanova contrived to take a room adjacent to the one Lucrezia shared with her teenage sister Angelica. Soon they were in each other's
arms, and Casanova describes what happened as indelibly precious:

> Happy moments that I no longer hope for, but whose dear memory
> only death could make me lose! I believe I never undressed more
> quickly. I opened the door and fell into the arms of Lucrezia, who said
> to her sister, "It's my angel; be quiet and go to sleep." She couldn't say
> anything more, for our mouths pressed together left no power of speech
> or passage for breathing. Becoming a single being at the same instant,
> we lacked the strength to hold back for more than a minute; our desire
> reached its fulfillment without any sound of kissing or even the least
> movement on our part. We were consumed by a fierce fire that would
> have burned us up if we had tried to restrain it.

When the encounter was over, it suggested analogies that were either blasphemous or else—as in Casanova's own philosophy—entirely appropriate for
a transcendent experience. "After a short respite, silent, serious, and tranquil,
eager for the fire that it would reignite in our veins, we dried the two copious
inundations that had followed the first eruption. We performed this sacred
service for each other with fine linen, devoutly, and observing a religious silence. After this expiation we paid homage with our kisses to all of those places
that we had just purified." The word he uses is *monder,* which is sometimes
mistranslated as "inundate," but in old French it did mean "purify," as *mon-
dare* still does in Italian. Italianisms often got into Casanova's French. His discreet language makes it hard to know why there were two inundations. Possibly he had withdrawn, as he sometimes did, to forestall pregnancy, and
Lucrezia must have added a contribution of her own.

They had thought that Angelica was asleep, but it turned out she had been
watching them all night, much aroused by the spectacle. So they resumed, and
at the moment when Lucrezia was "dying" she suddenly pushed Casanova
onto her sister, "who far from repulsing me, clasped me to her breast in such
a way that she achieved her happiness almost without my doing anything."

Just as with the angels Marta and Nanetta, Casanova had established a
guilt-free ménage à trois with a pair of sisters, and they eagerly played their

role. Or so he says. Was it really like that? Did the frustrated wife Lucrezia and the virginal Angelica both reach the summit of pleasure the very moment they fell into his arms? This is one of many places in the *Histoire* where one may suspect that whatever happened, he has given it a highly self-flattering and idealized shape.

Casanova claims that he apologized the next morning for going too far, and Lucrezia retorted that she was only doing Angelica a good turn. "Gazing at me like a goddess, she reproached me for ingratitude. 'I brought the light,' she said, 'into my sister's mind. Instead of complaining, she should approve of me now. She must love you, and since I'm about to depart, I leave her to you.'" But how plausible is that?

Whether or not he could have pursued an affair with Angelica, Casanova unexpectedly needed to get out of Rome. The church authorities were furious when they learned that he had helped his French tutor's daughter to elope with her lover, and had even concealed her for a night in his room in the cardinal's palazzo. At least, that's the high-minded reason he gives in the *Histoire* for how he got into trouble. His friend in later life, the Prince de Ligne, heard a very different story. "In Rome he abducted the mistress of a nephew of the pope, and about to be assassinated, he took refuge in a little town." But maybe he was just trying to impress Ligne when he told him that?[11]

At any rate, Father Georgi warned Casanova that there was no use protesting his innocence: "This episode will still be held against you forty years from now by the college of cardinals, in the event that you should be put forward for election as pope." Cardinal Acquaviva called him in and said, gently but firmly, that his days in Rome were over. He had been there less than a year. As he probably realized, the prospect of a career in the church was likewise over. The best the cardinal could do for him was to announce that he was sending him abroad on an important mission. Told to name a destination of his choice, he said, "Constantinople." The cardinal was surprised, but agreed.

The Malipiero philosophy had come to Casanova's rescue once more. "I named that city by the occult influence of my *génie,* which was calling me there in order to act out my destiny." It's possible, though—the chronology of his life at this time is extremely unclear—that he had been in Constantinople once before, which would make the choice less peculiar. Besides, that city had a long-standing commercial relationship with Venice, and he could hope to form useful connections there. Of course it had been called Istanbul for the past three centuries, but westerners went on using its former Greek name.[12]

It's impossible, really, to imagine that Casanova could have gone on playing the game of Roman politics. He says so himself in the *Histoire*. "A man so constituted as to make his fortune in this ancient capital of Italy must be a chameleon, responsive to all the colors with which the light suffuses its atmosphere. He must be supple, insinuating, a great dissimulator, impenetrable, obliging, often base, falsely sincere, seeming always to know less than he does know, using just one tone of voice, patient, a master of his expressions, and as cold as ice when someone else would be on fire. If unfortunately he has no religion in his heart, he must have it in his mind, suffering in silence, and if he's honest he'll be mortified to acknowledge that he's a hypocrite." To this Casanova adds dryly, "There's no Catholic city on earth where people are less bothered by religion than Rome."[13]

Casanova was indeed a chameleon, or slippery serpent, but he needed freedom to improvise in ever new situations, and with new companions each time. The clergy in Rome were bureaucrats and careerists, carefully ascending the ladder of success. By now—he was not yet twenty—Casanova understood that he would never again submit to a career.

CHAPTER 5

The Mysterious Castrato

Setting out for Constantinople, Casanova traveled to Ancona, where he had been detained in quarantine the previous year (no need for that this time, since he was arriving from inland). There he met someone who interested him so much that he described what happened at length in the *Histoire,* half a century later. He was still just nineteen, and his previous sexual experiences had been relatively straightforward. This time he would be aroused but also disturbed by erotic ambiguity.

At an inn in Ancona, Casanova met an officer who was commanding Spanish troops; they had been fighting desultory actions against Austrians as a minor sideline in the War of the Austrian Succession. This new acquaintance treated him to dinner and invited a family from Bologna to join them, a middle-aged woman with two young daughters and two sons, all of whom were strikingly good looking.

The girls, Cecilia and Marina, were not yet into their teens and were training to be musicians and dancers. Cecilia was twelve and Marina eleven; they struck Casanova as "living rose buds," and despite their youth, "one could see the signs of precocious puberty on their white bosoms." The sons were Petronio and Bellino. Petronio was a dancer and frankly homosexual; Casanova must have given him that name as an allusion to the male lovers in the *Satyricon* of Petronius. Bellino was a castrato singer.[1]

In Rome and in the Papal States that it controlled, it was illegal for women to perform on stage (Cecilia and Marina would have to pursue their profession elsewhere in Italy). Shown in blue on a contemporary map (color plate 8), the Papal States occupied a large area in the middle of the Italian peninsula. There, women's roles in plays were taken by boys, as they had been in Shakespeare's England, and in opera by male sopranos. These sopranos were not counter-tenors, but castrati—performers who had been castrated before puberty, usually by the age of nine, to preserve the pure and intense tone that can still be heard today in boys' choirs. When they grew into adulthood their larynxes and rib cages developed in an unusual way that permitted flexibility and power that boys don't have.[2]

It was illegal to castrate children, so in a macabre black market they were operated on in secrecy by surgeons whose identity was concealed. The musicologist Charles Burney "inquired throughout Italy at what place boys were chiefly qualified for singing by castration, but could get no certain intelligence. It is said that there are shops in Naples with this inscription: QUI SI CASTRANO RAGAZZI ('Here boys are castrated'), but I was utterly unable to see or hear of any such shops during my residence in that city."[3]

The operation was painful and dangerous, even if the boy didn't die of hemorrhage or sepsis. According to a treatise entitled *Eunuchism Displayed,* the least mutilating method was vasectomy. Often the boy would be rendered unconscious during the procedure by pressure on the carotid artery. It was also possible to remove the testes altogether, for which opium was given as an anesthetic, "but it was observed that most of those who had been cut after this manner died by this narcotic." At the time most people seemed not to understand that few castrati were actually eunuchs, and that many of them were still able to perform sexually in adult life.[4]

Horrifyingly, by the 1720s in Italy as many as 4,000 boys were castrated annually for this purpose. Few if any had a say in the matter. Most were born poor, and their parents saw it as a path to future income and possibly even wealth and fame. It was usual for the castrati to be employed in church choirs; the religious authorities were thus complicit in the crime of castration, but pretended to know nothing about it.

A tiny minority of castrati had musical talent as well as fine voices, and they were the ones who became rich and famous. The greatest was Carlo Broschi, who went by the stage name of Farinelli or Farinello (color plate 12). Someone who heard him perform in London recalled, "Farinelli drew everybody to the Haymarket [Theater]. What a pipe! What modulation! What ecstasy to the ear!"[5]

Casanova saw him in 1772, living in retirement in Bologna. Although extremely rich, he seemed pathetic. "Poor old Farinello fell in love with his nephew's wife, and what's worse he was jealous. Even worse than that, he was odious to his niece, who couldn't imagine how an old animal of his kind could flatter himself that she would prefer him to her husband, who was a man made like others, and to whom she owed her affection by every law human and divine. . . . A castrato (*châtré*) in love with a woman who detests him becomes a tiger."[6]

At the inn in Ancona, Casanova found himself forming a connection with one of the two boys. Petronio introduced himself with an open-mouthed kiss, but Casanova made it clear that he wasn't interested. What did interest him was Bellino. "He accompanied himself at the harpsichord with the voice of an angel and enchanting graces. His eyes were as black as carbuncles, and they cast a fire that burned my soul. His face looked feminine, and his male clothing didn't conceal the shape of his breasts. That put it into my head, in spite of what I'd been told, that this had to be a girl."

The two girls interested him too, and their mother had no objection to his making advances. She was clearly a *maquerelle,* a female pimp. Over the years Casanova would encounter many such people—women, often single mothers, who badly needed income and exploited their daughters to gain it.

"I touched and then kissed the developing breasts of Cecilia and Marina, and Bellino, with a smile, didn't prevent my hand from invading his shirt. I took hold of a breast that left no doubt. 'By this breast,' I said, 'you are a girl and can't deny it.'" Bellino replied, "It's the defect we all have." It was true that castrati did often develop breasts, but Casanova wasn't convinced. "I know enough to tell the two kinds apart. This alabaster breast, my dear Bellino, is that of a charming girl of seventeen."

If Casanova did say that, it was probably bluster. Castrati were seldom seen in Venice, where women could perform on stage; he never indicates how he could have acquired a familiarity with them. What he did know about was cross-dressing, a regular feature of Carnival, and it always stimulated him. He was convinced that he was encountering it in Bellino. That would mean that "he" was flouting the law by pretending to be a castrato and getting away with it.

The sisters turned out to be already experienced. Cecilia showed up in Casanova's room in a state of near undress, and aware of his curiosity about Bellino, said that if he would pay for the privilege he would learn everything. As was his habit when he happened to have some cash, he had been spending freely and gave the impression that he was rich.

He had been planning to depart at dawn, but he told her, "I won't leave until the day after tomorrow, if you want to spend the night with me." "You love me, then?" "Very much; but you must be nice to me." "Very good, for I love you too. I'll go tell my mother." This was frankly a transaction. Cecilia climbed into bed "all amorous," and after sex they slept in each other's arms. The next morning Casanova gave her three doubloons, Spanish coins that circulated widely in Europe and were equivalent to forty modern euros apiece. "She went to give the treasure to her mother, who wept with joy and declared her faith in divine providence."[7]

As presented in the *Histoire,* Casanova clearly regards this situation, the prostitution of a child, as amusing rather than ethically concerning. The mother's complicity absolves him of all responsibility. The next night, he adds dryly, Marina took her turn, and the girls' mother "was insatiable in contracting ever greater obligations to divine providence."

In Casanova's day there wasn't much criticism, let alone legal prohibition, of sex with children. The "age of consent" for boys as well as girls, meaning consent not to marriage but to sexual relations, was set at ten years old in English common law, and similarly defined elsewhere in Europe. Society's consciousness on this matter has only gradually evolved. A century after Casanova, in 1880 in the United States the legal age of consent was still ten or twelve in most states, and seven in Delaware. But in what possible way, even back then, could a child be thought of as "consenting"?[8]

To be sure, there were limits. The Venetian authorities did punish men who abused very young girls, even though the concept of child abuse was not yet clearly formulated. A historian explores the implications of a case that became notorious some years later. A wealthy man in his sixties named Gaetano Franceschini offered a washerwoman a ducat per month to employ her eight-year-old daughter Paolina as a servant. The mother was delighted at first, but alarmed when the neighbors realized that the child was spending the night with Franceschini. She told her parish priest, who in turn reported it to the authorities.

A medical examination determined that although the girl had been fondled in ways that bewildered and upset her, there was no actual penetration, so it wasn't legally rape. Franceschini was prosecuted instead by a Blasphemy Tribunal on a more general charge of causing scandal. After hearing secret testimony that survives in documents, the court ruled that even though Paolina was still a virgin, Franceschini had "taken her innocence." He spent three months imprisoned in the Ducal Palace, and was released only after paying the mother two hundred ducats—a very large sum in light of the monthly wage of a single ducat.[9]

All his life Casanova was attracted to young girls, and Cecilia and Marina were very young indeed. It's impossible today to treat his obsession lightly. Trying to see it from Casanova's point of view, Chantal Thomas suggests that what attracted him was a kind of naïve purity. "That may be what's at stake in his prevailing passion for young girls: not to defile their innocence, but to unite himself with their ignorance." Possibly that was true with the "angels" Marta and Nanetta in Venice. They were not much younger than himself, and he was almost as inexperienced as they were. This case was different. The girls were barely pubescent, their mother was cynically pimping them, and Casanova spent a lot of money to buy their cooperation.[10]

Young girls figure so often in Casanova's narrative, not just at this stage but throughout the years, that today his interest in them can only be called pedophilia. Someone who did love girls for their innocent "ignorance" was Lewis Carroll, who was deeply offended if anyone objected to his hobby of photographing them scantily clad. Casanova, however, saw girls as already sexual. What attracted him was rosebuds turning into roses; he was a Humbert Humbert, not a Lewis Carroll.

Cecilia and Marina made good on their promise by bringing Bellino to Casanova's room and leaving them alone together. When he tried to satisfy his curiosity by groping, however, Bellino indignantly fended him off. Casanova then took him by surprise by suddenly grabbing from behind. Somehow, he managed to get a glimpse that shocked him. "At that moment I saw he was a man, and I believed I had seen it against his will. Astonished, angry, mortified, and disgusted, I let him leave." Yet the next day he found his curiosity more inflamed than ever, and wondered if what he had seen was actually "a monstrous clitoris."

Bellino was not eager at first to gratify Casanova's obsession. However, he was about to travel onward to his next engagement at Rimini, sixty miles up the coast from Ancona, and he accepted Casanova's offer of a ride in a hired carriage. After a late start they stopped at an inn along the way, and at that point "the dénouement of the play" resolved everything. Bellino was unexpectedly prepared to yield, and after undressing wordlessly they retired to bed, where Casanova finally had proof that his companion was a girl.

This provoked one of those moments of transcendence that were so important to him. "I gave myself, body and soul, to a joy that flooded my entire existence, and I saw that it was shared. Excess of happiness seized my senses until it reached that point at which nature, drowned in supreme pleasure, is exhausted." Looking back, he remembered this as *ma première grande passion.*[11]

What that seems to have meant is that for the first time, he was not just enjoying himself, but was deeply attracted or even obsessed. Women would always be moved by how much he truly wanted them, but although his emotion was real, it was transient. He would tell himself each time that he really might stay with someone permanently, and she would be tempted to believe it, but he never did stay. In French a love affair is *une histoire d'amour. Histoire,* as in the title of Casanova's memoir, can mean "story," and every one of his love stories has a beginning, middle, and end.

After much tender lovemaking "an intermission was necessary," and they began to converse. "Bellino" admitted that her real name was Teresa, and that the purported mother and siblings weren't relatives of hers at all. Almost certainly Teresa wasn't her real name either, since Casanova regularly disguises his partners' identities; research has failed to establish hers.[12]

In Bologna she had studied music with a celebrated castrato, who initiated her sexually. Meanwhile a young castrato student named Bellino suddenly died, and the teacher formed the bold plan of passing off Teresa in his place. The real Bellino's mother was delighted, since she had been counting on her son's financial support in the future. "That was the good woman whom you met at Ancona, and whom everyone believes to be my mother."

To fool the monks who sometimes inspected castrati to confirm their sex, an artificial organ was constructed that could be attached when needed with sticky gum. Casanova insisted on seeing the appliance demonstrated, and fifty years later remembered it in fascinated detail: "It was a long, soft little tube, white and as thick as one's thumb, placed in the middle of an oval of soft transparent skin."

Far from dispelling sexual ambiguity, this revelation about Bellino-Teresa only made her more compelling. "A charming girl, who appeared to be one in every way, seemed still more interesting with this extraordinary attachment, for the white pendant offered no obstacle to the well of her sex. I told her she had done well not to let me touch her earlier, for that would have intoxicated me and made me become what I was not." But now, having learned the truth, he was touched to hear her ask if he had found her truly loving in bed. With her limited experience—the rosebud sisters had more—she was worried that he had been disappointed or bored.

With the fake penis, Bellino was not just androgynous but hermaphroditic as well. There was a celebrated ancient Roman sculpture in the Villa Borghese

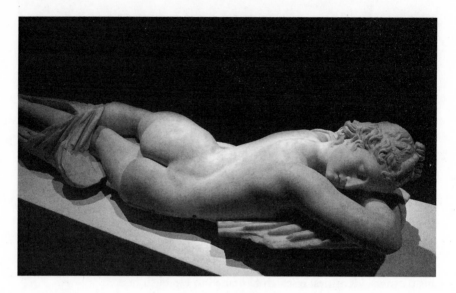

13. Sleeping Hermaphrodite

in Rome, *Sleeping Hermaphrodite*. Lying on its stomach—and on a mattress that was added by the great Bernini—the figure is strikingly ambiguous sexually. The English aesthete Horace Walpole, who was sexually ambiguous himself, had a bronze copy of it, and was amused when a lady friend called it "the only happy couple she ever saw."[13]

During that period there was intense interest in real-life hermaphrodites, with learned treatises that were graphically illustrated. A recent study concludes, "The uncanny combination of sensual poses and unlikely genitalia serves to produce both confusion and desire in the observer." That was exactly Casanova's response to Bellino. Androgyny always fascinated him, and a long novel that he published in later life is set in an imaginary world where all the people are hermaphroditic. Unfortunately the novel isn't any good and had hardly any readers.[14]

The son of Venetian actors had now found a person who completely blurred the difference between art and life. François Roustang puts it well: "Because men had to disguise themselves as women in order to play a feminine role on stage, Bellino had to pass for a man in the theater of life."[15]

As for Teresa, she was overwhelmed. For her it was a door opening to a possible new existence. "Take me with you! I don't ask to be your wife, I want only to be your tender lover. I don't believe I truly became a woman until I tasted the perfect pleasure of love in your arms." That, at any rate, is what

Casanova tells us she said. He confessed to her that he wasn't rich in the least, much less high-born. "My great treasure," he said, "is that I am my own master, and depend on no one." That's true; all his life he would be a rolling stone, escaping from every obligation—including every relationship that might become permanent.

As would often happen to Casanova, he briefly believed that the relationship could endure; and as would always happen, something occurred to stop it. At Pesaro they needed to cross a border separating Spanish and Austrian troops, and he discovered that he had somehow lost his passport. In those days there were no standardized passports, and travelers had to carry personal letters authorizing them to cross each specific border, usually with time limits before they would expire. He was told, therefore, that he would have to be detained until a new passport could be sent from Rome.

Meanwhile Teresa went on by herself to Rimini. There her singing enchanted a Neapolitan duke, and when he learned that she was a woman in disguise, he offered to set her up with a theater contract in Naples, where women were allowed to perform. Very likely she was fed up with impersonating a castrato, and happy for a chance to appear as herself.

When Casanova's passport eventually arrived, Teresa wrote to propose that he join her in Naples, but he balked. When he had been there previously he had been received as a distinguished visitor, but if he returned now it would be as the kept man of an actress, as well as recapitulating his father's role as humble consort to a star. "Sharing her lot either as husband or lover, I would have found myself degraded, humiliated, and forced to crawl. The reflection that in the finest moment of my youth I would give up all hope of the great fortune I believed I was born for gave the scales such a jolt that my reason silenced my heart." His reason didn't have to work very hard. And now that Bellino had been unmasked as Teresa, the mystery that had provoked the fascination was gone. So much for the *grande passion*.

Years later, in Rome, Casanova pondered anew the ambiguous attractions of castrati. He encountered a castrato there who took leading female roles on stage, and was well known to be the favorite of a Borghese cardinal. "Squeezed into a well made corset, he had the figure of a nymph, and one sees few women with bosoms as firm and pretty as his. The illusion he created was such that one couldn't resist it. One was stopped short, the illusion took effect, and one would either have to fall in love or else be the most stolid of Germans."

"The holy city," Casanova remarks, "obliges the whole human race to turn pederast, but won't admit it." A monsignor with whom he raised the subject agreed that it was absurd to allow castrati disguised as women to show their breasts while refusing to let real women do it. The churchman added, "Plenty of people with intelligence and good sense prefer these *messieurs* to all of the prettiest girls in Rome."[16]

CHAPTER 6

Casanova's Children

In the *Histoire* Casanova mentions, in a matter-of-fact way, that he some-times ran into a former lover and discovered that he was the father of a child. He seldom says much more than that, and it's not clear how often it hap-pened. Of course he had only the mothers' word, and sometimes good reason to be skeptical, but in a few cases he believed them and claims that he was delighted. He gives no indication, however, of wanting to establish an ongo-ing paternal relationship, with a single exception that will be taken up later in our story.

Nor does he acknowledge responsibility, and that was far from inevitable. Gentlemen in the eighteenth century frequently provided voluntary support, as James Boswell did when he was a young man in Edinburgh and a servant girl gave birth to their son and daughter. Boswell looked forward to knowing and helping them as they grew up, and was distressed when—as happened all too often in those days—they died of childhood illnesses.

Two meetings that Casanova does describe at length happened in 1760, and coincidentally, both of the children whom he met at that time had been conceived in 1744. Passing through Florence in 1760, he went to the opera, "taking a place close to the orchestra more to look at the actresses than to listen to the music. But what a surprise when I saw the principal singer! I immedi-ately recognized Teresa [i.e., "Bellino"]. After seventeen years I was seeing her on stage, beautiful, fresh, and seemingly just as young as I had left her."

Casanova wondered at first if it was merely his imagination, but when she began to stare at him he knew it wasn't. After the performance he caught up with her, "and we were both silent. I took her hand and placed it on my chest so she could feel my heart, which seemed to be struggling to burst out."[1]

Teresa told him her address, and after she left he asked a friendly bystander what her surname was and how to get there. "She has my name," the man answered, "because she's my wife. I'm Cirillo Palesi, at your service." Perhaps Casanova concealed the real name in the *Histoire,* since no Palesi appears in the marriage registers of Florence.

At their house Teresa embraced Casanova warmly, and told her husband that he was her father. The couple had gotten married very recently, and Palesi didn't seem to know much about her except that she was surprisingly well to do. Her money came from the duke who had originally invited her to Naples and was still giving her a generous allowance, as well as supporting her son Cesare, whom she called Cesarino. Palesi had been led to believe that the boy was her brother, not her son, and she still looked young enough for that to seem possible. By this time in her life Teresa was evidently as resourceful a con artist as Casanova.

Palesi offered to make some hot chocolate, which Casanova declared he "loved passionately." That gave him a chance to be alone with Teresa. She briefly described her life since they last saw each other, and then she said, "Just wait, my dear friend, for what will be one of the most interesting moments of your life." She now produced Cesarino.

"This alleged brother of Teresa's was my own portrait, except that he wasn't as dark, and I saw at once that he was my son. Nature has never been so indiscreet." Actually the resemblance was no problem. Since Casanova had been introduced as Teresa's father, it was natural that he and the boy should look alike.

The family group spent a pleasant evening with their guest, during which Cesarino accompanied himself at the harpsichord and showed real talent, just as his mother had done long before. "Thus I passed this day, one of the happiest of my whole life." Casanova repeats that formula often in the *Histoire;* every subplot has a happy ending. But he doesn't explain why the day was so very happy, and he gives no indication that he ever saw the talented Cesarino again, or had any interest in seeing him.

The very next day he was on his way, and although his path seems to have crossed Teresa's in later years, their encounters were casual. She was financially secure, and it was understood that the past was past. "Both of them knew,"

Michel Delon says, "that life is a theater where people sometimes forget they're onstage, and where they believe in their promises."[2]

This meeting may have been as agreeably unconflicted as Casanova says it was, but an encounter a few weeks later was different. Leaving Florence, he stayed briefly in Rome and then journeyed south to Naples to visit the Duke of Matalona, whom he had gotten to know in Paris. The duke had a lovely seventeen-year-old mistress named Leonilda, and as soon as he met her Casanova was smitten. "The seductive features of this girl seemed to me not unfamiliar, but I couldn't recall what woman might have given that impression."[3]

Casanova was so deeply in love, or so he claims, that he impulsively declared he wanted to marry Leonilda, and she was delighted with the idea. The duke was married himself, and far from taking offense, gave his approval. But when he sent for the girl's mother to sign a marriage contract, there was a great shock. "When she saw me," Casanova says, "she gave a piercing cry and fell back onto a sofa. I sat down, and I was seeing Donna Lucrezia Castelli." That was the married lady with whom he had trysted in the gardens in Rome, where they were visited by a glistening snake.

Lucrezia told Casanova that she had been pregnant when she left Rome but had never slept with her husband at that time. It's far from clear why he believed her, but if it was true, it meant that he himself must be Leonilda's father. She didn't resemble him as Cesarino did, but that was because she took after her mother; hence the sense of familiarity when he first saw her. Lucrezia added that she had given the girl the middle name Giacomina, in honor of Giacomo Casanova.

Marrying Leonilda was thus out of the question. Casanova being Casanova, why not sleep instead with Lucrezia? This led to a threesome—one of his favorite scenarios—that reproduced the earlier episode in Rome with Lucrezia and her sister Angelica, and the still earlier one in Venice with the "angels" Nanetta and Marta.

The three of them undressed and got into bed, with Lucrezia in the middle, and she made love enthusiastically with Casanova. Meanwhile Leonilda looked on with interest and commented, "So is that what you did eighteen years ago when you engendered me?"

Could it possibly have happened like that, this cheerful threesome with the cooperative daughter and the father she's just met for the first time? It certainly reads like conventional eighteenth-century pornography, and it's easy to suspect that the aged Casanova is inventing what he wishes could have happened. "Time seems forgotten," Delon says, "and the girl takes her mother's place in the arms of a lover who would never change." Only in his own mind. By 1760, though still only thirty-five, he was aging fast.[4]

Believe it or not—which is never just a routine expression where Casanova is concerned—there was a sequel to the sequel. Eight years later he was in Naples once again, and heard that Lucrezia and their daughter were now living in Salerno, where Leonilda had married an elderly nobleman and had become a marchesa. Lucrezia told him that it was genuinely a love match, but that the marchese, crippled by gout, seldom slept with his wife and had been unable to beget a son. This he wanted very badly, because if he died without an heir his fortune would go to grasping relatives whom he despised.

Casanova was invited to their estate, and found the old marchese to be courtly and intelligent. It turned out also that he and Casanova had something significant in common. "I was surprised when he kissed me on the mouth, which I returned with a sign that sufficed for us to recognize each other as fellow Masons." That membership, as we will see, would become an invaluable point of connection for Casanova after his initiation in 1750.[5]

In due course Lucrezia contrived to leave Leonilda and Casanova alone in a charming garden, reminiscent of the gardens in Rome. As she left she warned the two of them to resist any carnal impulses, and predictably, they failed. "Though we were determined not to consummate the alleged crime [i.e., incest], we came so close to it that an almost involuntary movement forced us to consummate it, so completely that we couldn't have done more if we had acted by premeditated design with the free use of reason. We stayed motionless, gazing at each other without changing our position, serious and mute as we reflected with astonishment, as we told each other afterward, that we felt neither guilt nor remorse. . . . If an angel had come down to say that we had monstrously outraged nature, it would have made us laugh."[6]

François Roustang comments that this experience echoes strikingly the one with the young angels in the dark. "In both episodes, the determination not to act is the necessary condition for the act to be committed involuntarily and forcibly. And as Casanova emphasizes, the fortuitous act is nevertheless as complete as if it had been premeditated. The effect of this cunning combination— and these are indeed Casanova's words—is to produce neither guilt nor remorse. As for the reminder of proper morality, it can only provoke laughter." Guilt and remorse are exactly what Casanova manages never to feel.[7]

Casanova strongly suspected that Lucrezia had only pretended to warn against carnal impulses, and had deliberately set the whole thing up, hoping to provide the marchese with the son he longed for. When he was departing soon afterward, the marchese declared that the visit had made him feel ten years younger.

And this sequel too had a sequel. A son was born. In 1791, when the son had grown to be a young man, Casanova met him at a coronation ceremony in Prague. He was highly intelligent, and had succeeded his father as the marchese. "What gave me the greatest pleasure was the resemblance of this lad to the late marchese, his mother's husband. That thought brought forth my tears, imagining the satisfaction that this resemblance must have given to that fine man, and likewise to his wife."[8]

Did friendship with the virile Casanova inspire the old marchese to recover his own virility, and to father the child he wanted so badly? Or was the young man's alleged resemblance to the marchese a way for Casanova to evade responsibility, as well as to congratulate himself on a good deed?

And what if the young man really was Casanova's son, which would make him his grandson as well? Then the incestuous plot gets more tangled than ever. Libertine philosophers argued that the taboo against incest was useful to stabilize social order, and for that reason illegal, but not based on any law of nature. It was based on religious law too, of course, but that never struck Casanova as relevant.

Cleverly, in the *Histoire* he puts this argument in the Duke of Matalona's mouth rather than his own, not at this point in the story, but eight years previously when he first found out that he was Leonilda's father. The duke remarks that incest is rightly prohibited by society, especially when a daughter has grown up with her father. But if two people are attracted to each other without ever knowing that they're related, that's another matter. "The incest that's such a perennial theme in Greek tragedy," the duke says, "far from making me weep, makes me laugh, and if I do weep at *Phèdre* it's Racine's art that makes me do it."[9]

Oedipus is one person who couldn't have had an Oedipus complex, since he was abandoned as an infant and had no way of suspecting that the woman he slept with was his mother. In the marchese's opinion, and presumably in Casanova's too, his reaction when he did discover that relationship should have been to laugh, not to gouge out his eyes.

As for Phèdre, she is a young queen who falls in love with her stepson, not with a biological son. In Euripides' *Hippolytus,* the tragedy that Racine adapted, her passion is cynically provoked by a cruel goddess; in *Phèdre,* more overtly misogynistically, she's tormented by original sin and the wickedness of the flesh.

Casanova didn't believe in that kind of wickedness, and certainly not in original sin. He accepted the libertine philosophy of doing what comes naturally, and as always in the stories he tells, a plot line exonerates him whenever he might seem to transgress. He and Leonilda made love in the garden because they couldn't help it. Nature was just taking its course. And since the marchese got the son he longed for, what did it matter whether he or Casanova was the biological father?

That's his way of rationalizing the episode of incest, but at another point in the *Histoire* he admits that even when a father and daughter know each other already, it might still be excusable. At one time in France a woman told him that when she was a girl her father used to join her in bed, and she thought it was just harmless play until she turned thirteen and he attempted intercourse. At that point she jumped up naked and fled for safety to her mother, who had been unaware of what was going on. On this Casanova comments, "It seemed to me that if I had been in her father's place, she wouldn't have gotten out of my hands so easily, and I forgave him if his love made him forget that he was her father." As always with Casanova, "love" is an ambiguous term.[10]

CHAPTER 7

Corfu and Constantinople

While Casanova was waiting for a ship to take him to Constantinople, his friend Signora Orio, the aunt of the angels Marta and Nanetta, invited him to stay at her house. The girls' room was adjacent to his, with its door securely bolted. Nevertheless "they took turns sleeping with me during the night, removing a plank in the wall so the amorous girl could come and go." Parting was emotional. "The evening before my departure I didn't leave Signora Orio's house. She shed as many tears as her nieces, and I didn't shed less than they. A hundred times during this final night they told me, expiring with love in my arms, that they would never see me again."[1]

Casanova had no plans as yet for what to do in Constantinople, but the Grimanis took care of that. They got him a position with the Venetian ambassador there, and until that began he was to spend some time on the island of Corfu, the last major Venetian holding in the eastern Mediterranean and an important military base. As shown on the map (color plate 8), it lay just eighty miles east of the Italian boot, and was a crucial point of defense at the mouth of the Adriatic. There Casanova would become an ensign in an army regiment. Such appointments obviously depended on patronage rather than training and experience, and had to be purchased, which the Grimanis no doubt did. He expresses no gratitude for that.

As it happens, in Bologna on his way back to Venice from Rome, it had already occurred to Casanova to pose as a military officer. Discarding his ecclesiastical costume, he engaged a tailor to make him what he calls a *uniforme de caprice*. A *caprice* is a whim, and since there were many different armies in Europe at the time, almost any outfit could seem plausible. However, the very term *uniforme de caprice* is an oxymoron, since uniforms imply uniformity, and Casanova belonged to an imaginary army whose only member was himself. He decided on a white costume with a blue vest and silver shoulder knots, and a hat with a black cockade such as Austrian officers wore. Looking in a mirror, his admiration was complete: "I had never experienced a pleasure like that." At the most popular café in town he was delighted that everyone gazed at him with respect.[2]

Playing his new role with cocky self-assurance, Casanova dismissed a nosy innkeeper's attempts to pry into his affairs. "He gave me a book in which to enter my name. 'Casanova.' 'Your occupation?' 'Officer.' 'In whose service?' 'No one's.' 'Your country?' 'Venice.' 'Where are you coming from?' 'None of your business.'"

When he arrived in Venice Casanova had gone right away to call on the abate Grimani, who greeted him with cries of alarm: "He beheld me in military uniform when he believed I was with Cardinal Acquaviva and on the road to a political career." Now he was going to be a real soldier, not a pretend one, and conceivably launched on a military career. But no career would ever suit him, and it has been well said that his true color was neither a priest's black nor a soldier's red—as in Stendhal's *The Red and the Black*—but the green of the gambling table.[3]

After the vessel set sail, it stopped off at Orsara in Croatia, where Casanova had stayed the previous year and picked up a venereal infection. The doctor who had treated him at that time recognized him and invited him to dinner. "You communicated a *galanterie* to Don Gerolamo's housekeeper, who gave it to a friend, who in good faith shared it with his wife. She in turn gave it to a libertine who passed it along so effectively that within a month I had fifty patients under my care, all of whom I cured for an appropriate fee. I still have a few, but in another month there won't be any, since the illness has ended. I saw you as a bird of good omen. May I permit myself to hope that you will stay here for a few days to renew it?"

During the voyage Casanova was greatly impressed with a role model who seemed to embody elegance and confidence. Giovanni Antonio Dolfin was on his way to serve as governor of a remote island, and struck him as "very eloquent, very polished, a daring gambler who always lost, loved by all women when he wanted to be, always intrepid, and even-tempered in good fortune and bad."

That was certainly what Casanova himself aspired to become, and Dolfin interested him in another way too, as an illustration of the stratification of prestige in Venice. He belonged to the nobility, but so did many hundreds of aristocrats who were relatively impoverished and didn't live in grand palazzi. They were expected to know their place, which meant that they should be inconspicuous and avoid showing off. Casanova's description of the way Dolfin was treated is striking, because it's essentially his own self-portrait:

> An aristocratic government can hope for tranquility only on the basis of equality among aristocrats. Now it is impossible to judge of equality, whether physical or moral, otherwise than by appearances, from which it follows that the citizen who doesn't want to be persecuted, if he isn't made like the others or worse, must employ all his care not to seem to be. If he has great talent, he must hide it; if he is ambitious, he must pretend to despise honors; if he wants to obtain something, he must ask for nothing; if he has a handsome face, he must neglect it. He must carry himself badly and dress still worse; his finery must have nothing unusual about it, since it's necessary to ridicule everything foreign; he must perform a bow awkwardly and not pride himself on politeness. He must not make much of the fine arts, must hide his good taste if he has any, and must not employ a foreign cook; his wig should be badly combed and rather unclean. Signor Dolfin had none of these qualities, and he was therefore unable to make his fortune in his native Venice.

Every word of that corresponds to the self-image Casanova was already cultivating. Flaunting his cleverness and style would indeed give offense in Venice, but in Paris and other cities it would serve him well.

This part of the *Histoire* is a reminder that we are reading a manuscript, unfinished at the time of Casanova's death. The section describing this stage of his life suffered from the action of an illiterate servant in Bohemia who thought the carefully composed draft was wastepaper and threw it out. Beginning all over again, Casanova commented gloomily, "I set about rewriting in a bad humor, and consequently very badly, what in a good humor I would have written well; but my reader may console himself that he will gain in time what he loses in force." Modern editors note that in this rewritten section "the legibility is not good: the paper has soaked up the ink, and the writing is hasty and heavy, with numerous crossings-out."[4]

Writing half a century after these early events, Casanova was sometimes inaccurate about dates, probably inadvertently. He seems to have been in Constantinople twice and conflated the two trips; some details clearly belong to 1745, and others to a previous visit in 1741. As already mentioned, that earlier episode explains why Constantinople was the name that sprang to mind when Cardinal Acquaviva asked him where he wanted to go.

An incident that happened on shipboard is narrated in a thought-provoking way. When a dangerous storm blew up, "a very ignorant and insolent" Slavonian priest declared that devils were at work and began to perform an exorcism. This alarmed the sailors so much that they gave up trying to save the ship. Casanova told them sternly that no devils were involved, but they weren't convinced, and one of them even tried to throw him overboard as a Jonah who was responsible for the storm.

Some soldiers rescued him, but the priest had a further idea. He demanded that Casanova turn over a parchment he had bought shortly before sailing, and threw it onto some glowing coals. "It went through contortions that lasted for half an hour, which convinced the sailors that it was diabolical. Its supposed virtue was to make all women fall in love with whoever had it. I hope the reader will have the goodness to believe that I gave no credence to philters of any kind, and had bought this parchment for half a scudo only for a laugh." At that very moment the storm died down, and "after eight days of pleasant sailing we arrived at Corfu."

Surely this is disingenuous. A spell to make women fall in love would have been an acquisition after Casanova's heart. Was it really a coincidence that the storm ended right when the parchment was burning? And how could it take so long to burn? The whole account smacks of careful framing to persuade readers that even as a teenager Casanova was a thoroughgoing skeptic. He wasn't, and throughout his life coincidences would make him wonder if something deeper was at work after all.[5]

On the way to Corfu the ship docked briefly at the island of Cerigo, and Casanova mentions that he met there a noble from Padua named Antonio Pocchini who was imprisoned for preying financially on women. The encounter is unimportant except that it presages the kind of repeated meetings over the years that will fill the *Histoire*. Between 1760 and 1783 Casanova would run into Pocchini again in Amsterdam, Stuttgart, London, Venice, Aix-la-Chapelle, and Vienna, sometimes losing money to him and once giving him a sound thrashing. Pocchini was what was known as an adventurer, a member of the shadowy underclass to which Casanova himself would soon belong.

After an unremarkable stay on Corfu, where the military duties were minimal, Casanova went on to Constantinople and reported to the Venetian embassy. That was located in the Pera district, where nearly all foreigners stayed. They rarely if ever penetrated into the heart of the city, and the Turks whom they did meet in Pera were exceptionally tolerant and cosmopolitan. Since European merchants had been coming there for centuries, Italian and French were widely spoken.[6]

Here too it turned out that Casanova had almost no duties to perform— just the kind of job he liked, of course—and he set about enjoying himself. He had a letter of introduction to a remarkable character known as Osman Pasha, who welcomed him warmly and soon became a friend, as older men regularly did. Osman was well known throughout Europe as an almost legendary figure, since before converting to Islam fifteen years previously he had been the Comte de Bonneval, a general serving in the French and then the Austrian armies, and only afterward in the employ of the Turkish sultan. He acknowledged freely that he had converted to Islam solely to promote his career, and everyone in his household, which was furnished in the French manner, spoke either French or Italian. It's an indication of the relaxed attitude in Rome that Cardinal Acquaviva had provided Casanova with a letter of introduction to the famous apostate, and that the pope himself sent his best regards.

Bonneval invited Casanova to dinner, and afterward "told me that he had never, since he became a Turk, passed two such agreeable hours as I had made him pass." That compliment is highly significant. A recent study of Casanova as a conversationalist stresses how often that gift brought him success in life. In the relaxed setting of dining with new acquaintances, he knew how to tune himself to their style and temperament, and then make himself liked without even seeming to try.[7]

A modern writer says romantically, "It was a summer of serenity for Casanova. The light of dawn dazzled upon the Bosphorus, and at night the stars seemed close to the earth." There's nothing like that in the *Histoire*. As usual, Casanova has little to say about the physical world, whether natural or manmade. Most Europeans, however, regarded Constantinople as romantically exotic, as captured in a painting by Casanova's brother Francesco (color plate 13).[8]

Although foreigners were in fact largely separated from Turkish culture, Casanova did form a friendship with a wealthy Turk named Yusuf Ali. Since it's the sexual episodes in the *Histoire* that tended to get emphasized by later writers, it's worth noting that most of the account of Yusuf concerns philosophical discussions that were conducted over water pipes. "Tobacco in perfection," Yusuf remarked as they puffed, "is certainly necessary to the pleasure in smoking, yet it's not the principal pleasure, since the kind it gives is merely sensual. True pleasures are those that affect only the soul, entirely independent of the senses." When Casanova protested that sensual pleasures were pretty good nevertheless, his host replied, "Forty years ago I thought like you. Forty years from now, if you succeed in becoming wise, you will think like me. The pleasures, my dear son, that stir the passions into movement trouble the soul, and so you must perceive that they cannot truly be called pleasures."[9]

This disquisition, which Casanova relates in great detail, may indeed have influenced him, since it has a lot in common with the way he would eventually talk about sexual experience in the *Histoire*—hollow and ephemeral unless the experience of the soul transcends the merely physical.

The discussion turned to theology, and Yusuf perplexed Casanova with a Muslim critique of the Christian doctrine of the Trinity, a God who is three and yet mysteriously one. "When I said that God, not being material, had to be spirit, he replied that we know what God is not, but not what he is, and therefore we cannot affirm that he is spirit, since we can only have an abstract idea of that. 'God,' he said to me, 'is immaterial; that's all that we know, and we can never know more.'" Casanova recalled that Plato, whom Yusuf had certainly never read, said much the same thing.

As his own thinking developed Casanova would become very much an Enlightenment deist, holding that a creator God exists but doesn't necessarily have any relationship with human beings. He also doubted that life after death was possible. Yet he regarded himself as a Catholic, in the sense that he accepted institutional religion as a bulwark for the social order. He also maintained friendships with many churchmen, and was never anticlerical like some of the French philosophes. But despite—or because of—his studies at Padua, theology never interested him. In a late unpublished essay he called Islam "more reasonable than Christianity" thanks to its doctrine of a single God.[10]

During a later visit the conversation came down to earth and turned to sexual morality, though still cast in an abstract light, questioning the Christian insistence on chastity. Yusuf commented further that prohibiting masturbation only tended to encourage it, and Casanova added that it might be more permissible in females than males: "Girls don't run so great a risk, since they can lose only a little substance, which doesn't even come from the same

source as the seed of life in man." Following these reflections, Yusuf unexpectedly declared that he had a beautiful fifteen-year-old daughter named Zelmi,
who would bring a great fortune in marriage, and that he was offering her to
Casanova so long as he would undertake to convert to Islam and spend the
next year learning the language. "You will become, I foresee it, a pillar of the
Ottoman Empire."

Casanova thought about accepting this extraordinary proposal, but he
wasn't ready to break with his entire past, or to put an end to his dreams of
success in Europe. "It seemed to me that I should not be indifferent to the
contempt of everyone who knew me, and whose esteem I aspired to deserve.
I couldn't make up my mind to renounce the hope of becoming celebrated
among the cultivated nations, whether in the fine arts, in literature, or in some
other way."

Most of all, Casanova believed that his success in life depended on exceptional facility in language. "I could not give up without pain the vanity of
being recognized as a *beau parleur,* as was already my reputation wherever I
had lived." He was fairly fluent in French by now, but that and Spanish were
the only foreign languages he ever tried to learn properly. During long stays in
England, Germany and Russia, he would never even consider learning their
languages, not because he looked down on them, but because he had no hope
of becoming witty and eloquent.

In any case Casanova wouldn't be permitted to see Zelmi until they were
married, and during his time in Constantinople he had almost no contact with
Turkish women. Christian slaves were a different matter. He had been given
a letter of introduction to a distinguished gentleman known as Ismail Effendi
("effendi" was equivalent to "sir" or "lord"), and they became friends. After a
dinner party some talented slaves were dancing before the guests, and Casanova was invited to demonstrate the furlana, a spirited dance from the Friuli
region north of Venice that was popular during Carnival. As a nineteenth-
century dancing master described it, "Love and pleasure are visible in this
dance; each movement and gesture is performed with the most voluptuous
grace. Animated by the accompanying mandolins, tambourines, and castanets, the woman tries by rapidity and vivacity to excite her partner's love. The
two dancers come together, separate, rejoin, throw themselves into each other's
arms, and then separate yet again. In all of their movements they display alternately love, coquetry, and inconstancy."[11]

Casanova was a good dancer and glad to show off, but he explained that
this would only be possible with a Venetian woman and a violinist who knew

the tune. Both were quickly found, and he was enchanted with his partner, who was obviously beautiful though partly concealed by a velvet mask like the ones worn during Carnival in Venice.

> The goddess took her position, I joined her, and we danced six furla-nas in a row. I was out of breath by then, for no national dance is more violent, but the beauty stood motionless, giving no sign of fatigue, and appeared to challenge me. During the whirl, the most exhausting stage in the dance, she seemed to glide; I was beside myself with astonish-ment. I couldn't remember ever having seen this dance performed so well, not even in Venice. After a brief rest, a bit ashamed of my weak-ness, I approached her again and I said, *Ancora sei, e poi basta, se non volete vedermi a morire*—"Six more, and then that's enough, if you don't want to see me die."

They performed the six dances, and then a eunuch opened a door and the mysterious partner vanished.

She was obviously a slave from Venice, and had shown interest in Casa-nova, but Osman/Bonneval warned him to leave her alone lest Ismail get fu-rious. It turned out, however, that Ismail had a plan of his own. He invited Casanova to join him one evening in a little garden house overlooking a foun-tain, where three slave girls stripped naked and bathed in the moonlight, very likely aware that they were being watched.

Casanova was sure that one of them must be the Venetian, though he couldn't tell which. He got so aroused that Ismail was able to carry out his own sexual designs on Casanova, although whatever happened is obliquely hinted at, not described. Earlier Ismail had made advances and been rebuffed, but this time, "I would have been impolite to refuse, and besides I would have repaid him with ingratitude, which my character is incapable of. Never in my life have I been so wild or so carried away . . . I never went back there, and I told no one about this adventure. The withdrawal of the three sirens put an end to the orgy, and as for ourselves, not knowing what to say, we burst into laughter. . . . It was the only pleasure of that kind that I had at Constantino-ple, and imagination played a greater part in it than reality."

This passage was evidently added after some reflection: in the manuscript it was written on a separate sheet pasted into the notebook with red sealing wax. Still, Casanova could have omitted it altogether if he felt embarrassed or ashamed.

While working on the manuscript of the *Histoire,* at some point Casanova crossed out a number of references to homosexual encounters. Those that can still be deciphered include: "At Corfu, the surgeon who masturbated me"; "My love for the *giton* [youthful lover] of the Duc d'Elboeuf"; "Pederasty with Bazin and his sisters." He mentions also that when traveling near Naples he always slept in his clothes, "a precaution I believed necessary in a region where *le goût antiphysique* [unnatural taste] is common." However, his attitude toward people who were bisexual or homosexual was completely tolerant, and he describes an encounter of his own in St. Petersburg with no embarrassment, let alone shame.[12]

When Casanova next visited Yusuf, he was treated to a fascinating but possibly risky sight. Before his host arrived a masked woman greeted him "in good Italian and in an angelic voice," saying that she was Yusuf's wife and had been told to entertain him. This she promptly did, crossing and parting her bare legs and revealing an enchanting bosom, which he recalls in luxuriant metaphor: "The two little globes were divided by a narrow and rounded space that seemed like a rivulet of milk made to quench my thirst and be devoured by my lips." This woman was a Greek from the island of Chios; a travel writer commented that skirts there were so short that they barely reached the knees, "and bosoms uncovered in a way that shocks modesty."[13]

Thrilled, he attempted to pull aside her mask to see her face, but that was going too far. "Do you deserve the friendship of Yusuf, when you violate his hospitality by insulting his wife?" He apologized abjectly, and she sat down again, giving him a brief glimpse of everything beneath her skirt. "You're on fire," she commented. "How could I not be," he replied, "when you're burning me up?"

The next day he reported the encounter to Bonneval, who only laughed. "'She was angry,' he told me, 'to find you were such a novice. You were playing a farce in the French style, when you should have acted like a man. Why did you need to get a look at her nose? You should have gone straight to the essential. The most reserved Turkish women have their modesty only on their faces; as soon as those are covered, they blush at nothing.'"

The biographer J. Rives Childs, a professional diplomat who had served in the Middle East, says sternly, "It is quite inconceivable that a Turk of any class or condition would have allowed Casanova access to a female member of his family." That's not so clear, however. Lady Mary Wortley Montagu was in Constantinople earlier in the century when her husband was British ambassador there, and commented that women pursued intrigues freely thanks to their burqas and shapeless robes: "This perpetual masquerade gives them entire liberty of following their inclinations without danger of discovery." Ian Kelly makes the plausible suggestion that foreigners associated only with sophisticated people and never had much contact with the more orthodox majority.[14]

As for Yusuf's wife, she may have had no fear of discovery; her husband might well have encouraged her in this little game. Thrown off balance by ambiguous cultural signals, Casanova was out of his element and knew it. He was not sorry that it was time to return to Corfu, where he could still expect employment. He told Yusuf on parting that he was going to have to refuse the offer of Zelmi, but there were no hard feelings about that. "My tears responded to his, and he told me that by not accepting his offer I had gained so much in his esteem that he couldn't have thought more highly of me if I had accepted."

Casanova always wept easily, and at convenient times; during the eighteenth century it was increasingly expected that men would expose a sentimental side by producing tears. A commentator notes their constant appearance in the *Histoire:* "We find tears of commiseration, sobs of gratitude, weeping from amorous melancholy, and tears of repentance; torrents of tears flow from separation, whether of love or friendship." Casanova always got over it fast.[15]

He traveled to Corfu on a huge Venetian galleass, a warship carrying forty cannons that combined sails with banks of oars and was managed by a crew of seven hundred. A dozen of these behemoths were stationed there, along with a fleet of smaller ships, all rowed by prisoners who were literally galley slaves. At a later point Casanova comments dryly that Venice would never give up its galleys not just for military reasons, "but because they wouldn't know what to do otherwise with the criminals who are condemned to row them."[16]

Despite their antique appearance—the ancient Greeks and Romans fought in galleys—those ships were well adapted to Mediterranean fighting, which often took place in narrow inlets and straits. Thanks to their oars, they were highly maneuverable in those conditions, and also in periods of calm or contrary winds that would have neutralized British and French sailing ships.

Casanova arrived in Corfu bearing valuable gifts from his friends in Constantinople, including quantities of superb fabrics, tobacco, mocha coffee from Yusuf, and two dozen bottles of rare wine from Bonneval. These he immediately sold for a handsome total of five hundred zecchini. Soon he was appointed a lieutenant in the service of "Signor DR," the admiral, whose real name we know to have been Giacomo da Riva. The only duties were carrying messages and performing other little tasks, and there was never any question of military training, much less of fighting. Consequently he had plenty of time for social life, gambling at cards and looking for interesting women.

Predictably, he was soon smitten, by a dazzlingly beautiful "Signora F." She was Andriana Foscarini, married to a galley captain and a few years older than himself, though with his usual tendency to make women in the *Histoire* younger than they actually were, he remembered her as seventeen. Because her identity is a matter of historical record, this is a rare case in which we can be sure of the identity of one of Casanova's lovers.

In due course he would make progress in Andriana's affections, but first there was a startling interruption, due to one of the explosions of temper to which he was always prone. He had acquired an insolent servant who had somehow persuaded everyone that he was a romantic figure, the son of a French duke traveling incognito and only pretending to be a servant. Amazingly, the Venetian officers were impressed, and began treating him with respect. Casanova questioned the man, easily detected holes in his story, and told him so. No doubt he was outraged that his servant should upstage him by performing as a rival con man.

When Casanova made that accusation, the servant responded with an indignant slap in the face, at which Casanova thrashed him with his cane and left him bloody and helpless. But this impulsive action created a sudden crisis. Since the authorities in Corfu believed that the man really was a duke in disguise, they were sure to punish Casanova for the beating. With characteristic resourcefulness he went straight to the waterfront and jumped into an unattended rowboat. Soon he was boarding a sloop that was about to sail, and when it reached the northern tip of Corfu he asked to be put ashore at Kassiopi, a resort today but a little fishing village then.

He had a gun with him, and fearing arrest, assembled a bodyguard of energetic young men who resented Venetian rule over Corfu and were glad to help. Since he had plenty of money, he was soon treating them to one of the splendid feasts that he describes so lovingly: "My table was exquisite. I ate only succulent mutton and snipes whose equal I had just once afterward, twenty-two years later at St. Petersburg. I drank only Scopolo and the finest muscats from the Greek islands." No one today is sure what Scopolo was like, but most of the wines Casanova mentions throughout the *Histoire* are still familiar. Just an incomplete catalogue is impressive: they included Refosco, Muscatel, vast quantities of Champagne, red and white Burgundy, Bordeaux, red and white Rhône, Malaga, Tokay, Rhine, Alicante, La Mancha, Montepulciano, Montefiascone, Orvieto, Languedoc, and Madeira.[17]

Casanova took advantage of his newfound prestige in Kassiopi to sleep with a number of young women (perhaps he paid them, though he doesn't say so). After a while an officer from the Venetian fleet turned up to say that the imposter had been exposed. Since the man was really a servant after all, Casanova was no longer blamed for the drubbing, and he was free to return. And now it was time to renew his pursuit of Andriana, with the happy reflection that "it's impossible to truly feel pleasure unless some pains have preceded it, and the pleasure is great only in proportion to the pains that were endured." In the manuscript he underlined that sentence.

Casanova excited Andriana's interest by recounting the story of the bathing girls in Constantinople, though she warned him to keep his language discreet. One day when a servant had cut her long hair he managed to pick some of it up, after which she sent him a little packet that turned out to contain still more. He had it braided into a bracelet and a collar that he wore around his neck, "excellent for strangling me if love should reduce me to despair." At first she refused even a kiss, meaning to be faithful to her husband, but that didn't last long. "She offered me her mouth, and so abandoned it to my own that I had to pull away in order to breathe. Recovering from my ecstasy, I threw myself at her feet, and my cheeks were inundated with tears of gratitude." This was the first aristocrat with whom he had been involved. She seems also to have been the first sexual partner who pondered the nature of desire as thoughtfully as he did, which produced one of the subtlest of all his accounts of erotic experience.

A doctor had ordered Andriana to rest in bed for a minor illness, and while arranging the cushions she tantalizingly revealed at least part of herself. "I saw two columns of ivory that formed the sides of a pyramid, and between them I would gladly have gasped out my dying breath. A jealous drape hid the apex from my eager eyes, that happy angle upon which all my desires were concentrated." When he visited the next day she asked him to hand her a chemise, "and I was in ecstasy admiring that lovely third of her person." Women were always enchanted by Casanova's unfeigned admiration. "I saw her gazing at herself attentively, ravished with herself, in a way that convinced me she delighted in her own beauty." This reflected the precocious insight that Casanova had expressed in Latin as a boy: the male organ is enslaved to the female.

Now at last Andriana permitted him to caress her naked, exchanging fiery kisses, "in a way that made it impossible for me to penetrate into the sanctuary." Her continued resistance bewildered him, since her desire was obviously keen, but she explained. Her husband had been the first man she had slept with, expecting to love him all the more afterward, but she had been sadly disappointed. "I felt only pain that wasn't compensated by any pleasure. I found that at the convent [where she had been educated] my imagination was my greatest resource." From this she concluded that imagination was always preferable to reality, which could only disappoint.

Casanova, who had thought a lot about the power of imagination, could see the force of the argument. What followed—elaborated, no doubt, in his narration—was a kind of philosophical dialogue. Meanwhile he and Andriana both experienced orgasms, but without penetration, which to his way of thinking wasn't really satisfaction at all. When he begged her once again to let him enter "the forbidden paradise," she exclaimed, "Oh, my dear friend! There's a furnace down there. How can you hold your finger there without being burned by the fire that's devouring me? Oh, my friend, stop! Hold me with all your might, come close to the tomb, but take care not to inter yourself in it."

A week later, when they next had an opportunity to be alone together, she did finally allow penetration, but only for an instant, after which she pushed him away abruptly and went to sit in an armchair. "Motionless and astonished, I trembled as I looked at her, trying to understand that what could have caused this movement against nature. I heard her say, gazing at me with eyes alight with love, 'My dear friend, we were about to lose ourselves.'"

Hurrying out into the night, Casanova committed an act of folly that wrecked everything. On the way back to his lodgings he was accosted by a courtesan named Melulla "whose exceptional beauty had enchanted all of Corfu for four months," and she had no trouble persuading him to go to her elegant apartment. "Her beauties were a hundred times beneath those of the divine woman I was desecrating, but this vile being had been placed there by hell to accomplish my dark destiny, and she attacked me at a moment when what had just happened made me no longer my own master. . . . I went home to bed detesting her and hating myself."

The consequences soon became apparent. Melulla had infected Casanova with venereal disease, and sleeping with Andriana again was now out of the question. He couldn't bear even to think of passing on the infection to her. When he went to tell her the truth, it turned out that she had been thinking things over and was ready to do whatever he wanted, but it was too late. She made it even more painful by saying that she was already aware of what he had just done. "While I was talking she never stopped denouncing the wickedness of the infamous Melulla. All of Corfu knew that I had paid her a visit [surely an exaggeration?], and they were astonished that I seemed to be a man in good health, since the number of young men was not small whom she had treated as she did me."

It was just as well that the stay in Corfu was about to end. An aristocrat's son was arriving to replace Casanova in his military role, and it was time to go home.

Reflecting in the *Histoire* on what it had all meant, Casanova concludes with a passionate exclamation about the nature of love, underlined for emphasis throughout. It's very much in the spirit of the old seventeenth-century libertines, epitomized for instance in the *Maxims* of La Rochefoucauld. Love is not just irrational but an illness, even insanity, yet nature makes it impossible to resist.

> What then is love? In vain have I read the alleged sages who have written about it, and in vain have I philosophized on it myself while growing old. I will never agree that it is a mere bagatelle or vanity. It's a kind of madness over which philosophy has no power, a malady that man is subject to at any age and incurable if it strikes in old age. Undefinable love! God of Nature! Bitterness than which nothing is sweeter, sweetness than which nothing is more bitter! Divine monster, that can be defined only by paradoxes!

CHAPTER 8

Metamorphosis

Back in Venice, Casanova was frustrated and unhappy. Still just twenty years old, he had made half-hearted attempts at the two most obvious professions for a young man of humble origins, the church and the army. But religious bureaucracy held no appeal for him, and he was never pious. As for the military, it had been fun to impersonate an officer in a nonexistent army, but his experience as a lieutenant in Corfu was far from encouraging. He did sign on as apprentice to a Venetian lawyer—after all, he had studied law in Padua—but nothing came of that, and it's clear he never wanted it to.

"I thought of becoming a professional gambler, but Fortune didn't approve of my project. After less than a week I was penniless, and for the time being I settled on playing the violin; Doctor Gozzi had taught me enough to scrape away in a theater orchestra." Accordingly Signor Grimani, who owned the theater of San Samuele, gave him a job, but it was a terrible comedown to play such a subordinate role. That was the very theater where his mother had been a star.[1]

Still, he held firmly to a conviction that Fortune was bound to favor him in the end. "I knew that she exerts her power over mortals without consulting them, so long as they're young, and I was young." It was tempting to personify luck as Fortune, who was worshiped as a goddess in the ancient Roman Empire. Gamblers have always been especially prone to this psychology; as the song has it, "Luck, be a lady tonight."

As he had at Padua, Casanova took up with bad companions, rowdy young men who roamed through Venice committing what they regarded as playful pranks. They untied gondolas and let them drift away, laughing at the curses of the gondoliers; they woke up midwives in the middle of the night and dispatched them to houses where no one was pregnant; they got into bell towers and rang the bells wildly as if there was some emergency. Most outrageously, they abducted a married woman from a tavern, stranded her husband and his friends for the night on the island of San Giorgio Maggiore, and returned her to him the next morning. What happened was unquestionably a gang rape, but Casanova claims it wasn't really rape because the woman had a good time. According to him, she laughed gaily when they were taking their turns with her, and thanked them politely when they took her home.[2]

What's astonishing is how casually Casanova describes this incident; he seems to class it with the other "pranks" like ringing the bells. It's highly relevant, too, that he claims the woman enjoyed it. That will be a pattern of his when encounters go bad, a convenient way of excusing himself from blame, let alone guilt.

In any case, he tells this story to illustrate how the rules in Venice depended on social class. Since he was hanging out with aristocrats, he was invulnerable to punishment. According to him, when the aggrieved husband reported what had happened to the judicial council, its members just laughed. "The tribunal wasn't going to do anything, since it would have had to punish a patrician."

Now came the gift of Fortune. During the spring of 1746 Casanova played in the orchestra at a wedding celebration. Leaving shortly before dawn, he happened to see a senator in a red robe about to climb into his private gondola. The robe was a sign of great distinction; this was one of the six consiglieri who advised the doge, the head of government. When the nobleman pulled out his handkerchief a letter fell to the pavement, and Casanova hastened to retrieve it for him. Gratefully, the stranger offered a ride in his gondola. Before it reached his palazzo, however, he was seized by a terrifying stroke. Casanova mentions that this happened at the very place where, three years previously, he had mugged Grimani's agent Razzetta.

With amazing self-confidence Casanova disembarked with the afflicted nobleman. If he hadn't guessed already who his companion was, he would know it now: this was the Palazzo Bragadin Carabba, and the nobleman was Matteo Giovanni Bragadin. He belonged to one of the most distinguished patrician families in Venice, with a colorful history. At the battle of Famagusta against the Turks in 1571, the defeated general was his ancestor Marcantonio Bragadin. The Turks flayed him alive, stuffed his skin with straw, and paraded it through the streets before delivering it to Constantinople as a gift for Sultan Selim II.

A doctor was urgently summoned and bled the patient copiously, as was usual in those days for almost any complaint. Meanwhile the sick man's two closest friends arrived, in despair because he seemed at the point of death. "They questioned me and I told them all that I knew; they didn't know who I was and didn't dare ask, and I told them nothing about that." The next day the doctor applied a mercury-impregnated plaster to the patient's chest; the medical theory was that excessive heat should be drawn out of a patient by overheating his skin.

By the day after that, the plaster had begun to cause fever and convulsions. The doctor had not yet arrived, and Casanova seized control of the situation. He ripped the plaster away, and after he bathed the place where it had been, Signor Bragadin fell peacefully asleep. It seemed to the two friends that this youth must possess extraordinary gifts, and indeed, his advice to let nature take its course was fortunate. From a modern perspective, the senator had suffered a transient ischemic attack or mini-stroke, which can pass off after a relatively short time.

Casanova had always taken an interest in medicine, which he originally hoped to study at Padua, and he had a skeptical opinion of physicians who followed rules of thumb from the ancients that generally did more harm than good. Years later he quoted a couple of sayings from Pliny: *Nihil ignorantius grammatico excepto medico,* and *experimenta per mortes agebant*—"No one is more ignorant than a grammarian, unless it's a physician," and also, "They get their experience by killing their patients."[3]

The recovering senator was enchanted with his rescuer, dismissing the doctor after telling him coldly "that the person who saved him from the mercury that would have killed him was a doctor who knew more than he." Casanova says, "So here I was, the doctor of one of the most illustrious senators in Venice." Always an improvisor, "I talked like a physician, I dogmatized, and I cited authors I had never read."

It soon emerged that there was another way in which Casanova could impress Bragadin and his friends, who were likewise noblemen, Marco Dandolo and Marco Barbaro. He realized that they were devotees of the occult, and he knew enough about that to play along. In fact they encouraged it; Bragadin declared that so young a man couldn't know so much unless he had access to secret knowledge. "I took the strange expedient of declaring, falsely and fool-ishly, that I had a mastery of numerical calculation. After translating a written question into numbers, I would receive an answer telling everything I wanted to know, and that no one in the world could have told me."

Casanova would continue to exploit this oracular game for the rest of his life. Modern attempts to explain how it worked are too complex to describe here, but it's clear that he pulled it off because he possessed exceptional facility at mental calculation. As he translated the letters of a question into numbers, following a well-known code of equivalences, he would arrange them on paper in the form of a pyramid. Then, like a chess master looking several moves ahead, he would translate the numbers back into letters that spelled out the desired answer. He claimed that an informing spirit named Paralis guided him, and in the years to come Paralis would be a useful fiction whenever he had occasion to pose as a magus.

Signor Bragadin said that this oracular power was undoubtedly the Cla-vicule of Solomon, "which the common people call the Cabbala." Casanova claimed that he had learned it from a hermit near Rimini during his travels. When the three friends begged him to teach them what he knew, he realized that his cover was about to be blown. With impressive resourcefulness, he replied that he would love to do so, but the hermit had warned him that if he did tell anyone he would meet a sudden death. "I don't believe in this warn-ing," he said, which prompted Bragadin to reply that he most definitely must believe it. "From that moment on, none of the three of them ever asked me to reveal the Cabbala."

Venice was a place where the Cabbala (or Kabbalah) was of particular in-terest. It had originated as a mode of biblical interpretation in medieval Spain, with an emphasis on secret relationships among numbers. The Clavicule ("Lit-tle Key") of Solomon was a collection of magic spells that supposedly went back to the biblical king; Goethe mentions it in *Faust*. Cabbala became known in Venice after 1492 when the Sephardic Jews were expelled from Spain.

In fact Casanova did what any fortune-teller does, letting the questioners lead him to the desired results and then telling them what they wanted to hear. It was a scam, of course, but he was entirely without remorse. At various points in the *Histoire* he insists that people who let themselves be fooled de-serve what they get, and anyway, if he was clever enough to get away with it, he had every right to. "Deceitfulness is a vice, but an honest ruse is nothing but prudence of mind. It's a virtue. It's true that it resembles rascally behavior (*friponnerie*), but it's necessary to proceed in that way. Whoever doesn't know how to do it is a fool."[4]

At this stage in the development of modern science, chemistry was still disentangling itself from alchemy, and advanced thinkers could pursue both. That was the shadowy underside of the Enlightenment. Isaac Newton, one of the greatest physicists who ever lived, sought to recover the occult knowledge of the ancients, with particular attention to alchemy. John Maynard Keynes said that Newton "was not the first of the age of reason, he was the last of the magicians." Among Newton's belongings at his death in 1727 were nearly two hundred books on alchemy, such as *The Secret Booke of Artephius and the Epistle of Iohn Pontanus: Containing both the Theoricke and the Practicke of the Philosopher's Stone.* That was a mysterious primal material, the chief goal of all alchemists, that could turn base metals into gold.[5]

In *The Alchemists* (color plate 14) by the Venetian Pietro Longhi, these are not sleazy con men, but serious scientists laboring to reveal nature's secrets. The man in the fur-lined robe is evidently explaining what has just occurred in his glass vessel, while at the left his colleague tends the crucible. The church frowned on alchemy, which it considered akin to magic, but the man in the middle is a Carmelite monk. On the floor an open book displays conventional astrological symbols; the sun is at the top, followed in pairs by the moon and Mercury, Mars and Venus, and Jupiter and Saturn.

Fourteen years after meeting Bragadin, Casanova would run into an elderly lady in Switzerland who dabbled in chemistry and had been a good friend of Hermann Boerhaave. That was a distinguished Dutch physician who genuinely believed that he knew how to transmute base metals into gold. "She told me that he had presented her with a manuscript in which the entire process was explained, but which she found obscure." Casanova also met in Switzerland the distinguished poet and scientist Albrecht Haller, who had been Boerhaave's student. When asked whether he believed in the existence of the philosopher's stone, he said that he personally doubted it, but couldn't deny that it might be possible.[6]

It might seem that if someone actually did possess the philosopher's stone, with its awesome powers, it would be hard to keep it secret, but gifted con men had a clever answer. They said that they were disguising themselves as fakes in order to keep the powers that be from catching on and robbing them. They were thus charlatans who protected their ruse *by pretending to be charlatans.*[7]

Casanova gives the impression that he never believed for a moment in his occult power, but that's because when he was writing the *Histoire,* he wanted to be seen as an altogether rational intellectual. Yet the supernatural was never far away in the Venice of his youth, beginning with the witch on the island of Murano and the mysterious lady in the night. And the exorcism of Bettina in Padua, even if her fits were staged, confirmed that demonic possession was a perfectly genuine aspect of Christian belief. The Church, of course, insisted that there was no similarity whatsoever between belief and superstition, but to many people that was a distinction without a difference. For that matter, Protestant theologians regarded much of Catholicism itself as superstition.[8]

One might assume that a successful con man must be a calculating actor, skillfully managing his performance. According to Diderot, stage acting was itself a kind of con: the best actors study their expressions and tones of voice objectively and avoid any emotional involvement with the characters they play. Casanova, though, was the opposite of that. He was a method actor before there was such a thing: when he assumed a role, he felt that it *was* him. He convinced others so well because he first convinced himself.[9]

A critic offers this reflection: "People talk about Casanova's 'inner void' as if, once the mask and costume came off, there was nothing left. In truth nothing is more full than the character of Casanova. . . . Our viscera, nerves, and glands respond to the emotions that appear on our face; authentic reactions within the body follow from the actor's external simulation. Casanova had a body that spoke the truth." Another commentator adds, "Surprising though it may seem, the success of an adventurer like Casanova, in deception as in love, is linked to his profound tendency to empathize."[10]

Casanova's three new aristocratic friends were bachelors. There were two reasons for that. One, as has already been mentioned, was that it was customary in Venice to keep aristocratic fortunes intact by expecting just one son and one daughter to marry. The others would live comfortably enough, as Bragadin did in his palazzo, but if they did marry they would be legally barred from bequeathing money to their children. The other reason was specific to the practice of the occult. The friends were convinced that their access to hidden secrets depended on sexual abstinence. "All three of them," Casanova says, "had become irreconcilable enemies to women after giving them up. According to them, that was the principal condition that the elemental spirits required of anyone who wished to have to do with them. The one excluded the other."

There were four of these "elemental spirits." They were sylphs in the air, gnomes in the earth, nymphs in water, and salamanders in fire (Aristotle had claimed that salamanders were invulnerable to burning up). Alexander Pope made playful use of these spirits in *The Rape of the Lock,* and in later years Casanova would exploit an extremely rich French lady who fully believed in them.

The immediate consequence of Casanova's encounter with Bragadin was remarkable. Just as Yusuf in Constantinople had wanted Casanova to be his son-in-law, Bragadin announced that he would treat him henceforth as an adopted son. Suddenly he found himself installed in an apartment in the palazzo with elegant clothes, a gondola all his own, and a regular supply of cash.

Located on a side canal not far from the Grand Canal, the Palazzo Bragadin Carabba—a hotel today—was impressive. Its main entrance was on the Campo Santa Maria in the northern Castello district, a short distance from the Rialto Bridge. There was also a water gate on a small canal, the Rio di San Lo (beneath the balcony, color plate 15), and that was where Casanova first entered the palazzo with Bragadin on the night of their memorable meeting. Centered above the four Gothic windows was the family coat of arms, a simple cross upon a shield—somewhat distorted today by a streak of dark discoloration. By a decree of 1562, incidentally, all gondolas were required to be black, as they still are to this day.

It has been suggested that when Bragadin dropped the letter he was offering to pick Casanova up for sex, but that's pure conjecture, and on the whole it seems unlikely.[11]

Their relationship would prove to be enduring. For the remaining twenty-one years of his life, Bragadin did treat Casanova like a son, and his room in the palazzo was always waiting for him whenever he returned to Venice. Even after Bragadin's death, his friends continued to send Casanova a regular stipend, modest but welcome. It's obvious that his appeal went much further than his cabbalistic mumbo-jumbo. The three aging ex-playboys, Félicien Marceau says, appreciated "his flow of talk, his good humor, his amorous adventures—in short, his youth." Throughout his life Casanova knew how to make himself lovable to men as well as women—perhaps even more so to men, since sexual tension and fear of betrayal weren't present to compromise the relationship.[12]

First with Malipiero and now with the Bragadin circle, Casanova was mixing on easy terms with patricians. They were just 2 percent of the population of Venice, but it was the 2 percent he felt he belonged in. It has been calculated that 140 Venetian patricians are mentioned in the *Histoire,* some in passing but many repeatedly. Most were men; Casanova never had much success with patrician women.[13]

14. The Palazzo Bragadin

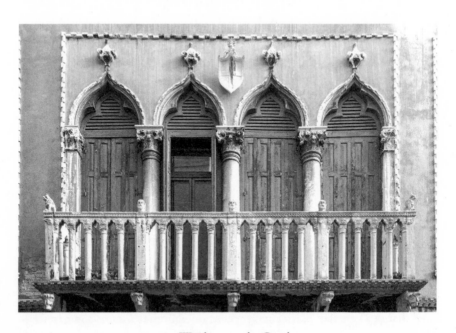

15. Windows on the Canal

When Bragadin announced that henceforth Casanova would be his adopted son, it was as if a fairy tale had suddenly come true. "I immediately threw myself at his feet to assure him of my gratitude, and to call him by the sweet name of father. I swore that I would obey him as a son. The other two friends, who were staying in the palazzo, embraced me, and we swore eternal brotherhood. There, my dear reader, is the whole story of my metamorphosis, and the fortunate moment that saw me soar up from the vile trade of a fiddler to that of a *seigneur.*" The caterpillar had become a butterfly, as he always believed he would.

CHAPTER 9

Playboy

Thanks to the chance encounter with Signor Bragadin and the relationship that developed, Casanova suddenly had an entirely new life. No need now for half-hearted attempts to become a priest, much less a soldier; his mission was the one he felt born for, to enjoy himself to the full. Whether or not he was actually the illegitimate son of Michele Grimani, believing that he was had let him feel that he was a prince in disguise. Now he was being rewarded as he deserved to be, with a fairy-tale rescue from ignoble status. And he could hope now to get involved with upper-class women who wouldn't have looked twice at a theater violinist.

By his own admission, Casanova didn't just take advantage of this opportunity, he abused it. He was still just twenty-one. "I began to live in freedom from anything that could set bounds to my inclinations. So long as I respected the laws, I felt that I could despise all prejudices. I believed I could live in perfect freedom in a country that was subject to an aristocratic government." He couldn't, of course, but he started behaving as if he really was an aristocrat, and the government soon began to keep a close eye on him. Most Venetian nobles weren't wealthy, but the important thing was that they were all nobles. That status and its accompanying prestige were strictly guarded. We have already noted that marrying a commoner meant automatic loss of noble status, and even if Bragadin chose to treat Casanova like an adopted son, actual adoption would not have been permitted.

"During that year," Casanova says, "I began to beat a path that would end up in an impenetrable prison of the State." He was aware of surveillance, and he mentions a habit of changing gondolas three times to throw spies off his track. But in any case the prison was still a long way off. Much travel and many adventures would happen before he found himself there.[1]

Bragadin counseled him genially to behave more respectably, but having led a scandalous life in his own youth, he thought that these follies would soon be outgrown. Meanwhile, "wealthy enough, naturally endowed with a striking appearance, a confirmed gambler, a leaky basket [i.e., pouring out money], a great talker with a sharp tongue, not at all modest, bold, chasing pretty women, supplanting rivals, and regarding no one as good company except those who amused me, I could only be hated." And why not behave like that? Casanova's quick wit had gotten him out of many a difficulty already.

It's worth noting that he wasn't conventionally good-looking, but somehow all the more compelling for that. The Prince de Ligne said, "He would have been a very handsome man if he hadn't been ugly; he's tall and built like Hercules, but with a dark complexion." He seems to have been somewhat swarthy at a time when fair complexions were favored, but that too made him interestingly different.

Few authentic portraits of Casanova survive—most experts think there are only two, or at most three—but we do have one made when he was thirty by his brother Francesco (color plate 16).[2]

As for his height, he once recorded it as "five feet and nine thumbs," which translates to 1.88 meters or a bit over six feet one. A passport he obtained in his early thirties made him even taller, "five feet and ten and a half thumbs," which would be close to six feet three, but of course he might have misrepresented his height at that time. In any event he was exceptionally tall, during an era when the average male adult stood five and a half feet.[3]

An acidic description of Casanova at this time—the only one that we have from his early life—survives in a novel by Pietro Chiari, who was a rival of Goldoni and hated Casanova for being Goldoni's ally. Chiari also suspected, possibly correctly, that Casanova was the author of an anonymous satire against himself. The actress who narrates the novel calls him Signor Vanesio, "conceited," and starts out by alluding to the rumors of his parentage:

Among others there was a certain Signor Vanesio, of unknown origin, and by many said to be not of legitimate extraction. He was well-made in his person, with an olive complexion, affected manners, and indescribable boldness, and he claimed to be my *cicisbeo* [gallant, accepted companion], but he didn't possess the first quality to be lovable. . . . Always as polished as a Narcissus, puffed up like an inflated balloon, and in continual motion like a windmill, he made it his business to get involved with everything, playing the gallant with all women, and adapting himself to everyone who might offer an opportunity to make money or to be fortunate in love. With misers he played an alchemist, with beautiful women a poet, and with the great a politician. . . . His system was to be everything to everyone, although since he always adjusted himself to each person's humor, he couldn't be a friend to anyone.

Like all effective caricatures, this one highlights some very recognizable characteristics of Giacomo Casanova.[4]

An anecdote in the *Histoire* illustrates the new power Casanova was experiencing. He needed to pay a gambling debt of one hundred zecchini—ten times his monthly stipend!—and Bragadin suggested that he try to borrow the money from a French soldier who was hoping for a lucrative appointment in the Venetian army. Casanova made the attempt, and the soldier turned him down. Soon after that the soldier's application was rejected, very much to his surprise, since he knew he was well qualified.

This turned out to have been a deliberate setup by Bragadin. In Venice everything was done through influence, and the Frenchman should have grasped that if he did Casanova a favor, Casanova would tell his patron and the appointment would duly follow. Bragadin had proposed asking for the loan as a test. "I realized," he told Casanova, "that this man wasn't intelligent enough for the appointment he wanted. Could he have had good judgment when he refused to lend you a hundred zecchini? Doing that made him lose an income of three thousand scudi that would have been his right now."

Casanova's debt was enormous, equivalent to 11,000 modern euros, and it's not clear how the Frenchman could have afforded the loan. Still, 3,000 scudi would have meant an annual income of more than 100,000 euros, and accommodating Casanova would have been well worth it. "This man," Casanova says complacently, "was useful to me by telling everyone what had happened. From then on, anyone who needed the senator's help knew the way to get it. I paid all my debts."[5]

Well aware that the affection of Bragadin and his friends was an invaluable asset, Casanova was on guard against anyone else who might try to horn in.

A Milanese swindler named Antonio della Croce once tried to enlist him to persuade Dandolo to marry a widow, who would in turn pay off Croce. Casanova thought that that would be "a ridiculous marriage," and told him frankly, "Every man is something of an egotist, and I'm permitted to reflect that if Signor Dandolo should take a wife, her credit with him would have some weight, and whatever she might gain over his mind would be so much lost for me. . . . Understand that so long as I'm with these three friends, they will have no wife other than myself." Croce replied, "You're caustic this morning," but he dropped the idea. In later years, however, the two of them would run into each other from time to time, and would become good friends.[6]

Always an inventive role-player, Casanova now tried his hand at a new role, the benevolent savior of innocents in distress. By chance he happened to be present when a masked young woman emerged from a boat that plied between Ferrara and Venice by way of the Brenta Canal. She was clearly lost and confused, and he offered to help. Impulsively trusting him, she revealed that she was a countess; she had succumbed to an unscrupulous seducer who promised to marry her but then suddenly disappeared. Knowing that the seducer was from Venice, she had come to demand that he keep his promise.

Did it actually happen by chance, or was Casanova more calculating than he acknowledges? At any rate, he chose not to take advantage of the lady in distress. After convincing her that immediate confrontation with the seducer was a terrible idea, he found her lodgings with a virtuous widow while he sorted things out. Bragadin and his friends agreed to help, and the culprit was soon detected. In due course the woman's father, her brother ("handsome as the god of love"), and her uncle arrived in search of her, and Casanova effected a heartwarming reconciliation. Fortunately they never realized that she had actually slept with the villain. Trapped and facing a forced marriage, the seducer became a monk, while the woman went home with her family. Casanova adds that he fell in love, as usual, but virtuously refrained from abusing her trust.

Relating this story in the *Histoire*, Casanova was writing as a sentimental novelist would. His description of the family reunion could come right out of the popular fiction of the day, and he presents it as a masterful feat of stage management. "What a *coup de théâtre!* Fraternal love expressed on two angelic faces formed from the same mold. . . . My role was as the principal architect of this noble edifice." Always a hair fetishist, he did ask for a lock of her long blonde hair, which he had admired when he surprised her combing it at a mirror. A year later she wrote to say that she was now living in "one of the loveliest cities in Italy" and had married a marchese.[7]

A somewhat similar episode happened when Casanova encountered another stranger in town, a gorgeous country girl named Cristina who was visiting with her uncle, an elderly priest. She was intelligent but charmingly naïve, and it didn't take long to get her to sleep with him after he promised to marry her. As so often, he believed he really meant to do that, and counted on his patrons to make it happen: "It would be up to me to convince my three friends, on the strength of oracles, that my marriage was written in the great book of destiny." Pretty soon, however, he had second thoughts about such an irrevocable step. But now he was in a fix, since he couldn't callously desert Cristina. And what if she should be pregnant? "To abandon this innocent girl would have been a black action that was not in my power. The very idea made me tremble."

Fortunately the uncle revealed that Cristina would bring a big dowry to a husband, and Casanova set about finding her a suitable one, relying as usual on his friends. They selected a worthy young man who was delighted at this unexpected gift of fortune, and as it turned out it suited Cristina too; marriages were commonly arranged in those days, after all. She proposed a farewell kiss, which Casanova tried to refuse, "since we're alone, and my virtue is weak. Alas, I still love you!" She replied, "Don't weep, my dear friend, in truth I'm not worried about it."

On her wedding day Cristina was "beautiful as a star," and Casanova had to go into another room to hide the tears that flowed so promptly on emotional occasions. But the upshot was another opportunity for self-congratulation. "Her gratitude pleased me, and I certainly had no thought of taking advantage of it. I was delighted to see that I had been able to make two people happy."[8]

The young playboy was learning how to be another eighteenth-century type, a man of feeling. In traditional morality, you must do good to other people because God commands it, and may even punish failure to do it. As that stern ethic began to fall into disfavor, moralists recommended doing good because it will make you feel good about yourself.

Apart from these sentimental performances, Casanova spent most of his time gambling and roistering. One horrible exploit got him in serious trouble, when he was staying with friends in a village near Treviso on the mainland. "We gambled, we chased women, and we played tricks on each other. Some of them were cruel, and bravery consisted in laughing about them. One could never take offense; not to appreciate joking was to seem like a fool."

One day Casanova was crossing a plank bridge over a slimy ditch when the plank snapped in two and he plunged in, ruining an elegant new suit. Everyone roared with laughter and he was forced to join in, though he was furious and suspected that someone must have sawn the plank partway through. He always had a hair-trigger temper when he felt insulted. Later he bribed a peasant to reveal that a Greek merchant named Demetrio was the culprit.

Casanova regarded revenge as entirely appropriate after a public insult. Italian aristocrats were indeed famous for their hotheaded reaction in such cases, and he no doubt felt he was acting in character. It would be too easy, however, simply to pick a fight, and too easy to win since Demetrio was close to fifty years old. An appropriate revenge called for a trick "that would be the equal of his, both in inventiveness and in the pain it would cause him." For a while nothing came to mind "until I happened to see a burial. Here is what I planned while I was actually looking at the corpse."

Casanova waited until midnight, stole into the churchyard, and dug the cadaver up. With a hunting knife he amputated an arm, and carried it back to the lodgings where he and Demetrio were both staying. Creeping cautiously into the Greek's room, he tugged the bedclothes partway off, at which the sleeper stirred and reached out to grab at the intruder's hand. Instead he seized the dead one, after which Casanova retired complacently to his own bed.

He assumed that the only consequence would have been a bad fright, but not so. The next morning he learned that the terrified victim had had an apoplectic fit, and a priest declared that Casanova had committed an appalling crime. "They told me they had had the Greek bled, after which he was able to move his eyes but not his limbs, and he couldn't speak. A day later he did speak, but I heard afterward that he remained stupid and spasmodic; he passed the rest of his life in that state. The priest reburied the arm the same day, filed a complaint, and sent an indictment to the episcopal chancellery at Treviso."

A doctor confirms that the unfortunate Greek's fate makes medical sense. "Sudden intense terror can provoke a vascular attack, a slowing of the heart rate and drop in arterial tension; this is the famous 'syncope.' If it's long and intense enough the drop in blood pressure can lead to irreversible brain damage. It is therefore entirely possible that poor Demetrio remained 'stupid and spasmodic' for the rest of his life."[9]

Casanova had not only injured Demetrio, he had committed blasphemy as well, since it was considered blasphemous to violate a grave. Even the distinguished medical faculty at the University of Padua was permitted to dissect just four cadavers a year, and those had to be newly executed criminals, not corpses exhumed after interment.[10]

In relating this episode Casanova doesn't condemn his behavior, but he doesn't try to justify it either. In the preface to the *Histoire* he declares that he will give an unvarnished account of what he was like in his impulsive youth, merely admitting that it was sometimes truly disgraceful, and now he lets the reader be the judge.

We have remarked on Casanova's gift of empathy, but it had its limits. He could tune himself effortlessly to another person's temperament, so that he or she would feel right away that he was a kindred spirit. There was genuine sympathy between himself and Malipiero (until the abrupt rupture of that relationship) and permanent affection with Bragadin and his friends. But he shows no trace whatever of sympathy, let alone remorse, for what he did to the unfortunate Greek. The man had humiliated him before his friends, and Casanova paid him back. He didn't care that that the payback turned out to be grossly disproportionate—avenging a trick, malicious though it may have been, by ruining a man's life.

There's a further point to make about the episode of the dead arm, which has the folk-tale flavor of an old fabliau. A sixteenth-century Florentine author, Antonio Francesco Grazzini, known as Il Lasca (the name of a hard-to-catch fish), wrote a collection of stories in the manner of Boccaccio. Many of them center on acts of punishment and revenge, and one is remarkably similar to Casanova's appalling prank. Grazzini's collection *Le Cene* ("the dinners," stories told to amuse a group of friends) remained unpublished until 1756. That was seven years after Casanova was in Treviso, so he couldn't have known about it when he was there—but he could certainly have known about it when he was writing the *Histoire*. Still, there seems no doubt that the incident really happened. Among the mass of papers he left at his death was this note: "The man in the cemetery whose arm I cut off."[11]

Thanks to the priest's complaint, Casanova knew he could expect prosecution, and sure enough when he got back to Venice he was summoned for trial. But surprisingly, it had nothing to do with the dead man's arm. A woman charged that he had lured her daughter to a garden on the island of Giudecca, raped her, and afterward beaten her up.

Casanova's defense was that he never committed rape, and he claimed indignantly that the mother knew perfectly well what she was doing and had accepted six zecchini to bring the girl to the island and leave her alone with him. If he really did pay her that much—it's not clear why he would have—it was the equivalent of 700 euros today. The reason he beat the girl, he explained, was that after accepting this implicit bargain, she refused her favors and pretended to virtue she didn't possess. "If I'm guilty," he declared, "it's only for beating an infamous girl, the pupil of a still more infamous mother."

In the *Histoire* Casanova admits to only one other occasion when he was violent toward a woman, in London sixteen years later. There too he would be led to expect sexual favors and would find them withheld. The incidents have something else in common, though. In each case teenagers were being used by their mothers as bait, and very probably they hated that role. Here on Giudecca, the girl may well have been alarmed or even terrified when she found herself alone with this powerful older man. Whether or not her mother was responsible for sending her there, his behavior was appalling, and he doesn't recognize that it was.

We will never know what would have happened if the case had come to trial. Just at this time the outrageous story from Treviso became known, and Casanova was still deeper in trouble. "Signor Bragadin advised me to give way to the storm, and I immediately packed my bags." The three friends assured him that a year later his misbehavior would be forgotten and it would be safe to return; evidently the authorities preferred to have him disappear for a while rather than go on trial. A lower-class offender who lacked aristocratic patrons would not have gotten off so easily.[12]

This would be Casanova's first involuntary exile from the city he loved, though not the last. It was probably just as well. His pampered life in the Palazzo Bragadin was turning him into an unpleasant character, and learning to survive on his own in the wider world would broaden and deepen him.

CHAPTER 10

Libertinism

Casanova wasn't just a bad boy, he was a particular kind of bad boy. "In Venice," he recalled cheerfully in the *Histoire,* "there was no greater libertine than myself." What did that mean? The term could be applied to a wide range of temperaments and lifestyles, sometimes with approval, usually with indignation.[1]

A recent survey lists possible implications: "The libertine is sometimes interchangeable with, and sometimes distinguished from, the Priapean, the spark or ranter, the roaring blade, the jovial atheist, the cavalier, the sensualist, the rake, the murderous upper-class hooligan, the worldly fine gentleman, the debauchee, the beau, the man of pleasure, and even the 'man of sense.'"[2]

At one extreme, libertines were cynical seducers, sociopaths even, like the Marquis de Valmont in *Les Liaisons Dangereuses* and his collaborator the Marquise de Merteuil. Jean Giraudoux famously said that every copy of that novel should have a warning on the cover, "For External Use Only." But at the other extreme, libertinism claimed to be a genuine philosophy of life, and that's how Casanova understood it.

The key to this philosophy was an emphasis on freedom from repression, the liberty implicit in "libertine." It claimed to follow nature, arguing that what our instincts prompt us to do can't possibly be wrong. That was of course an explicit rejection of orthodox religious teaching. "God saw every thing that he had made," the first chapter of Genesis tells, "and behold, it was very good." As far as Casanova was concerned, the story should have stopped right there. He never accepted the doctrine according to which Adam and Eve wrecked the primal goodness by committing the original sin. Pleasure, he says in a draft preface for the *Histoire,* "is a gift of God; anyone is monstrous who believes that God could take pleasure in the pains, sorrows, and abstinence that people offer in sacrifice to him."[3]

In *The Invention of Liberty* Jean Starobinski says that eighteenth-century libertines "desired their freedom in order to seek alike immediate pleasure and fundamental truths; they sought enjoyment, but also critical understanding." Robert Darnton, in an account of eighteenth-century forbidden books, likewise confirms that while some were pornographic, others were serious discussions of philosophy and religion that would seem completely innocent today; the reason they were forbidden is that they were intellectually dangerous. "To French readers in the eighteenth century, illegal literature was virtually the same as modern literature."[4]

Casanova did share the intellectual interests, but for him libertinage was, above all, liberation of the senses—all five of the senses. In the final version of the *Histoire* preface he mentions his love of strong flavors, and extends the thought frankly to sex. "I like highly seasoned dishes—macaroni made by a good Neapolitan cook, *olla podrida* [a spicy Spanish dish], cod from Newfoundland that's good and sticky, game with a high aroma, and cheeses whose perfection appears when you begin to see the tiny creatures that live in them. As for women, I've always found that the ones I loved smelled good, and the stronger their sweat was, the sweeter it seemed to me."

He knew perfectly well that many readers would find this shocking, and he added, "What a depraved taste! How shameful to recognize it in oneself and not blush! That criticism makes me laugh. Thanks to my gross tastes, I'm shameless enough to think I'm luckier than other people, since I'm certain that my tastes make me susceptible to more pleasure." In an earlier draft he declared, "I'll allow people to call me a pig. When I consider a real pig, I'm more inclined to congratulate it for not having the mental qualities of a man, than to complain that a man has the qualities of a pig." He would have appreciated Winston Churchill's remark, "Dogs look up to you, cats look down on you. Give me a pig! He looks you in the eye and treats you as an equal."[5]

Epicurus was the patron philosopher of libertinism, and the pig was an

Epicurean example of a creature entirely comfortable in its life—unlike most humans. According to Horace, a follower of Epicurus,

> *Me pinguem et nitidum bene curate cute vises,*
> *Cum ridere voles, Epicuri de grege porcum.*

In an eighteenth-century translation, "When you would be merry you may visit me, whom you will find fat and sleek and in good plight of body; in short, a hog of Epicurus's herd."[6]

Horace was in fact one of Casanova's two favorite poets, together with Ariosto, and he knew much of their poetry by heart. They represent the essential poles of his imagination: in Horace an epicurean meditation on life, in Ariosto a combination of daring heroism and romance. He may also, as Marie-Françoise Luna suggests, have felt a personal affinity with Horace. Born in socially marginal circumstances, they received fine educations and were taken up by highly placed patrons. Bragadin was Casanova's faithful maecenas, and the term derives from the real Maecenas who was Horace's friend. But Horace also enjoyed the friendship of the emperor Augustus; Casanova would never succeed in getting close to kings and princes, though he often tried.[7]

From Casanova's unpublished writings, we know that he doubted the immortality of the soul, and even the existence of the soul. For him the only certainty was living each moment to the fullest. In the *Histoire* he says, "I've loved, I've been loved, I felt well, I had plenty of money and spent it; I was happy and I said to myself that I was, laughing at the stupid moralists who claim there's no true happiness on earth. It's the expression 'on earth' that makes me laugh, as if one could seek it anywhere else. *Mors ultima linea rerum est.*"

Horace's line means "death is the end of all things"; and Casanova goes on to quote two more favorite lines. One begins with an expression that has become familiar in English: *Carpe diem quam minimum credula postero,* "Seize the day, and put little trust in the next." The other is suggestive of the stream of life as he experienced it: *Quod adest memento componere aequus: caetera fluminis ritu feruntur,* "Remember to deal serenely with what is present; everything else flows away like a river." If the moments of perfect happiness are necessarily fleeting, that just makes them all the more precious. "This happiness passes," Casanova says, "but its ending doesn't mean it didn't exist, or that someone who enjoyed it can't bear witness to that."[8]

It should be stressed that despite the porcine analogy, there was nothing hoggish about sex as Casanova understood it. He made a distinction between simple appetite and a complex and thoughtful experience of pleasure. Gratifying appetite, he said in some unpublished reflections, is common to all creatures, "which must perpetuate their species through the act of generation, and they would certainly not perform this duty—no matter what Saint Augustine says—if it weren't pleasurable to do it." Augustine does indeed claim, in *The City of God,* that before the Fall Adam and Eve activated their organs deliberately with no need to enjoy it. "Only man," Casanova continues, "is capable of true pleasure, since being endowed with the faculty of reason, he anticipates pleasure, he seeks it, he shapes it, and he reflects about it after enjoyment." Ideally, one should experience three distinct gratifications— anticipating, experiencing, and reflecting afterward. When that happens, "These three gratifications become pleasure, pleasure, pleasure."[9]

These ideas were very much part of the Enlightenment campaign against the repression which Freud would later claim is essential to civilization. Casanova and the philosophes would have laughed at that. One writer who especially interested him was Julien Offray de La Mettrie, best known for his notorious *L'Homme Machine,* in which he held that mind is simply a function of body. Casanova did believe that, and equally relevant for his thinking was La Mettrie's *L'Art de Jouir,* which argues that we need to distinguish between three different types of gratification. *Plaisir* is a simple instinctual response. At the other extreme, *débauche* is vulgar debauchery that selfishly exploits other people. The ideal is *volupté,* in which the heart joins with the senses and physical pleasure is exalted by imagination.

Denis Diderot develops similar ideas in an article entitled *Jouissance* in the great *Encyclopédie* that he edited. Then as now, *jouissance* meant "enjoyment," but could also mean "orgasm." It is Nature's gift, Diderot says, just as Casanova does, to ensure the perpetuation of the species. "Do you imagine that your mother would have risked her own life to give you life, if she had not felt an indescribable charm in her spouse's embrace?" And ideally it is more than that, a true merging of two people. "Tell me," Diderot continues, "you who have a soul, what could be more worthy of our pursuit than a being who thinks and feels like yourself, who has the same ideas, who experiences the same heat and the same transports?"

In an unpublished dialogue entitled *D'Alembert's Dream* and its sequel, Diderot went still further: no common human practice is unnatural, masturbation and homosexuality included. What *is* unnatural is repression. "Nothing that exists can be against nature or outside nature, and I don't even exclude chastity and voluntary continence, which, if it were possible to sin against nature, would be the greatest of crimes against her, as well as the most serious offences against the social laws of any country in which acts were weighed in other scales than fanaticism and prejudice." Clerical celibacy and monasticism were regular targets of the Enlightenment philosophers, and they thought it unsurprising that vows of chastity were often broken.[10]

There are thus two very different expressions of libertinism. Catherine Cusset puts it well: one kind encourages manipulative seduction, while the other is immersion in the moment, "a point in time when circumstances suddenly make you oblivious to any other reality but physical pleasure." Those exalted moments are what Casanova celebrates all the way through the *Histoire*.[11]

Or exalted hours—as, for example, "We spent six happy hours, as the reader can imagine for himself. Sleep had no part in it." And again, "We had before us six hours which the reader may imagine well filled. We got out of bed highly satisfied, and laughing because we were dying of hunger." Two points are significant. One is that six hours is a lot of lovemaking—this was mutual and protracted pleasure. The other is that Casanova invites the reader to fill in the details in friendly complicity. He imagines his ideal reader as a kindred spirit, not moralistic and judgmental.[12]

Wholesome as Casanova thought such experience was, his treatment of it is never free from special pleading. Even though he claimed to pursue high-minded *volupté*, often he was simply a *débauché*. Nor can he be believed when he claims that he never seduced anyone who wasn't just as interested as he was. In one of his draft prefaces he admits, "I have sometimes deceived women." He adds ruefully, "They've had their revenge, and most cruelly; they love me no more, and I love them still." But that was an imagined collective revenge at a time when he had grown old and no women wanted him. That would have been small consolation for the women who did get hurt by him in earlier days.[13]

Still less high-minded is a popular Italian saying that Casanova invokes repeatedly in the *Histoire, Il cazzo non vuol pensieri*—"the prick doesn't want thoughts." It has a counterpart in the *Oxford Dictionary of English Proverbs:* "A standing prick has no conscience."[14]

And then there were the bouts of venereal disease (it seems to have usually been gonorrhea, not syphilis) that sometimes interrupted Casanova's amorous campaigns, as had happened in Corfu. It generally took him six weeks of self-medication to get well, but he did get well, and he sometimes represents the result as a kind of trophy. "The disease which we call French doesn't shorten life when one knows how to cure oneself. It leaves only scars, for which one finds easy consolation by reflecting that they were won by pleasure. In the same spirit soldiers take pleasure in the traces of their wounds, which are witnesses to their valor and the source of their glory."[15]

Casanova doesn't give details about how his condition was treated, but it seems to have involved rest, moderation in diet, and of course abstention from sex. The favored medications were cubebs, a dried pepper from Indonesia, and copaiba balsam from a South American tree. Those were taken internally and did stop the discharge, but they didn't kill the bacterium, and later outbreaks often occurred even without reinfection. Unfortunately, the difference between gonorrhea and syphilis was not well understood, and both diseases were sometimes treated with highly toxic mercury chloride. On several occasions Casanova mentions its use in his own case.[16]

Casanova distinguishes convincingly, however, between casual episodes with prostitutes—the usual source of his venereal infections—and more deeply felt experiences of sex as mutual and exalting. He repeatedly fell in love, even if it seldom lasted long, and in a late essay he describes what that was like:

> I was in love almost to madness, and I remember perfectly what passed through my mind at that time. I saw all imaginable happiness concentrated in the one I loved, and I couldn't believe that any other happiness was possible beyond living with the woman I adored. We would spend whole hours tête à tête, speaking only of our passion and imagining the happiest future, holding each other tightly breast to breast, inundating each other with kisses without ever moving on to the extreme gratification which, after the crisis, produces a calm in every mortal. Overwhelmed with satisfaction, we perhaps feared that that fatal calm would have shown that in spite of ourselves, our fire could diminish.

Consummation was deferred because the pleasure that precedes it was too sweet to give up. Conventional libertines never talked that way.[17]

At its best, Casanova's tribute to mutual enjoyment is in the spirit of a little four-line poem by William Blake:

> What is it men in women do require
> The lineaments of Gratified Desire
> What is it women do in men require
> The lineaments of Gratified Desire[18]

A contrast with a very different libertine, the seventeenth-century Earl of Rochester, highlights how affirmative Casanova's treatment of sexuality is.

Rochester regularly expresses disgust for the act itself, and revulsion against his own body. His poem entitled *The Imperfect Enjoyment* treats premature ejaculation as a hateful betrayal:

> Worst part of me, and henceforth hated most,
> Through all the town a common fucking-post,
> On whom each whore relieves her tingling cunt
> As hogs on gates do rub themselves and grunt,
> May'st thou to ravenous chancres be a prey,
> Or in consuming weepings waste away.[19]

Casanova could never write like that, or think like that.

Libertinism for him was above all a game of teasing flirtation, in no hurry to reach consummation because the game was a pleasure in itself. A famous painting by Jean-Honoré Fragonard, *The Happy Accidents of the Swing* (color plate 17), embodies a sophisticated version of this ethos. Swings were ubiquitous in fashionable gardens, and they furnished a metaphor for pleasurable letting go, along with repetitive oscillating motion.

Fragonard's picture is set in a secluded bower at a *petite maison,* a private hideaway used for dalliance. An older man in the shadows is pulling a rope to make a young woman fly ever higher, while a young man in the bushes gazes raptly up her billowing pink dress. Making eye contact with him while kicking off an impossibly tiny shoe, she undoubtedly intends this provocative "accident." Contemporary viewers would know that a dropped shoe often symbolized lost virginity, and the sculpture at the left would make them recall a well-known statue called *Menacing Cupid* that was made for Mme. de Pompadour.

In the original statue, not fully visible in this painting, Cupid or Eros is drawing an arrow from a quiver behind his back; he must be about to impale one or both of the young people. This was not Eros the beautiful adult of the Cupid and Psyche myth, but instead the mischievous pre-adolescent son of the goddess of love, who amuses himself by randomly provoking people to fall in love with each other.

But why is he holding a finger to his lips? Is he urging silence so that an illicit affair can remain secret? Or is he warning that this dangerous game is going to turn out badly? And who is the man pulling the rope? Some have thought that he is a clergyman, others that he is the woman's oblivious husband. It's known that Fragonard executed this painting at the request of an aristocratic patron who wanted it to depict himself and his mistress.[20]

In a study entitled *Le Savoir-Vivre Libertin,* Michel Delon stresses the freeze-frame effect. "Fragonard's painting refuses to tell a story; it magnifies a moment, a 'happy accident.' The spectator of the painting is in the situation of the voyeur: if he doesn't enjoy a direct view of the woman's sex, he enjoys the ensemble in the scene, the triangular situation and the suspense. Liberty overcomes weight, the lovers escape prohibitions, and art escapes interpretation. Libertinage is located in this suspense."[21]

This vision of libertinism, however, is highly idealized—flirting and teasing arrested in a graceful moment, surrounded by nature shaped and tamed. Less charmingly, a philosophy that treated pleasure as the highest good could easily rationalize self-serving behavior and even abuse. But at its best it was a philosophy that encouraged mutuality and generosity. That was how Casanova understood it, and throughout his life it would be his guide when conventional morality seemed repressive and life-denying. On a few occasions— but only a few—he would find a partner who understood libertinism in the same way he did. Those encounters remained alive in his memory, and he recreates them vividly in the *Histoire.*

CHAPTER II

"*You Will Also Forget Henriette*"

Even if Casanova hadn't been forced to leave Venice, he might have done it anyway. A rhythm was already established that would persist for most of his life: each period of temporary stability would be followed by a leap into the unknown. New places and new people energized him, and he loved to improvise roles, as would happen frequently during the coming year. In addition there would be a love affair with a mysterious woman whom he would miss for the rest of his days.

A few days after setting out, Casanova reached Milan in the Duchy of Lombardy, far away from Venetian justice. There he encountered someone from his past and made a friend for the future. The figure from his past was Marina, Teresa/Bellino's supposed sister with whom he had briefly dallied five years previously, who had become a professional dancer. She was seventeen now, lovely, and the mistress of a gambler who called himself a count but wasn't. In fact, Marina said, he was a pimp and she was his whore. Not surprisingly there was a quarrel, and that led to an absurd duel in which Casanova saw that his opponent was a coward and thrashed him soundly with the flat of his sword. After he and Marina spent "a most agreeable night" together she offered to travel on with him, but he urged her to proceed instead to her next engagement in Mantua.

The new friend was a dancer named Antonio Stefano Balletti, one year older than Casanova, who would later introduce him to Paris and the milieu of Italian actors there. "I developed a very strong friendship that would influence a great part of what happened in my life, as the reader will see at the appropriate time and place."[1]

Casanova went on to Mantua by himself, and fell in with some raffish officers in the Austrian army. In an era when soldiers of fortune were common, most of them weren't Austrian themselves, and one was an Irishman named O'Neilan (his historical reality has been verified). After spending a night with a prostitute Casanova was disgusted to realize that he had contracted gonorrhea yet again, for the fifth time. O'Neilan laughed and said that he had too, from the same woman. He added that he was so accustomed to repeated infections that he had given up being treated for them. "What's the point of being cured of a *chaudepisse* ("hot piss") if one catches another right afterward?"

Here the narrative pauses for an unusual encomium. "O'Neilan, the brave O'Neilan, perished several years afterward in the Battle of Prague. Such as he was, this man was sure to perish as the victim of either Venus or Mars. . . . One has to respect these great warriors, since their indomitable courage comes from greatness of soul, and from a *vertu* that places them above all mortals." Casanova was capable of courage, but had no intention of dying on a battlefield. The French term *vertu* implies not virtuousness in the ordinary sense, but moral integrity, and although he admired it in others, he also saw it as a sad waste. "O you who despise life, tell me if you believe that by despising it you make yourselves worthier of it."

O'Neilan's contempt for medical treatment wasn't as obtuse at it may seem. "Cures" were often dangerous, and likely to be temporary rather than permanent; libertines did regard repeated infections as simply the price one had to pay. A book with the cheerful title *Casanova: The Contagion of Pleasure* turns out to be about venereal disease, and the author calculates that he was treated for it at least a dozen times.[2]

What came next was one of Casanova's impromptu scams, cooked up just to have fun with a credulous victim. The opportunity arose when a young man invited him to see a collection of rarities that had been assembled by his father, a pompous official called a commissario. These included relics of saints, coins that allegedly dated from before Noah's flood, and "an old knife with a bizarre shape that was eaten up by rust." Reverently, the owner disclosed that this was the very sword with which St. Peter cut off the ear of the high priest's servant when Jesus was being arrested.

Casanova, who knew his Bible well, responded that one thing was still missing to make the object a priceless treasure, for which the pope himself would pay a fortune. That was the sheath that went with it, for did not Jesus tell Peter to let the arrest proceed, saying *Mitte gladium tuum in vaginam,* "Put thy sword into the sheath"?[3] No doubt the double meaning of *vagina* amused him. Fortunately, he continued, he knew exactly where that sheath was, and he could get it if they would pay him what it was worth.

Up until now Casanova was just having fun, but the commissario and his son eagerly took the bait. They told him they knew a rich farmer in the town of Cesena, beneath whose cellar a great treasure was concealed that could be recovered by "a skillful magician" if they could find one. With this they would be able to purchase the sheath. Naturally, Casanova became the magician. After boiling an old boot and rubbing it with sand he created a plausible sheath, and he spent some time in a library forging a document that purportedly recorded its history ever since the Crucifixion. The document ended by revealing that during the night of a full moon, "a sage philosopher will be able to raise the treasure above ground while standing within the Great Circle." Books of magic described the Great Circle as protection against invisible spirits.

When they got to Cesena the farmer turned out to have a pretty daughter. Naturally Casanova enlisted her, explaining that the ceremony required the participation of "a virgin seamstress between fourteen and eighteen years of age." Shyly, she said she was just fourteen and did know how to sew; she blushed furiously when he asked her to confirm that she was a virgin. Next a ritual bath was necessary, "and she interested me because while washing her breasts I found a firmness of which I had no conception." She even shared his bed and permitted some sexual attentions; he claims she did it willingly.

When the night of the full moon arrived, what happened is extremely interesting, for it reveals Casanova's tendency to be taken in by his own act. It also illustrates the tendency to superstition that he experienced all his life, much though he wanted to regard himself as an enlightened philosopher.

The girl stitched together a big circle out of sheets of paper, and Casanova chanted some meaningless gibberish, but no sooner did he take his place inside the circle than a violent thunderstorm blew up. "The lightning flashes were all around me and froze my blood. In the terror that seized me, I was certain that if the thunderbolts didn't crush me, it was only because they couldn't enter the circle, so I didn't dare leave it to save myself. . . . I recognized an avenging God who had been waiting to punish all my villainies and to put an end to my unbelief by death. What convinced me that it would be useless to repent was that I found myself positively unable to move."

By the next morning Casanova had gotten over his fright, but it occurred to him that if any peasants had seen him performing magic they could report him to the church authorities, and he decided to drop the game of treasure-seeking, "disgusted with this comedy." It had indeed been, as a commentator says, "a masterpiece of theatricality." He told the gullible commissario that he regretted not having obtained the treasure, but he did demand a down payment on the sheath. "I didn't know what to do with it, and I didn't need the money, but it seemed to me I would be dishonored by letting him have it for nothing, which would show him that I didn't actually care about it at all." As so often, Casanova convinced himself that he was doing the victim a favor by not dispelling his delusion.[4]

After this episode Casanova stayed on in Cesena, whiling away his time with casual gambling—at this point calling himself Count Farussi, using his mother's maiden name—when the love affair materialized. In his inn at dawn he was awakened by shouting in the next room. Policemen were demanding to know if the guest there was with his wife or someone else; he had been seen arriving at the inn with a young man and they suspected it was really a woman in disguise. Although Cesena was within the Papal States and subject to religious supervision, it's still not obvious why such a commonplace occurrence would provoke a police raid. Maybe there was more to the story than Casanova understood, or at any rate told.

The guest, meanwhile, was sitting up in bed and shouting back, but in Latin which no one there understood. Casanova was fluent in that language and soon figured out what was going on. The offended guest was a Hungarian officer who had documents to prove he was carrying out a mission for a cardinal; Casanova went to the local bishop's residence and soon straightened everything out. Meanwhile he was eager to get a glimpse of the man's companion, who was still hiding under the covers. Casanova inquired what country this companion came from; the Hungarian replied that he was French, and understood no language but his own. "You speak French, then?" Casanova naturally asked. "Not one word." "That's amusing! So you communicate entirely by gestures?" "Exactly so."[5]

The companion now appeared, and as Casanova had suspected, was female. "Emerging from under the covers came a smiling, tousled head, fresh and attractive, that left no doubt as to her sex, though her hair was cut like a man's."

Having learned French in Rome, Casanova had no trouble speaking with her. When they went to dinner a bit later she and her companion were both wearing uniforms, but the disguise was ineffective. "To know that this girl was no man, it was enough to look at her figure."

Cross-dressing always interested Casanova; he was totally smitten, and disgusted that she was with a companion who had to be at least sixty. At dinner with a group of other guests a lady remarked in French that it was strange to be entirely unable to converse with one's companion, and the young woman's reply made everyone laugh: "Why strange, Madame? We understand each other just as well; words aren't needed for the business we have with each other."

The couple were about to leave for Parma, which made sense because it had recently come under French influence and she would be able to speak her own language there. With his usual impulsiveness Casanova decided to join them. He had been planning to go to Naples to see Teresa/Bellino again, but that was no longer relevant; he was certain that he could soon win this woman away from her Hungarian. He was surprised to discover that she spoke highly cultivated French; he still had no idea who she might be, but she was evidently well born. Her name, she said, was Henriette, but that was probably no more true than that his was the Count de Farussi.

That night at an inn Casanova had an exceptionally powerful dream. In it Henriette declared, "I've come to tell you that I love you, and to prove it," which she proceeded to do ferociously. Two things struck him as significant. This dream didn't stop short of consummation as such dreams usually did, and it was so vivid that he had trouble afterward believing it wasn't real.

In dreams of this kind, ordinarily the dreamer wakes up a moment before the crisis. Nature, jealously protecting reality, won't permit the illusion to continue. . . . But, oh miraculous! I didn't wake up, and I spent the whole night with Henriette in my arms. And what a long dream! I couldn't recognize that it *was* a dream until daybreak forced it to dissolve. I stayed motionless in a stupor for a quarter of an hour, going over the details in my astonished memory. I remembered that when I was asleep I had said several times, "I am not dreaming"; and I would have gone right on doubting it if I hadn't found that the door of my room was bolted from inside. Except for that I would have believed that Henriette really did spend the night with me, leaving before I woke up.

It was like a message from the unconscious. "After this happy dream, I was in love to perdition."

Casanova now wasted no time. He told Henriette that he was in love with her, and that if she would leave the Hungarian they could travel on together, but if not, he would go to Naples after all. "Shall I come with you to Parma? Shall I stay here? One of the two—decide!" Laughing, she observed that this peremptory manner was a strange way to win a woman's heart, but he replied that he was not interested in playing the languishing lover of some novel. "The word 'decide' shouldn't seem harsh to you. On the contrary, it honors you, since it makes you the arbiter of your fate, and of mine." She relented, he fell before her and kissed her knees repeatedly, and the thing was settled. As for the Hungarian, it had always been a temporary connection, and he wished them both well.

Rather than conducting a careful campaign of seduction, what always intoxicated Casanova was delicious surprise. Later on in the *Histoire* he says, "Those have been the finest moments of my life: happy meetings that were unforeseen, unexpected, totally fortuitous, due to pure chance, and all the more precious for that." He might have added that he would never have met Henriette at all if the absurd scam about the buried treasure hadn't brought him to Cesena.[6]

That night the dream became reality, and following his usual practice, Casanova describes what happens with great tact. "What a night! What a woman was this Henriette whom I loved so deeply, and who had made me so happy!" Her story came out, too, though not in any detail. She was on the run from an abusive husband and his father whom she called "monsters"; evidently she had been unfaithful, and would have been consigned to a convent if she hadn't escaped. That was somewhere in France, but she never said where. As for the cross-dressing, she left that unexplained. One guess is that she had fled to Italy with a lover, parted from him, and kept some of his clothing as a disguise since a woman traveling alone would be at great risk. She then took up with the Hungarian in order to have a male protector.

Casanova and Henriette were soon settled in Parma, and he arranged to have splendid clothes made for her; he was thrilled to realize from her demeanor that she really was an aristocrat. "We went to bed in love, and got out of bed in the morning more in love than ever. I spent three months with her, always just as amorous, constantly congratulating myself on it." Three months was a long time for Casanova. Writing half a century later he still remembered the relationship as unique. "Anyone who believes that a woman can't make a man happy twenty-four hours a day has never known an Henriette. The joy that flooded my soul was even greater when I conversed with her during the day than when I held her in my arms at night."

Their conversations often turned on the nature of happiness, that perennial theme of eighteenth-century thinkers, and they found that they were in perfect agreement. People were simply wrong who claimed that happiness is illusory because it's not continuous. On the contrary, Henriette said, it's the calm that follows moments of intensity that allows us to appreciate our happiness to the full. She came up with a striking analogy: "This happiness, which does endure throughout our lives, can be compared to a bouquet of various flowers in a mixture so lovely and so well combined that one would take it for a single flower." The word *mixte* is defined in the *Encyclopédie* as a chemical union so indissoluble that it can't be separated into its component parts. Casanova comments, "It was thus that the divine Henriette gave me lessons in philosophy, reasoning better than Cicero."[7]

His own philosophy developed somewhat differently. It emphasized not the retrospective appreciation of happiness, as in Henriette's interpretation, but its absolute fullness while being experienced. In his classic *Studies in Human Time,* Georges Poulet captures the distinction: "This is the perfect moment for Casanova: a moment of pure newness, where nothing else matters, neither past nor future. . . . Happiness cannot be a permanent state of existence. It's a means of experiencing in the instant what by its very nature is instantaneous."[8]

That, in turn, raises a potential problem: what if happiness is not just momentary, but illusory? When it's over, is gratified recollection the only possible result? In *Les Liaisons Dangereuses* the Marquise de Merteuil tells Valmont that she despises prudish women, including the one he's trying to seduce, because "they hold back at the very heart of rapture and offer nothing but half-pleasures. That entire abandonment of the self, that delirious ecstasy where pleasure becomes purified by excess, all this wealth of love is unknown to them."[9]

But in what way does excess "purify" pleasure, and why should it deserve the name of "love"? Whatever the moments of excess may mean to Merteuil, at all other times she is a cold and vicious sociopath, delighting in ruining people's lives. In mainstream eighteenth-century thought, pleasure was thought of not as an intensification of happiness but as virtually its opposite. Pleasure burns itself out, and often leaves pain behind. Happiness, more tranquil, is an ongoing state of being. Perhaps Casanova did experience that state of being with Henriette, but if so, it's the only time in his long erotic history that it happened. The rest of the time it burned out.

Still another talent of Henriette's was revealed, to Casanova's delight. The lovers had been lying low for fear that her family might track her down, but they accepted an invitation to a party at a country house. After dinner there was an orchestral piece, and a cellist played a concerto to warm applause. "But here is what astonished me. Henriette got up, and after praising the young man for his performance, she took up his cello [it was probably the more popular viola da gamba] and said serenely that she would make it show off its qualities even better." Sitting down, she placed the instrument between her knees and asked the orchestra to begin again, while the guests were all silent with surprise. Casanova suspected at first that she was just joking, but as soon as she began to play the applause almost drowned out the orchestra. She sight-read the score perfectly, even though she had never seen it before. Casanova was so moved that he went out to weep in the garden "where nobody could see me."

Afterward Henriette charmed the guests with her wit. Asked how she learned to play the cello, she said she took lessons when she was a convent girl, but the mother superior forbade her to play it until her parents got an explicit order from a bishop. "What reason could the abbess give for not consenting?" "This pious bride of our Savior claimed that I could only manage the instrument by putting myself into an indecent posture."

"Who then," Casanova reflected, "*is* this Henriette? What is this treasure whose master I've become? It seemed impossible that I could be the lucky mortal who possessed her." Calling himself master was just a conventional expression; they were mutually in each other's thrall. But her mysteriousness did indeed stimulate his desire, and although he eventually learned her real identity he was careful to cover it up in the *Histoire*. Researchers have claimed to have proved that she was a certain Jeanne-Marie d'Albert, or Marie-Anne d'Albertas, or else Adélaïde de Gueidan, or possibly Jeanne Marie d'Albert de Saint Hippolyte. As usual in such cases, nothing significant is known about them, if indeed they are all different people.

Back in town Casanova hastened to buy a cello for Henriette and encouraged her to play it often for him. "The cello's human voice is superior to that of any other instrument, and went straight to my heart." There were several more weeks "plunged in happiness," and then it all came to a shocking end. Henriette let herself be persuaded to attend an outdoor celebration, and she was recognized there by a gentleman from Provence who turned out to be a relative. He may have been sent to find her, and in any case the game was up. Together they wrote to her family to negotiate terms for a return home, and the family's response was acceptable. "What need was there to have stayed so long in Parma!" Casanova exclaims. "What blindness on my part!"

They set off at once for Milan, and after crossing the alpine pass at Mont Cénis they reached Geneva. There Henriette drew a large sum of money from a well-known banker, which confirmed that she came from a distinguished family and could be trusted. At an inn called Les Balances, "The Scales," she informed Casanova that she would now travel on by herself, and he watched her setting off at dawn. "I didn't go back to our room until I had followed her carriage with my eyes, and long after I could see her no more."

Henriette had told him to expect a letter from her. When it arrived it contained just one word: *Adieu.*

What happened next is reproduced here from Casanova's manuscript, in which he underlined the crucial phrase. *Ne pouvant partir que le lendemain, j'ai passé tout seul dans ma chambre une des plus tristes journées de ma vie. J'ai vu écrit sur une des vitres des deux fenêtres qu'il y avait: Tu oublieras aussi Henri-ette. Elle avait écrit ces mots à la pointe d'un petit diamant en bague que je lui avais donneè.* "Unable to leave until the next day, I spent one of the saddest days of my life alone in my room. I saw, written on one of the panes of its two windows, *You will also forget Henriette.* She had written those words with the point of a little diamond in a ring that I had given her." She used the intimate *tu,* not *vous,* and she must have been remembering something he had said to her back in Cesena: "'Forget me' is easy to say. You should know, Madame, that a Frenchman may be capable of forgetting, but if I may judge by myself, no Italian has that singular ability."

Incidentally, Casanova habitually used a grave accent in the Italian manner, where French would expect an acute, and placed it rather casually—*donneè* should have been *donnée.*

One might suppose that Henriette's letter was something of a challenge, predicting that he would easily get over her, but she may actually have wanted that; the relationship had run its course and now belonged in the past. "It's an invitation to oblivion," a commentator says, "not an expression of regret."[10]

Another letter followed, which Casanova says he copied out from the original; he did keep most of his correspondence. "Don't make your grief worse by thinking of mine. Let us imagine that we have had a pleasant dream, and not complain about our destiny, for no dream was ever so pleasant and so extended. . . . Don't try to find out about me, and if by chance you do learn

16. Henriette's Farewell

who I am, act as if you don't know. . . . I don't know who you are, but I know that nobody on earth knows you better than I do. I will have no more lovers in the future, but I don't want you to think of doing the same. I want you to love again, and even find another Henriette. Adieu."

In the days that followed, Casanova says, he was all but paralyzed with grief. Crossing the Saint Bernard pass, he noted that misery at least insulates a person. "I felt neither hunger, nor pain, nor the cold that freezes Nature in that dreadful part of the Alps, nor the fatigue that's inseparable from that dangerous and difficult passage." He really was deeply in love, in a very different way from his usual easy come, easy go relationships.

Years later Casanova happened to be in Geneva, lodged in the same room, and found that the words on the windowpane were still there. "Ah, my dear Henriette! Noble and tender Henriette, where are you?" With regret he reflected that although he had had many lovers in the meantime, "I found myself less worthy to possess her than in those days. I did still know how to love, but no longer with the same delicacy, with the emotions that make one lose one's heart, the gentleness of manners and integrity. And what appalled me was that I no longer had the same vigor." For Casanova declining virility was a tragic loss of self.[11]

In 1763, fourteen years after their parting, there was a painful reprise. Casanova was traveling with a beautiful woman named Marcolina, whom he had detached from his despised youngest brother Gaetano. When their carriage broke down near Aix-en-Provence, they were taken in at a country château, but didn't get a good look at the widowed countess who owned it. Right after they arrived she tripped over a dog, sprained her ankle, and retired to bed. They were invited to meet her there, but it was dark and she was so well muffled that it was impossible to see her face. She invited Marcolina to share her bed, however, and the next morning Casanova heard all about it. "I saw her entirely naked," Marcolina reported, "and we kissed each other all over. . . . I tickled her adroitly you know where, and she did the same for me." He was predictably delighted. "Nearly all the women in Provence incline to that taste, and they're all the more lovable for it."

After the carriage was repaired and they moved on to Avignon, Marcolina produced a letter that the countess had instructed her to give him. "My heart was pounding. I unsealed it, and saw the address, 'To the most honorable man I have known in the world.'" The letter itself was a blank sheet of paper with just one word on it: "Henriette." She had recognized him, all right, but he had been in her presence without suspecting it. And it was Marcolina, not himself, with whom she made love.[12]

We can only guess what Henriette meant by "honorable man." In the original French it's *honnête homme*, which meant much more than mere honesty; a seventeenth-century writer defined it as "a gentleman who joins to birth the gifts of body, culture, and mind, a taste for poetry, courage, and probity." Casanova had all of that except birth, as he never forgot, but he knew how to simulate birth. Above all, Henriette may have meant that in love he gave at least as much as he took.[13]

Now that he knew who the widowed countess was, it might be thought that he would have hastened back to her château, but he didn't. No doubt he understood that she didn't want him to, and he may also have felt that the relationship should remain safely in the past, not compromised by the changes time had made.

Years later there was one more non-encounter. Casanova was in Aix once again, undergoing a cure for a dangerous attack of pleurisy, and although he was sure that this time he would run into Henriette, it never happened. After recovering he made up his mind that he would go to her château and compel her to see him. When he got there, however, a servant told him that she was still in Aix and had been there all along. In fact, she had paid for the nurse who took care of him.

He didn't go back to Aix to find her, but sent word that he hoped she would finally write to him and that he would wait for her letter in Marseille. When it arrived she acknowledged that she did indeed see him in Aix, though he never realized it. "Nothing, my old friend, is more like a romance than the story of our encounter six years ago at my château, and at the present moment twenty-two years [it was actually eighteen] since our parting in Geneva. We have both aged. Would you believe it, even though I still love you, I'm not sorry that you didn't recognize me? It's not that I've become ugly, but putting on weight has changed my appearance." They agreed to correspond from then on as friends, and they did, though before his death Casanova burned her letters along with many others.[14]

This turned out to be the most satisfying romantic relationship of Casanova's life. Neither lover knew the other's real name, neither was hampered by commitments, and they could simply be themselves. No doubt they were both still performing, but at least they weren't consciously putting on an act. "She conducted their affair," Lydia Flem says, "as though they were living a pure fiction, almost a work of art, outside space and time." Judith Summers adds, "Henriette brought out the very best qualities in Casanova—selflessness, kindness, empathy and generosity."[15]

Why did she write "you will *also* forget," anyway? Did she mean that he would forget her just as he forgot all other women? But the *Histoire de Ma Vie* is enduring proof that he remembered them all—and Henriette was the one he never got over.

A century later, travelers in Geneva could still see the scratched windowpane, and Michel Delon evokes its symbolic significance. "This most fragile of inscriptions becomes the unalterable mark of the diamond—passion and a passing affair, eternity lived in a moment."[16]

CHAPTER 12

Paris at Last

At this point, in the spring of 1750, there was a strange interlude, during which Casanova succumbed to a highly untypical attack of piety. Passing through Parma on his way back to Venice, he had consoled himself for the loss of Henriette with a casual encounter with an actress, and she gave him yet another venereal infection.

A doctor put him through the usual treatment, and meanwhile a pious older man named Valentin de la Haye, who had been Henriette's Italian tutor, urged him to mend his godless ways. "He made me devout, so much so that I agreed I should think myself fortunate to have gotten sick, since that brought salvation to my soul. I gave sincere thanks to God for making use of mercury to bring my soul out of darkness into the light of truth."

When Casanova traveled on to Venice, De la Haye accompanied him, and delighted Bragadin and his friends since they were pious themselves. "Their surprise was extreme at my prodigious change of life. I went to Mass every day and often heard sermons, I was eager to attend the Forty Hours Prayers [commemorating Christ's time in the tomb]. There was no more gambling, and no cafes unless the company was respectable." His three patrons "gave thanks for the crimes that had compelled me to spend a year far from my homeland, and were thrilled to see me an enemy of gambling of every kind."[1]

Before long, however, it became obvious to Casanova that De la Haye was a hypocritical Tartuffe, skilled at extracting money from the rich. Already something of a con man himself, Casanova was disgusted to have been taken in by someone else's con, and he decided that it had only happened because of mental confusion brought on by the mercury. Before long he was growing weary of life in Venice and ready, once again, to move on.

Antonio Balletti, the dancer he had met in Milan, turned up at this point and proposed that they go together to Paris—a mecca for artists and performers, and for adventurers too. Rome was the Eternal City, a monument to the past; Paris was excitingly modern and dynamic. "A new model for urban space and urban life was invented," a historian says, "a blueprint for all great cities to come. . . . Speed and movement were its hallmarks." There were more than half a million inhabitants, ten times as many as in Venice.[2]

Paris was also dominated by a royal court, which Venice never had and which Casanova found exciting. A print of the royal family in the Tuileries Garden is a virtual hymn to aristocratic elegance, with formal plantings beyond the group and the Louvre in the background. The scene exhibits perfect (not to say oppressive) symmetry, in the classical French style. It had been a royal palace until Louis XIV moved the court to Versailles; in the eighteenth century it housed the Académie des Inscriptions et Belles-Lettres and the Académie Royale de Peinture et de Sculpture. Paris also had leafy refuges like the *allée ombreuse* in a drawing by Jean-Honoré Fragonard. Unlike the Tuileries, this scene is an example of nature tactfully shaped by art.

Shortly after setting out Casanova and Balletti stopped at an inn in Ferrara, where there was an opportunity for a spontaneously improvised scene. A group of people were dining there, and a beautiful young woman jumped up, embraced Casanova, and announced that he was her cousin and a distinguished Venetian musician. Falling in with her game, whatever it might be, he recognized her as an actress named Cateria Lazari with the stage name Cattinella. The poet Giorgio Baffo, who had been Zanetta's companion on the boat to Padua long ago, called Cattinella one of the most scandalous women in the whole of Venice.

After introducing Casanova to her fiancé and his parents, she asked him why her mother hadn't come too. Picking up on the cue, Casanova replied that she was indeed on the way and would arrive in a couple of days. He still had no idea what they were talking about. Cleverly, when he was offered wine he held out his hand awkwardly and explained that he had badly sprained his wrist. Cattinella exclaimed what a pity that was, since the injury would keep him from showing off his skill on the clavier. She correctly grasped that he didn't know how to play it.

17. The Tuileries Gardens

When they were finally alone together she explained it all. Finding herself totally broke while performing in Ferrara, she had manipulated a young man into proposing marriage, on the promise that her mother would soon be bringing a big dowry. Since then she had been living at his family's expense, knowing that an Alsatian count was about to arrive to spirit her away. "Women like Cattinella," Casanova comments, "are born enemies of dupes; they are pitiless."

Having carried off the impersonation, he was counting on a reward in bed, but before that could happen the count arrived. He turned out to be shockingly obese, and after watching his inept fumbling with Cattinella through a crack in the door, Casanova lost all interest. "It humiliated me to think that one day I might become as old and fat as this count." He would live to be old, but not fat.[3]

Cattinella was an *aventurière,* a female example of the adventurers who circulated throughout Europe, as Casanova himself was beginning to do. In his last years the Prince de Ligne, who enjoyed his stories and encouraged him to write the *Histoire,* actually gave him the nickname "Adventuros." These characters were a mobile assortment of card sharps, grifters, and con men of all kinds—mobile because they regularly got into trouble with the authorities and had to leave every town in a hurry. A number of them turn up repeatedly in the *Histoire de Ma Vie,* sometimes offering to join forces, often trying to scam each other. We have already encountered one of them in Cyprus, Antonio Pocchini.

18. Fragonard, *L'Allée Ombreuse*

While he was working on his memoirs Casanova wrote to another friend, "When you want to know the truth about all the adventurers in the world, come to me, because I've known them all *funditus et cute*—totally and under the skin." The Latin was a jab at Rousseau, who claimed in his *Confessions* that he would reveal himself *intus et cute,* "within and under the skin." Casanova didn't care for Rousseau, with his boast of utter honesty, and beyond that he never showed much interest in psychological speculation. His claim was that he knew what his fellow adventurers were like when their masks were off, not that he had access to some deeper truth.[4]

In his own mind Casanova may have been one of this tribe, but he was also superior to it. Adventure for him was not just a way of swindling dupes, it was an existential quest for freedom. Guillaume Simiand puts it well: "Adventure promised a rupture with the everyday order, a moment of super-existence liberated from the common lot of humanity, from the Sisyphean path." When the first (and very defective) French edition of Casanova's *Histoire* was published in 1838, the great critic Sainte-Beuve commented: "The man who is clever at expedients, the genius of metamorphoses, the Mercury in politics, finance, or gallantry, in a word the adventurer, *ne dit jamais non aux choses*—he never says no to things."[5]

One stop on the way to Paris was Lyon, and there Casanova made a permanently important connection. That city was a center of Freemasonry, and he became friendly with a Mason "who thought I was worthy, as he put it, to see the light." Very likely they were introduced by Balletti, who was a Mason himself, as many itinerant Italian performers were. We don't know which of two Lyon lodges Casanova joined, but their names were *L'Amitié* and *Les Amis Choisis*—Friendship and The Chosen Friends. Later on, in Paris, he would be initiated into another lodge and quickly rise to the levels of companion and then master, "than which there is no higher grade."

The reason this mattered was that Freemasonry was an international network that would make him welcome among privileged individuals wherever he might be. Vowing a commitment to fraternity and universal peace, its members from every social status were connected throughout Europe as "artisans of the moral and scientific progress of humanity."[6]

Due to its ideal of universal fraternity, Freemasonry was held in deep suspicion by political authorities, as well as by the Catholic Church (a papal bull denounced it in 1738). *Fraternité* would indeed be one of the slogans of the French Revolution, along with *liberté* and *égalité,* and to this day Masonic symbols appear on the United States dollar bill. In a comedy by Casanova's friend

Goldoni, who may have been a Mason himself, *Le Donne Curiose* are "curious ladies" who believe their husbands are up to no good and manage to sneak into their meeting hall, only to find them talking about mutual support and help for the unfortunate.[7]

The script for a Masonic initiation in Lyon has been preserved in the Bibliothèque Municipale there, not printed but handwritten for greater security. If, as seems probable, Casanova submitted to this very ritual, he was required to surrender all of his money, jewels, and items made of metal, including belt buckle and even pins. Next he was blindfolded, since "to open the eyes of the soul, you must close those of the body." After a warning to depart if he wasn't ready to make an irrevocable commitment, a sword point was held against his naked breast while he vowed to treat all fellow Masons as brothers and to give them assistance when possible. The blindfold was then removed and his valuables returned, with the understanding that he should contribute them whenever needed for mutual assistance.[8]

At this stage a new initiate would not be admitted to secret rituals and symbols, but over time Casanova must have become familiar with those, an obvious attraction given his fascination with magic. Indeed, the Masons traced their origins back to the builders of King Solomon's temple in Jerusalem, and the Bragadin circle had credited him with possessing the magical Clavicule of Solomon. In the *Histoire* he mentions the ancient Greek Eleusinian Mysteries, which indeed remain mysterious to this day, and says solemnly, "The secret of the Masons is such that it cannot be communicated to anyone, no matter who, because no one can be sure of knowing it. It is thus inviolable by its very nature. Beyond that I will say that the truth veiled within this secret is such that someone who lacks the talent to guess it is not competent to learn it from anyone else. . . . The secret of the Masons will forever be secret." In short, the deep truth can be known only by intuition. Casanova's fascination with magic and spells now had a respectable home.

A similar claim of incommunicable wisdom lies at the heart of Rosicrucianism, which Casanova would practice later on, as is brilliantly developed in Borges's story "The Rose of Paracelsus." A would-be disciple tells the magus, "I want to walk beside you on that path that leads to the Stone." That meant the alchemical "philosopher's stone" that could turn base materials into gold. Paracelsus replies, "The path is the Stone. The point of departure is the Stone. If these words are unclear to you, you have not yet begun to understand." Defiantly, the visitor demands that he prove he is no imposter by resurrecting a rose from its ashes after it has been burned. A flower is accordingly thrown into the fire and burns to a crisp. Sorry to have exposed the old man's hollow-ness, the visitor leaves, after which "Paracelsus poured the delicate fistful of ashes from one hand into the concave of the other, and he whispered a single word. The rose appeared again."[9]

It should be added that there is little about Masons in the *Histoire,* because by the time Casanova was writing, in the aftermath of the French Revolution, they were regarded throughout Europe as subversive. In Vienna, where he maintained close connections, most lodges were shut down by government decree. Some friends who read his manuscript held high positions and shared that suspicion. He personally hated the Revolution and lamented the fall of the Ancien Régime, but all the same he thought it prudent, as a historian says, "to include only ironic references to his membership in the secret fraternity, veiling the social importance of this international network throughout his life of wandering." It's known that there were active lodges in Germany, Switzer-land, England, and Spain, and he undoubtedly made contact with them.[10]

When Casanova and Balletti arrived in Paris they encountered another carriage, and Balletti exclaimed that it was his mother's. "We got out, and after the usual transports of delight between mother and son, he introduced me. His mother, who was the famous and unique Sylvia, welcomed me with these words: 'I hope, Monsieur, that my son's friend will dine with us this eve-ning.'" She then got back into her carriage with her son and her ten-year-old daughter.

Balletti's mother was Rosa Giovanna, known as Sylvia after her most cele-brated role, and a favorite actress of the great Marivaux. Casanova remembered her with admiration: "They've never found an actress capable of replacing her, and they never will, for she would have to unite all the qualities Sylvia pos-sessed in the too-difficult art of theater—action, voice, expression, wit, bear-ing, pacing, and knowledge of the heart. In all of those she seemed natural, and never revealed the art that created and perfected them." He adds that "her morals were pure. She wanted male friends but never lovers, and the opinion was unanimous that Sylvia was a woman absolutely above her station in life."[11]

The daughter he noticed only in passing, but seven years later that would change. She was Manon Balletti, with whom he would have a long engage-ment, and whose poignant letters are the only ones that have survived from any of his lovers.

Sylvia's husband appears only dimly in the story. He was Giuseppe An-tonio Balletti, with the stage name of Mario. By a remarkable coincidence, his mother was an actress named Giovanna Balletti whose stage name was La

Fragoletta, "Little Strawberry," and it was falling in love with her that had impelled Casanova's father to become an actor himself. Only after that relationship ended did he move to Venice and meet Zanetta Farussi.

In Mantua Casanova had encountered Little Strawberry herself, growing old by then, and was revolted by her flirtatiousness, gaudy makeup, false teeth, and flabby breasts, on which she proudly displayed the birthmark that inspired her nickname. But when he was writing the *Histoire* he was painfully conscious of his own aging body, and that provoked philosophical reflections. Long ago, after all, she must have been irresistible. "I beheld the object whose attractions had seduced my father thirty years previously, the object without whom he would never have left his parents' house, and would never have begotten me with a woman in Venice."[12]

Soon Casanova was virtually a member of the Balletti family, dining with them most days and gaining access to the exciting milieu of expatriate Italians. As a child of the theater himself, he got friendly with performers wherever he went, and they formed a kind of international community; it's been calculated that all told he mentions over two hundred actors and musicians in the *Histoire*.

It's not clear how Casanova was supporting himself at this point. There would have been remittances from Bragadin from time to time, but it's likely that he was also living off the Ballettis.

Because Paris was much less conservative than Venice, Casanova also found it easy to be accepted by aristocrats of both sexes. At the opera he even encountered the great Marquise de Pompadour, Louis XV's official mistress (there were countless unofficial ones). At one moment Casanova burst into laughter when a singer practically shrieked, and a duke asked coldly where he came from. He answered that he was Venetian and that in Venice everyone was free to laugh at the theater, which was perfectly true. "My rather blunt reply made the marquise laugh. 'Are you really from down there?' she said. 'Pardon me, Madame, but I am from *up* there.'" A portrait of Pompadour by François Boucher (color plate 18) shows her in repose in the artfully "wild" Trianon gardens, dressed in a torrent of satin, with a book in her hand and more under her elbow to signify her status as an intellectual and patron of the arts.

Saying "up there" was a faux pas, since Paris thought of itself as the summit of the world—she reminded Casanova of it years later—and he proceeded to make two more blunders. He had a cold and kept blowing his nose, which led the duke to ask politely whether the windows of his room might not be properly closed. "I replied, asking his pardon, that actually they were tightly stopped up." At least that was what he meant to say, but instead of the correct word, *calfeutrées,* it came out *calfoutrées.* That meant they were well fucked. And he even topped that when he was asked which of two singers pleased him most, and after naming his choice was told that she had ugly legs. "I replied that in judging a woman's beauty one must first set aside her legs." His meaning was that beauty is an overall effect and not confined to specific parts, but when he used the word *écarter* he was inadvertently saying that the first thing to do is to spread her legs.[13]

It was clear that Casanova's French, though serviceable, needed work. In this highly competitive culture points were scored by deft turns of phrase, and sly insults were masked under apparent compliments. The playwright Marmontel said, "The weapon of raillery and malicious gossip is like the arrows of savages that are dipped in poison, but so finely sharpened that the prick is imperceptible." Casanova was brilliantly witty in Italian, and that was an essential element in his charm, but he still had a long way to go in French. "Being able to make a woman laugh," he remarks at one point, "is the most beautiful of all declarations of love."[14]

Fortunately Casanova was taken up by a distinguished writer, the eighty-year-old Prosper Jolyot de Crébillon, who offered to tutor him informally (surrounded by his twenty cats) and did so for two years. No doubt he was flattered to hear that Casanova had translated one of his plays into Italian. This was yet another older man who was taken with him.

At first, Crébillon said, minor errors would contribute to his Italianate charm, "but after two or three months the same people who applaud you today will make fun of you." Casanova warned that he wouldn't be an easy student to manage—"I am questioning, curious, demanding, and insatiable"—but they got along well and he made rapid progress. At one point he demonstrated his mastery by writing a poem in French. Crébillon said that the individual parts were fine but the whole thing was bad—"it didn't have balls."[15]

Prosper Crébillon, incidentally, is known as Crébillon *père* because his son Claude was also a writer, of rather licentious novels including *Le Sopha* in which a sofa gets a voice and reports everything that happens on it. In an anecdote that was much appreciated, Crébillon *père* once said sarcastically that he only regretted making two things in his life, his failed play *Sémiramis* and his son. "That's all right," Crébillon *fils* replied, "nobody believes you did either one of them yourself."

Casanova never did speak or write French flawlessly, and when he showed the draft of his memoirs to the Prince de Ligne, his friend called his French "bizarre and barbarous." The prince found it charming all the same, and told him so with a clever pun: "Don't regret your Italianisms: they have more strength than the stupid French grammar, an old driveler who has lost her *règles.*" The word *règles* has two meanings: rules, but also menstrual periods.[16]

Though his French might sometimes embarrass him, Casanova had the advantage of a truly compelling physical presence. Stefan Zweig, with a novelist's eye, imagines him making an entrance at a Parisian concert: "He is tall and broad-shouldered, his hands are strong and sinewy, his frame is tense as steel without a line of softness in it. He stands lightly poised, his head a little lowered, like that of a bull before the charge."[17]

Soon Casanova felt comfortable expressing sharp judgments. He and a new friend, a lawyer and poet named Claude-Pierre Patu, went to an opera entitled *Les Fêtes Vénitiennes* that was set in Venice. Casanova laughed at the backdrop, which depicted the Piazza San Marco as seen from the lagoon, but with the Ducal Palace on the left and the campanile on the right instead of the other way round. After the overture there were Carnival revelers in inauthentic costumes, a formal dance by the doge and his counselors wearing absurd Roman togas, a ballet dancer who performed stylized leaps to huge applause, and a ballerina who was famous for wearing no underclothes. Casanova asked Patu how he knew what she wore or didn't wear, and was told, "Oh! that's the sort of thing one has to know. I can see that Monsieur is a foreigner."

The performance lasted for four hours, and Casanova found the declamatory style of singing repellent. When it finally ended he asked Patu innocently, "When is the singing going to begin?"[18]

Patu and Casanova took to each other warmly, and strolled around Paris admiring the sights. At one point they visited a famous brothel called the Hôtel du Roule after the name of its street, run by a Madame Paris, who was known as "the abbess." The house had a dining room with a skilled chef and first-rate wine, well furnished bedrooms, masters who taught the girls writing, dance, and music, and a doctor who visited every other day to confirm their health and cure them if necessary. The abbess had fourteen "nuns" dressed in identical white muslin, all young and pretty but otherwise catering to different tastes—"tall, middle-sized, and petite; blonde, chestnut-haired, and brunette."

Casanova asked why there were always exactly fourteen of them and was shown a line from Virgil inscribed over the front door, *Sunt mihi bis septem praestanti corpore nymphae.* It had been suggested by Voltaire when he visited there, and means "I have twice seven nymphs of exceptional beauty." There was a fixed price for dining with a girl and another for spending the night; virgins were much in request and were more expensive.[19]

Establishments like the Roule were exclusive, patronized by the titled and wealthy, and there were only twenty of them. Ordinary streetwalkers were considered disreputable and often arrested, but the high-class brothels were protected by the police as deliberate policy. They received regular reports from the madams and wrote up information gathered by spies of their own; the goal was to make sure that the customary system ran smoothly, and the madams regarded the police virtually as colleagues. "More than anything," Nina Kushner says in a deeply researched study, "the police helped to enforce the demi-monde's own rules." Parents could accept a fee for consigning their daughters to a brothel, in effect selling them, so long as they didn't come from middle- or upper-class families. They were generally around fourteen when they arrived; the sale of girls younger than twelve was illegal and regularly punished.

Still, prostitution itself was technically illegal; the police expected to be paid off, and exploitation was endemic. Kushner adds that the madams needed "a steady stream of young women whom they could compel to engage in activities that were illegal, socially stigmatized, physically dangerous, and personally disgusting to many of them." Casanova has nothing to say about that.[20]

He also formed a connection with his landlady's teenage daughter Mimi. She was lively and amusing, with a good voice, and she had a big repertoire of popular songs. Mimi turned up regularly in his room, all by herself, and they started sleeping together. Before long she announced that she was pregnant and told her mother, who took Casanova before a magistrate to force him to marry her.

He was convinced that it was entrapment. It wasn't likely that the girl was spending all that time in his room without her mother's knowledge; more probably it was actually encouraged. The magistrate agreed, and Casanova was free to go. When the birth happened, however, he paid for it, and arranged for the infant to be delivered to the Hôpital des Enfants Trouvés.

The Enfants Trouvés—"found infants"—was a hospice run by nuns where fully a quarter of newborns in Paris ended up. Rousseau, much to his shame when the story eventually became known, had forced his mistress Thérèse to place all five of their children there, though because of malnourishment and infectious disease few could have survived for long. His defense was that all young bachelors did that, and Casanova clearly felt the same way. Rousseau felt guilty, though, and Casanova did not.

As for Mimi, he says that things worked out all right for her at first. With good looks to go with her voice, she went on stage, and might have done well if she hadn't fallen for a violinist who somehow wrecked her life. "She disappeared after that, and I never found out what became of her."[21]

After Casanova had been in Paris for a year, his younger brother Francesco turned up, the only sibling for whom he ever had any use, and they shared an apartment. Francesco was an aspiring painter, and noting that battle scenes were much admired—the Seven Years War had recently begun—he decided to specialize in those. Eventually he would gain fame for them, but when he exhibited his first attempt it was jeered at. Humiliated, he brought it home, "gave his innocent painting three or four blows with his sword," and resolved to improve his skills elsewhere before tackling Paris again.[22]

Among Casanova's stories from this time is one about helping out an innocent girl, which he enjoyed doing from time to time as a sentimental interlude. Her name was Annette-Louise Solari-Vésian, and she happened to take lodgings with her brother right next to his own. They were hoping the brother could get a commission in the army, but meanwhile they were broke and at a loss how to survive. She admitted to Casanova that although she hated the idea, she might be forced to sell herself for money. He was genuinely moved and resolved not to attack her virtue himself. "When I reflect today that I stayed with this girl until three in the morning, ardent with love but never coming to the point, I don't recognize myself."[23]

Casanova counseled Annette in strategies for finding a rich protector, and before long she did succumb to the advances of a count, but he turned out to be fickle and dropped her after a week. Balletti's help was now requested. He thought she had potential as a dancer and undertook to train her himself, and that proved successful. It was common for young women to enroll in the ballet or opera with the chief intention of attracting a well-to-do admirer.

Meanwhile, predictably enough, Annette was willing to reward Casanova for his help and encouragement. They had a long discussion of the nature of happiness, much as had happened with Henriette; he no doubt improved the dialogue in the *Histoire* long afterward, but it's very possibly true to what happened. Annette was concerned that she would be forced into an immoral way of life, and Casanova replied that pleasure is the ultimate good and can only be achieved by overcoming conventional prejudice. When she asked what true pleasure was, he replied that it's immediate *jouissance* of the senses, followed afterward by imagination. And when she asked him to define prejudice, he said, "It is every so-called duty for which we can find no reason in nature." The discussion ended predictably. He devoured "her eyes, her mouth, and her alabaster breasts," and they spent the night in bed.

Before long Annette did find a protector, a generous count. "She lived with him until his death always happy, and making him always happy too; he left her wealthy." Thus was fulfilled a prophecy that Casanova and Balletti had made when they began coaching her: "We will see you one day covered in diamonds."

Annette had become a courtesan or *dame entretenue,* a "kept woman," a well-recognized class whose members got signed contracts from their lovers for lodging, upkeep, and clothing, and usually generous stipends as well. Their stories, Kushner says, reflect "misfortune and desperation," but also "hard work and manipulation, love, and above all individual agency."[24]

Casanova had one further interesting relationship during this time. He and Patu were planning to spend the night with an actress from Flanders named Victoire Murphy (her father had been Irish). Victoire didn't interest Casanova, but he was much taken with her little sister Louise, not quite fourteen, who let him fondle her naked. They stopped short of consummation because both sisters told him that that would cost much more. Even so, they got a lot of money out of him during the next two months until he became fed up with *enfantillages,* childish fooling around.

This would have been a casual, passing encounter except for a painting of Louise by the celebrated François Boucher that has become famous (color plate 19). Casanova had commissioned a miniature from some other artist, and the Boucher version—discreetly titled *Reclining Nude*—was probably inspired by it. In Casanova's description, "She was lying on her stomach, supporting herself on her arms with her little breasts on a pillow, turning her head as if she had been lying on her back. The skillful artist depicted her legs and thighs in such a way that the eye couldn't desire to see even more. In London I've seen a hermaphrodite, attributed to Correggio, in the same pose." Underneath his miniature he wrote *O-Morphi,* punning on a Greek word meaning "beauty." There is no known painting like that in London, but he probably saw a copy there of the Roman statue that was illustrated previously in connection with Bellino (see figure 13, page 80 above).[25]

Remarkably, when Louis XV saw the Boucher painting (in which the girl's head is not turned as in Casanova's miniature) he recruited her as a mistress, "after assuring himself, with his royal finger, that she was perfectly intact." She was installed at Versailles, "where His Majesty kept an absolute seraglio," and stayed there for three years until she unwisely insulted the queen and was banished forever.

It should be added that Casanova felt an almost involuntary enthusiasm for monarchs. Though Venice had no hereditary ruler, it definitely had a patrician class, and ever since he moved into the Palazzo Bragadin he had identified with it strongly. Kings and queens had still greater charisma, at the very top of the social hierarchy.

This is how Casanova describes his first sight of Louis XV, in the palace at Fontainebleau: "I was in a gallery and saw the king pass by, supported by an arm across the shoulders of M. d'Argenson [a former minister of foreign affairs, now retired]. The head of Louis XV was ravishingly handsome, supported on a neck that could not have been finer. Not even the most gifted painter would be able to capture the sudden impulse with which he would turn to look at someone. One felt compelled to love him at that instant."

It's interesting that Jean Laforgue, the 1826 editor of the *Histoire,* not only bowdlerized the erotic passages but added political reflections that were entirely his own. Right after the rapt tribute to Louis XV comes this statement, which Casanova didn't write and would never have written: "'Oh, servility!' I thought within myself; 'can a man submit to the yoke like this, and can another man believe himself so much above the rest that he puts on such airs!'" Laforgue approved of the French Revolution; Casanova despised it.[26]

Casanova may have been in awe of kings, but not necessarily of queens, who were often unimpressive and had been selected for reasons of state. He was permitted to be present when Queen Marie partook of a public luncheon. Pious and timorous, she was the former Marie Leszczyńska, daughter of the deposed Polish king Stanislaus I who was now Duc de Lorraine; she had been chosen from a list of nearly a hundred candidates when she was twenty-one and the boy-king was fifteen. After eating in silence for a quarter of an hour she called out, "Monsieur de Lowenthal." Casanova says that he was "very curious to see the face of the famous warrior who had taken Berg-op-Zoom." That was a fortified Dutch town, thought until then to be impregnable, that had fallen during the recent War of the Austrian Succession to a French army under his command.

"Hearing himself named by the queen, Lowenthal advanced three paces toward her, saying 'Madame.' 'I believe,' she told him, 'that the dish preferable to all others is a chicken fricassee.' 'I am of the same opinion, Madame.'

After this response, which he gave in the most serious tone, the great warrior returned to his place, repeating the same three paces backward. The queen did not speak again."[27]

Paris was the only city besides Venice where Casanova would live for extended periods of time, and he thought of it as a second home. Remembering it nostalgically after the Revolution, he felt as the statesman Talleyrand did, who wrote in his own memoir, "Whoever hasn't lived in the eighteenth century before the Revolution doesn't know *la douceur de vivre,* the sweetness of living."[28]

Nevertheless, after two years in Paris Casanova was ready to move on. Francesco proposed that they go to Dresden and visit their mother, and he agreed. They arrived in the fall of 1752 and Giacomo stayed for several months, but in the *Histoire* he says nothing about the reunion with Zanetta except that she was *enchantée* to see her sons. This was the first time he had been with her in fifteen years; he last saw her when he was twelve. Francesco signed on to study with an eminent painter, and would live in Dresden for several years. Giacomo had no interest in remaining there, and he departed during the spring of 1753. After stopping briefly in Prague and Vienna to add to his collection of European cities, he was on his way to Venice once again.

By now, at the age of twenty-seven, he had accumulated a truly remarkable breadth of experience. As Angelo Mainardi says, it was acquired in almost every possible milieu: "literary circles, courts, aristocratic mansions, and theaters; among professional gamblers, prostitutes, and adventurers; in ecclesiastical palaces and secret societies, with philosophes and followers of Cabbala—all the contradictions of the age."[29]

CHAPTER 13

Nuns and Lovers

Casanova was returning from Paris chagrined and defeated. He had imagined that he would launch a brilliant career there, but nothing happened. He was going back to Venice not because of homesickness but for financial support.

In Padua, just before taking the canal boat to Venice, he happened to see a pretty woman falling from a carriage. He caught her, and noticed appreciatively that her skirt flew up, "exposing all of her hidden marvels to my eyes." (The nineteenth-century bowdlerizer of the *Histoire* makes him say that he "repaired with a chaste hand the disarray that the fall had caused in her clothing.")[1]

The next day in Venice the woman and her male companion were masked for Carnival, but she tapped Casanova with her fan as he was passing by and they introduced themselves to him. The man was "P. C.," whose real name was almost certainly Pier Antonio Capretta. He had had a falling-out with his wealthy merchant father, and was now seeking a backer for a scheme he had. Casanova was disgusted that this fellow could mistake him for an easy mark, but he agreed to help, because he was presented with an interesting proposition. The scheme involved P. C.'s fourteen-year-old sister. If Bragadin would come through with funds to underwrite a marriage, maybe Casanova could be that husband. P. C. would of course cash in himself as a result.

Several things had to happen for this scheme to work. First, Casanova had to find the girl sufficiently desirable. After that, her affectionate mother needed to approve of him. And even then it was far from obvious that her father would give his consent. Casanova might be living as the adopted son of a wealthy nobleman, but he was well known in town as something of a ne'er-do-well.

Casanova calls the girl C. C., and if the Capretta identification is correct, we know that her name was Caterina. She was virtuous and innocent, never left the house without her mother, and hadn't even read a novel. As Chantal Thomas remarks, without her slimy brother she would probably never have fallen into Casanova's orbit. But innocence always appealed to him, and as soon as he met C. C. he was smitten. "What struck me above all was a lively, fresh spirit in which shone candor, ingenuousness, simple but elevated feelings, and gay and innocent vivacity." That combination, he claims, "always had the power to enslave me." No doubt there is some truth to that, but what was really enslaving him must have been the prospect of marrying into wealth.[2]

After a second visit and three hours of conversation, Casanova left her house "so much in love that I knew it was incurable." He agonized about what to do. "I couldn't proceed with C. C. either as an honorable man or as a libertine, and I would have killed anyone who dared to persuade me to seduce her." She was "an angel incarnate," and when at the opera her revealing dress pulled open and "let me glimpse her nipples beneath the lace," he was terrified of offending and stared only at her face.

P. C. saw his chance: maybe Casanova was an easy mark after all. Now that Casanova was falling in love, he couldn't refuse P. C. the promissory note he had been pressing for. At least that's the way Casanova narrates the story in the *Histoire,* but as occasionally happens, evidence has survived that exposes his tendency to reorder events for dramatic effect. Since his relationship with C. C. would never have occurred but for the chance encounter with P. C. and his companion when she fell from the carriage, he comments solemnly, "If I had set out from Padua ten seconds earlier or later, everything that has happened in my life would have been different. My destiny, if it's true that it depends on combinations of circumstances, would have been otherwise. The reader will judge of that."

That's indeed impressive, but documents prove it's just not true. Casanova first got financially entangled with Capretta in 1748, five years previously, and it was a subsequent involvement in 1753 that led to the relationship with C. C. Why, then, did he scramble the chronology in the *Histoire?* Very likely for dramatic effect, to make the story more gripping; certainly it gave him an opportunity to quote the maxim he had first learned from Signor Malipiero, *fata viam inveniunt,* "the fates will find the path." But also, no doubt, he wanted to cover up the fact that he and P. C. must have been in on the caper together from the very start.[3]

At this point the mother, who was known to be thinking about marriage for her daughter, gave her son permission to take C. C. and Casanova out to dinner. There P. C. encouraged his friend to kiss the girl. Casanova politely refrained, but to his surprise her feelings were hurt—she was falling for him too, and she thought it meant he didn't like her. "What!" I said, "you're wrong, heavenly C., and if you need a kiss to be sure I love you, here's how I'll print it upon your lovely laughing mouth." Thus began a love affair that would turn later into two love affairs and eventually into a threesome.

C. C.'s mother was impressed by the charming suitor, and allowed him to go alone with her daughter to a garden on the island of Giudecca. There they played a game in which they ran mock races; Casanova had brought some elegant stockings and garters as a gift, and he was permitted to put them on her. "Carried away with gratitude, she sat on my lap and gave me the same kisses that she would have given her father if he had been there. I returned them, stifling with supernatural strength the violence of my desires."

On the garters were verses in French that the girl asked to have translated. Their message was that the lucky garters were well placed to see her jewel all the time. He may well have been thinking of Diderot's notorious novel *Les Bijoux Indiscrets,* the "indiscreet jewels." A sultan has a magic ring which, when pointed at a woman, prompts her jewel to speak up and relate its sexual history. After Casanova explained what was meant by the jewel, she blushed and said she knew that that was reserved for her future husband. He was emboldened to reply, "I'm thinking that these fortunate garters enjoy a privilege that I may never have. Why am I not in their place!"

What happened next was predictable. They were made for each other, he declared, their intentions were pure, and they would be marrying in the sight of God even if they didn't wait for church formalities. That wasn't true legally, although during the previous century a promise of marriage had been sufficient to legitimize a sexual relationship. More recently, the church and the legal establishment had been cracking down on that practice.[4]

There was an inn next to the garden, the couple took a room, and soon they were in bed. "C. C., white as alabaster, had black hair, and her puberty appeared only in wispy hair divided into little curls that formed a transparent fringe above the little entrance to the temple of love." Shyly, she confessed that she had been making love to her pillow every night, pretending it was him. "I only touched myself there, my dear friend, for one moment at the end, and very lightly, but a pleasure I can't explain rendered me immobile and as if dead."

He explained the pleasure, and soon she was a virgin no longer. There was some pain, but (he says) not a bad kind: "C. C. became my wife like a heroine, as every girl in love should, since pleasure and the fulfillment of desire make even pain delicious. I passed two whole hours without ever separating myself from her. Her continual swoonings made me immortal"—like a pagan god, not a Christian saint. Afterward she said that she hoped she would get pregnant, since in that case her father might be likelier to give his consent.

What isn't clear is why her mother ever let her set off alone with Casanova, and why she wasn't alarmed when they took so long to return. Perhaps she liked the idea of a marriage with the adopted son of a distinguished senator, and covertly approved.

The next step was to persuade Bragadin to negotiate with C. C.'s father. He and his two friends agreed to the plan so long as "Paralis"—the spirit Casanova always invoked as his oracle—would give the necessary instructions. So they went through two hours of the usual rigamarole with number pyramids, Paralis approved, and Bragadin then promised to guarantee an income sufficient to satisfy C.C.'s father. However, the father had always insisted that his daughter wait until the age of eighteen to get married, and not even Bragadin's prestige could change his mind. As Venetian parents often did, he immediately consigned the girl to a convent to keep her away from temptation. She would be a novice at first, not taking formal vows, and free to leave the convent later on if she and her family chose.

That happened in the early summer of 1753, after which C. C. was able to communicate with her "husband" only by letters that a servant was paid to smuggle. Her father probably believed that Casanova wouldn't find out which of the many convents was hers, but thanks to her letters he knew; it was on the island of Murano, where the witch had cured him long ago. He doesn't identify it in the *Histoire,* but erasures in the manuscript show that it was Santa Maria degli Angeli. It no longer exists today, but the picture shows a similar Murano convent. And so the next act of the drama begins.[5]

Venetian convents were not much given to self-denial. Many of the nuns were there simply because of the custom of allowing just one daughter and one son in a family to marry, and had no particular sense of religious vocation; if anything they found convent life less repressive than their experience

Veduta di S. Mattia di Murano.

19. A Murano Convent

at home. The mothers superior counted on generous donations from the girls' families, and had no inclination to impose strict propriety.[6]

Casanova had no clear plan as yet, but he commissioned a painter and a jeweler to make a gift for C. C., a ring with a hidden secret. It had an enamel portrait of her patron saint, but if a tiny dot was pressed with the point of a pin, "the saint jumped up and my own face appeared underneath, an excellent likeness." He intercepted C. C.'s mother at church and persuaded her to take the ring to her daughter, who wrote afterward that she kissed it constantly. When other nuns came in she would let the cover fall shut, and they were impressed by her devotion to St. Catherine.

C. C. did turn out to be pregnant, but she had a miscarriage followed by a terrifying loss of blood. When the servant brought Casanova this news, "I was in utter despair. Realizing that I was the executioner of this innocent girl, I felt that I didn't have the strength to survive her. . . . My horrible incontinence had done this to an angel incarnate."

The servant managed to carry away the tell-tale bloody rags, and the other nuns knew only that C. C. was ill, not why. A discreet doctor was called in, the hemorrhaging abated, and soon she was recovering. Overjoyed, Casanova resolved to go to the convent during visiting hours, when they could at least glimpse each other. Since he often dates episodes in his life by religious holidays, we know exactly when he did so. It was All Saints' Day, November 1, 1753. (Our Halloween is the Eve of All Hallows, which has no special name of its own in Italian.)

Visiting hours at Venetian convents were much like fashionable gatherings elsewhere. A painting by Francesco Guardi (color plate 20) shows the *parlatorio* at the convent of San Zaccaria near San Marco, so called because it was intended for conversation (the root meaning of "parlor" as well). The painting can be seen today in the Ca' Rezzonico museum in Venice.

The visitors are opulently dressed, aristocrats no doubt, while the nuns—inmates, really—look out from behind a screen. There's a booth with a puppet show to keep children entertained. The only glimpses of ordinary life are at the margins of the picture: a beggar on a crutch at the far left, and a nun in a light-colored habit accepting a gift of food at the far right.

The lady in the opulent hooped skirt teasingly holds out a ring toward a tiny lapdog, which contemporaries would have known how to interpret. Rings often had sexual connotations in art, and lapdogs signified faithful lovers but also servile flatterers, as in Alexander Pope's line "When husbands or when lapdogs breathe their last." Several Venetian sayings embodied that thought, such as *non dare del pane al cane ogni volta che dimena la coda,* "don't give the dog bread every time it wags its tail."[7]

When Casanova got to the convent, "I thought I would die with pleasure when I saw her gazing attentively four paces from myself, astonished to see me there. I found her taller, more fully formed, and even more lovely than I would have believed possible. I had eyes only for her, and I didn't return to Venice until they closed the door."

He may have had eyes only for her, but someone else had eyes for him. C. C. had written earlier that the most beautiful of the nuns "loved her to distraction," and added that when they were alone together they shared kisses "which he had no reason to be jealous of." To see her as often as possible Casanova started attending Mass in the adjacent church, and one day as he was leaving a woman dropped a letter at his feet. It was written in French, and he says he is copying it "word for word":

> A nun, who has seen you for two and a half months every feast day at her church, desires you to know her. . . . She will direct you to a casino here on Murano, where you will find her alone at nightfall on a day that you will indicate. You may stay and have supper with her, or you can leave after a quarter of an hour if you have business. Or would you

rather give her supper in Venice? Name the day, the hour, and the place where she should go. You will see her get out of a gondola wearing a mask, and you should be on the quay all alone, likewise masked, with no servant, and carrying a candle

There was no signature. As mentioned previously, a casino was a hideaway that might be used for various purposes, including sex of course.

Casanova was surprised, he says, that "these holy virgins could get out of their cloister so easily"—there was a secret door in the convent garden that those in the know made use of—and he decided to make sure he wasn't being set up in some way. So he wrote back to request that some person trusted by the mysterious nun accompany him to the convent and let him see her for himself. She nominated a countess who went with him from Venice in a gondola, and when they arrived asked to speak with M. M., "which astonished me, for she who bore that name was celebrated." An affair with a patrician was still a thrilling novelty for Casanova.

Scholars have tried as usual to establish who M. M. was, and as usual they've failed. Most believe that she was Marina Maria Morosini, but some identify her instead with Maria Elenora Michiel. Only obsessive fact collectors could care which, since we don't know anything about either one. The editors of the *Histoire* rightly say, "Let us leave to these persons their masks, who now exist only in Casanova's narrative."[8]

In response to the countess's request, M. M. came to a little window to speak with her, and Casanova was overwhelmed.

She was a complete beauty, very tall, white inclining to pale, with a manner that was noble and at the same time reserved and shy. She had big blue eyes, a sweet and smiling face, and lovely lips moist with dew that revealed two rows of superb teeth. Her nun's habit didn't let me see her hair, but whether she had any or not [some nuns were shaved] her eyebrows showed that it had to be a light chestnut. What I found admirable and surprising were her hand and forearm that were visible up to the elbow; one couldn't see anything more perfect. No veins could be seen, and instead of muscles I saw only hollows.

While M. M. chatted with her friend she never looked directly at Casanova, and that pleased him because it seemed tactful and discreet. Now that he had beheld her she was no longer just words on paper, and he desired her desperately. He even rationalized being unfaithful to C. C. "It seemed to me that an infidelity of this kind, if she were to find out about it, couldn't displease her since it was necessary to keep me alive, and thus preserve myself for her." Anyway he suspected correctly that M. M. had to be the companion with whom C. C. had been exchanging passionate kisses.

Casanova and the countess rode in silence while the gondola carried them back to Venice, until she remarked with a smile, "M. M. is beautiful, but her mind is even more rare." Casanova answered, "I've seen the one, and I believe the other." The word commonly translated as "mind" is *esprit,* which can also mean "wit," and the countess's compliment implied liveliness as well as intelligence.

As it turned out, the affair got off to a rocky start. When Casanova arrived at the casino for the promised assignation, M. M. didn't show up, but sent a message by a lay sister that she was "busy." Certain that he was the victim of a willful prank, he waited over a week to reply and then sent a chilly note. In return she said she had been misunderstood—she did get cold feet about the assignation, but had claimed to be ill, not busy—and she was deeply wounded by "the cruel, barbarous, and unjust letter you sent." Bitterly, she added that if he couldn't imagine "the dire effect your infernal letter had on the soul of an innocent woman, allow me to pity you. You would not have the slightest knowledge of the human heart."

Already they were living a romantic novel with obstacles and misunderstandings to overcome. Probably they enjoyed the challenge. It was also an epistolary novel, since they had yet to exchange a single word in person. Casanova sent an abject reply and then went out to the convent to speak with M. M. through the little window. She blushed furiously when she saw him, "and I finally broke the silence by asking if I could count on being forgiven. She extended her lovely hand through the opening and I bathed it with tears and kissed it a hundred times. She said that since our acquaintance had begun with so fierce a storm, we should hope now for eternal calm."

It was time to meet at the casino. Casanova was told to arrive well after sundown, wearing a mask. After letting himself in and ascending the stairs, he should enter a room that would be well lit. "You will find me there, or if not, wait for me. I won't delay more than a few minutes. You may take off your mask, sit down by the fire, and read. You'll find books there." The reason M. M. had access to this retreat was that it belonged to her current lover, who had no objection to her new affair. "What a man your lover must be!" Casanova exclaimed. "I imagine he's old." "Not at all. I would be ashamed of that. I'm sure he's not yet forty."

Although M. M. tried at first to keep the man's identity secret, Casanova soon figured out that it had to be the French ambassador to Venice. He was François-Joachim de Pierre de Bernis, already quoted earlier, just turning forty and ten years older than Casanova (color plate 21). An aristocrat and intellectual, he had been elected to the Académie Française at the early age of twenty-nine, and thanks to an affair with Mme. de Pompadour had received this diplomatic post. He was also an abbé in the church, and in later years would become a bishop and then a cardinal. All the same he was notorious for licentious living, and according to a contemporary "he devoted himself entirely to the fair sex in Venice, instead of occupying himself with affairs of state." M. M. was no doubt merely one of those women.[9]

M. M. was indeed waiting for him in the casino, her beautiful long hair flowing freely, illuminated by candles backed by mirrors. After they conversed for a while she rang for a servant, who brought in a superb dinner cooked in the French style along with excellent wine. Then at last she permitted liberties, but for now she resisted fulfillment, clearly in order to stimulate desire. "With a trembling and timid hand, gazing at her with eyes that begged for charity, I unlaced six large ribbons that fastened her dress in front, and was ravished with joy when she didn't stop me. I found myself master of the most beautiful of all breasts. It was too late; after I had contemplated them, she had to let me devour them. I raised my eyes to her face and saw the sweetness of love with which she said, 'Content yourself with this, and learn from me to endure abstinence.'"

The dress, of course, was secular clothing, which wasn't permitted in the convent. M. M. kept a wardrobe in the casino.

They slept through the night, and when church bells awakened them M. M. quickly dressed to return to the convent. "I will enjoy," he said, "the sight of watching you disguise yourself again as a saint." She promised to meet him the next time in Venice and "make us both entirely happy."

Soon afterward a letter from C. C. arrived, declaring encouragingly that she would have no objection if Casanova should take a lover. If that did happen, "You will find me ever more worthy to be your wife. You must believe that despite my age, I'm able to keep a secret, and discreet enough not to be offended by your reticence. Sure of your heart, I'm not jealous of someone who can divert your spirit and help you to endure our separation." Of course C. C. and M. M. were already lovers themselves.

Casanova now invited M. M. to dine at his own casino in Venice, and she agreed to meet him in the Castello district outside the church of San Zanipolo

20. Bartolomeo Colleoni

(Venetian for Santi Giovanni e Paolo) at the foot of a statue honoring the fifteenth-century condottiere Bartolomeo Colleoni. That was a reminder of the glory days when Venice maintained a mighty army as well as navy, and Casanova would doubtless appreciate an art historian's opinion that the statue, by Andrea del Verrochio, "is bursting with titanic power and energy."[10]

Casanova didn't actually have a casino, but that sort of thing never stopped him, and he quickly found an opulent one near San Marco that was once the English ambassador's. It now belonged to a chef who rented it to him for a hefty fee, with the stipulation that he himself should provide the meals. To audition him as a chef, Casanova had him prepare a banquet in advance, which turned out to be satisfactory. The costliness is significant. Casanova was intimidated by patrician women, and he intended to do everything he could to impress this one. Even in later life, when he liked to convey the impression that he was a patrician himself, he was always aware that at bottom he was an impostor.

When M. M. arrived, she was disguised in male dress to avoid detection, much as Henriette had been. She was suitably impressed by the casino, which was a virtual stage set. The rooms were exquisitely furnished, and in one of them the walls were tiled with painted porcelain, "interesting for the amorous couples in a state of nature whose voluptuous postures inflamed the imagination." Another room was octagonal and its walls, ceiling, and floor were all covered with mirrors, whose purpose was obvious. The magnificent dinner was served through a dumbwaiter so that no person intruded, and Casanova, always happy to recall experiences of eating, describes it in loving detail: game, sturgeon, truffles, and oysters which were believed to be aphrodisiac. There were also "perfect wines."

They spent the rest of the night in bed, and as always with the relationships that meant the most to him, he describes what happened only allusively. It's clear, at any rate, that he was by far the more experienced of the two. "She was amazed to find herself capable of so much pleasure, after I showed her many things that she had believed were merely imaginary. I did things to her that she didn't believe she was allowed to ask me to do, and I taught her that the least constraint spoils the greatest pleasures." When church bells announced the arrival of dawn she raised her eyes to the Third Heaven "to thank the Mother and Son for having so well repaid the effort she made when she declared her passion to me." The Third Heaven was not the Christian one, but the realm of the goddess Venus. She was the Mother and Eros was her son.

Throughout the *Histoire* Casanova has two favorite terms for the female organ. One is *champs*, "field," meaning sometimes a verdant meadow, sometimes a field of battle. The other is "the temple of Venus," in which he longs to sacrifice himself, though the worshiper is sometimes denied entrance to the holy of holies. In one of his reminiscences a woman playfully uncovers her sleeping sister, "revealing the cornice and frieze of the altar of love where I wanted to die." And we have already seen Andriana in Corfu holding herself "in a way that made it impossible for me to penetrate into the sanctuary."[11]

In his youth a countess had shown him her drawing of Adam, but not the matching Eve. Adam was splendidly muscled, she said, "but in the woman there's nothing to see." "But it's precisely that nothing that will interest me," he replied. Lydia Flem calls attention to the difference between this and conventional male writing: "The 'emptiness' of the female sexual organ never frightens him; on the contrary, he fills (and fulfills) it."[12]

It was exciting, too, to make love with a bride of Christ. "I was about to taste the forbidden fruit; I was going to encroach upon the rights of an omnipotent spouse, seizing the most beautiful sultana in his harem." In a brilliant aphorism Nietzsche says, "Christianity gave Eros poison to drink; he did not die of it, but degenerated into Vice."[13]

The erotic life of nuns, with each other and with male lovers, fascinated Casanova's contemporaries. One of the most popular "forbidden books" was *Vénus dans le Cloître, ou la Religieuse en Chemise,* translated into English as *Venus in the Cloister, or, the Nun in Her Smock.* Those books, however, laid a heavy emphasis on masochism: "Sister Dorothea found by experience that these whippings and flagellations of her posteriors rather augmented than diminished her fires." In all of Casanova's writings he shows no interest in sadomasochism as an end in itself. What he wanted was shared enjoyment.[14]

The contemporary eroticizing of nuns is captured in an English painting by Henry Morland, *The Fair Nun Unmasked* (color plate 22). It's also known as *A Lady in a Masquerade Habit,* which she obviously is: a lady (or perhaps a courtesan) pretending to be a nun. She does have a veil and a cross, but the low-cut dress and jewelry are a giveaway, as is the mask itself. There's nothing nunlike about that, with its elegant eyebrows, lipstick, and prominent beauty spots. Venice was of course the world headquarters of masking, but masked balls were popular in London too, as Casanova would see for himself some years later.

Actually, Casanova was so indifferent to orthodox morality that there may not have been much of a thrill in flouting it. La Rochefoucauld famously called hypocrisy the tribute that vice pays to virtue, and Félicien Marceau comments, "The hypocrite is someone who conceals his actions or at least disguises them, adorning them with the colors of virtue. Casanova doesn't conceal and doesn't adorn. Is he beyond sin, or below it? I believe he never gave it a thought."[15]

Like D. H. Lawrence, Casanova saw sex at its best as transcendent, virtually a religious experience. It was more than just a metaphor when he called the casino "the temple of my amour." As quoted previously, a commentator concludes, "In Casanova's writing, to mention God or the saints to express a pleasure doesn't represent a desire to defile the sacred with lust. On the contrary, it indicates a desire to render voluptuousness sacred."[16]

Casanova was gratified to learn that M. M. shared his skeptical view of religious orthodoxy. Bernis, churchman though he was, had assembled a library of two kinds of books. One group was pornographic, for example illustrating the notorious thirty-five "postures" of Pietro Aretino; that was presumably where she learned of the practices that she assumed were merely imaginary. The other group was treatises of libertinism. Reading those, she told Casanova, had freed her from the clouds of superstition. "The greatest happiness is to live and die in tranquility, which we can't hope to do if we believe what the priests tell us. . . . I can say that I didn't begin to love God until I was disabused of the idea of him that religion gave me."

During their next night together, in the Murano casino this time, M. M. indulged in a bit of playful blasphemy. She arrived in her nun's habit, which Casanova found so arousing that when she was about to change her clothes he begged her not to. "She replied '*Fiat voluntas tua*—thy will be done' in the most devout manner, letting herself fall back on the great sofa."

And now she had a further surprise. When Bernis had originally acquiesced in her affair with Casanova, there was one proviso: at his casino he watched them secretly through a tiny spyhole in the wall. Now he was going to do it again, but he had warned M. M. not to tell Casanova. She did tell him, however. Now he had a new challenge: to avoid revealing in any way that he knew they were being observed.

Some people might have felt upset or even betrayed at this revelation, but not Casanova. His only concern, he told M. M., was that their performance might disappoint Bernis. But he was proud of his sexual powers, he knew that she would be equally passionate, and he was happy to be admired doing what he did best. He especially liked the idea of impressing a distinguished French aristocrat, and may well have guessed that Bernis could be helpful to him in the future, as indeed would happen.

It would also, as Ian Kelly notes, be acting out a favorite theme in libertine fiction, in which "characters observe each other from behind muslin and masks, through keyholes or spyholes, in gardens or via mirrors."[17]

That night M. M. put on a lot of rouge, a French custom that Venetian women didn't practice. Casanova explains its purpose: "The charm in painting lies in the carelessness with which it's applied to the cheeks. The rouge isn't intended to seem natural; they use it to please the eye with signs of an intoxication that promises amorous fury." She showed him the spyholes—there were a number of them in the centers of decorative flowers painted on the walls—and soon after that she winked to indicate that Bernis was now in place.

They enjoyed a leisurely dinner that included taking oysters from each other's mouths; "There is no game more lascivious and voluptuous between two lovers." Finally, as midnight struck, "I showed her my little Gabriel, who was sighing for her." That was deliberately blasphemous; the angel Gabriel announced the birth of Christ to the Virgin Mary, and was also one of the creative forces called *sephira* in the Cabbala.

21. A Casanova Illustration

   After performing energetically on the sofa, they got to their feet to enact
one of the "postures" of Aretino. Casanova's description is tactfully metaphor-
ical: "I had her do the 'straight tree,' raising her up so I could devour her
chamber of love, which I could do only by putting her in a position to devour,
in her turn, the weapon that wounded her to death without depriving her of
life." M. M. reported later that Bernis greatly enjoyed the spectacle, admiring
Casanova's tirelessness and also a "delicacy" unusual in the male sex.
   Illustrations for Casanova's memoir have tended to be stylized and emo-
tionally distancing, with wigs and lace and elegantly fashionable furniture. In

22. An Aretino Illustration

a typical example, a bed awaits, but the gentleman, fully clothed to put it mildly, is still holding his hat. Casanova's experience of sex was much hotter and grittier than that. On the other hand, the graphic explicitness of the Aretino illustrations, with heroically endowed gods and goddesses, can be off-putting too. The resources of language actually gave Casanova a wider scope for evoking experience than pictures could. Nabokov once said that most pornography is the copulation of clichés. What Casanova wanted was to avoid clichés and to invent metaphors of his own that could be suggestive without being obscene, using language that enhances rather than deflates erotic excitement.[18]

Inevitably, it was time to invite C. C. into the game. By now she was a freethinker too. "M. M. had initiated the girl not only into the mysteries of Sappho, but into high metaphysics." But first there was an awkward misunderstanding. When Casanova went again to the Murano casino, expecting to

spend a night with M. M., he was astounded to find C. C. there, dressed as a
nun. He imagined that after finding out about his previous relationship with
C. C., M. M. had set up this confrontation to humiliate him. "I felt by turns
played upon, deceived, entrapped, and despised." He gazed silently and re-
morsefully at C. C. "I was her husband, I was the one who had seduced her.
These reflections wounded my soul." But soon all was resolved. She explained
that her friend had created this scene as a gift to their mutual lover—"her soul
is as grand and noble as her heart is generous." Besides, she added, she herself
was M. M.'s "wife, or her little husband."

One final act in the drama remained, and that was to literalize the ménage
à trois that had been only symbolic until now.

> *Nous voilà* all three of us in a state of nature, in thrall to voluptuous-
> ness and love. The women began their labors with the ferocity of two
> tigresses who seemed eager to devour each other . . . C. C. was thinner
> than M. M. but broader in the hips and thighs; her ornaments [i.e.,
> hair] were brunette, the other's were fair; and they were equally skilled
> in this struggle that exhausted them both without being able to push
> it to a conclusion. Able to resist no longer, I fell upon them under
> pretext of separating them and got M. M. underneath me, but she es-
> caped and made me fall instead on C. C., who received me with open
> arms and made me yield up my soul in less than a minute, accompa-
> nying my death with her own, with no thought of taking precautions.
> Recovering from the ecstasy, we both attacked M. M.

In the sheer intensity of the moment, they were "devouring with desire all
that we saw, and finding that all three had become a single sex in all the trios
we performed." For him this was a truly transcendent state. As Lydia Flem
says, "At the moment of supreme pleasure, distinctions are obliterated. Casanova sees himself as having the same sex as his partner or her as having his; he
no longer knows to what gender he belongs."[19]

In the introduction we noted that Casanova endorsed an older "one-sex"
model of sexuality, as contrasted with a "two-sex" model that was gaining
ground in his own day. In the older view, men and women experienced exactly the same desires and gratifications, rather than fundamentally different
ones. All his life he was fascinated by androgyny, and in this ecstatic threesome with the pair of nuns, the one-sex model was realized to the full.

There will be many more pages in the *Histoire* before Casanova is finished
with the story of M. M. and C. C., but after this peak the narrative energy

flags. He was also terrified that one or both might be pregnant. When that had happened with a landlady's daughter in Paris the problem was easily dealt with. But C. C. came from a wealthy family and M. M. from a noble one, and they were nuns who supposedly never got out of their convent.

There had actually been a supply of condoms in the casino, but they were awkward and crude in those days, and neither he nor M. M. cared to use "precautions." Anyway she was sure that if she did get pregnant she could feign illness and Bernis would spirit her away somewhere for a "cure." But now Bernis was gone—he had been called away to Vienna on an important diplomatic mission, which meant that M. M. had lost her protector. He did let her keep his casino for the time being, but if either nun got pregnant she would be disgraced and expelled from the convent, and Casanova would be held responsible. To everyone's relief, however, time went by and there were no pregnancies.

One emergency occurred that struck Casanova afterward as a crucial turning point in his life. No longer able to use Bernis's gondolier, they were afraid to hire one who might betray them, so he bought a small gondola of his own and not very expertly rowed it himself. After one of their nights together a fierce storm blew up, and because M. M. had to be back in the convent by dawn, he struggled desperately against the wind while making almost no progress at all. Then a bigger boat came by, and in return for payment the boatmen agreed to help them reach the convent. Otherwise Casanova and M. M. would have had no choice but to let the wind blow them back to the casino, and their relationship would have been exposed. "I would have had to leave Venice with her and never gone back, and her fate would have been joined with mine. My life would then have followed a destiny totally different from the one whose vicissitudes have led me to find myself now, at the age of seventy-two, at Dux." That was the town in Bohemia where Casanova spent his final, deeply unhappy years and wrote the *Histoire de Ma Vie*.

Back in the convent, M. M. fell gravely ill with a fever and even received the last rites; Casanova was distraught, and immensely relieved when word came that she was on the mend. But it was really all over. He went out to Murano to see M. M. and C. C. again, but without enthusiasm. "The time was approaching for our eternal separation." Not only that: he had taken an apartment of his own on Murano, and suddenly fell for his landlady's daughter Tonina, and then for her little sister Barberina.

In Paris several years later, Casanova reconnected with Bernis and learned that he had stayed in touch with M. M. She had remained a nun, "unable to

see either of the two men she might have counted on." That certainly sounds
like a reproach.

Meanwhile C. C.'s father had taken her out of the convent and she had
married a lawyer, with whom she was unhappy. A few years later Bernis told
Casanova that M. M. had mentioned the marriage in a letter, and he eventually heard it from C. C. herself. That reunion came after the point where the
narrative in the *Histoire* breaks off, but what he does say there deserves to be
quoted:

> She had left a letter for me in which she said that if I would promise
> once again to marry her when I found it possible, she would wait, and
> firmly resist giving her hand to anyone who offered himself. I replied
> straightforwardly that having no position in the world and no likeli-
> hood of achieving one soon, I left her free, and indeed I encouraged
> her not to refuse anyone who she believed could make her happy. . . .
> I never saw her again until nineteen years later. She had been a widow
> for ten years, and unhappy. If I were in Venice now I still wouldn't
> marry her, since marriage at my age is a farce, but I would certainly
> have united her fate to mine.

If Casanova doesn't show remorse or even regret, he at least acknowledges
some responsibility, and claims that he had been acting in her best interest.[20]

It's possible, anyway, that there weren't really hard feelings afterward. Recently discovered records show that in 1758 Caterina Capretta married Sebastiano Marsili (who was actually a timber merchant and not a lawyer) and
Casanova may have remained on good terms with both spouses; Marsili was
one of the subscribers to his translation of the *Iliad*. Marsili didn't die until
1783, just at the time of Casanova's final expulsion from Venice. Thus Caterina
couldn't have become a widow as early as he says she did, but in the *Histoire*
he frequently got muddled about dates.

That's all we know; the researcher who turned up this information concludes, "And thus Caterina vanishes." As for her nasty brother, after a continued series of misdeeds he was condemned to prison at hard labor, and died
there.[21]

A musicologist, Patrick Barbier, says appreciatively of the story of the nuns,
"For us this remains one of the most savory of Casanova's narratives, and
certainly one of the most piquant illustrations of the freedom of morals that
reigned in those days on the shores of the lagoon." Not every reader will feel
included in Barbier's "us."[22]

There is another sidelight to the story, and since it evidently reflects the
way Casanova described it to friends, it bears thinking about. The Prince de
Ligne, to whom he was close in his final years and who read the manuscript
of the *Histoire,* sent him a satiric poem in French, highlighting the irreligious
aspect of the ménage à trois.

> When I read about your amorous adventures at the convent
> I see that the Father and the Son had the same windfall:
> They were both cuckolded by the Holy Spirit,
> And their wives enjoyed forbidden pleasures.
> M. M. in passion should have known herself better,
> And the Blessed Virgin didn't make much of an appearance.
> You had more delicacy than the divine pigeon:
> The bride of Christ didn't conceive a baby.

Ligne must have been remembering Casanova's comment that he showed
M. M. "my little Gabriel, who was sighing for her." Mary was impregnated by
the Holy Spirit in the form of a dove, but the bird was now Giacomo Casa-
nova, and not a biblical dove but a bathetic pigeon. In Joyce's *Ulysses* Stephen
Dedalus recalls a French joke in which Joseph demands to know who put
Mary in such a wretched position and she answers, *C'est le pigeon, Joseph.*[23]

The story of this ménage à trois as Casanova tells it is a self-contained
novella, but richly detailed though it is, he may have chosen not to acknowledge the lesson it taught him. Forty years ago Félicien Marceau, himself a
novelist, proposed a plausible hypothesis that no one seems to have picked up
on. To begin with, why was M. M.'s original letter of invitation written in
French? She was a Venetian and could easily have written in Italian, or Veneziano. Why would she suppose Casanova even knew French? He mentions
that she may have seen a pamphlet in that language that he happened to drop,
but that could be part of his cover story.

So here is the hypothesis. Bernis, an experienced voyeur, commissioned
M. M. to recruit a lover to perform in his peephole-equipped casino. C. C.
was already M. M.'s lover, and could have told her all about Casanova right
from the beginning, alerting her to size him up during his visits to the convent church. C. C. did, after all, write to tell Casanova that she would be
happy if he took another lover. She may have known very well who that was
going to be.

"The real master of the game," Marceau concludes, "was Bernis." Once
Bernis had enjoyed C. C. as well as M. M., the game was essentially over, and

what happened after he was called away to Vienna seems to confirm that. With Bernis absent, why weren't the two nuns freer than ever to pursue their affair with Casanova? Perhaps it was they who cooled off and decided it had gone on long enough.[24]

If this was the case, then far from being fickle when he dallied with Tonina and Barberina, Casanova was consoling himself; as Angelo Mainardi says, it was a way to recover his freedom of action. In effect he had been the pawn of two patricians, M. M. and Bernis, and may well have had some feelings of humiliation. The novella in the *Histoire* is his revenge. He may have been used, but he had nevertheless been rewarded with an exalting experience to which he could give permanence in art.[25]

The convent of Santa Maria degli Angeli (though not the adjacent church) was demolished in 1832, but the garden wall, with its little door through which M. M. used to slip out, could still be seen well into the twentieth century. A Casanova scholar went to see it and met an elderly gardener who was taking care of the place. "When I returned from the war in 1919," the gardener said, "a well-dressed gentleman came here, like yourself, and spent a long time gazing at that door in the wall. I don't know what there was about that door, it's not beautiful. It had something to do with Casanova, the gentleman told me. Perhaps he was a monk there?"[26]

CHAPTER 14

The Great Escape

In July of 1755, a shocking event overturned Casanova's life of pleasure. He says, "It took me by surprise at the age of thirty, *nel mezzo del cammin di nostra vita,* 'midway in the journey of our life.'" The famous first words of Dante's *Inferno* introduce the beginning of his descent into Hell: "Midway in the journey of our life, I found myself in a dark wood, for the straight way was lost. Ah, how hard it is to tell what that wood was, wild, rugged, harsh; the very thought of it renews the fear! It is so bitter that death is hardly more so."[1]

On the 27th of July Casanova was arrested and committed to solitary confinement in a cell in the Ducal Palace. He was given no explanation of why he was there or when he might be released. On the top floor of the palace, beneath the metal roof that gave it the name of *I Piombi,* "the Leads," this prison was popularly known as the Inferno.

In the weeks before the disaster Casanova had ingratiated himself with a family next door to his lodgings on the Fondamenta Nuove, which borders the lagoon on the northeast side of the city. Evidently he had taken an apartment of his own to enjoy greater freedom than in the Palazzo Bragadin. The family's teenage daughter had become frighteningly pale and gasped for breath, and had not yet begun to menstruate. The doctor who came to bleed her—the standard remedy for everything—diagnosed chlorosis, which the English called greensickness. That form of anemia was thought to result from sexual frustration, one feature of which was retention of the blood that menstruation should have released.

Casanova saw his chance, and at night he managed to get the girl alone on a balcony. "After a quarter of an hour of amorous talk, she permitted my eyes to enjoy all the charms that starlight made still more interesting, and she let me cover them with kisses." Before long "she made me happy, with a fervor by which I recognized that she believed she was receiving much more than she gave. I immolated the victim without bloodying the altar."

They went on making love for the rest of the night, and the girl never once had trouble breathing. Not long afterward she even experienced her first period. They continued to sleep together for the next three weeks (did her family condone it, given his high social connections?), and he claims he would have married her "if toward the end of the same month catastrophe had not intervened."

The evidence that led to Casanova's arrest came from Giovanni Battista Manuzzi, a jeweler who was secretly an informer for the Inquisition. In Venice the Inquisition was a political, not religious, committee of three patricians who oversaw a system of surveillance and could order arrests without charges or trial. Prior to his arrest Casanova had run out of funds, and had thought of selling some of his books, but since they were prohibited due to intellectual or erotic content, he didn't dare. Manuzzi gained his confidence by offering to sell the books for him, claiming that he knew a buyer who would keep quiet about the transaction.

Manuzzi had in fact been observing Casanova for quite some time. When the Inquisition's records were searched in modern times his written reports came to light, beginning in November 1754, eight months prior to Casanova's arrest. At first Manuzzi mentions him merely as one playboy among others, most of them Masons, who were thought to harbor subversive ideas.

In subsequent reports a more detailed portrait emerges. The biographer Laurence Bergreen, incidentally, declares that Casanova "remained devout throughout his life," but his unpublished writings refute that completely, as do these reports. Manuzzi declares firmly that he is irreligious, or if he does have a religion, no one knows what it is. It can hardly be orthodox Christianity, since he has been heard to say that "only weak minds believe in Jesus Christ." Despite having no employment he gambles constantly and loses huge sums of money, which can only come from exploiting patrons. "By means of his damnable impostures concerning the [Rosicrucian] Rosy Cross and angels of light, he bewitches people, including the N. H. Messer Zuanne Bragadin and other noble patricians, in order to extract money from them." N. H. stood for *nobile homine,* "noble gentleman"; Zuanne was the Venetian version of Giovanni.[2]

Casanova was also known to have written a satiric poem which the Inquisitors were eager to see. Manuzzi had heard him read parts of it, but couldn't get his hands on a copy. He did know that it treated extensively *del usar il coito nelle vie rete e indirete,* "coitus by direct and indirect paths." He also got a glimpse of a white apron that would be worn in a Masonic lodge. In sum, "When you talk with Casanova you find united in him *la miscredenza, l'impostura, la lascivia, e la voluttà*—unbelief, imposture, lasciviousness, and voluptuousness—to a degree that raises horror."

A bureaucrat appended a note to each of these reports. The one for July 23 says, "Ask Manuzzi where Casanova lives," and the next day, "Order the Messer Grande [the chief of police] to arrest Giacomo Casanova, seize all his papers, and incarcerate him under the Leads."[3]

Venetian surveillance seldom produced anything that provoked such drastic action. Mostly the Inquisition's secretaries had to read through endless reports like this one by a spy named Gerolamo Mazzucato: "I kept the N. H. Pietro Giacomo Foscarini under close observation throughout yesterday. He stayed at home all day and nobody, so far as I could see, came to the house. At about the twenty-fourth hour he went to the Della Nave. Ordered a coffee. Stayed half an hour or so, but spoke to no one. Went to the Vecchie Procuratie, to the snuff merchant's for an ounce of snuff. Walked in the Merceria for perhaps fifteen minutes, and then home." The triviality was really the point. You could expect to be watched everywhere, all the time.[4]

One possible reason for his arrest that Casanova fails to mention is that his friendship with the French ambassador Bernis may well have become known. Near the beginning of his relationship with M. M. she had asked him anxiously whether he was Bragadin's son, and was greatly relieved that he wasn't. The reason was that to protect Venice from foreign entanglements, noblemen were forbidden to associate with ambassadors under pain of death. Casanova had replied, "You were right to be concerned about my rank, since if I were a patrician the Inquisitors of State would have gotten involved in earnest, and the frightful consequences make one tremble. Me beneath the Piombi, you dishonored, the abbess, the convent, good heavens!"[5]

It should have been a tip-off when Casanova arrived at his lodgings after a night on the town and found that the front door had been smashed open and his belongings ransacked by the police. Before leaving they told his landlady that they were searching for a trunk full of contraband goods, which she believed. Even after this he failed to act. Bragadin warned that he had served as an Inquisitor himself and knew their ways all too well. He urged Casanova to leave Venice at once, and offered a generous sum of money, but Casanova objected that that would seem to confirm guilt. Besides, he wasn't prepared "to bid my fatherland an eternal farewell."

Bragadin embraced him and said they might never see each other again. That would turn out to be true. "Go then, my son, *sequere deum, fata viam inveniunt*, "follow the god, the fates will find the path." Casanova often quotes this maxim in the *Histoire,* and usually he means that his inner *daemon* showed him the way. This was not going to be one of those times.

Bragadin encouraged Casanova to stay the night in the palazzo, where he would be safe from arrest. But there was an assignation he wanted to keep, and he went back to his own place for a few hours of sleep. At dawn the police chief, Mattio Varutti, appeared in his room and informed him that he was under arrest. Waiting outside were at least thirty "archers," the French word for guards who carried firearms but still kept the name from an earlier era. In Venice they were known as *sbirri.*

Courteously, Varutti permitted Casanova to shave, have the landlady's daughter comb his hair, and put on an elegant costume "as if I was going to a wedding" (perhaps he hoped that that would impress his interrogators). As it would turn out, he would be very glad, much later, to have those fancy clothes. He was also permitted to take money with him, and that would be important right away.

Before they left, Varutti collected Casanova's papers and some incriminating books, which in the *Histoire* he claimed he kept only for show—"anyone who knew I had them would have thought I was a magician, which didn't displease me." They included the cabbalistic *Clavicule of Solomon,* a *Picatrix* that explained how to conjure up the devil, and an astrological guide to "the planetary days best suited to prepare the perfumes and spells necessary to converse with demons of all classes." There were also the collected poems of Horace and Ariosto, Aretino's sexual *Postures,* and a pornographic favorite entitled *L'Histoire de Dom Bougre, Portier des Chartreux.* Charterhouses were Carthusian monasteries, and *bougre* means "bugger."

Casanova was taken by gondola to the Piazza San Marco, and was brought into the Ducal Palace by the Bridge of Sighs, beloved by modern tourists but so called because it was there that condemned prisoners had their last glimpse of the outside world. Once inside, he was turned over to the Inquisitors' sec-

retary, who looked at him carefully and said, *È quello; mettelo in deposito*—
"That's him; put him away."

Varutti must have felt great satisfaction as he submitted his report. "To the
illustrious and excellent Lords of the Inquisition, July 27, 1755: in accordance
with the greatly honored command of Your Excellencies, I have done my duty
and have had Giacomo Casanova committed to prison. In a thorough search
of his dwelling I found the papers which I am transmitting to Your Excellencies with my most profound respect. Mattio Varutti, Capitan Grande."[6]

Casanova was not taken to the chamber where the three Inquisitors conducted interrogations; they already knew more than enough. Their decision
was recorded in the official register: *Venuti a cognizione del Tribunale le molte
rifflessibili colpe di Giacomo Casanova, principalmente in disprezzo publico della
Santa Religione, SS. EE. lo fecero arrestare e passer sotto li Piombi*—"the Tribunal being cognizant of numerous and repeated offenses by Giacomo Casanova,
principally in publicly disrespecting the Holy Religion, their Excellencies had
him arrested and imprisoned under the Piombi."

A further note indicated that his sentence was for five years, but nobody
ever told him that. For all he knew he might have to spend the rest of his life
there. The document was signed by the full panel: "Andrea Diedo Inquisitor,
Antonio Condulmer Inquisitor, Antonio da Mula Inquisitor." Casanova mentions that Condulmer suspected him of trying to seduce a lady whom the
Inquisitor himself was pursuing.

Casanova would now be incarcerated in a rudely constructed cell within
the grandest edifice in Venice, a masterpiece of splendor and ostentation. Ian
Kelly says, "Prisoners had the bizarre status of living in the same palace as a
potentate, and within feet of the judges who condemned them."[7]

Far below the Piombi was the Hall of the Great Council, 180 feet long
and 80 wide (color plate 23). The walls and ceiling are filled with paintings
depicting the glory days of Venetian history, set off by lavish gold leaf. In the
distance in this picture, behind the doge's throne, is a *Paradiso* by Jacopo
Tintoretto that is said to be still the longest canvas painting in the world. And
along the top of the walls around the room are portraits of the first 76 doges,
with a black cloth (not visible here) in the space where the executed traitor
Marin Falier would be. As shown in a contemporary print, the hall could ac-
commodate the entire body of 1,800 patricians who were entitled to vote.

Above these spectacular rooms were more practical chambers occupied by
bureaucrats, and then a torture room that Casanova was shown as he was led
past it. The guard cheerfully explained that a winch was slowly turned that

23. The Hall of the Great Council

tightened a cord around a prisoner's neck "until the patient gives up his soul to Our Lord, for the confessor never leaves him, praise be to God, until he's dead." Casanova remarked, "That's most ingenious, and I imagine, Signore, that you yourself have the honor of turning the winch." The guard made no reply.

There were in fact three separate prisons. The largest, known as the New Prisons, was on the other side of the Bridge of Sighs, and most prisoners went there. Another, in the cellar of the Ducal Palace, was for those convicted of the gravest crimes. It was known as *i Pozzi*, "the Wells," since every high tide filled it with water and immersed the prisoners up to their knees unless they clambered onto stone ledges. Actually most of those cells were empty in Casanova's time, but as a historian says, "The terrifying threat of the almost deserted Pozzi was kept alive as part of the government's settled plan of scaring everybody out of their wits." Unchanged to this day, the dungeons are a formidable scene of iron and stone.[8]

The cells in the Piombi were reserved for "prisoners of state," mostly upper class, who were allowed to keep any money they brought with them, given a modest allowance if they needed it, and permitted to send out for decent meals and wine. There were prisoners in some of the other cells there at the time, but

24. The Dungeons in the Ducal Palace

Casanova was told nothing about them. This most gregarious of men would now live in total solitude, with human contact only with the guard who would bring him his meals. "A man in solitary confinement longs for Hell, if he believes in it, just to have companions."

Getting undressed confirmed Casanova's fall. "I placed on a shelf my beautiful silk cloak, my handsome outfit that was starting out so badly, and my hat trimmed with golden Spanish lace and a white feather." The cell was narrow and barely furnished, with a hard bench along one wall and a bucket for a latrine. The ceiling was so low that he couldn't stand upright. That seems not to have been an intentional inconvenience, but he was much taller than most Venetians. There were no windows and hence no circulation of air, which made the place a furnace in hot weather; Venice in summer can be scaldingly hot. The next day, after paying the guard, he was able to get a bed and armchair. "The sweat poured from my skin onto the floor on either side of my chair, in which I sat stark naked." In winter it was correspondingly frigid.

Incidentally, the cells in the Piombi were all demolished after Napoleon conquered Venice in 1797. When visitors today are shown "Casanova's cell," it's a reconstruction that he might not recognize if he could see it—not that he would want to.[9]

The only light came in through a small barred grill in the door. Casanova was permitted no lamp or candles, and the gloom was oppressive even in daytime. At night it was total, which made scrambling rats "as big as rabbits" especially appalling. He had already been revolted by rats in his boyhood bedroom in Padua. To keep them out, he shut a little flap over the grill, but the rats had brought in fleas and there was no getting rid of those. "A million of them spread joyously all over my body, avid for my blood and skin which they pierced with a tenacity I had no previous notion of. These damnable insects threw me into convulsions and poisoned my blood."

The guard, whose name was Lorenzo Basadonna (writing in French Casanova calls him Laurent), had held that position for only a few months, and assured him that he was far kinder than his predecessors. He was willing to do what he could about the fleas by having the cell swept every morning, but that didn't make much difference.

Rats were ubiquitous in prisons in those days. Prisoners lived in fear that while they were sleeping their ears and noses would be bitten off. Freud, of course, gave rats a prominent place in his symbolism, and a writer on the eighteenth-century fear of rats says, "The accursed rodent bears a heavy symbolic charge, and his scuttling travels through the catacombs of the mind."[10]

During his first night, obliged to sleep on the hard floor while he waited for the bed, Casanova had a terrifying experience. When he was awakened at midnight by the bell in the nearby Campanile, he realized to his horror that in the darkness he was touching a hand that was "cold as ice." He imagined that to warn him of his fate, the corpse of some recently executed criminal had been deposited there. Eventually he got up the courage to grasp the hand again and discovered it was his own—it had gone completely numb while he was asleep. This was like a macabre reprise of the dead man's arm that he played a practical joke with years before.

"This adventure," he says, "though comic enough, did not amuse me." As a materialist he took it for granted that bodily sensations of the external world are the proper guide to reality. His body had never let him down; indeed he rejoiced in its powers. Now, however, "I realized that I was in a place where if the false appeared true, realities must seem like dreams; where the understanding must lose half its privileges; and where a distorted imagination makes reason the victim of chimerical hopes or dreadful despair."

He wasn't permitted writing materials. He begged to be given some reading matter, dim though the light through the grating might be, but he didn't get his own books back. Instead he was brought a couple of pious treatises. One, by a Jesuit, was a celebration of the Sacred Heart of Jesus, still familiar in Catholic iconography as shining in the bosom of the risen Christ. That held no interest for Casanova: "The heart did not seem to me an organ any more respectable than the lungs." The other was *The Mystical City of Sister María de Jesús, known as de Ágreda,* recounting the visions of a Spanish nun.

Casanova's reaction to this book was the usual one of Enlightenment philosophes, diagnosing the visions as caused by sexual repression. "I read in it all the extravagance of the heated imagination of an extremely devout Spanish virgin, melancholic in temperament, closed up in a convent, with ignorant and flattering directors of conscience." It was in reality a displaced love story—she was "*amoureuse* of the Holy Virgin"—but the miracles that the Virgin Mary related to the nun were preposterous. For example, when Christ's mother was three years old and was ordered to sweep the house—surely a daunting challenge for a small child—she was assisted by nine hundred angels sent at the express command of the Archangel Michael.

Soon Casanova began to run a dangerous fever. While ill he began to experience wild delusions that were not unlike those of Sister María. He says in the *Histoire,* "Although it rarely happens that a man goes mad, it's true all the same that it can easily happen. Our reason is like gunpowder, which is easy to ignite, but never does ignite unless somebody puts a flame to it; or it's like a drinking glass that never breaks unless somebody breaks it. This Spanish woman's book is all that's needed to drive a man crazy, but for the poison to take effect, he should be imprisoned all alone beneath the Leads and deprived of any other occupation."

A doctor was summoned, who prescribed some sensible remedies, and the fever abated. There was a welcome consequence. For the sake of his health, Casanova would be permitted to walk in the attic outside his cell for five or ten minutes every day. Piled here and there he saw various odds and ends, such as furniture left behind by previous occupants. He also noticed an iron bolt a foot and a half long, and a fragment of black marble. These he smuggled into his room, where he concealed them in the stuffing of his armchair. It occurred to him that they might be useful someday.

He also enjoyed reading through a pile of notebooks he found that recorded long-ago criminal cases, "which permitted me to read what in their own day would have been extremely secret. I saw the seduction of virgins, gallantries pushed too far by men employed in the orphanages for young women, confessors who abused their female penitents, schoolmasters convicted of pederasty, and guardians who cheated their wards. These were two and even three centuries old, and their style and manners gave me hours of pleasure." It was much more entertaining reading than the *Mystical City* or the adoration of the Sacred Heart.

For a while Casanova told himself that he would soon be set free. He surmised that it would happen on the last day of September when a new panel of Inquisitors would take over. Perhaps the reason he was never interrogated was simply that there was no crime and nothing to confess, and the current Inquisitors were too embarrassed to admit it. But when the auspicious day arrived nothing happened, and he grasped that the methods of the Venetian Inquisition were unlike those of legal systems elsewhere.

"When this tribunal proceeds against an offender, they are already certain that he is one. What need, therefore, to talk to him? And after he's been condemned, why give him the bad news of his sentence? They don't need his consent, and it's better, they say, to let him go on hoping. The condemned man is a machine who has no role to play in the process. He's a nail that needs only a few blows of a hammer to go into a plank."

Casanova also began to suspect, as was indeed the case, that for a time Bragadin didn't know what was happening to him and was unable to communicate with him, let alone bring about his release. Only after a bitter winter had set in was Bragadin permitted to send him warm clothes and bedding, as well as money to order books and other things. According to Lorenzo, Bragadin "had appeared in person before the Inquisitors, and kneeling in tears had begged the favor of sending me this mark of his constant affection, if I was still in the number of the living. They were so moved that they were unable to refuse."

Clearly Casanova was not going to be set free any time soon, if ever. He decided to free himself.

This dreadful idea made me laugh, because I was certain I was free to remain there no longer, once I was determined to win liberty at the risk of my life. Either they would kill me, or else I would reach my goal. *Deliberata morte ferocior.* It was at the beginning of November that I resolved to escape by force from a place where I was being held by force. That became my sole thought, and I began to search, scheme, and examine a hundred ways of achieving a goal which many others might have attempted before me, but no one had ever carried through with success.

It was true: not one prisoner had ever escaped. The quote from Horace means "more intrepid because prepared to die." Or as one commentator puts it, "paradoxically, he was prepared to die, the better to live."[11]

Casanova tells us that on November 1 a remarkable event occurred. Suddenly the entire building began to sway, and a huge beam in the attic roof twisted first in one direction and then in the other. It was obviously an earthquake. Casanova cried out hopefully, *Un' altra, un' altra, gran Diu, ma più forte*—"Another, another, great God, but even stronger!" The guards were appalled at this apparent blasphemy, but what was going through his mind was this: "As it collapsed, the palace might eject me without the slightest injury safe, sound, and free on the beautiful pavement of the Piazza San Marco. It was thus that I was beginning to go mad."

He learned afterward that the shock, which was felt throughout Europe, came from the celebrated earthquake that demolished the city of Lisbon and killed tens of thousands of people. And in fact that was an important stimulus to Enlightenment religious skepticism. The Inquisition—the official "Holy Office," not the secular tribunal of Venice—declared that Lisbon had been punished for exceptional sinfulness. Voltaire wrote a bitter poem asking why people were dancing merrily in Paris, surely not a less sinful city, while the Portuguese perished. And in *Candide* he made his anti-hero visit Lisbon and observe the solution that was implemented by the Catholic Church, "it having been decided by the University of Coimbra that the spectacle of a few individuals being ceremonially roasted over a slow fire was the infallible secret recipe for preventing the earth from quaking."

This is a striking episode in Casanova's account, but significant for another reason: it never happened. Tremors were indeed felt far from Portugal, but almost certainly not as far away as Venice, and anyway not until a year after Casanova was in prison. Evidently, a commentator says, "Casanova wanted to establish a symbolic connection *a posteriori* between the epochal earthquake and his own escape."[12]

Having resolved to escape, Casanova devised a plan. He calculated that his cell must be directly above the room to which he had first been brought, when the Inquisitors' secretary had said, "That's him; put him away." The chances were good that that office would be vacant in the early morning, if only he could get into it. He decided, therefore, to carve a hole through the floor, after which he could make a rope out of bedclothes and descend. What would happen after that must be left to chance and improvisation.

Now it was time to transform the iron bolt into a usable tool. With infinite pains, using the piece of marble as a whetstone, he managed to grind the end of the bolt into an octagonal point "so well proportioned that one couldn't have asked a cutler to do it better." Whenever Casanova made up his mind to do something he was indefatigable, and he was undaunted by the prospect of weeks if not months of labor.

It was also necessary to get some sort of lamp so he could see what he was doing in the dim light. That too was a problem he enjoyed solving. He would need oil and some kind of container, material for wicks, a piece of flint and steel to strike it on, and finally sulfur and amadou. That was a kind of tinder which an eighteenth-century dictionary defines as "a spongy and inflammable substance derived from certain mushrooms."[13]

The container he already had, an earthenware pot in which food had been brought. Cotton from his coverlet could serve to make wicks. Steel was ready to hand in the form of a belt buckle. As for the oil, he requested it for use in salads. The gun flint and sulfur presented a bigger problem, but with his usual plausibility he convinced the gullible Lorenzo that flint soaked in vinegar could relieve an agonizing toothache, which he didn't actually have, and that an ointment mixed with sulfur would help a skin rash. As it turned out he was able to get hold of some matches and didn't need the flint after all.

Now he had his makeshift oil lamp, which he would keep hidden whenever he wasn't using it, and everything was ready except the amadou. What pretext could he think up for that? He suddenly remembered that he had asked his tailor to sew a layer of amadou in the armpits of his taffeta coat, to prevent stains. With characteristic vividness, he recreates the emotions of that moment, changing from past tense to present for immediacy.

> I had my coat right there before me, which was entirely new, and my heart was palpitating, torn between hope and fear. I had to take just two steps to reassure myself, and I didn't dare to. I feared not finding the amadou and having to give up so dear a hope. At last I make up my mind. I approach the plank where my coat is, and suddenly feeling unworthy of such grace, I throw myself on my knees and pray to God that the tailor had not forgotten. After this fervent prayer I unfold the coat, unstitch the oilcloth, and find the amadou. My joy was great. It was natural that I should thank God, since I had sought the amadou confident of his goodness, and I was praying in an effusion of my heart.

Equipped now with his lamp, Casanova set to work with a will, digging into the floor with his bolt, and tying up the fragments of wood in a napkin so he could discard them in the attic the next time he was allowed to walk there. Each morning he concealed the growing hole by putting his bed on top of it. Under these planks there turned out to be a whole second layer, and that too he bored through. Yet another setback appeared, since those planks rested on top of a mosaic of marble. Here memory came to his aid. He recalled that Hannibal used vinegar to soften rocks in the Alps, and sure enough, his vinegar was helpful now. One final layer of planks remained, and since they must be the ceiling of the room below, he chipped at them with extreme care.

One afternoon, Casanova was lying on the floor, working stark naked because of the heat and dripping with sweat, with his lamp lit so he could see what he was doing. Suddenly he heard a door scraping open in the corridor outside. "What a moment! I blow out the lamp, I leave my bolt in the hole, I throw my napkin in with it, I spring up and hastily replace my bed, I throw the pallet and mattresses on top of it, and with no time to put on the sheets I fall on it as if dead at the very instant when Lorenzo enters my cell. A single moment earlier and I would have been caught."[14]

Casanova had decided to make his break on the night of August 27, 1756, thirteen months after his arrest, since the feast of St. Augustine would be celebrated the next day and the palace offices would be deserted. Religious feast days were faithfully observed, and that enabled him to keep track of the calendar. But on August 25 there was a horrible surprise. Lorenzo entered the cell and exclaimed cheerfully, "I congratulate you, Signore, on the good news I'm bringing you!" This was that his punishment was being relaxed, and he would be transferred to a more spacious cell where he could stand upright, and look out from a pair of windows at the lagoon and the island of San Giorgio Maggiore that faces San Marco from across the water. Even better than the view was the fresh air that flowed through the windows. When Casanova begged to remain where he was, Lorenzo only laughed. "Have you gone mad? They want to take you out of Hell and put you in Paradise, and you refuse? Come on, you've got to obey, get up. I'll give you my arm, and I'll have your clothing and books brought to you."

Now there was a double problem. Not only was all of Casanova's labor thrown away, but Lorenzo was bound to discover the hole. When he did, he rushed to the new cell to accost Casanova, incoherent with rage. But the sharpened bolt was concealed as usual in the armchair, there was no sign in the old cell of a tool of any kind, and Lorenzo couldn't imagine how the hole ever got made. As Casanova pointed out, the authorities were bound to believe that the guard had been complicit in some way, and under interrogation Casanova would certainly tell them so. "Keep quiet," Lorenzo said with alarm, "and remember that I'm a poor man with children."

At this point someone less determined might have given up, but not Casanova. Lorenzo and his fellow guards systematically pounded the entire floor of the new cell to reassure themselves that it was sound. But there was another possible way out—through the ceiling. Well aware that he would be kept now under even greater surveillance, what Casanova needed was an accomplice. With his usual luck he got one.

Lorenzo told him that a nearby cell was occupied by someone who also had books and would no doubt be willing to share them. Sharpening a fingernail to use as a pen and writing with mulberry juice, Casanova sent a message concealed within one of his books, with a note on the cover, *Latet*—"something is hidden." Soon he and the other prisoner were corresponding regularly. His name was Marin Balbi, a patrician and monk in the Somaschian order, which had been founded in the sixteenth century as "the Company of the Servants of the Poor." Its members vowed to live simply and to practice bodily mortification, but Balbi had been in the Piombi for four years because he got three young virgins pregnant and then—with flagrant lack of discretion—baptized their infants under his own name. If he hadn't acknowledged them, his transgressions might have been overlooked.

Balbi was very willing to take part in a jailbreak. His assignment would be to cut a hole in his own ceiling, concealing it with a large religious print that he might seem to want for meditation when lying on his bed. Of course it was now necessary to get the bolt to him. The method Casanova came up with was both daring and ingenious. He ordered a big dish of hot buttered gnocchi. After concealing the bolt between the pages of a large Bible, he balanced the Bible on top of the dish of gnocchi, and then called for Lorenzo and asked to have it taken as a gift to Balbi.[15]

The bolt was long, and protruded a bit on both sides, which meant that Lorenzo could easily have noticed it. Casanova's hope was that to keep his balance and avoid spilling the hot contents, he would look straight ahead and not down. Incredibly, the scheme worked, and the bolt reached its destination undetected.

After a week Balbi finished cutting a hole in his ceiling big enough to climb through. Casanova heard footsteps above his own ceiling, and then the three knocks that were their agreed-upon signal. By the following day Balbi had bored into the planks in Casanova's ceiling until just a few more thrusts would open a gap. They agreed to make their attempt two days after that.

But at this moment there was a new setback. From time to time Casanova had to share his cell with a temporary companion, and one arrived now. This was a scruffy character who turned out to be a Franciscan friar named Francesco Soradaci, who had been acting as a spy for the Venetian government but was suspected of double-dealing.

October was nearing an end, fifteen months since Casanova's arrest, and he decided that despite this latest complication, it was now or never. The previous year he had observed that during the first three days of November the Inquisitors, along with most of the Venetian aristocracy, went on holiday to their villas on the mainland. While they were away Lorenzo was sure to get drunk and would need to sleep it off.

It occurred to Casanova to seek the kind of oracular confirmation favored by people who used to open the Bible or the *Aeneid* at random and regard whatever verse they hit upon as intended personally. He no longer had a Bible, since Balbi was keeping his, but he did have "the divine poem *Orlando Furioso* by Messer Ludovico Ariosto, which I had read a hundred times, and which was still my delight." He did not, however, open at random. Instead he drew up one of his numerical pyramids, from which he deduced that the prophetic line must be the first one in the seventh stanza of the ninth canto.

The result could not have been more auspicious. It read *Tra il fin d'Ottobre, e il capo di Novembre*—"between the end of October and the first of November." In context the line merely introduced a bit of description: "It was the end of October and the onset of November, the season when the trees can be seen shedding their leafy raiment until they stand stripped and shivering in their nakedness, and the birds fly together in tight flocks. This was when Orlando began his amorous quest." The line must have spoken directly to Casanova. It was a long time since he had enjoyed an amorous quest. And in another way *Orlando Furioso* was highly relevant. Casanova loved the ideal of fearless heroism in the poem, and that was what he was about to enact.[16]

One final challenge remained: what to do about Soradaci? His offense was relatively trivial and he expected to be released soon, so he was unlikely to want to take part in the escape. Yet it was essential to keep him quiet. Fortunately he was deeply superstitious, praying constantly, and Casanova saw a solution. After sharing a bowl of soup with Soradaci, he proclaimed in a solemn voice, "Eat this soup, and afterward I will reveal your good fortune to you. Know that the Holy Virgin of the Rosary appeared to me at daybreak and commanded me to pardon you. You will not die, and you will escape from this place with me."

This declaration was only the prologue, for it was still necessary to prepare Soradaci for the arrival of Balbi through the ceiling. Casanova said that the Virgin had declared to him, "I will command one of my angels to take the form of a man, and I will send him immediately from heaven to break through the ceiling of the cell and convey you out of it. This angel will begin his work today at nineteen o'clock [two hours after sunset in Venetian reckoning] and will keep on working until half an hour before sunrise." Casanova had confirmed this timing with Balbi, and when the banging on the ceiling began as predicted, any skepticism Soradaci still felt was dispelled. Playing on his pious gullibility had been a masterstroke.

When Balbi broke through the ceiling, Casanova helped him down. Admittedly he didn't look much like an angel, but that was because he was appearing in human form. Balbi had even brought a pair of scissors, and with those Soradaci trimmed their hair and beards. That was a good idea, since they didn't want to look like disheveled convicts. The scissors had been obtained from an elderly count in a neighboring cell, which meant that he had to be told about the plot. When he was asked if he wanted to escape with them, however, he declined, remarking that he couldn't imagine how they would get down from the roof unless they grew wings. Soradaci likewise decided to stay.

Just before leaving Casanova wrote a letter for the Inquisitors to read after he was gone. It began with a Latin quote from the Psalms, "I shall not die, but live, and declare the works of the Lord." After that came a frank statement of his right to escape if he could manage it. "Our lords the Inquisitors of State must do everything they can to hold a guilty person in prison by force. The prisoner, happy that he hasn't given his word to stay there, must do everything he can to gain his liberty. The basis of the law is justice; the basis for the guilty person is nature. Just as they didn't need his consent to lock him up, he doesn't need theirs to save himself."

As a postscript he added, "If he does have the good fortune to save himself, Casanova makes a present of all he is leaving behind to Francesco Soradaci, who remains a prisoner because he is afraid of the dangers I'll be exposing myself to, and does not love, as I do, his freedom more than his life." Casanova doesn't explain, and perhaps didn't care, whether Soradaci would be suspected of complicity in the escape.[17]

Once Casanova and Balbi had climbed up through the hole in the ceiling, the roof remained to be penetrated. If it had been sheathed in solid lead it would have been impossible to cut through, but the plates of lead were three feet square and it wasn't difficult to pry them loose with the bolt. After making a hole, Casanova and Balbi put their heads out into the open air. It must have been an intoxicating moment. But immediately they realized that the moon was shining brightly, a danger they hadn't foreseen. If they went further up on the roof, they would be visible to anyone who happened to look up from below. There was no alternative but to wait inside until the moon set several hours later, and then at last they clambered up to the peak of the roof.

On one side below them was the courtyard, where guards would see anyone trying to come down. On the other side was a canal. Before leaving their cells they had knotted sheets and clothing into a long makeshift rope. Their plan was to use it to descend to the pavement or the canal. But now they discovered that there was nothing whatever on the roof to which they could attach the rope.

Casanova decided that their best hope would be to crawl down the sloping roof to reach one of the dormer windows, climb in through the window, and then find a way downstairs to the palace doors and freedom. A thick fog had made the roof dangerously slippery, but still it had to be attempted. Shinnying along the top of a dormer, he leaned down and pried loose a metal grill and then smashed the glass. Balbi joined him, and cautiously descended inside while Casanova held on to the rope. Once inside, Balbi called up that it was a long drop to the floor. Casanova now had no one to hold the rope for him. How could he get in without risking a dangerous fall?

Yet again he had a stroke of luck. Going back up to reconnoiter the rooftop, he spotted a ladder that some workmen had left behind. If he could manage to maneuver the ladder into the window, he could climb safely down. But as he was struggling with it in the near-darkness, disaster struck. He lost his footing and slipped down to the very edge of the roof. His legs were now dangling into empty space, and all that prevented him from falling to his death was the pressure of his elbows in the gutter. With infinite care he began to raise one leg up, but that effort brought on a paralyzing cramp. "Terrible moment! After two minutes I tried again, and thanks be to God, I did get one knee onto the gutter and then the other knee." Soon he was inside the palace with his greatly relieved companion. They pulled the ladder in after them to prevent detection when daylight arrived.

This dramatic moment was illustrated in *The Story of My Escape from the Prisons of the Republic of Venice, Known as the Leads,* a miniature epic that Casanova published in 1787, after having narrated the tale orally for many years. The illustrator, incidentally, could never have seen the actual place. The domes

25. Casanova's Escape

of the church of San Marco at the top should really be out of sight at the left. And the boat at the bottom is preposterous. Casanova had his emergency above the interior courtyard, not the canal outside.

Once inside, things went surprisingly smoothly. Casanova, desperately fatigued, fell asleep for four hours in the room they had entered, until Balbi woke him at dawn. They found themselves in some sort of archive. From there they went down a staircase to a larger set of offices, where the door was locked from the outside. Casanova laid hold of a sharp instrument that secretaries used to make holes in parchment records, and with this tool he managed to shatter an opening in the door. The wood was so full of knots that he had to stop when the hole was barely big enough. He lacerated his thighs badly squeezing through it, but they were now close to freedom.

At the bottom of another couple of staircases, they arrived at the massive front door of the palace. Not surprisingly, that door too was locked, and was much too formidable to think of trying to force. Luckily Casanova was dressed in the fancy clothes in which he had been arrested, and he concealed Balbi's monastic robe by putting his cloak over it. "I looked like a man who had been at a ball and after that in a place of debauchery where he got beaten up." A watchman outside in the courtyard saw them through a window, and hurried over with a bunch of keys. Casanova was prepared to attack him if necessary, but the watchman assumed they were courtiers who had a right to be in the palace and had just fallen asleep. Casanova's rose-colored silk suit with lace trim was incongruous for a chilly November morning, but he could plausibly be someone dressed for a party who had accidentally gotten locked in.

Hurrying past the watchman before he could ask questions, Casanova and Balbi descended to the interior courtyard of the palace by way of the majestic Giants' Staircase, flanked by heroic statues of Mercury and Neptune that symbolized commerce and the sea. At an inquiry afterward the watchman claimed that Casanova had knocked him unconscious as he rushed past. As for the guard Lorenzo, Casanova learned later that he was imprisoned for negligence in his duty, and had died there.[18]

All that remained now for Casanova and Balbi was to walk with forced calm across the Piazzetta in front of the palace, and onward between the columns with the winged lion and the dragon slayer to the nearby quay known as the Molo. An eighteenth-century engraving (color plate 24) gives a good sense of the massiveness of the palace from which they had just escaped; the twin columns can be seen in the middle distance. Further away, the Customs House and the church of Santa Maria della Salute mark the entrance to the Grand Canal, and beyond them is the broad Giudecca Canal that would be the route to freedom.

They hired the first gondola they came to, and Casanova loudly commanded the two gondoliers to take them to the mainland town of Fusina. That was a ruse to throw off pursuit in case he had been overheard; once they

26. The Giants' Staircase

were underway he told them that he had changed his mind and wanted to go to Mestre instead. Mestre appears in the distance in a modern photograph, though today it is heavily industrialized. With wind and tide in their favor, the trip would take barely an hour.

Passing through the canal, Casanova turned for a farewell look at the city he loved, and was destined not to see again for eighteen years.

> I gazed behind me at the beautiful canal, and seeing not a single boat, I admired the loveliest day that one could possibly wish. The first rays of a superb sunrise emerged from the horizon, the young gondoliers rowed energetically, and I reflected on the cruel night I had passed, the place where I had been the previous day, and all the combinations of circumstances that had been favorable to me. Emotion overwhelmed my soul, which lifted itself up to the God of mercy, inspiring me with gratitude and moving me so powerfully that my tears opened up the fullest means of relieving my heart. Suffocating from an excess of joy I sobbed, I wept, like a child being dragged by force to school.

27. The Piazzetta

28. The Giudecca Canal

A child being dragged to school—what a strangely negative analogy! But it was accurate in a way. Casanova's carefree life was over, and now he would have to submit to the demanding school of the world beyond.

Over the years he saw this episode as a defining experience in his life, and if he did transform it into a heroic myth, still it was based on truth. He was an inveterate role player, and for that very reason he placed the highest value on experiences that can't be faked. Stendhal, a great admirer of the *Histoire,* felt the same way. For both of them those experiences took the form of courage in situations of great risk, and also occasions of intense physical pleasure.

When, after eighteen years, Casanova was finally permitted to return to Venice, there were no hard feelings. He was invited to dine with each of the three current Inquisitors, who "wanted to hear from my own lips the fine story of my escape." He also ran into the Inquisition's secretary, who told him he should have been patient since he would soon have been set free. He objected that for all he knew he would have remained in the Piombi for life, and received a mysterious reply: "I ought not to have imagined that, because a small fault gets a small punishment. I interrupted him with some feeling and asked him to be so good as to tell me what my fault was, since I had never been able to guess. He responded sagely by placing his right index finger against his lips. I didn't question him further."[19]

Something he did learn later on was that he had been accused of devil worship, on the preposterous grounds that when he lost money gambling, "at a time when all believers blaspheme God, I was heard only to utter imprecations against the Devil." He was also wicked enough to eat meat on Fridays.[20]

Casanova learned a permanent lesson from his imprisonment: never to say openly what he believed on dangerous subjects. Voltaire had gone into self-exile from France to avoid prosecution for skeptical views, and Casanova wrote to one of Voltaire's admirers, "In Venice they put me under the Leads for having said a lot less than you're telling me. . . . I'm persuaded that the Republic of Venice acted justly in imprisoning me for my indiscreet petulance. I assure you, Monsieur, that if I deserve my liberty it is only because I've learned to shut up."[21]

CHAPTER 15

In Search of the Blind Goddess

When he reached the mainland at Mestre, Casanova was still in Venetian territory. There were miles to go before he would be safe, but setting off on foot, he felt thrillingly free. Starting from scratch was in fact what he loved best. Eighteenth-century adventurers were like sharks that die if they can't keep moving. There were many cases in which they refused advantageous appointments or marriages to avoid being pinned down. "Each time," a historian says, "the adventurer starts over again at zero." Casanova had already done that several times, and it would become the permanent pattern of his life.[1]

In a draft preface for the *Histoire* that has only recently been published, Casanova says, "The incidents are always surprising, even though they ought to have been foreseen, and even a philosopher is agreeably surprised, because he perceives their novelty precisely in their being always the same." That's one way of putting it. Another would be to say that Casanova's life illustrates what psychoanalysts call repetition compulsion. With compelling charm, nimble intelligence, and a chameleonic gift for mirroring other people's feelings, he repeatedly initiated cons or scams that brought him success and sometimes wealth, but they never lasted long. And the same is true of his erotic relationships.[2]

As for where to go, the obvious destination was Paris. Casanova knew the city well after his two years there, spoke French fluently, and could count on being welcomed as he had been before by the Ballettis, the star actress Sylvia and her son Antonio. There was a good chance too that Bernis, who had become his friend in Venice when they shared the nun M. M., would be willing to help him. More generally, he looked forward to resuming "my career as an adventurer in the one city in the universe where the blind goddess dispensed her favors to those who abandoned themselves to her."[3]

The blind goddess was Fortune, but soon Casanova had a strange experience that seemed due instead to the mysterious daemon that sometimes guided his life. He and Balbi had split up to make detection less likely, agreeing to meet again at a town in the north. Thirty miles from Mestre he arrived at a village called Valdobbiadene, in the Alpine foothills, and decided to seek a night's lodging at a farmhouse. When he asked a passing shepherd who owned it, he was startled to learn that it was none other than the chief of the *sbirri*, the police, who must have been combing the countryside for him at that very moment.

Nevertheless, that's where he went. "It's inconceivable that I headed for that terrible house, which by reason and nature I should have avoided. I went straight there, and I know it wasn't by conscious volition. If it's true that a beneficent invisible presence pushes us toward our happiness, as sometimes happened to Socrates, I have to believe that that was what made me do it. I admit that in all my life I never took so bold a step." This "happiness" apparently depended on going to the one place Casanova should have avoided at all costs. He may have felt that having achieved the impossible at the Ducal Palace, he could now count on a charmed life. And he always loved the thrill of taking risks.

When he knocked at the door, a pretty woman in an advanced state of pregnancy said she was sorry her husband was away and asked politely what he might want. Taking note of her condition, he replied with his unfailing resourcefulness, "I'm disappointed, Madam, that my *compère* isn't here, charmed as I am to meet his beautiful wife." *Compère*, literally "father with," was a term shared affectionately by the father and godfather of a child (he used an Italian equivalent, of course). Identifying himself in that way was a dangerous gamble, but it worked. "Your *compère!*" she replied. "I'm speaking, then, with His Excellency Vetturi? My husband told me you've kindly promised to be godfather to my baby." Vetturi was the mayor of nearby Treviso, whom she had fortunately never met.

As for why her husband wasn't there, "Then you don't know that two prisoners have escaped from the Piombi? One is a patrician, and the other is an individual named Casanova. My husband received a letter to search for them.

If he finds them he'll take them to Venice, and if not he'll come back here, but he'll be away searching for at least three days."

Casanova ate well and spent a pleasant night. Not only that, the woman's mother called him "my son," and skillfully dressed the knees and thighs that he had lacerated when he forced his way through the shattered door in the Ducal Palace. He told her he got hurt when he fell in the mountains while hunting.

This was a region where he could expect to run into people who knew him, but by now he was fully trusting his luck. Attending Mass in a village church, he was accosted by Marcantonio Grimani, a relative of his former guardian. Evidently they were friends, since far from exposing him, Grimani just said, "Tell me how you managed to break through the Piombi!" Casanova replied that it was an interesting story but too long to relate, and moved on.

At the town of Bolzano in the Tyrol, beyond Venetian territory at last, he called on a banker who wrote to Bragadin and a week later received authorization to give him a hundred zecchini. With these funds he bought some new clothes and continued northward to Munich. There he ran into a lady he had known in Paris, who was headed to Paris herself and offered him a seat in her coach.

When Casanova later encountered Balbi again, he found him more repellent than ever, "not just ugly, but with a face that expressed baseness, cowardice, insolence, and stupid malice." He wasn't sorry in later years to learn the rest of Balbi's story. Claiming repentance, Balbi turned himself in to the Venetian authorities, but was imprisoned in the Piombi all over again, and after his release died in poverty as a village priest.

In January of 1757, two months after his escape, Casanova reached Paris and went straight to the Ballettis. Antonio greeted him with open arms and said he was certain, even though he had heard nothing from Casanova, that he would soon show up. His mother Sylvia was equally warm. Now Casanova was struck by the young daughter Maria Maddalena, known as Manon. He hadn't paid much attention to her during his previous stay in Paris, but he definitely paid attention now. She was seventeen, talented and beautiful, and would soon play a significant role in his life.

A biographer punningly entitles his account of this period *Nouveau Pari(s)*; *pari* means a wager or bet. For an ambitious young man, the best way to get ahead was to find a powerful patron who could make connections for him, or even establish him in some well-paying employment. When Casanova had been in Paris previously he had no useful contacts and no way to make any.

Now he knew Bernis, who had become foreign minister of France and would soon be a cardinal as well.[4]

For success here, it was necessary to adopt an altogether different persona from the one that had gotten Casanova into such trouble during his playboy years in Venice. "I saw that to get ahead I needed to put all of my faculties in play, both physical and moral, get acquainted with the great and powerful, exercise mastery over my mind, and take on the coloration of those whom I needed to please." In Rome in his youth he had learned that the key was to be a chameleon, and it was time to relearn the lesson. In addition, "I must keep away from what is called bad company and renounce all my former habits."

Casanova called on Bernis, and was received exactly as he had hoped. Bernis already knew about the escape from the Piombi, since M. M. had written to him about it. "He let me know not only the pleasure he felt at seeing me triumphant, but also his joy at being in a position to be useful to me." Indeed, Bernis may have known or suspected that his own involvement with Casanova and M. M. had been a reason for the imprisonment, in which case he would definitely have felt some responsibility.

In addition to some money that Bragadin had sent, Casanova now received from Bernis a roll of a hundred louis, gold coins that were so called because the king's head appeared on them. That was generous indeed, equivalent to 2,500 modern euros, with far more buying power in those days.

Casanova was now able to acquire the clothes that would be necessary to carry on his quest for success. "Paris was, and is, a city where they judge everything by appearances, and there's no country on earth where it's easier to make an impression." Accessories mattered just as much as clothing, since they were visible evidence of wealth. An eighteenth-century adventurer's usual props, a historian says, were "furs, rings with diamonds of high value, gold chains, medallions, and snuffboxes or watches studded with diamonds—which might sometimes turn out to be paste." Casanova acquired all of those. An inventory of his luggage a couple of years later listed numerous rings, gold boxes, and crystal flasks, as well a blue suit lined with ermine, another suit of velvet in four colors, and muslin shirts with lace cuffs.[5]

For a gifted actor, this was literally costuming for a role. His exceptional height and striking features were important too. A lady who met him in Paris described him as "tall, with a dark complexion, dressed as a rich seigneur, with heavy rings adorning his fingers." Throughout the *Histoire* Casanova's fullest descriptions are of costumes, both male and female. Chantal Thomas comments that they exist *en soi (et en soie)*—in themselves, and in silk, which along with satin and velvet plays a starring role.[6]

It was important for a gentleman to treat his hair with ointment and powder, which needed to smell good as well as look good. Casanova favored powder made from a mixture of iris, coriander, cloves, calamus, and souchet (the last two were plant roots). He also perfumed his handkerchiefs with rose essence, which he kept in a small flask attached to his watch chain.[7]

To add spice to his story for contemporary readers, Casanova says that by chance he arrived in Paris on the very day when an attempt had been made on the king's life. The would-be assassin was a servant named Damiens, mentally unstable and with some kind of religious grudge, and the knife wound he inflicted turned out to be trivial. All the same, he was subjected to an appalling public torture that lasted for four hours, and finally dismembered.

In the *Histoire* this event provokes a tale that is really impossible to believe. Casanova says that he rented a room overlooking the execution site and invited two women to watch it with him. Also invited was an Italian acquaintance, Edoardo Tiretta, nicknamed by women "Count Six Times" for his sexual prowess. While their companions gazed in horror at the scene of torture, he and Tiretta took advantage of them from behind, and they were too engrossed to object. Casanova did have a habit of claiming to have been present at well-known events even when he wasn't. This may well have been one of those.

Thanks to Bernis he immediately fell into a perfect situation, although as usual he pulled it off only through his uncanny ability to make people believe he knew much more than he did. Bernis told him that the government was looking for a way to finance a military academy that the royal mistress Mme. de Pompadour wanted to establish, without having to draw on current funds in a time of financial strain, and suggestions would be welcomed. What Casanova should do, Bernis advised, was to present himself as an expert in finance. Of course he agreed, though he had not the least idea what kind of scheme to propose.

He was then introduced to the comptroller general in charge of all expenditures, who said that Bernis had praised his financial mastery. Casanova "could barely keep from laughing," but replied solemnly that he had a plan in mind to bring in huge sums, but wouldn't reveal it until they came to a more concrete understanding. At this point he was told that somebody else had also put forward a plan, and if he would come to a meeting the two plans could be considered together.

With amazement, Casanova realized that it might actually work. "I went to walk in the Tuileries, reflecting on the extraordinary stroke of fortune that was presented to me." All he had to do was size up the other applicant and see if there was a way to enlist him as an accomplice—and that kind of manipulation was just what he did best.

The rival turned out to be Giovanni Antonio Calzabigi, a diplomat representing the Kingdom of the Two Sicilies (Naples as well as Sicily itself). Calzabigi was a gifted mathematician who hoped to start a state lottery to finance the military academy, but was having trouble making it sound like a good idea. The officials were deeply skeptical, due to a conservative impression that the state was being asked to become a gambler.

Lotteries were already in widespread use in Italy, and as for gambling, that was one subject Casanova knew all about. He argued convincingly that the proper analogy was with the casino or bank, which always came out ahead in the long run. It was the people who bought the lottery tickets who would be the gamblers, and enough of them would make a killing for everyone else to be eager to get into the game, even though most would inevitably lose. Looking over Calzabigi's calculations, Casanova had enough mathematical knowledge to see that they were well conceived. He pretended he had already come up with exactly the same scheme, with some improvements of his own.

He had a further convincing argument. Insurance companies that handled maritime trade had to allow for unpredictable disasters, such as violent storms that could sink a ship. Yet by estimating probabilities, they were very successful. After all, most ships didn't sink. In the case of a lottery it would be a matter of pure arithmetic, with no unknown variables at all.

Calzabigi was delighted to take Casanova on as a partner, and for once, a scheme of his was above board. After the lottery was established, it worked exactly as they said it would. The state raked in money, and the two of them were given such a generous cut of the profits that they became rich. It was indeed a partnership that benefited both. Calzabigi had provided the crucial details of the plan, but Casanova provided the plausibility that induced the government to adopt it. At this moment he was as close to launching a real career as he would ever be in his life. But once the lottery was up and running—and its descendant, the French National Lottery, exists to this day—he was ready to move on to something else.[8]

Meanwhile someone turned up who really was launching a career. That was Casanova's brother Francesco, who had worked hard in Dresden for several years copying paintings and felt prepared to tackle Paris once more. His

29. Francesco Casanova, *Cavalry Charge*

previous attempt at an exhibition had been a failure, but he mounted one now that was a big hit.

Francesco was on his way to lifelong distinction; four of his paintings still hang in the Louvre. The Seven Years War had begun in 1756, and battle scenes were especially topical at the time. An etching entitled *Cavalry Charge,* with a dead horse and rider in the foreground, gives a good sense of his energetic style.

No less a critic than the great Denis Diderot treated Francesco's work with respect, in his reviews of the biennial Salons. He wrote in 1761 about one of the battle scenes, "You need to see it. For how can one render the movement, the melee, the tumult of men hurled in confusion against each other; how depict this man who has been knocked down with a shattered skull and blood escaping between his fingers against the wound, or this horseman on a white steed trampling the dead and dying, prepared to lose his life before he'll surrender his flag? This Casanova is a man of imagination, a great colorist, a warm and bold spirit, a fine poet, and a great painter."

At the next show, however, two years later, Diderot felt that the greatness had evaporated. "Ah, Monsieur Casanova, what has become of your talent?"

The answer seemed obvious. "They say that for years Casanova kept a young painter named Loutherbourg confined in a house in the country, who finished his paintings for him." Philippe Jacques de Loutherbourg had indeed been Francesco's student, and went on to success with battle scenes of his own, as well as brilliant scenic effects for David Garrick at the Drury Lane theater in London.[9]

In a letter to a lady, Diderot quoted something Francesco said about the uncertainty of life, which suggests that he shared Giacomo's wit. Francesco had stepped aside in the street to let a companion urinate against a wall, when a collapsing chimney fell from above and killed the companion. "I always recall Casanova's comment," Diderot wrote. "Believe that our fate is enveloped in utter darkness, and step aside for someone who wants to take a piss."[10]

While the lottery was being set up, Bernis found another government employment for Giacomo: to act as a secret agent. He was to go to Dunkirk, make friends with French naval officers there, and find out whether they were telling the truth about their state of military readiness. That was important because at some point an invasion of Britain might be attempted. Casanova was able to draw on his naval experience at Corfu, and he turned in a report that was considered satisfactory. Plenty of other people could have done the same thing, but Bernis was still a great favorite of Mme. de Pompadour, and his colleagues were glad to do him favors.

On the return trip from Dunkirk, the always mercurial Casanova flew into a rage when the gatekeeper in a fortified town wouldn't let him in. No doubt his role as a government agent had gone to his head. He refused to show his passport, and got even more furious when a customs officer demanded that he pay a big fine for some perfectly legal snuff he had with him. Once he did get in, he stormed into a dinner party to complain, astounding all the guests, and by his own admission made a dreadful scene. Fortunately everyone calmed down and he proceeded to Paris to submit his report, but Bernis, after laughing at his account of the contretemps, reminded him that secret agents were expected to avoid trouble, and that if something serious did happen the government would say it never heard of him.

It has always been suspected that Casanova had other secret missions during this period, and that he didn't choose to reveal them in the *Histoire*. We do know that an extensive network existed outside the normal diplomatic service, known as the king's secret, *le Secret du Roi*. It's unlikely that Casanova was a member of it, but some of his activities probably paralleled theirs.

What he does describe, at rather wearisome length, is financial transactions in Amsterdam on behalf of the French government, which was always looking for new ways to finance the costly Seven Years War. As with the spying, they preferred to use foreigners who could always be disavowed if something went wrong.

In the manuscript of the *Histoire* there were originally two brief mentions, afterward deleted, of having been granted French citizenship. It's not clear why Casanova removed those, and if he really did receive naturalization, it never seems to have done him any good.[11]

Amsterdam was the financial center of Europe. Securities issued by countries with stronger credit than France could be bought there, even if with a financial penalty, to be then converted to cash. One example in the *Histoire* can stand for many: "Boaz [a banker], astonished at the advantageous sale I had made of my sixteen Gothenburg shares, told me that he could get them discounted in shares of the Swedish East India Company if I could persuade the ambassador to sign an agreement by which I would agree to deliver the French royal securities at a loss of 10 percent, taking the Swedish shares at 15 percent, as I had already done with my own sixteen shares." There is a lot more of this, and it's evident that Casanova was once again making himself useful to people in power.[12]

During this period Casanova also attached himself to a patron, the elderly Marquise d'Urfé, who was immensely rich. He had already enchanted a countess named Mme. du Rumain, convincing her that he possessed extraordinary spiritual powers. They may well have become lovers, though he wouldn't have acknowledged that in the *Histoire,* since he was careful to protect the reputations of people whose identity was known. Soon she was writing him deeply admiring letters: "I am profoundly touched, Monsieur, by the happy wishes you've made on my behalf. You promise me happiness, and I'm so accustomed to believe what you tell me that I'm honored by this promise. If only, in return, I could procure all the good things you deserve!"[13]

Mme. du Rumain did procure them, by connecting him with Mme. d'Urfé. A passionate student of the occult, Mme. d'Urfé maintained an alchemical laboratory for her own use. Casanova knew a great deal about those arts and could talk convincingly, and she came to believe that he had real supernatural powers.

In particular, Mme. d'Urfé was obsessed with a belief that instead of dying she could be magically reincarnated in a young boy, and that Casanova could make it happen. He had come to her attention not just through Mme. de Rumain but because a nephew of hers suffered from painful sciatica and believed that Casanova had miraculously cured him. Actually sciatica can resolve spontaneously, and he was just letting nature take its course, as he had with Signor Bragadin.

Casanova claims that at some point he and Mme. d'Urfé paid a visit to Jean-Jacques Rousseau, and found him disappointingly dull. But scholars have shown that this almost certainly never happened. Rather than admit he never bothered to meet that great writer, Casanova seems to have drawn on other people's recollections of him.

While he was in Amsterdam he carried out financial transactions for Mme. d'Urfé as well as for the French government. He also made an unexpected connection with someone from his past that he would exploit in his relationship with the marquise. This was Teresa Imer, the girl with whom Casanova's first patron Malipiero had been besotted; it was when they were caught together that Malipiero thrashed him with a cane and threw him out of his palazzo. A few years before this meeting, Casanova and Teresa had seen each other in Venice, "where we made love once or twice, not as children but as real lovers."

She was now a singer and *aventurière* going by the name of Trenti, and she had two children. One was Giuseppe or Joseph, a handsome lad of thirteen, who used the name of Pompeati after his late father, a Venetian dancer named Angelo Pompeati to whom Teresa had been married. The other was a pretty five-year-old girl named Sophie who looked startlingly like Casanova himself. Teresa explained that he was in fact the father, and produced a birth certificate to confirm that the timing was right. Pleased rather than shocked, Casanova smothered the child with kisses and proposed to take her with him, but Teresa refused. He surmised that she was counting on Sophie as a source of income after she grew up.

Surprisingly, however, Teresa did permit Casanova to take charge of her son, whom he promised to take back to Paris with him. They both had their reasons. Casanova's reason was that Joseph could be the boy in whom Mme. d'Urfé would believe she was being reincarnated. And if she responded favorably to that idea, she might well give Joseph an education and set him up as a gentleman. Teresa was pleased with this scheme for launching him in life, and for some time it did work out like that.

There was also a flirtation with the seventeen-year-old daughter of a rich merchant; he calls her Esther. "With her white complexion, unpowdered black hair, and large eloquent black eyes, she struck me greatly. She spoke French very well, played the harpsichord with a light touch, and was passionately fond of reading." For some reason Casanova crossed out a further detail in his manuscript: "a smile that showed the greatest *finesse* of mind." In this context *finesse* has multiple connotations, all of them positive—delicacy, sensitivity, and perceptiveness.[14]

Casanova enjoyed a bit of sexual play with Esther, but didn't take it very seriously. Two things about the relationship are interesting, though. One was the effectiveness of his numerological scam even when he was deliberately trying *not* to fool someone—he was so good at it that it worked even so. And the other was his capacity for charming older men. He had already seized upon a chance occurrence to demonstrate his occult powers. Arriving at their lodgings, he noticed a wallet on the stairs and bent over to pick it up, but inadvertently knocked it into a space between the steps. When he joined Esther and her father, he found them lamenting the loss of the wallet, at which point he solemnly constructed his usual number pyramids. Sure enough, they revealed that it would be found under the fifth step of the staircase.

Esther was gifted at arithmetic, and just for fun Casanova began showing her how his pyramids worked, explaining frankly that they weren't really prophetic. As so many other people had done, however, she soon became convinced that the oracle was genuine, and a spur-of-the-moment prediction that he made seemed to prove it. Her father was pondering whether to purchase, as a speculation, a ship that was late arriving from the East Indies. If it was safe he would make an immense profit, but if it had sunk he would absorb a corresponding loss.

Casanova agreed to perform his usual rigamarole, which Esther helped to interpret, and to his horror it somehow came out confirming that the ship was safe. If it wasn't, he would be responsible for the financial blow. But his luck ran true. The ship did arrive, its valuable cargo was now the property of Esther's father, and he told Casanova that he would make him his agent and give him Esther in marriage. It can't just be because he was right about the ship. He had an innate appeal that set him off from other young men.

As always in such cases, he declined the offer. Félicien Marceau remarks that a "vulgar adventurer" would have leapt at the chance to marry a rich girl, but Casanova resisted that temptation whenever it arose. He valued his freedom, and knew that he would make a bad husband. Besides, he didn't like Holland much.[15]

Returning to Paris from Amsterdam, he turned entrepreneur and launched an ambitious business venture. He met someone who claimed to have a secret process for painting silk in indelible colors. If Casanova would provide the

capital to set up a little factory, they would both get rich. He agreed enthusiastically, using his proceeds from the lottery.

The factory was established with frames on which the fabric was painted
by twenty young women following patterns. The employees were all pretty,
and they soon understood how to supplement their modest salaries. Casanova
housed many of them in apartments of their own, as well as lavishing gifts on
them. That was expensive, but there were worse financial problems as well.
The war was paralyzing commerce; no one wanted to buy the finished product, and bankruptcy ensued.

This would be the last conventional money-making project in Casanova's
life. But while his money lasted he was able to set himself up in an elegant villa
in Little Poland, a then-rural district where the Gare Saint-Lazare is today,
with his own horses and carriage, a coachman, lackeys, and a chef. There he
entertained like some free-spending aristocrat; it was a grander version of the
casini back in Venice.

A painting entitled *The Oyster Lunch,* commissioned by Louis XV for the
private apartments at Versailles (color plate 25), evokes the kind of convivial
feast Casanova loved—and he repeatedly mentions that he especially loved
oysters. Every guest (they're all male) is richly dressed. They've obviously had
plenty to drink and aren't finished yet, with more champagne waiting on ice.
Empty oyster shells are tumbled haphazardly on the elegant marble floor;
there will be plenty of work for the servants to do, and the man in red at the
left is asking one of them to clean his shoe. It's not at first obvious why a
number of people are gazing upward. A closer look reveals a cork popping
into the air; the gentleman to the left of the waiter has his thumb on the bottle to keep the champagne in.

The pleasures of the table interested Casanova so much that in the *Histoire*
he describes over two hundred meals, and Ian Kelly has a chapter in his biography entitled "Casanova—Food Writer." There is a handsome illustrated
volume devoted entirely to *Casanova: Un Vénitien Gourmand,* which includes
forty pages of recipes with which he would have been familiar. We know, incidentally, that he carried a little portable stove with him on his travels.[16]

During these years Casanova had affairs with women, naturally, but none
as memorable as the ones with Teresa/Bellino, Henriette, or C. C. and M. M.
In the *Histoire* he describes several, not very interestingly. In Amsterdam there
was Esther, who was fascinated by his number pyramids, and in Paris there
was a Mlle. M—re who was about to get married. His interest in them wasn't
deep.

There was also a Miss XCV (no one knows why he chose the Roman nu-
meral) who has been identified as the half-English Giustiniana Wynne. She
too was going to be married, but had unluckily gotten pregnant by someone
who wasn't her fiancé. This was an opportunity for one of Casanova's good
deeds. First he took advantage of an opportunity by persuading Giustiniana
that she would miscarry if he inserted a special ointment he had prepared, so
long as it was combined with fresh sperm. "We undressed quickly, with none
of the preliminaries that always precede the act when it's prompted by love.
Both of us played our role to perfection. With deeply serious expressions, we
were like a surgeon undertaking an operation and the patient who submits
to it. . . . The astonishing thing is that we didn't laugh or even want to laugh,
so completely were we involved in our role."

That was enjoyable, but of course it didn't work, and as the pregnancy
became obvious Giustiniana was in despair. This time Casanova actually did
find a way to rescue her. With the sympathetic help of Mme. du Rumain, he
arranged to have her concealed safely in a convent until after she gave birth.
The infant was then consigned to the foundling home where one of his own
had been placed years previously, and Giustiniana was reconciled with her
mother. Casanova had had the satisfaction of doing a good deed.

The one relationship of significance during this time was also the most
troubling. From 1757 until early 1760, Casanova was engaged to Manon Balletti, daughter of the actress Sylvia and sister of his friend Antonio. Manon
was deeply in love, but his feelings are harder to know. In the *Histoire* he treats
the relationship in a quite perfunctory way, which has encouraged biographers to do the same. But many of her letters to him have survived, the only
ones we have from any of his lovers, and the story they tell is painfully moving. For once, we can hear the unmediated voice of one of his partners in love,
and get a glimpse of Casanova through her eyes.

CHAPTER 16

Manon

In the background of Casanova's account of his Paris years—very much in the background—is his three-year engagement with Manon Balletti. This was the only time in his life that he ever got engaged, and it seems clear that he did so without much enthusiasm. The best guess is that he wanted to keep on good terms with the Ballettis, who were treating him like a member of the family, and he found it convenient to acknowledge an engagement without being in any hurry for marriage. He's altogether unclear about that.

However, we have a unique perspective on this relationship, because he kept forty-one of Manon's letters, and after his death they were found among the masses of paper at the castle in Bohemia where he spent his final years. No one knows why he kept them. He tells us that he saved Henriette's letters too, but he evidently destroyed those toward the end of his life in order to protect the secret of her identity. There was no secret about Manon Balletti.

As Manon's portrait confirms (color plate 26), she had grown up to be stunningly beautiful. She was also highly intelligent. Seventeen years old when their relationship began, she was in training to be a musician, showing talent on the harpsichord and guitar.

When Casanova arrived in Paris after his escape from prison, Manon was engaged to her music teacher, a much older man named Charles-François Clément. She lost her heart, however, to the romantic Venetian. Her parents agreed to end the engagement to Clément, but they stipulated that marriage with Casanova must wait until he had a secure place in the world. Since he was launching his lucrative lottery and carrying out other assignments for the government, that seemed likely enough to happen.

Among his previous relationships, Casanova had been most aroused by M. M. for her erotic freedom, by Teresa/Bellino for her androgynous ambiguity, and by Henriette for her mysteriousness. Manon was entirely different, so far as we can tell. She had no sexual experience at all, and was vulnerable without being exciting. They usually saw each other only in the family group. When they would say goodbye in her room there was undoubtedly kissing and fondling, but apparently no more than that.

Although Manon was inexperienced, she had grown up in a theater milieu and was far from naïve. She knew nothing about Casanova's other women, but she certainly suspected that they existed. Meanwhile she was determined not to surrender sexually, which both frustrated and annoyed him. As he saw it, she was deliberately playing hard to get. "Sylvia's daughter was in love with me, and she knew that I loved her, even though I had never told her so; but she took care not to show it. She was afraid of encouraging me to demand favors, and not being sure that she was strong enough to refuse, she feared she would lose me afterward."

Casanova precedes this comment with a generalization right out of the libertine playbook: "If we get what we desire, it's certain that we won't desire it anymore, since one doesn't desire what one possesses. Women are quite right therefore not to yield to our desire." And he adds, "A man who declares that he's in love with a woman otherwise than *en pantomime* [i.e., not verbally] really needs to go to school."[1]

If all we had was Casanova's interpretation of what happened, it would be easy to see Manon as manipulative, but her letters give a deeper and more affecting insight into what happened between them. He mentions that there were originally over two hundred letters, which means that only a fifth of them have survived. Did he destroy the others because he knew they would make him look bad? And if so, did he fail to grasp how bad the surviving ones make him look?

Written in lucid and often eloquent French, Manon's letters begin in April 1757 and end in February 1760. Since she didn't want her family to know that they were corresponding, her brother Antonio or a trusted servant would smuggle letters in and out of the house.

In the very first one that we have, Manon tells Casanova that what had begun as an agreeable friendship is turning into something more. She usually writes after midnight, when she can be alone, and this one ends, "Good night, *mon cher ami,* I'm dying with sleepiness, my pen drops from my hand." In a P.S. she adds, "If you want to make me happy you will burn our letters; I think I'm telling you that I love you."

The next letter is dated two months later, with an engaging sense of happening in real time. Manon expects his arrival at any minute, but keeps talking to him on paper meanwhile. "Hush! I hear someone moving. Oh, it's nothing yet, I'm being impatient. . . . If you love me, arrive! I'm putting down my pen every moment to listen—here you are!"

Not long after this, however, Manon indicates that whenever they're actually together, they keep getting on each other's nerves. "How is it then! We write the most agreeable things in the world, and we constantly quarrel! But why, *mon cher?* You love me so much, or so you say, yet you hold grudges against me!" But she ends hopefully, "Adieu, adieu, love well your *petite amie.*"

It was evidently in writing that Casanova reassured her most successfully. "Your latest letter is so full of love and feeling, *mon cher ami,* that it fills me with joy, and convinces me completely of your love for me." At this stage she is still addressing him with the formal *vous* and calling him by his surname, *mon cher Casanova.*

Did Casanova express more passion in writing than he really felt? Equally important, how strong a commitment did he make to the prospective marriage? Was he leading Manon on or fobbing her off? Even if we did have his letters, we would still have to guess at the answers. We do know that he later called marriage "the tomb of love."[2]

Before long it was obvious that the ups and downs were going to continue indefinitely. "Your letter gave me renewed life," Manon writes in September. "I experienced an anxiety that I can't express, I even began to suspect you of indifference, but your letter has brought balm to my soul and I breathe again." Half a year later she tells him that she wants him to return her letters, "which must have little value for you." For whatever reason, he didn't. She ends bleakly, "Adieu, soon you'll no longer remember whether you loved me, and I—I will remember it forever."

Manon was in way over her head with this man and knew it, but she was trapped by the intensity of her feelings and by his intermittent encouragement. In October of 1758 she signs off, "Good night, *mon cher ami,* remember always that you have a very tender little wife, who expects the greatest fidelity from her husband." He was in Holland at the time, and she must have guessed that he was involved with some woman there. Why was she calling herself his wife? Was it to charge him with a promise he had made and was probably break-ing? Or because he had actually encouraged her to think of herself that way?

Less than a week later she writes, "Oh, what a letter have I just received from you! But is it really from you? Truly, *mon cher ami,* you're very violent, and you know me all too little if you dare to tell me that I don't love you." By the time she finishes the letter, though, she's prepared to accept blame. "Re-ally I'm what they call a little good for nothing, and I don't know how you *can* love me. . . . As soon as I see you I'll feel better. No more bad humor. *Je vous désire, je vous désire.*" She adds, "When you say that 'I know my power over you,' you're totally wrong, for I've never believed I had any."[3]

What Casanova tells us about Giustiniana Wynne ("Miss XCV") reveals just how easily he could transfer his attention from one woman to the next.

> After an hour that I spent alone with her, she had me in her chains. I told her so, and she seemed very pleased. She took the place in my heart that Esther had occupied less than a week before, but she wouldn't have gained it if Esther had been in Paris. My attachment to Sylvia's daugh-ter Manon was of a kind that didn't prevent me from being in love with someone else. Without a certain kind of nourishment a libertine's love soon grows cold, and women who have had any experience know that. The young Balletti was a total novice.

The "certain kind of nourishment" was what Manon withheld; her portrait shows her with a rose symbolizing innocence, and although a famous seduc-tion poem begins "Gather ye rosebuds while ye may," Casanova never did gather hers. Actually she was faced with a true double bind, since by Casa-nova's own account, if she did yield he would quickly lose interest.[4]

By this time her parents could see that Casanova was never going to be an appropriate spouse, and they began to look for a match with some stable and affluent older man. Through a go-between, negotiations began with a distin-guished architect, a widower named François-Jacques Blondel who was thirty-five years older than Manon (Casanova was fourteen years older). Meanwhile her mother Sylvia, who suffered from tuberculosis, died in September of 1758 at the age of fifty-seven.

Still Manon went on hoping that it would work out with Casanova, and she did her best to delay the new engagement with Blondel. While Casanova was away in Amsterdam, her family agreed to let her stay in his villa in Little Poland. From there she wrote to him reporting malicious gossip that they were living together. "*Mon cher ami,* I am filled with rage, indignation, and grief that can't be described. I've just come from Paris where I had the pain of hearing that everyone claims I'm here with you, and that you're in hiding here. Isn't that the most disgraceful, frightful, and horrible calumny? What monsters are black enough to invent such falsehoods? I can't bear it, I'll collapse under it with a broken heart, for the honor they want to rob me of!"

That was in October of 1759. Two months later Manon is joyously optimistic, writing with new frankness, "*Mon cher Casa, mon cher Giacomo,* lover, husband, friend, whatever you please, believe truly that I love you with all my soul, and you are *tout mon bien.*" She is thinking of the Italian expression *mio bene,* "my beloved." In January an even happier letter ends with an overflowing of Italian: "Adieu, my entirely lovable husband, be always as you were in your last letter and you will be loved by *Nena, Nenotola, Ballettina,* who is crazy about you. *Addio viscere mie, core, core, core*—farewell my vitals, my heart, my heart, my heart."

But at this point the surviving letters dry up. We don't know when or why Manon made up her mind that it was really all over. Or rather, we do have one letter, but not in the same collection; Casanova quotes it in the *Histoire* without making the date clear. At any rate it must have been in 1760, when he was in Amsterdam yet again. Manon's language is blunt: "Receive with *sang-froid* the news I'm giving you. This packet contains all of your letters and also your portrait. Send back mine, and if you keep my letters, burn them. I am counting on your decency. Think of me no more. For my part I will do all I possibly can to forget you. Tomorrow at this hour I will be the wife of M. Blondel, architect to the king and member of his Academy. You will oblige me when you return to Paris if you seem not to know me wherever you may encounter me."[5]

However ambivalent Casanova may have felt about the engagement, "this letter left me stunned for two whole hours." He drafted a series of replies to "the faithless one" and tore them all up. "I decided to go to Paris and kill this Blondel whom I didn't even know, who was daring to marry a girl who belonged to me, and who was thought of as my wife. I was furious with her father and her brother for not telling me about it." After a sleepless night he thought better of the murder plan, and consoled himself instead by going to visit Esther.

Esther read through the whole series of letters, which at this stage still included his own, and told him she had never read anything so interesting. "'These damnable letters,' I replied, 'are going to kill me. After dinner you'll help me to burn them all, even the one that tells me to burn them.'" Her answer was, "Make me a present of them for now, I'll never let them out of my hands, and I'll give them back to you tomorrow." She also looked at Manon's miniature portrait in a gold snuffbox, and pleased him by saying that such a vile soul didn't deserve to have such a pretty face. "I passed with her one of those days which one could call happy, if happiness consists in shared and tranquil satisfaction, without any tumultuous passion." Casanova was never one to blame himself for long when things went wrong. "Only Esther could make me forget Manon, who was already seeming unworthy of everything I had wanted to do for her." It's far from clear what that was supposed to mean.

At some later time, at a social event in Paris, Casanova realized that Manon was about to show up and tactfully left. They never saw each other again.

Manon's marriage contract with Blondel lists among her possessions clothing and jewelry, 250 books (mostly plays) bound in calfskin, and a number of musical instruments: "a harpsichord painted green and gilded, a harp with its case, two guitars, and a violin." Their union seems to have been pleasant if unromantic; they had one son who died at birth and another who grew up to be a distinguished architect himself. Blondel died in 1774 and Manon in 1776, aged only thirty-six. If Casanova knew about that he doesn't say so.[6]

Even though we have some of Manon's letters, understanding the relationship must still be a matter of guesswork. Most biographers have treated her in a cursory way, since Casanova himself does that in the *Histoire*. Ian Kelly concludes that her letters display "a cool sense of self-worth and a serene unwillingness to risk much in love." Casanova did apparently believe that she lured him into the engagement and perhaps exaggerated her own passion. Judith Summers gives Manon a full chapter in *Casanova's Women* but is disgusted with both participants: on the one hand Casanova establishes "a pattern of psychological abuse," but on the other hand Manon is "clingy, obsessive, and chronically insecure."[7]

Both interpretations depend on reading between the lines, since the letters themselves don't suggest cool serenity. In order to be sure that Manon was clingy we would need to know much more than we do about the encouragement Casanova gave her—or failed to give. My own impression is that she was deeply in love, and kept overcoming her doubts about him until it was impossible to do so any longer.

For Casanova, at any rate, a relationship was something that ran its course and left little damage behind. Chantal Thomas says, "He is unaware of the weight of amorous complications, for which the English term 'affair' gives an accurate idea; he likes to escape every time through the too-loose mesh of his net." He wanted to believe that in each case, the woman was as willing as he was to move on. Manon's letters suggest that we're right to doubt it.[8]

Histoire de ma vie
jusqu'à l'an 1797

Nequiquam sapit qui sibi non sapit
Cic: ad Treb:

Preface

Je commence par déclarer à mon lecteur que dans tout ce que
j'ai fait de bon ou de mauvais dans toute ma vie, je suis sûr d'avoir
merité ou demerité, et que par consequent je dois me croire libre.
La doctrine des Stoiciens, et de toute autre secte sur la force du Destin est
une chimere de l'imagination qui tient à l'atheisme. Je suis non
seulement monotheiste, mais chretien fortifié par la philosophie,
qui n'a jamais rien gâté.

Je crois à l'existence d'un Dieu immateriel auteur, et maitre de
toutes les formes; et ce qui me prouve que je n'en ai jamais douté,
c'est que j'ai toujours compté sur sa providence, recourant à lui
par le moyen de la priere dans toutes mes detresses; et me trouvant
toujours exaucé. Le desespoir tue: la priere le fait disparoitre; et a=
près elle l'homme confie, et agit. Quels soyent les moyens, dont l'
Etre des etres se sert pour detourner les malheurs imminens sur ceux
qui implorent son secours, c'est une recherche au dessus du pouvoir
de l'entendement de l'homme, qui dans le meme instant qu'il contem=
ple l'incomprensibilité de la providence divine, se voit réduit à l'a=
dorer. Notre ignorance devient notre seule ressource; et les vrais heu=
reux sont ceux qui la cherissent. Il faut donc prier Dieu, et croire d'
avoir obtenu la grace, même quand l'apparence nous dit que nous ne l'
avons pas obtenu. Pour ce qui regarde la posture du corps dans laquelle
il faut être quand on adresse des voeux au créateur, un vers du

2. Venice from the South

3. Arlecchino and Arlecchina

4. The San Samuele Theater

5. Carnival Costumes

6. Guardi, *The Ridotto*

7. Caravaggio, *The Card Sharps*

8. Italy in 1730

9. Guardi, *Venice from the Bacino di San Marco*

10. Tiepolo, *Il Burchiello*

11. Pope Benedict XIV

12. Farinelli

13. Francesco Casanova, *Audience Given by the Grand Vizier*

14. Longhi, *The Alchemists*

15. The Palazzo Bragadin

16. Francesco Casanova, *Giacomo Casanova*

17. Fragonard, *Les Hasards Heureux de l'Escarpolette*

18. Boucher, *Mme. de Pompadour*

19. Boucher, *Reclining Nude (Louise Murphy)*

20. Guardi, *The Parlor of the San Zaccaria Convent*

21. Greuze, *Cardinal Bernis*

22. Morland, *The Fair Nun Unmasked*

23. The Hall of the Great Council

24. Nathaniel Parr, *A View of the Doge's Palace*

25. Jean François de Troy, *The Oyster Lunch*

26. Nattier, *Manon Balletti*

27. Huber, *Le Lever de Voltaire*

28. Soho Square

29. Sans Souci

30. King Stanislaw August Poniatowski

31. Dueling Pistols

32. Mengs (?), *Giacomo Casanova*

33. Dux (Duchkov) Castle

Dux bei Töplitz.

34. A View of Dux

Rolling Stone

To this day nobody is sure why Casanova suddenly hit the road in early 1760, still less why he continued to ricochet around Europe for the next two years. A possible clue survives in a report that was sent at the time to the Duc de Choiseul, who had replaced Bernis as foreign minister (Bernis had offended Mme. de Pompadour, his onetime lover, by trying to rein in her financial extravagance, and was banished from court). According to this report, a general in the Austrian army "claims that [Casanova] should be watched closely, and for some time he has kept him under strict surveillance. He suspects him to be a most dangerous spy, capable of the greatest crimes." Alarming though that sounds, Choiseul ignored it and the Paris chief of police told the informant that no further investigation would be needed. An obvious inference would be that Casanova was acting covertly on behalf of the French government, whether as a spy or in some other way.[1]

At some point during this year Casanova began calling himself the Chevalier de Seingalt, a name he would use regularly from then on; he had run away from enough debts to need a new identity. He had already claimed to be the Count de Farussi, which would have been a title of nobility; this new alias was less pretentious. A *chevalier* or "knight" was often a younger son in an aristocratic family, not likely to inherit the title.

Adventurers routinely adopted aliases, changing them whenever convenient, and that was easy to do when there was no such thing as a standard passport. The record for aliases was probably held by a certain Stjiepan Zanovich, who at various times was Count Babbindon, Castriotto prince of Albania, the abbé Warta, and twenty other identities, or non-identities.[2]

There have been many guesses about how Casanova came up with "Seingalt," none very convincing. There is apparently no territory or town of that name anywhere in Europe, and perhaps he chose it for that very reason. Attempts to associate it with the famous Swiss abbey of Saint Gall seem groundless. People who met him often wrote it like that, however, which shows that he must have pronounced "Sein" in the French rather than the German way, rhyming with "man," not "mine."

He may simply have liked the sound of it. He always asserted defiantly his right to rename himself at will. Voltaire, he noted, made up that name for himself and "couldn't have achieved immortality with the name Arouet"— though that ignores the difference between a pen name and an alias.[3]

A German mayor once pressed Casanova on this point, insisting that he had to be either Casanova or Seingalt but not both. He denied it. "We are all free to dispose of the alphabet. Thus I've chosen eight letters which I've combined to form the word 'Seingalt,' I've taken this word for my name, and I will prove to anyone who lays claim to it that it belongs only to me." When the bewildered mayor protested that one has to bear the name of one's father, Casanova remarked slyly, "Even your own name may not be authentic, since it may well be that you're not the son of the man you take to be your father." He must have had his own story in mind, with the possibility that his real father was the theater owner Grimani.[4]

A rare contemporary mention of Casanova has survived in a Berne library, a letter of recommendation to the poet and scientist Albrecht von Haller:

> For a couple of months we've had a foreigner with us named the Chevalier de Seingalt. This foreigner is worthy to meet you, and you'll find him a true curiosity. He's an enigma we've been unable to decipher, or even to discover what he is. He doesn't know as much as you do, but he knows a lot, speaks with much fire about everything, and appears to have seen and read prodigiously. It would seem that he doesn't want to be known. He tells me that he's a free man, a citizen of the world, and observes the laws of each sovereign under whom he lives. He has given me proof of his learning in the Cabbala, astonishing if true, that makes him almost a magician (*un sorcier*).[5]

"He doesn't want to be known" was a shrewd insight.

Casanova's first stop after leaving Paris was a six-week stay in Cologne and nearby Bonn, the capital of the Electorate of Cologne, one of the members of the loose confederation known as the Holy Roman Empire. Whatever he may have been doing there, he had plenty of money and carried himself like a person of distinction. His preening gave offense to Baron Friedrich Wilhelm Ketteler, the Austrian military attaché, who was doubly annoyed because he had his eye on the pretty wife of the mayor of Cologne, and Casanova began to look like competition. In the *Histoire* Casanova calls this lady Mme. X; her real name was Marie ("Mimi") van Groote. It was Ketteler who reported that Casanova was a dangerous spy.

Once Casanova started paying attention to Mme. X, she made a demand that could lead to big trouble but could also show off his social savoir-faire. Baron Ketteler was giving a big supper ball and had pointedly failed to invite Casanova. "I will consider myself dishonored," Mme. X told him, "if you're not at this supper. You could never give me a better mark of your affection and esteem." He replied that he would obey her, even though "this fatal order may cost me my life, since I'm not a man who can feign indifference if this brute should offend me." With his equivocal social status, it was important never to ignore an insult. Whether or not Ketteler was a brute, Casanova despised him. "He was advanced in age, with disagreeable features, and with no quality of mind that could lay claim to being loved."[6]

Casanova really did fear a duel, and "passed two hours in hell" before the ball began, but he then showed up and behaved with easy politeness. Ketteler ignored him at first but finally confronted him: "Monsieur, I did not invite you." "I responded, very respectfully but firmly, 'That is true, *mon général,* but being certain that you merely forgot to do it, I've nevertheless come to pay my respects to Your Excellency.'" The general was checkmated, and as Rives Childs says, "Casanova's handling of so delicate a situation was in every respect characteristic of him: adroit, bold, but at the same time respectful, and preserving a perfect sangfroid."[7]

Having passed this chivalric test, he was duly rewarded. Mme. X gave him a tour of her house, in which a little staircase led down to an attached chapel, and arranged for him to hide there when she knew her husband would be asleep in a different room than her own. Needing a place of concealment until the chapel was locked for the night, he decided on a booth where priests heard confessions. "Choosing the darkest confessional, I got into it at four o'clock and stayed crouching there, commending myself to God." The irony has to be intentional. Any God worth acknowledging would encourage love-making, not punish it.

At five the chapel was locked, and Casanova crept up the unlit stairs in the dark and waited at the top for Mme. X to appear with a candle. "One may imagine the shared delights of this happy night. . . . We spent seven hours in intoxication, interrupted often by amorous talk before renewing our delights." To describe her beauty in romantic metaphors he invokes his favorite Ariosto, quoted in verse: "Her small rounded breasts were like beads of milk newly pressed from a reed. They were so set apart that they resembled two little hillocks, and between them was a pleasant shady dell in the season when winter snow still lies in the hollows. The prominent hips, the flat belly, more limpid than a looking glass, those white thighs, they all seemed the work of Phidias or of an even finer hand." Casanova ends the quotation with "etc. etc." and omits what follows: "Am I to describe to you those parts, too, which she was so vainly hoping to conceal?"[8]

After another delicious night Mme. X had to leave for the country, and Casanova could congratulate himself on a passionate affair that supposedly left no sourness behind. Ever since Lucrezia in Rome and Andriana in Corfu, he had especially enjoyed episodes with married women. According to him, episodes is exactly what they were—brief holidays from ordinary existence that carried no weight of future obligation.

Soon after Mme. X. departed, Casanova ran into an Italian actress he knew. She was coaching her young daughter, "a real jewel," to attract the attention of a duke and become his mistress. The duke was known to insist on virgins, so there was no chance for Casanova to sleep with the girl, but the mother and daughter both cheerfully allowed him to verify her virgin condition. This led to yet another encounter à trois, but with a new twist: he had sex with the mother while gazing at the daughter. "She seemed not in the least annoyed that I needed this tableau to perform as a lover with her. Evidently she thought of the girl she adored as part of herself, but was sure that hers was the leading role. She was wrong about that." All three of them were playing roles.

Then it was on to Stuttgart, where some card sharps rendered Casanova helpless with drugged wine and robbed him. The next day he thought of fighting them, but decided that the best plan was to get out of town fast, which he did by climbing down a rope from a window that overlooked the city walls—a sort of parodic reprise of the escape from the Piombi. He stopped this time in Zurich, "the richest city in Switzerland," and paused for some self-examination.

"I saw that I had brought upon myself all the misfortunes that oppressed me, and I had abused all the favors that Fortune had given me. I decided to stop being Fortune's plaything and escape her clutches entirely." He thought he might purchase a country estate and settle down, but that was a totally improbable fantasy, as if the rolling stone could ever stop rolling.[9]

In Zurich Casanova pawned most of his ostentatious wardrobe for eighty French louis, and the receipt has survived in the archive in Czechoslovakia— he kept it for the rest of his life. Upon repayment, the pawnbroker wrote,

> I will return to him a blue jacket lined with ermine, a white embroidered waistcoat and trousers, a velvet suit in four colors, a lace muff, a varnished toothpick case decorated in gold, two muslin shirts with lace cuffs, a pair of English lace cuffs, a signet ring showing a coat of arms, a Hercules signet, a Galba signet, a signet showing a Roman chariot, a two-sided signet with two heads, another with a compass on one side and a head on the other, a little gold shoe gusset, a gold charm depicting two legs, another with three towers, a rock crystal flask mounted in gold and enameled, a gold box, a gold and steel knife, an amethyst needle surrounded with small gems, and a golden corkscrew.

All of this was what Dickens's Wemmick would call "portable property," easily converted into cash and back again as needed.[10]

Setting out on foot with no destination in mind, Casanova happened upon a grand edifice that turned out to be the famous Benedictine monastery of Einsiedeln. The abbot, who was also a prince in the Empire, listened courteously to his scandalous confession and entertained him with a sumptuous dinner. This was clearly not a place of austere self-denial, and Casanova impulsively declared that he was ready to enroll as a monk. The abbot told him to go back to Zurich, think it over for two weeks, and then come back if he hadn't changed his mind.

All that was needed to change his mind was the sight, from the window of his inn, of four women getting out of a carriage. Three didn't interest him, but the fourth was very pretty and made eye contact. Dressed *en amazone,* in a riding costume, she had big black eyes "under intrepid eyebrows," a lily complexion, and rosy cheeks. "Defend yourselves, mortals, from an encounter like that, and hold on fanatically—if you can—to the crazy notion of burying yourselves in a monastery."

He must pursue this lady, but how? Talking with a waiter, he learned that she and her companions were on their way home to Soleure (Solothurn in

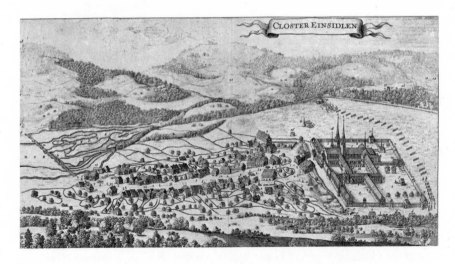

30. The Monastery at Einsiedeln

German) and would be dining in their room that evening. Immediately he decided to pose as the waiter himself, after paying the man suitably. "I took his carving knife, tied back my hair, removed my collar, and put on an apron over my scarlet vest trimmed with gold. Looking in a mirror I could see that I had the plebeian air and false modesty of the character I was going to play."

At table Casanova impressed the guests with his skill in carving the capon, and was even allowed to kneel down and unlace the pretty one's boots, despite her polite protest: "I'm sorry to have to put you to this trouble." "Am I not made for that, Madame?" Recalling the incident in the *Histoire* he adds, "These are the pleasures in my life that I can no longer obtain, but I do have the pleasure of remembering them. And in spite of that there are monsters who preach repentance, and foolish philosophers who say they are merely vanities. In my imagination I slept with the amazon. . . . This angel was sent expressly to me from Soleure to deliver me from the temptation of becoming a monk."

How could he turn imagination into reality? He hadn't been planning to visit Soleure, but he certainly would now. There he was welcomed by the Marquis de Chavigny, the French ambassador to the sixteen Swiss cantons, who was amused by the story of his performance as a waiter. From Chavigny he learned the lovely amazon's name; in the *Histoire* he calls her Mme. =, but a definite identification is possible. She was Maria Antonia Ludovika von Roll, twenty-two at the time, and recently married to the Baron Viktor Joseph von Roll, who was nearly thirty years older.[11]

She and her friends remembered Casanova well from the inn. Soon the story of the faux waiter was the talk of the town; apparently upper-class people thought it was a daring prank. The lady's husband "thanked me courteously for having done his wife the honor of unlacing her boots."

There was an opportunity for a closer approach through taking on a role in some amateur theatricals. The play was a comedy by Voltaire that had just been published, *L'Écossaise*. Lindane, the Scotswoman of the title, was played by Mme. von Roll. Casanova played a Lord Murray. It turned out to be a rare occasion when he was disconcerted by dissonance between a role and reality, since far from playing an irresistible lover, he was playing a rejected one.

> My blood ran cold during the third scene of the fifth act when Lindane said to me, "What? *You!* You *dare* to love me?" She pronounced those words so strangely, and in such a marked tone of contempt, that the spectators applauded wildly (*à l'outrance*). The applause annoyed and disconcerted me, for I felt that her performance had demeaned my honor. When they quieted down and I had to reply, as my role called for, "Yes, I adore you, and I must," I said those words so movingly that the applause was redoubled. A cry of *bis* (encore!) from four hundred voices forced me to repeat them.

What was acting and what was real? Did Mme. von Roll really despise Casanova, or was it merely the fictional Lindane despising Murray? Were they sending covert messages to each other under the cover of Voltaire's lines?

It soon became clear that she was indeed interested in an affair, and Casanova sought advice from the worldly Chavigny, who was familiar with Swiss ways. He should rent a country villa, Chavigny told him, and find a good excuse for doing so. The solution was to pretend to have some serious illness and retire there for his health. To support his story he should complain of symptoms that would be impossible to disprove, and call in a doctor Chavigny knew who prescribed country air and medicinal baths for pretty much everything. The second thing was to make friends with Baron von Roll, so that he would bring his wife to visit the invalid. Further developments would be up to Casanova.

The actual villa has been identified, a few miles from Soleure on the banks of the river Aar. Along with it came a pretty housekeeper, a widow named Mme. Dubois. In due course Mme. von Roll and her husband arrived for a visit, together with an unpleasant Mme. F. whom Casanova had disliked when he first saw her in Zurich, and who was furious during *L'Écossaise* because she didn't get to play Lindane.

Casanova and Mme. von Roll agreed that he would come to her apartment after midnight, when darkness would be complete, and that they would keep very quiet lest her husband in the next room wake up. As he groped his way through the door, a hand covered his mouth and he was pushed down on a couch. Knowing that sunrise would come early, "I had only two hours before me, and I didn't waste a single minute. . . . Her furies seemed to surpass my own and raised my soul to heaven."

And then it all blew up. The next morning Mme. von Roll asked him sadly why he never showed up, a question "that froze my blood." In the dark he must have made love instead with Mme. F., "a monster from hell." It was what was known in the Elizabethan theater as a bed trick.

After Mme. F. departed she sent him a letter explaining that she had punished him for slighting her in public at the play. She also taunted him for having been so passionate. "I've had my revenge by unmasking your plotting and the hypocrisy of Mme. von Roll, who can no longer treat me with the air of superiority she gets from her fake virtue. . . . You can no longer believe that she's a miracle of nature, since if you mistook me for her, I must not be any different from her, and that should cure you of the mad passion that possessed you."

This was bad enough, but what she went on to say was worse. "You must know, Monsieur, that for ten years I've had a little indisposition that I've never been able to cure. You did enough last night to contract it, and I advise you to seek treatment right away. I'm warning you so that you will avoid infecting your beauty, who in her ignorance might then give it to her husband. . . . It's up to you to bury this story in silence, and I urge you to do so."

Casanova was desperate to get back at the monster from hell, but at a loss how to do it. With unexpected resourcefulness, the housekeeper Mme. Dubois came to his aid. He had been traveling with a clever and mischievous manservant named Leduc, who had just confessed that he had a bad case of venereal disease. Mme. Dubois' suggestion was to send Leduc to Mme. F to declare that it was he who had slept with her, not Casanova, and to demand a hefty payment to keep quiet about the infection she had given him.

Mme. F took the bait, paid Leduc off, and said she would be leaving town for a while. The tables were thus turned once more. "It's you," Casanova gratefully told Mme. Dubois, "who are the author of this farce, masterfully played." She cheered him up further by saying she was sure the "little indisposition" was nothing but *fleurs blanches,* a harmless discharge known as leukorrhea, and that turned out to be correct.

No one has been able to determine who Mme. Dubois was. Casanova doesn't mention her first name, and if he did he would probably have made it up, and for that matter "Dubois" as well. He refers to her as "la Dubois"; as *ma gouvernante,* "housekeeper"; and as *ma bonne,* "maid." She was very intelligent and, having lived in England, liked to read John Locke.

What was most upsetting was the reaction of Mme. von Roll when she understood what had happened. "But how could you spend two hours with that woman without perceiving, in spite of the darkness, that it wasn't me? I'm humiliated that the difference between us made no impression on you. She is much smaller than me, much scrawnier, and ten years older, and what really astonishes me is that she has bad breath." It was a killing shot. Casanova always acknowledged the role of imagination in sex, but he also prided himself on appreciating the individuality of each of his partners. The best response he could come up with was: "I was intoxicated with love, my dear friend, and it was you alone whom I had before the eyes of my soul."

This passage of dialogue, incidentally, may help to confirm that Casanova didn't make the whole thing up. Why would he invent such a humiliation if it didn't really happen?

Casanova was about to move on, but he did get one opportunity to be alone with Mme. von Roll. Her husband was briefly away on a day trip. "With just one hour before me, which would have to be the last, I fell at her feet, and she made no resistance to my desires, which to my great regret had to be restrained by the concern I had to have for her health. In what she did allow me to do, the great pleasure she experienced convinced me how wrong I had been in imagining myself happy with Mme. F."

So, as Casanova prefers to end his stories, all's well that ends well. He and Mme. Dubois chatted while she was helping him get over his infection, and she said that although she had been married she had never had "the misfortune to fall in love." Soon they were sleeping together, companionably more than romantically.

Right at this point in the *Histoire,* about halfway through the massive manuscript, there is a noticeable flagging of energy in the narration. There will be numerous high points still to come, but the accumulation of names and places grows endlessly with less frequent passages of vivid re-creation. It's evident that life itself was starting to feel repetitive. In this summer of 1760 Casanova was thirty-five years old, Dante's age when he was lost in the dark wood, and he was beginning to feel that he was just going through the motions.

Accompanied by Mme. Dubois, who was planning to return to her family home in Lausanne, Casanova set out for Berne. There she went with him to a bath house that doubled as a brothel, and they were both fascinated by a pair of girls who performed much as C. C. and M. M. once did in the casino on Murano. "The coupling of these girls, even if comical, didn't fail to arouse the most intense voluptuousness in us. My *bonne* was carried away and abandoned herself completely to nature, anticipating everything I could desire. The party lasted for two hours, and we returned to our inn very satisfied." By now he had fully recovered from his infection, whatever it was.[12]

From then on, according to Casanova, "We regarded ourselves as husband and wife, and I couldn't foresee that the day would come when we would part. When one is in love one thinks of that as unbelievable."

A curious episode followed. They had gotten to know a gentleman named Ludwig de Muralt-Favre who had two young daughters, the older of whom was thirteen, "brunette and very pretty." Casanova calls her Sara, perhaps as a disguise; that was actually her little sister's name, and hers was Marguérite. She was giddily playful, pretending to be much more naïve than she actually was, and one morning jumped into bed with Mme. Dubois. "Putting her hand under the covers, she tickled her and declared, while kissing her, that she was her little husband and wanted to give her a baby. My *bonne* laughed."

The next morning the girl stripped naked, uncovered Mme. Dubois, "and showed off so many postures that I felt a desire to let her see the thing itself. She watched most attentively until the end, seeming astonished. 'Do it again,' she said. 'I can't,' I replied, 'since as you can see, I'm dead.' Counterfeiting innocence, she undertook my resurrection, and succeeded so well that my *bonne* said that it was up to her to make me die again." No doubt Sara knew exactly what she was doing. Records in Berne show that Muralt-Favre got into trouble with the law for prostituting his daughters. "Sara" would turn up again in Casanova's life in London, four years later.[13]

The relationship with Mme. Dubois ended pragmatically. Chavigny's majordomo, an older man named Lebel, wrote to her to propose marriage, offering a generous financial settlement. She told Casanova that she wanted to turn him down, but they both began to wonder if that was a good idea. They respected Chavigny and wrote to ask his advice, which was, predictably, that she would make a big mistake if she threw this opportunity away. It wouldn't be a love match, but Lebel was a good man, and after some hesitation they agreed that she should accept him. In Lausanne Lebel met them at her mother's house and the thing was settled.

Casanova and Mme. Dubois shed some tears, but he ended by feeling good about himself. "I regarded her as a treasure who had been mine, and after giving me happiness would become another man's, with my full consent." She did tell him, or so he claims, "Be sure that I have never loved anyone but you, and that you are the only one who has made me understand the power of the senses."

Casanova went on by himself to Geneva and stayed there at Les Balances, the inn where he had parted from Henriette. It was at this time that he saw the words that were scratched into the windowpane eleven years before, *Tu oublieras aussi Henriette.*

CHAPTER 18

Jousting with Voltaire

Casanova stayed in Geneva for several days, with the sole purpose of visiting the great Voltaire at his estate just outside the city (he lived there to be safe from potential arrest in France). Born wealthy, and wealthier still thanks to shrewd investments, he lived like a grand seigneur, receiving hundreds of visitors a year from all over Europe, accepting homage and dispensing witticisms.

Voltaire was surrounded by a large entourage when Casanova delivered a carefully planned opening speech: "This is the happiest moment of my life. At last I see my master. For the past twenty years, Monsieur, I have been your student." The great man replied, "Honor me with another twenty, and then promise to bring me my fee." Already they were sparring, in a desultory way. "I promise," Casanova said, "but you must promise to wait for me." Voltaire was sixty-six at the time, so that was a complimentary way of saying he should live to a great old age. "I give you my word," he replied, "and I'll give up my life rather than fail to keep it." This unremarkable exchange had the entire group applauding and roaring with laughter, which they continued to do whenever their hero fired off a bon mot.[1]

Casanova regarded the encounter as momentous, and he narrated it at great length in the *Histoire*, working from detailed notes. "I spent part of the night and the next morning writing down the three conversations I had with him, which I have now copied in abridged form." The two of them were concerned mainly to impress each other, and their audience of course.

A historian calls this "a veritable jousting match," and another says, "To prove oneself an illustrious man's equal, one must engage him in polemics. Voltaire, that literary divinity, provoked the revolt of rebel angels, all trying to build up their reputations by dethroning him. They rarely succeeded."[2]

During the first of Casanova's several visits they mostly recited poetry, at great length. Casanova claimed to have the whole of *Orlando Furioso* by heart (and all of Horace as well); Voltaire in turn recited a long passage from Ariosto in excellent Italian. Casanova, always the method actor, wept copiously when delivering some lines about tears flowing down the hero's cheeks, which prompted Voltaire to embrace him and exclaim, "I've always said, if you want to make people weep, weep yourself; but to do that, the tears must come from your soul."

It was going well until Casanova's final visit. They began talking about religion, whose abuses Voltaire always denounced; he used to sign his correspondence with *Écrasez l'infâme,* "Crush the infamous thing," meaning the institutional church. Casanova told him that he was wasting his time attacking superstition, since people were never going to give it up, and challenged him to say what he proposed to put in its place. Voltaire retorted, "I like that! When I deliver the human race from a wild beast that's devouring it, how can I be asked what I would replace it with?"

Casanova's rejoinder was cynically realistic: "It doesn't devour them; on the contrary, it's necessary to their existence. . . . Between two evils, one must choose the lesser. A people without superstition would be philosophical, and philosophers never want to obey. The people can be happy only if they are crushed [he used the Voltairean word *écrasé*], trampled underfoot, and kept in chains."

Voltaire clearly thought he was scoring a point when he asked, "Are you free in Venice?" True to his conservative politics, Casanova replied, "As much as one can be under an aristocratic government." And he added provocatively, "My detention, for example, was an act of proud despotism, but knowing that I had myself abused my liberty, I sometimes felt that they were quite right to imprison me without the usual formalities."

Voltaire was no radical—at one time he lived in Potsdam as the house philosopher of Frederick the Great—but he was critical of the abuses of the Ancien Régime. For Casanova, however, that was the milieu in which he thrived. However much he may have transgressed the rules, he needed them to be predictably in place. Eighteenth-century adventurers, Alexandre Stroev says, exploited a privileged society and couldn't have existed without it. "Society creates its adventurers, gives them their form, suggests their roles and their actions. . . . The adventurer fights for liberty, equality, and fraternity, but for himself only. He needs limits so he can exceed them, and a hierarchy in order to climb up it."[3]

Casanova's visit was intended to establish him as a serious intellectual in Voltaire's eyes, and when it did nothing of the kind he was bitter. He recalled with satisfaction what the scientist Haller had told him on the way to Geneva, that Voltaire was worth knowing, "but contrary to the laws of physics, he's bigger when seen from afar." In later published writings Casanova kept coming back obsessively to Voltaire, in what one writer describes as "love-hatred," piling up critiques that harp constantly on the same themes: he was proud, greedy for fame and money, vindictive, and an intolerant fanatic in his own way. Most cutting of all was Casanova's judgment that Voltaire was a popularizer, not an original thinker—which was perfectly true.[4]

All the same, by the time Casanova was writing the *Histoire* he regretted his campaign against Voltaire, who was after all a great "athlete of reason." He admitted that he had been writing from anger, and anticipated that "posterity will number me among the Zoiluses [a Greek grammarian who criticized Homer]; the humble reparation I'm now making will perhaps never be read." He would have been delighted to know that the twentieth-century statesman François Mitterrand would call the *Histoire* "a very great book, probably the greatest book of the eighteenth century," and would add that it was rivaled only by Voltaire.[5]

Casanova thought of Voltaire as a poet, playwright, and thinker, not as the immortal satirist we admire today. He makes no mention of *Candide,* which came out the previous year, or for that matter of the Seven Years War that was raging at the time. Voltaire's mordant critique of warfare in *Candide* was altogether different from Casanova's indifference: "Climbing over heaps of the dead and dying, Candide came to a village in ashes. It was an Abar village which the Bulgars had razed to the ground, in accordance with international law. Here old men riddled with wounds or lead shot looked on as their wives lay dying, their throats cut, clutching their children to their blood-stained breasts; over there lay young girls in their last agonies, disemboweled after having satisfied the natural urges of various heroes." From Casanova's *Histoire*—and for that matter from Rousseau's *Confessions*—one would hardly know that the war took place at all.[6]

Two portraits give a good sense of Voltaire, and also of the ways Casanova was out of his depth with him. One of them shows him at the writing desk

31. Voltaire

where he spent endless hours, corresponding with intellectuals all over Europe who looked up to him as their hero. A warm coat and hat defend him against the chilly Swiss winter, and his keen expression and wry smile reflect the ironist who wrote the immortal *Candide*. He's smiling because it appears the passage of time is bringing progress to the world; the book on the table is labeled *Changemen(t)s arrivés dans le Globe*.

The other portrait, *Le Lever de Voltaire* by Jean Huber (color plate 27), shows him beginning his day. The royal levee (the usual English form) was the ceremonial reception of visitors by a king, and Voltaire was a kind of intellectual monarch. Here, however, he's awkwardly putting on his trousers like anyone else, one skinny leg at a time, and is already dictating to his secretary.

This image illustrates the creation of modern celebrity as it was developing during the eighteenth century. People who knew Voltaire through his writings were eager to see him in private life, as an individual rather than an icon.

Huber was a member of Voltaire's circle for twenty years, and painted him so many times that he acquired the nickname "Voltaire Huber." When Voltaire complained that he was being made to look ridiculous, Huber countered that a touch of ridicule was exactly what was needed to humanize him. "The painting's appeal," the Voltaire Foundation says, "rested on the impression it created of a voyeuristic glimpse into Voltaire's intimate life."[7]

Voltaire's influence was not just literary, but moral and political too. After the Revolution his monument would stand next to Rousseau's in the Panthéon in Paris. As a popular song had it (a character in Hugo's *Les Misérables* sings it at the barricades),

> *Je suis tombé par terre,*
> *C'est la faute à Voltaire,*
> *Le nez dans le ruisseau,*
> *C'est la faute à Rousseau.*

"I've fallen to the ground, it's the fault of Voltaire, my nose in the ditch, it's the fault of Rousseau." Casanova could only dream of making a difference in the world like that, and even if he did, he would never have allowed a painter to depict him struggling into his trousers.

The encounter with Voltaire might have gone better if he and Casanova had talked about life rather than about books and ideas. What Voltaire once wrote in a poem could have furnished a fine meeting point for them: *La véritable sagesse / Est de savoir fuir la tristesse / Dans les bras de la volupté*, "True wisdom is knowing how to escape sadness in the arms of sensual pleasure."[8]

Significant as the encounter with the great man may have felt to Casanova, his long account sparkles only when he pauses for a vivid portrait of a nobleman who happened to be present, the Duc de Villars.

I thought I was seeing a woman of seventy dressed as a man, thin, emaciated, and feeble, who might have been beautiful in her youth. His cheeks, streaked with veins, were covered with rouge and his lips with carmine, and his eyebrows were blackened. He had false teeth, and false hair was glued firmly to his head by a pomade scented with ambergris; a big bouquet in his top buttonhole reached to his chin. He affected gracious gestures, and spoke in such a low voice that I could hardly understand what he was saying. All the same he was very polite and affable, with manners that went back to the time of the Regency [forty years earlier]. I've been told that when he was young he loved women, but when he got older he took on a modest role as wife to three or four pretty minions, who took turns enjoying the honor of sleeping with him.

The deft portrait ends with a deadpan statement that crystallizes the privileges of the Ancien Régime: "This duke was governor of Provence."

Not surprisingly, the theme that does come to life in the account of the visit to Geneva is sex. Having formed an acquaintance with a distinguished Genevan syndic, one of the chief magistrates, Casanova accepted an invitation to spend an evening at an Orgy, which he spells with a capital O. The syndic quoted the church father Clement of Alexandria, who held that "modesty, which seems so deeply rooted in women, goes only as far as their underwear, since as soon as you get them to take it off, there's no longer even a shadow of it." The saint was condemning this, of course, not appreciating it.

His new friend introduced Casanova to a pair of young sisters and their cousin "who were made for love, even though they couldn't be called beauties. They had an easy and welcoming manner, intelligent faces, and an appearance of gaiety that did not deceive." He was warned that it would be disastrous for them to get pregnant, in view of the strict morality of Geneva, so he settled for "an ejaculation of which I was truly in need. I kissed again and again the lovely hands that had condescended to this task, always humiliating for a woman who is made for love; but it couldn't be humiliating in the farce we were playing, since after kindly sparing them I did them the same service, assisted by the voluptuous syndic. They thanked me endlessly."

For the next evening Casanova had another plan. The syndic was happy to use a condom, but Casanova refused "to envelop myself in a dead skin." So he gave a jeweler six Spanish pieces of eight, to be melted down into three golden balls weighing two ounces apiece. These, he assured the young women, once inserted into "the cabinet of love," would be an infallible contraceptive, as he had proved during fifteen years of experience. Somehow the chemical action of the metal would do the trick. They were skeptical but agreed to try, fearing however that the balls might drop out. No problem, he declared: he would teach them a posture that would make that impossible.

A candle was brought for close inspection, the "charming cousin" made the experiment, and sure enough the ball did drop out. So as before, Casanova refrained from penetration, and "on parting from them, I saw that the three girls were full of gratitude." They thanked the syndic earnestly for setting the whole thing up.

In retrospect the encounter with Voltaire had been a sad, even embarrassing disappointment. Casanova liked to think of himself as an intellectual, and he was one, but politics and ideas occupied only part of his thinking, whereas they were the element Voltaire lived in. What he was still learning was that his own genius was for recreating lived experience in his writing, whether in the portrait of the Duc de Villars or the game with the golden balls.

CHAPTER 19

Still Rolling

After leaving Geneva in August of 1760 Casanova was on the road again, pausing at various places that happened to appeal to him. He was thinking of going to Italy, though not to Venice where he was still in danger of arrest. During the next four months he would stay in Aix-les-Bains, Grenoble, Avignon, Marseille, Genoa, Florence, Rome, and Naples. The itinerary would be impossible to summarize in detail even if it were all interesting, which it's not. Of the most memorable episodes, the first was an affair of the heart. But when that was over, and it didn't last long, it left plenty of unanswered questions.

Aix-les-Bains was a fashionable spa, and Casanova went there from Geneva because it was a well-known haunt of gamblers. He still had a lot of money, which he kept in a locked casket, and he plunged enthusiastically into gambling. He also dallied casually with a Mme. Z whose husband had no objection—"he was one of those men who would rather pass as cuckolds than as fools." That was a common game: the female partner would engage a victim's interest while the card sharp was fleecing him. Casanova understood that, and was in no danger of being fleeced, but he didn't mind taking advantage of Mme. Z's availability.

And then he was stopped short by romance. He introduces it by declaring, "Here, my dear reader, is an altogether novelistic event, but for all that it's no less true. If you believe that it's fantastic, you're mistaken." Credible or not, the story is disturbing, in ways that Casanova seems not to grasp. Long ago on

Murano, M. M. had picked him out from a crowd and planned their assignations, along with her lover Bernis who was very much in on the game. This time another nun was involved, but it was a seduction by Casanova, and she resisted at first.[1]

After three weeks in Aix he happened to see a pair of nuns wearing veils, one young and one elderly. He was struck that their habit was the same sky-blue color as M. M. used to wear, which meant that they belonged to the same religious order. What really staggered him was a glimpse of the young one's face when she momentarily lifted her veil. "I was seeing M. M. herself! It was impossible to doubt it!" He watched them leave town and go to an isolated farmhouse, and he was desperate to know more. What could she possibly be doing here, so far from Venice? Perhaps she was pregnant and had come to Aix to deliver the baby in secrecy?

Soon afterward a peasant woman approached him and said that the mysterious nun had seen him staring at her, and asked that he visit that evening to talk. When he got to the farmhouse he seized her in the darkness, covered her face with kisses, and asked in Veneziano why she was there. She replied in French, and he was staggered all over again: he didn't recognize the voice. After she lit a candle he could see that although the resemblance to M. M. was astonishing, she was definitely someone else, with black hair and eyes whereas M. M. had light chestnut hair and blue eyes.

Her story was soon told. Her convent was in Chambéry, ten miles away. Just twenty-one, she had yielded to an admirer who climbed the wall into her convent garden, even though she didn't feel much for him, and was horrified to find that she was pregnant. In her innocence she thought that that could only happen if you did it three times. The reason she had asked to see Casanova was that she thought he might be an emissary from the seducer.

She wasn't entirely ignorant about sex, however. When Casanova asked if the desires of the flesh never showed themselves, she replied, "That's an inclination that we satisfy easily in the convent. When we accuse ourselves of it to our confessor, because we know it's a sin, he treats it as mere childishness and gives us absolution without even any penance. He's a wise and learned old priest, and austere in his morals."

She was indeed here to give birth in secrecy, though she had taken care to conceal that fact. She claimed to be suffering from hydropsy, a swelling due to fluid retention, and with that excuse had been permitted to come to Aix for a water cure. The older nun was her chaperone, and was now sound asleep because the peasant woman had surreptitiously given her a dose of opium as a soporific. "This viper wants me to return to our convent three days from now, since my malady has turned out to be incurable."

Here was a chance for Casanova to rescue a beautiful woman in distress, which he always enjoyed, and hopefully to sleep with her as well. He promised to return the next night, and advised her to make sure the chaperone got a double dose of opium to make sure she stayed asleep. That turned out to be a mistake. She didn't just go to sleep, she remained unconscious, and it seemed likely that she would die. But there could be no calling in a doctor, since then the secret would be out. "You must see," Casanova said, "that your happiness may depend upon this misfortune. Do not weep, Madame; let us submit ourselves to the will of God."

The old nun did indeed die. But neither Casanova nor the young nun thought of it as murder, or at any rate involuntary manslaughter. Rather, they had just let nature take its course—or perhaps it was even the will of the Almighty. Casanova often persuaded himself that events in his life were divinely sanctioned. "It seemed to me that in saving her I was carrying out an order from God. God had wanted her to appear to me as M. M. God had made me win a great deal of money. God had provided me with Mme. Z so that curious people wouldn't wonder why I was putting off my departure from Aix. What have I not attributed to God throughout my life! And yet the rabble of thinkers have always accused me of atheism." This isn't just rationalization; it's total disingenuousness. In the *Histoire* Casanova poses as more of a believer than we know he really was.

A priest was summoned. He agreed that the death must have been caused by apoplexy after too much alcohol, and arranged for burial.

When Casanova next visited, the young nun had already given birth, and the peasant woman had taken the infant to a hospice in Annecy twenty miles away. He then produced a double portrait of M. M., first dressed as a nun and then naked; evidently he always carried it with him. "That's *my* portrait," she exclaimed, "apart from the eyes and eyebrows. That's my habit! It's amazing! What a coincidence! I owe all my happiness to this resemblance. . . . Inscrutable providence divine!" She asked to borrow the portrait, and with money Casanova had given the peasant woman—the nun never accepted any for herself—she sent it out to have a local painter retouch it. As directed, he made the hair and eyes black.

Casanova always fell in love easily, but this time it felt genuine, certainly more than it had with Mme. Dubois or poor Manon. It was the uncanny resemblance to M. M. that first triggered his feelings, but by now they belonged

Et nous auſi nous ferons meres, car.........!

32. *Et Nous Aussi Nous Serons Mères, Car . . .*

to this new nun and not to a ghost from the past. She still dreaded committing a mortal sin by sleeping with him, but laughingly allowed him to relieve
her milk-swollen breasts. "It is sweet, my dear friend," he told her, "and the
little that I've swallowed has filled my soul with balm."

Casanova must have enjoyed the thrill of nursing at the breasts of a bride
of Christ, like an impious baby Jesus. The transgressive resonance of that idea
in his culture is captured in a drawing by Jean-Jacques Lequeu, *Et Nous Aussi
Nous Serons Mères, Car . . .* , "and we too, we will be mothers, for. . . . " Ostensibly this image celebrates the liberation of nuns from their convents after
the Revolution, looking forward to a future of domesticity. Rousseau, whose

first names Lequeu shared, had celebrated breast feeding as the maternal ideal. All the same, the drawing is nothing if not erotic.

This mingling of religion and eroticism was not uncommon at the time. When Casanova was in a Madrid church later on, "I saw an image of the Holy Virgin with the infant Jesus at her breast. Her uncovered breast, skillfully painted, inflamed the imagination. There was not a nobleman passing by the holy place who didn't order his carriage to stop so he could take a moment to pay homage to the goddess, and contemplate *beata uber quae lactaverunt aeterni patris filium.*" The quotation, adapted from the Vulgate Bible, means "the blessed breast that suckled the Son of the eternal Father." Orthodox theology, of course, does not consider the Virgin Mary a "goddess."[2]

When Casanova returned to the farmhouse the nun lamented that her resolve was weakening. "I've passed the cruelest of nights! I couldn't fall asleep without finding myself in your arms, and I would wake up with a start at the moment when I was about to commit the greatest of crimes." She was still determined not to yield, even though he assured her that she couldn't get pregnant so soon after childbirth.

That night they drank some wine and she went to sleep. At first he wondered if she was just pretending, which might be meant as an invitation; but no, she was definitely sound asleep, murmuring unintelligible words in her dream.

> Lying down next to her, I had no fear of awakening her by taking her in my arms; the movement she then made to receive me convinced me that her dream was continuing, and that everything I might do would only help to make it real. I managed to pull down her delicate chemise, and she stirred and took a deep breath as a child does that feels its vest being removed. I consummated the sweet crime in her, and with her, but before reaching the extremity she opened her lovely eyes. "Ah, God!" she exclaimed in an expiring voice, "then it's true!" After uttering those words she brought her mouth to mine to receive my soul.

This anticipates a classic male fantasy of a later generation, Keats's *Eve of St. Agnes,* in which a woman dreams that her lover is present and awakes to find it true. It also repeats a favorite theme of Casanova's: women find him so compelling that orgasm overtakes them spontaneously. All the same, even in his own telling, the episode is deeply disturbing. M. M. had been a practiced libertine, and it was she who initiated and managed their affair in Murano.

But Casanova took advantage of this vulnerable young woman in her sleep, knowing full well that she believed it would be a mortal sin. We have only his account of the dream to show that he was doing what she "really" wanted—in effect, to be raped. Biographers have either glanced at this story in passing or have simply retold it from Casanova's point of view. Most troublingly, she was in an immediate postnatal condition, and he gives no indication that he felt concerned about that. He claims that when they woke up the next morning, she told him earnestly, "We love each other, and we have crowned our love. I find that that I'm freed at last from all my anxieties. We have followed our destiny by obeying the precepts of imperious Nature."

That sounds more like his language, though, than the young nun's. And although he tries to gloss over his guilt, this may be the ugliest episode in the entire *Histoire*. Angelo Mainardi's severe judgment is entirely justified: "It has a double title to be called a descent into the Inferno, with the homicide and the betrayal of innocence."[3]

For his next visit Casanova brought a condom that he hoped to use, and admitted that he hadn't done so in the old days with the original M. M. "I was fortunate," he said. "I didn't give her a child, but if I had, I would have abducted her and taken her to Rome, where the Holy Father, seeing us at his feet, would have released her from her vows, and my dear M. M. would now be my wife." At this she cried out, "My God! M. M. is my name!" Presumably she meant the name she had taken as a nun, though Casanova doesn't say what it was. Is it conceivable that until now he still didn't know her name? More likely he did know it, but chose this moment of revelation to make the narrative more dramatic.

He put the condom on so she could understand its use, and when she stroked it she was startled by what happened. "O my God, what a pity! Unhappy me, he's dead!" He told her cheerfully, "Your alarm is enchanting. In a moment you'll see the little fellow revive, and so full of life that next time he won't die so easily." "That's incredible," was her reply.

Word now came that two nuns were coming to fetch her back to the convent, and he begged her to run away with him to Rome. He insisted that he would marry her there, and he meant it, or thought he did. She was adamant. "No. I have lived enough. Let me return to my tomb." This would not be a spouse she could put any trust in, and in any case, it's far from obvious that her religious doubts had been dispelled.

That night "we spent a dozen hours in bed making love, sometimes sleeping for a bit." At dawn they parted in tears and he returned to his inn, aware that she would be leaving the following morning. He got up early and set out on the road he knew they would use. "A short distance from Aix I saw my angel walking slowly, together with two nuns who begged alms from me in God's name. I gave them a louis and wished them *bon voyage*. M. M. didn't look at me."

In the *Histoire* Casanova recreates this brief relationship as a love affair, and he clearly needed to remember it that way, but it remains opaque and disturbing. In any case he got over it fast. After all, it was immediately before he went to Aix that he had been startled to see Henriette's message on the windowpane. He had reflected then, "I did still know how to love, but no longer with the same delicacy, with the emotions that make one lose one's heart, the gentleness of manners and integrity." That's confirmed by the story of this second M. M.[4]

The next stop was Grenoble, where Casanova decided to stay for a while. He went there because he had arranged to have letters waiting for him at a *poste restante*. One letter was from Mme. d'Urfé, the rich eccentric who hoped he might effect a magical resurrection for her, and she gave him the name of a congenial officer in the local army garrison. He was the Baron de Valenglart, who could give him an introduction "to all the good houses in town."

They hit it off well, and Valenglart helped him to find an elegant villa for short-term rental, along with its concierge or caretaker who was an accomplished chef. Soon Casanova was entertaining his new friend to a lavish banquet with a selection of superb wines, including "ratafia that was superior to the Turkish visnat that I drank with Yusuf Ali seventeen years before." That seemed extravagant, but he declared grandly, "Don't worry at all—I love expense." They finished off the evening with "a bottle of the divine liqueur of Grenoble, which consists of brandy, sugar, cherry, and cinnamon."[5]

The Casanova scholar Marie-Françoise Luna, a professor at the University of Grenoble, has successfully identified the villa, and it was spectacular. Named La Tronche after a nearby stream, it belonged to Charles Gabriel Justin de Barral, who often rented it out to suitable tenants. Luna says it was the largest and most luxurious property in the area, with extensive formal gardens running down to the river Isère. She adds that Grenoble itself "had been known since the seventeenth century for libertine thought and morals." A few years later Choderlos de Laclos was stationed in an army garrison there, and conceived the idea of *Les Liaisons Dangereuses*.[6]

The second M. M. was apparently pretty much forgotten, and Casanova was feeling good about himself. "I couldn't resist looking within and finding

33. The La Tronche Estate

that I was happy. In perfect health and in the flower of my age, with no duties and no foreseeable needs, provided with plenty of money, dependent on no one, fortunate in gambling, and willingly received by women who interested me, I was not wrong to say to myself, *Saute Marquis.*" He was quoting a popular line from a comedy by Jean-François Regnard, *Le Joueur,* in which a gambler tells himself that everything is going wonderfully well, "So come on, jump, Marquis!"

If Casanova knew the actual play, the full quotation would have appealed to him. The gambler is about to marry a rich widow and breaks into a dance for joy, exclaiming, *Près du sexe tu vins, tu vis, et tu vanquis; / Que ton sort est heureux! Allons, saute, Marquis!*—"With the fair sex you've come, you've seen, and you've conquered; how happy is your lot! Come on, jump, Marquis!" However, Casanova was never going to get married, and he might have remembered also that in the play the hero's hopes are abruptly dashed. In that case the allusion would be ironic.[7]

Before setting forth in quest of upper-class women, Casanova tried his luck with the servant girls at his villa, the caretaker's two pretty daughters and their pretty cousin. Leduc, the servant who had assisted in the scheme against Mme. F. in Soleure, was still with him, and understood without being told that he should pretend to be ill. That way the girls would have to take his place, and wait on Casanova in his bedroom. "Leduc was bold, insolent, malicious, and a libertine, but he could keep a secret and was faithful, so I had to endure him." Casanova made repeated attempts to get one of the girls alone with him—it didn't matter which—but they understood his game and flirted without risking anything.

Meanwhile he was making acquaintances in town, and was smitten by a tall, dark, gravely serious young woman who had black hair and black eyes—"I don't remember ever seeing more beautiful ones." We actually know her name: Anne Roman-Coupier. She was the impoverished daughter of an office clerk and on the lookout for a path to a comfortable life. Casanova was clearly not that path, and she fended off his rather tentative advances, but he thought up something more interesting. Discovering that the aunt she lived with was fascinated by astrology, he decided to exploit that. "Already a savant in the Cabbala, I might be one in astrology." He pored over a textbook and produced "eight pages of learned charlatanism."

According to the horoscope Casanova concocted, Anne would infallibly become the mistress of Louis XV, but only if she went immediately to Paris and found a way to meet the king. If she waited beyond her next birthday it would be too late. She was understandably skeptical, but her aunt was thrilled and began helping to make concrete plans. Meanwhile Casanova was equally thrilled, at the prospect of adding a new weapon to his arsenal. "The idea of becoming a celebrated astrologer in my century, when reasoning had discredited it so well, filled me with joy. I rejoiced, foreseeing myself sought by monarchs."

Incredibly, the fake prophecy came true. Anne went to stay with a sister in Paris and did get an introduction to Louis XV. She became his mistress for five years, bore him a son, and received the title of Baronesse de Meilly-Coulonge. After Louise Murphy, this was the second mistress Casanova had provided for the king; but then, the king had a great many of them. When he tired of Anne he endowed her with an enormous pension, and at her death in 1808 she was still a millionaire.

A historian comments, "Our man had bent destiny to his caprice, and one does not know what is most to be admired in this adventure: the audacity with which he forged predictions of this kind, or the course of events that undertook to transform the product of his imagination into reality."[8]

Or was it in fact transformed into reality? We have only Casanova's word for it. Why isn't this a possibility: he did meet Anne in Grenoble, and later on he heard that she had become the king's mistress. She might easily have decided on her own to seek her fortune in Paris, with the help of the sister who was already there. When he was writing the *Histoire* long afterward, it might have amused Casanova to invent his inspired prophecy. With the stories he tells, one never knows.

The night before he left Grenoble, Casanova managed to get all three of the girls at his estate—the caretaker's daughters and their cousin—into bed with him at the same time. That was not a problem from the point of view of the caretaker, who had profited handsomely from his spendthrift guest; when the possibility was broached "he replied, laughing, that that was their affair." The account of this foursome is so perfunctory, however, that it's hard to take it seriously. "After we passed four or five lively hours, nature sent us to sleep." Perhaps it's what Casanova wished had happened, not what actually did.

The next stop was Avignon, which had been the seat of the papacy in the fourteenth century during the so-called Babylonian Captivity, when there was a rival pope in Rome (not until 1791 did Avignon become part of France). Casanova went there for one reason only, to make a pilgrimage to nearby Fontaine de Vaucluse, where four centuries previously Petrarch had fallen in love with the unattainable Laura and immortalized her in his sonnets. A single line of verse, Casanova says, could move a heart of stone: *Morte bella parea nel suo bel viso*, "Death would seem beautiful on so lovely a face."

Unusually for Casanova, he pauses to describe the setting, which is indeed spectacular: the river Sorgue bursts from a cavern in a limestone cliff and then flows through the town. That sight provokes another quotation from Petrarch:

> *Chiare, fresche, e dolci acque*
> *Ove le belle membra*
> *Pose colei che sola a me par donna—*

"Waters clear, fresh, and sweet where she immerses her lovely limbs, she who is to me the only woman." Casanova climbed a steep hill to a ruined castle that was believed (wrongly) to have been where Petrarch lived. "I threw myself upon the ruins with arms outstretched, kissed them, and watered them with my tears."[9]

Among Casanova's unpublished papers is a brief essay critiquing the assumption that Petrarch's passion for Laura was purely platonic. Granted, she may have always resisted his advances, but the result was not exalted purity but sublimation. "Finding himself more in love than ever, he persuaded himself easily that sensual *jouissance* could not be the chief object of his passion, and being inclined to flatter himself, he sublimated himself in Platonic contemplations. By making the object of his passion divine, he made himself divine as well."[10]

No doubt Casanova picked up the concept of sublimation from his studies in alchemy, in which it was the process by which a solid is transformed into a gas without passing through a liquid state. Modern chemistry has retained the term, which in turn became the source for Freud's psychoanalytic usage. Casanova was not interested, however, in sublimating his own desires. He would never have wasted his time yearning for the unattainable.

He found no Laura in Avignon, but he did have a brief dalliance with a pair of actresses, one ugly and the other hunchbacked. He found the deformity fascinating, and had no trouble getting both of them in bed. He claims that the encounter was mildly amusing.

From Avignon Casanova proceeded to Marseille, where he rescued a pretty girl in distress; he calls her Rosalie. He was first attracted to her at a theater, and when he got directions to her house he happened to arrive in the middle of a drama, or farce. A woman was spinning flax, and when he asked for her daughter he got an angry reply: "Do you take me for her pimp?" He narrates the scene in the present tense: "At that moment the girl arrives, and her infuriated mother hurls a bottle at her that would have killed her if she hadn't missed her aim. I get in between them, raising my cane, the infants scream, and my valet comes in and shuts the door. The woman doesn't calm down, she calls her daughter a whore in a loud voice, orders her to leave, and says she is no longer her mother." Casanova pulled the girl away and went to find an apartment where he could set her up by herself.[11]

Rosalie's story was that she was a good girl who had slept with only one man before, an honorable merchant from Genoa who had gone back home but promised to return in the spring and marry her. Meanwhile she was glad to enjoy Casanova's protection and be his mistress. "There is no city in France," he remarks, "where the girls push libertinism as far as in Marseille. Not only do they pride themselves on refusing nothing, they are the first to offer what a man might not dare to ask for." Quite possibly Rosalie wasn't inexperienced at all.

The next step was to outfit her in a style befitting his companion. "I spent a whole morning on that, and the valet brought her a little trunk with two dresses, chemises, skirts, stockings, handkerchiefs, bonnets, gloves, slippers, a fan, a sewing bag, and a cape. I was charmed at having prepared such a delicious spectacle for my soul." Two things especially pleased him: Rosalie's delightful proportions, and his own expertise in clothing. "At the age of fifteen, she had the figure of a woman of twenty, with a perfect bosom and everything marvelously proportioned. I didn't make a mistake in a single measurement."

Casanova had dressed Henriette as a fine lady because she was one; he was dressing Rosalie as if she might become one. He was acting as Pygmalion. "I took pleasure in elevating this girl, and I rejoiced to foresee that with the education I would give her, she would become perfect."

Rosalie was appropriately grateful, and began addressing him with the familiar *tu*, not the formal *vous*. "She devoured me with kisses, and completed my happiness. Since nothing in life is real but the present, I relished it, dismissing images from the past and abhorring the shades of the future, which is always frightful since it presents nothing as certain except death, the *ultima linea rerum*." He quotes that line from Horace often—"Death is the end of all things."

Rosalie agreed to travel with him to Genoa, where her previous suitor lived. There Casanova paid a friendly call on the marchese Gian Giacomo Grimaldi, with whom he had been friendly in Avignon. What he didn't realize was that Grimaldi was the godfather of Rosalie's suitor Paretti; Casanova calls him P——i, but his identity is known.

Grimaldi was immediately struck by Rosalie's charms, and concocted a plot that Casanova understood only afterward. He provided Rosalie with a gorgeous servant named Veronica, in the hope that Casanova would transfer his attentions to her. Paretti was invited to a dinner party at which Casanova and Rosalie were also present. Rosalie was staggered at first when she saw him, but he made it clear that he still wanted to marry her.

Rosalie was no fool, and although she told Casanova she was willing to stay with him, she could see the obvious advantages in marrying Paretti. Casanova had to admit that her decision made sense. "My fortune, despite its apparent grandeur, was not solid. As my story continues the reader will be convinced of that."

He did indeed turn his attentions to Veronica, and when she resisted he moved on to her sister Annetta. His night with Annetta was followed by still another performance *à trois*, the sisters taking turns this time as attentive spectators. The only upsetting thing was that he found himself impotent, and nothing they could do revived him. Not only did he take pride in his virility, he practically defined himself by it, and this was an alarming intimation of decline. "It was something I couldn't conceive of, and it positively filled me with despair."

From Genoa Casanova moved on to Florence, where he spent three weeks. The most significant encounter there was his meeting, described earlier, with Teresa/Bellino and their sixteen-year-old son Cesarino. Casanova also ran into the abbé Gama, the Portuguese cleric who had been so friendly years before in Rome, and they enjoyed each other's company now. Watching Gama flirt with a couple of young women, however, provoked another of Casanova's rueful comments about aging. "I could see that he thought he was pleasing them, and I understood very well that vanity prevented him from realizing that he was making himself ridiculous. What I didn't foresee was that when I myself reached his age I might resemble him. In truth I never gave it a thought."

Gama, always insatiably curious, asked a leading question: how had Casanova come by his great fortune? "My fortune, Monsieur l'Abbé," he replied, "is not great, but I have friends whose purses are always open to me." That must mean Bragadin and his companions Barbaro and Dandolo in Venice. In addition there are indications that he was getting support from Mme. d'Urfé. It's most unlikely that the French government was still subsidizing him.

A new acquaintance was Sir Horace Mann, the British chargé d'affaires, who proudly showed off his impressive collection of art. Casanova's mention of that is notable for vagueness: "I saw marvels in painting, sculpture, and engraved gems." Though he had grown up in a city of great art and had two brothers who were painters, visual art seems to have left him indifferent. James Boswell was just the same. When he saw the celebrated Apollo Belvedere in the Vatican a few years after this, his only reaction was: "Baddish knees." They shared a lack of interest in landscape, too. After climbing Vesuvius Boswell wrote, "Monstrous mountain. Smoke. Saw hardly anything."[12]

Casanova's stay in Florence came to an end when he was abruptly expelled. It had to do with passing a forged bill of exchange, in which he claims that he was the unwitting victim of somebody else; that seems unlikely. At any rate the chief of police ordered him to get out of town at once. "I left the next day, and in thirty-six hours I arrived in Rome."

Even if Casanova was guiltless in this instance, he had developed a dubious reputation during his wanderings. He was known to be a gambler and libertine, and suspected of being a trickster or con man. And whereas the story of his great escape was received with appreciation elsewhere in Europe, Florence wasn't far from Venice, whose good will it was important to keep.

In Rome he reconnected with his brother Giovanni, whom he hadn't seen for ten years. Giovanni was studying painting there with the famous Anton Raphael Mengs, and would eventually become the director of the Academy of Fine Arts Dresden. Giacomo never cared much for him. "We spent an hour recounting our adventures, his little ones and my great ones."

Through a cardinal he knew, Casanova obtained an audience with the Pope.

"I liked and esteemed him when he was a cardinal," the recommender said, "but since he became pope he's made himself known too much as a *coglione*"— literally, "testicle." This was Clement XIII, the former Carlo Rezzonico from Venice. He was humorous and friendly, and permitted Casanova to kiss his slipper, but was noncommittal when asked to persuade the Venetian authorities to let him come home. Not until fourteen years later would that happen.

The pope did bestow on him the Order of the Golden Spur, symbolized by a cross (not a spur) that he wore around his neck on a red ribbon. This may have been a papal gift, but often the award was given out indiscriminately in return for a fee. Still, it looked impressive, and would contribute over the years to Casanova's peacock persona. It also gave him the right to call himself a *chevalier*, though he was already doing that anyway.

In Rome Casanova was invited to an orgy, mostly homosexual, at which he claims to have been the only nonparticipant. He calls it "an infernal debauch" and says that "during this whole incredible performance I was never affected by the slightest sensation, unless it was to laugh." That may be the truth. What he loved was shared intimacy, ecstasy if possible, and not an indiscriminate free-for-all.

He was amused also when he dropped in on the art historian Johann Joachim Winckelmann just as a young man was leaving, hastily adjusting his clothes. Winckelmann explained, untruthfully, that he was not homosexual but had simply been conducting research. Since most of the ancients "were buggers without hiding it," he felt that he couldn't really appreciate their art unless he acquainted himself with what they must have felt.

Casanova's most memorable encounter at this time was not in Rome but in Naples. That was when he unexpectedly encountered Lucrezia Castelli, together with her daughter Leonilda, and discovered that in all likelihood he was the girl's father. He also slept with them both, or so he claims; but that story too has been told earlier.

CHAPTER 20

Magus

Running out of funds and ideas, Casanova was ready to exploit Mme. d'Urfé's fantasy, with himself presiding as magus. The fantasy would develop in stages, with increasingly weird features, and he himself marveled at the credulity of an otherwise intelligent and sensible person. It was the phenomenon of the true believer who strenuously resists being disabused.

Drawing on his knowledge of alchemy and magic, and orchestrating a number of bizarre sexual performances, Casanova would succeed in relieving this immensely wealthy noblewoman of staggeringly large sums over the course of six years. In a novel such behavior might be entertaining; in real life it's an ethical challenge for those who may want to defend Casanova, and it has attracted much perceptive commentary.

In hindsight he expresses remorse at times for having swindled Mme. d'Urfé, but only at times. More usually he offers the same rationalization that he had with Bragadin and his friends: if he didn't do it somebody else would. Besides, he was doing the victim a favor by humoring an obsession she had nurtured long before she met him. A common sentiment among adventurers was that a fool's purse was the patrimony of a man of wit. Ian Kelly comments, "Casanova enjoyed the ridiculousness, the ingenuity, the fecundity of his own imagination and stagecraft."[1]

A widow since her youth, the former Jeanne Camus de Pontcarré, now the Marquise d'Urfé, was a deep student of Cabbala and the occult. Formerly a

beauty, she was in her late fifties now and terrified of death. Rosicrucianism—
the Ancient and Mystical Order of the Rosy Cross—though condemned by
the Catholic church, offered a seductive promise: someone who possessed the
secret of the philosopher's stone could not only transmute base metals into
gold, but could live forever in this world, not the next. As was mentioned
previously, the great physician Boerhaave believed he had that secret, though
as Casanova noted, in his case it failed to work, since he died in agony at the
age of seventy.

Casanova was not the first self-styled guru to enter into Mme. d'Urfé's
fantasy life, which had been nourished by the books in her massive collection
and by elaborate chemical experiments in her state-of-the-art laboratory. She
had already taken an interest in two previous adventurers, the shady Count
de Cagliostro and the equally shady Count de Saint-Germain, and both had
extracted a lot of money from her. Far from inventing a previously unheard-of
scheme, Casanova was a latecomer to the game, and rather in awe of these
celebrated role models.

Of these two predecessors, Cagliostro interested him less, perhaps because
as a fellow Italian the resemblance was uncomfortably close. Cagliostro was
not a count, of course, but a Sicilian whose real name was Giuseppe Balsamo.
He specialized in psychic healing, and like Casanova was well versed in magic,
alchemy, and Cabbala, as well as being a Mason. In another work years later
(not the *Histoire*) Casanova described him as "a buffoonish charlatan, ignorant, not good looking, uncultivated, who speaks only the jargon of his own
country, and doesn't even know how to write, showing that his education is
equal to his birth."[2]

Saint-Germain was much more formidable. He may not have been a count
either, but he knew how to act like one, with easy aristocratic grace. He was
fluent in an amazing number of languages, and spoke each with so perfect an
accent that no one could tell what his native language might have been. Saint-
Germain was widely thought to be the illegitimate son of some royal house,
of which there were a great many in those days. He also claimed to have been
alive for hundreds of years, and with his mastery of alchemy and magic could
help chosen initiates to live indefinitely if not forever. Louis XV gave him a
big stipend and an apartment in the château of Chambord for his "scientific"
work.

The original caption for an engraving (reproduced below) confirms his prestige: "Le Comte de Saint Germain, Celebrated Alchemist," followed by verses
in French: "Like Prometheus he stole the fire by which the world exists and

Alexandre Comte de Cagliostro.

34. Cagliostro

everything lives. At his voice Nature listens and moves; if he is not God him-self, a powerful god inspires him."

When Casanova met Saint-Germain at Mme. d'Urfé's he was genuinely impressed. "He gave himself out to be a prodigy in everything; he wanted to astonish, and he positively did astonish." Many years later Casanova published a pamphlet that ends with a paean to Saint-Germain. "What a man! One could be his dupe without being dishonored. He had an agreeable counte-nance and noble manner, he was a fine speaker if sometimes boastful, he spoke all languages well, a great chemist and musician, rarely showing off, reserved, polished, bantering, full of wit, and such that those who admitted to being his dupes were not ashamed to admit it." Casanova deeply wished to be like that himself. "The imposter," he says in the pamphlet, "sees the human race beneath his feet and rejoices in his superiority."[3]

With his own insinuating charm and unfailing plausibility, Casanova couldn't resist this new opportunity, and he soon got closer to Mme. d'Urfé than either

35. Saint-Germain

Cagliostro or Saint-Germain. In addition to Rosicrucian and cabbalistic knowledge, he had a gift the others didn't: the ability to manipulate his number pyramids with apparently oracular results. She was enchanted by that, and placed
implicit faith in Paralis, the spiritual guide he used to invoke with Bragadin and
his friends. She gulped down his fictions, Félicien Marceau says, like a glass of
water.[4]

When it was all over Mme. d'Urfé's grandson wrote, "She ended up falling
into the hands of another Italian imposter named Casanova, who had the tact
never to ask for money, but only for rich jewels with which to form 'constel-
lations.' He managed to convince her that she would become pregnant at the
age of sixty-three, under the influence of the stars and of cabbalistic numbers,

after which she would die in childbirth but be reborn *as herself* at the end of seventy-four days."

There were two errors in this account, in addition to adding a few years to her age. Since she believed that only males could possess the philosopher's stone, she originally expected to be reincarnated as a boy. Teresa Imer's son, the so-called Count d'Aranda, was slated at first to be the vehicle for that, but eventually Casanova thought better of it. The other error is more significant: she already harbored this belief in reincarnation when Casanova met her, and all he needed to do was encourage it. This writer added that the grandchildren, who of course looked forward to inheriting her fortune, "regarded her as an old madwoman, and Monsieur le Chevalier Casanova as a notable thief."[5]

Casanova was an accomplished con man, but his cons were most successful when he was also conning himself. Rationally, he knew that the philosopher's stone was a fiction and reincarnation impossible. But there was nothing rational about the whole business with Mme. d'Urfé. François Roustang makes an interesting suggestion:

> I tend to think that Casanova's hoax would not have been possible if Mme. d'Urfé had not reactivated the dream that lies at the very heart of his personality. The unique man to take on a powerful state, friend to Bernis, the man who, lacking any means or knowledge, nonetheless fills the king's treasury with gold—this man is closely akin to the little boy who was revived by the witch, and all the personas that make up the man Casanova find it quite normal that Fortune should shower her favors on him.[6]

While Casanova was developing this scheme, a more pragmatic opportunity to make money appeared. Back in Florence the abbé Gama, who was Portuguese, had made an interesting proposition: he could get Casanova an appointment with the Portuguese delegation at a forthcoming peace conference in Augsburg that was intended to end the Seven Years War. Such an appointment actually made sense, since Casanova was a persuasive speaker in French, the language of diplomacy, and was well connected with the bureaucracy of the church.

While he was waiting for the peace conference to begin, Casanova spent the spring of 1761 in Turin, and after leaving there he decided to stop off in Chambéry. There he would visit the nun from Aix-les-Bains, the second M. M., in her convent. "I sighed for her," he claims, "whenever she came into my memory." The first step was to get in touch with her aunt Mme. Morin in Grenoble, who had seen his portrait of the original M. M. when he was there previously, and had exclaimed that it was her niece. Startled, he had assured her it was someone else entirely whom he had known in Venice, but that was only partly true, since the second M. M. had had the portrait retouched to look even more like herself. "If you go to Chambéry," Mme. Morin said, "pay her a visit on my behalf, and your surprise will be as great as mine." So he wrote now to ask her to accompany him there, and she agreed.[7]

As Casanova describes it, the reunion with M. M. was curiously untroubled. She was naturally astonished to see him, and to cover her reaction she told her aunt that she had noticed him when she was in Aix for her alleged health cure. Casanova says, "I admired her presence of mind and her tact. I thought she had gotten even more beautiful."[8]

The next day Casanova arranged to treat M. M. to a dinner with several of her companions. A grill divided a large table in half, with visitors on one side of the grill and nuns on the other. "The abundant dishes, the bottles of wine, and the conversation lasted for three hours, and we all got tipsy. Except for the grill I could easily have taken advantage of all eleven of the females there, who were in no condition for reason." In addition to nuns there was a pretty boarder at the convent who was just about to turn twelve, and accompanying Casanova were Mme. Morin and her daughter. It's an understatement to say, as Rives Childs does, "The picture he has left us of the relative freedom permitted at this time in some convents could not be more revealing."[9]

The day after that Casanova was able to have a private conversation with M. M. He declared that he was ready to climb over the garden wall as her first seducer had done, but she told him calmly that he had to leave town at once. "Believe me, you're already being watched. They're sure we must have known each other in Aix. Forget everything, my dear friend, in order to spare ourselves the torment of useless desires." He wondered how she could bear continual sexual abstinence, and she replied, "I won't hide from you that I'm in love with my young boarder. It's a love that gives me tranquility, an innocent passion."

He did visit her again, and she brought the little boarder with her to avert suspicion. If what Casanova relates really happened, he was able to grope the girl through the grating, which she and M. M. both enjoyed. And at a final meeting the day after that, the girl asked him to kneel down on the sill that separated them, "and with a desire to devour me, may have thought she could succeed in swallowing me; but the excess of pleasure she aroused in my soul distilled my heart." After that, "I pressed my lips upon the delicious mouth that had sucked out the essence of my soul and heart."

That's so improbable, in fact unbelievable, that one wonders why he bothered to write it. By now many of his encounters are described as impromptu threesomes, and it's easy to suspect that fantasies are increasingly pervading the actual past. But telling about it in this way may have served a psychological purpose. If M. M. and her little friend really did enjoy themselves, that might exonerate him from feeling guilty for what he did in Aix-les-Bains.

Next Casanova proceeded to Paris for a brief reunion with Mme. d'Urfé before going to Augsburg for the peace conference, telling her in confidence that his attendance at the conference was only a cover story. His real purpose would be to make contact with Rosicrucian sages who could help him prepare for the great event, and she sent him off with a collection of priceless jewelry as "gifts" for them. He claims that a servant later absconded with them; very possibly he sold them off himself to cover gambling debts.

As it turned out, the peace conference was called off; the war would continue for another two years. Back in Paris in the spring of 1762, it was time for the long-awaited mystical ceremonies with the eager Mme. d'Urfé. The first stage began at her château (which no longer exists) at Pontcarré, twenty miles east of Paris. Teresa Imer's son Giuseppe, now known as d'Aranda, would play the role of the boy into whom Mme. d'Urfé's soul would pass. Marianna Corticelli, a young dancer Casanova had met in Florence at the time of his reunion with Teresa/Bellino, had been recruited to play the role of surrogate mother: Casanova would impregnate her with the reincarnation of Mme. d'Urfé. It would be easy not to believe this incredible story, but the indignant comments of the grandson and heir show that Casanova did get her to believe it.

Unfortunately, Marianna didn't get pregnant, and meanwhile she and Giuseppe were getting entirely too interested in each other. The oracle Paralis now informed Casanova that Giuseppe was not only unnecessary, but was somehow blocking the success of the procedure. Casanova thereupon banished him, after which Marianna ran away too, taking a treasure trove of jewels the marquise had given her.

It was time to invent a new plan, and outrageously, Casanova told the aging lady that he had been instructed to impregnate her himself, with no need for an intermediary. They must now go to Aix-la-Chapelle, he explained, where they would take a bath in moonlight and seek instructions from the lunar goddess Selene.

When they got there, Mme. d'Urfé wrote a letter to the goddess which they reverently burned, in order that its message could fly up into the heavens. A reply duly appeared, floating on the surface of the water where Casanova had secretly placed it. This disclosed that the performance had to be postponed for a year, and should then take place at Marseille (it's not clear why he wanted it to be there). On that occasion a new virgin would be provided to witness the ceremony, and so would a supernatural being with the Rosicrucian name of Querelinth.

Meanwhile, in July of 1762 Casanova headed for Italy once more. In Turin and Milan he engaged in heavy gambling, which he describes in exhaustive detail, and some sexual adventures that he relates in a perfunctory way. Marceau comments, "We are beginning—or at least I am beginning—to be exasperated. With his sure writer's instinct, Casanova knows it, and maybe he's exasperated himself."[10]

What he describes most vividly, as so often, is clothing and food. He recalls with relish how he appeared when a friend from Venice introduced him to a distinguished family in Milan: "He announced me as rich, and I looked it. My luxuriousness was dazzling. My rings, my snuffboxes, my watch chains covered with diamonds, not to mention the diamond and ruby cross hanging from a ribbon around my neck, all made me an imposing personage. It was the Order of the Golden Spur that I had received from the pope himself."[11]

During Carnival at Milan there was a masked ball to which he escorted a pair of young noblewomen. In preparation he purchased extremely expensive dresses in satin and silk, deliberately ripped big holes in them, and then paid a tailor to patch them up with incongruous materials. They were thus costumed as beggars but dressed in preposterous finery; he himself went as Pierrot, the sad, lovelorn character from commedia dell' arte. The result, as Angelo Mainardi says, was a theatrical comment on illusion and reality, "showing riches and poverty inverted in order to humble and conquer two cousins who were arrogant in their nobility. All was appearance, all was impermanent. Theater illustrates the great pretense that is life, the false rituals on which society rests."[12]

As for food, "I've always believed that one eats nowhere as well as in Turin, but it's true that the land itself produces exquisite foodstuffs, to which able cooks apply every art to make them succulent. The wines too are preferred by many gourmets to those from elsewhere. Game, fish, fowls, veal, greens, milk products, truffles—all are exquisite there."[13]

There's a fascinating aside when Casanova happened to pass through the town of Lodi, and stopped to buy some books. "Until then I thought Lodi deserved respect only for its excellent cheese, which all of Europe ungratefully calls Parmesan. It comes from Lodi, which I added that same day to an article on Parmesan in the dictionary of cheeses I had begun, but afterward abandoned when I found it was beyond my powers." Casanova was no dilettante in pleasures. He really did intend to compile a dictionary of cheese, but there would be no point if it were not comprehensive. No trace of his dictionary has survived.[14]

In Milan there was a strange episode, in fact alarming. Casanova had made friends with a Milanese count whose Spanish wife was offended by his hints of sexual interest, treating him with scorn if he even presumed to look at her. His narrative doesn't make clear why this made her so very indignant, but at any rate she attempted a weird kind of revenge.

When Casanova called one day, her husband was away, and the countess offered him a pinch of snuff, taking some herself. He was startled when he inhaled it, since it wasn't snuff at all but a "sternutative" intended to cause sneezing and then nosebleeds, which were supposed to promote good health. Both of them did sneeze forcibly and did bleed. Waving his handkerchief away, the countess held out a silver basin and they each dripped some blood into it. "'Our mingled blood,' she said laughing, 'will cause an eternal friendship between us.'"

That was peculiar, but he thought no more about it until the next day when a priest asked to speak with him, and said earnestly that while his lips must be sealed after hearing a confession, he did feel justified in revealing enough to save Casanova from mortal danger. "It can only be your guardian angel who, unable to speak to you himself, is making use of me to preserve your life." He must go at once to a certain address, ascend to the top floor, and tell the old woman there that he would pay whatever she demanded for a bottle that a servant would have brought to her the previous night. And not just the bottle, but "*all that goes with it.* Remember that well: *all that goes with it.*"

When Casanova found the old woman and delivered this message, she seemed scared, but he showed her his knife and insisted. Accordingly she opened a closet that contained a bizarre collection of objects—vials, tongs, a small furnace, and strangely deformed statues. She was obviously a witch. She then gave him a bottle, and when he asked what was in it, "Your blood mingled with the countess's." Next she opened a box, "and I saw a wax figure lying on its back, entirely naked. I read my name on it, and although they were badly executed, I could recognize my own features, and my cross around the idol's neck. The simulacrum resembled a monstrous Priapus in the parts that characterize that deity." After it had been smeared with the blood and melted in a fire, he would infallibly die.

What was especially disturbing was the way this episode recalled those nosebleeds in Venice long ago, and that other witch on the island of Murano. Still, the sight of the effigy made him burst out laughing. Chantal Thomas says, "The priapic representation of himself was a prefiguration of his role as myth."[15]

Afterward it occurred to him that it was fortunate the countess believed in witchcraft, since otherwise she might have hired professional killers. He decided that the best course was to pretend to know nothing about it, and when he saw her next he gave her a mantle lined with ermine. "Accepting it, she asked most graciously why I had made her such a lovely present. I said I had dreamed that she was so angry with me that she had spoken with assassins to murder me. She replied, blushing, that she hadn't gone mad. I left, seeing her plunged in dark reflections."[16]

By the time the reunion with Mme. d'Urfé in Marseille came around, Casanova was badly in need of financial support, and more than ready to get on with their plan. She would now assume the ceremonial name of Semiramis. For the virgin he selected a new girlfriend of the moment, Marcolina, who had turned up in the company of his disreputable youngest brother Gaetano, an abbé by now but not religious in the least. Giacomo sent him off to Paris with enough money to get there. (Gaetano left a letter accusing Giacomo of being "inhuman, unjust, and an unnatural brother.") As for "Querelinth," that would be an actor and adventurer named Giacomo Passano, who also called himself Ascanio Pogomas, and who might plausibly play the role of a distinguished visitor from the heavens.

After Passano arrived, however, Casanova was alarmed to realize that although his looks were impressive, he was far from competent to impersonate "the wisest and most powerful man in the universe." Fortunately, that didn't matter. Bowing deeply, Mme. d'Urfé addressed Passano as "Your Divinity" and led them to dinner, where he got drunk and fell asleep. Casanova explained that she had asked forbidden questions, and that withdrawal into sleep was Querelinth's way of indicating it.[17]

Before Passano dozed off, Mme. d'Urfé announced that for the ceremony she would provide jewels worth 100,000 French livres, a truly staggering sum worth over a million modern euros. As soon as they were alone together, Passano warned Casanova that unless they split the spoils equally, he would write to Mme. d'Urfé and tell all. Always brazen, Casanova told him to go right ahead.

Now, however, he had to figure out how to get rid of this treacherous accomplice. He told Mme. d'Urfé that according to his oracle, "Seven Salamanders [Rosicrucian spirits of fire] had transported the real Querelinth up to the Milky Way, and the individual who was now downstairs in bed was in actuality the evil Count Saint-Germain, whom a gnome had sent to be the executioner of Semiramis. The oracle said that Semiramis should leave everything in the care of Paralisée Galtinarde (that was me) to get rid of Saint-Germain."

If Mme. d'Urfé could believe that Querelinth was now in the Milky Way, she certainly had no trouble believing that her unwelcome guest was Saint-Germain—a deft blow by Casanova against a formidable rival. To confirm this startling revelation they spent a couple of hours with the number pyramids, and of course the confirmation appeared. Passano was sent packing.

Following Casanova's instructions, Mme. d'Urfé now filled a big casket with seven enormous jewels, one for each day of the lunar week: a diamond, a ruby, a sapphire, an emerald, an opal, a topaz, and a yellow chrysolite, each weighing seven carats. In due course these would be an offering to the spirit world.

It was time to involve young Marcolina, who would play the role of an Ondine or water spirit. It might have been a problem that she spoke no French, but Mme. d'Urfé had previously mentioned that Ondines were mute since it was impossible to speak under water.

The real reason Casanova wanted Marcolina there was that he was going to have to impregnate Mme. d'Urfé, or pretend to, and he was afraid that with his waning sexual powers he might not perform convincingly. The girl's only function was to stand by, fetchingly naked, to arouse his imagination while he went through with it. That worked at first, but he had incautiously told Mme. d'Urfé that the act had to be repeated two more times, and try as he might he could no longer sustain an erection. The result, as Judith Summers says, was "the first faked male orgasm in literature." Fortunately Mme. d'Urfé didn't suspect, and was joyously certain that she was pregnant.[18]

Possibly she was disappointed in another way, but if so, Marcolina took care of that. The three of them entered the ceremonial bath up to their waists, "and the Ondine enchanted Semiramis by the kinds of caresses she gave her, of which the Duc d'Orléans [her early lover] never had the least idea. She believed that they must be natural for river *génies,* and applauded everything that this female *génie* accomplished with her fingers." Casanova was aware that although Marcolina had no objection to sex with men, she preferred it with women.

The oracle then revealed that the pregnancy would succeed only if Mme. d'Urfé remained in bed for the next hundred and seven hours, which she promised to do. That gave Casanova a chance to return to his inn and prove to Marcolina that although no longer young he was still far from impotent.

> "But why were you so stupid as to commit yourself to three times?"
>
> "I thought it would be easy so long as I was looking at you, but I was wrong. The flabby flesh I was touching was not what I was seeing, and the excess of pleasure refused to arrive. Tonight you'll see the truth. Let's go to bed together."
>
> "Let's go."
>
> The force of the comparison made me pass a night with Marcolina that was the equal of the ones in Parma with Henriette and in Murano with M. M. We stayed in bed for fourteen hours, four of which were consecrated to love.

After Mme. d'Urfé completed her allotted time in her own bed, she and Casanova carried the heavy jewel casket down to the Mediterranean and solemnly cast it in. He had, however, provided himself with an identical casket filled with lead, and that was what went into the sea. Now he had possession of the fantastically valuable jewels, and looked forward to converting them to cash.

The oracle decreed that Mme. d'Urfé should next await Casanova at a place where two rivers flowed together, and pour some water from the Mediterranean into them. That not very mysterious directive obviously meant Lyon, where the Rhône and the Saône join, and she proceeded there. He made his own journey northward in easy stages with Marcolina as his companion. It was on that occasion that they stopped at the villa of Henriette, and Marcolina spent the night in her bed.

Marcolina's role had now concluded, and she was dispatched to Venice. As Casanova continued traveling by himself, there was one of the sudden emergencies that he likes to relate, showing both his courage and his generosity. Roads were generally bad, thieves lurked on them, and a traveler was well advised to carry loaded pistols. Casanova always did. He had bought a small carriage called a *solitaire,* and was preparing to set out before dawn when he was informed that its lanterns were broken and he would have to pay for repairs before leaving. His servant, however (no longer Leduc), suspected that the lantern maker himself had damaged them in order to get paid. "I knew that trick," Casanova says. "I called the lantern maker a scoundrel, he answered insolently in French, and I gave him two kicks in the belly with a pistol in my hand." Next he filed a complaint, slipped the customary bribe into the local police chief's hand, and watched the prisoner being marched away.

But this apparent resolution was followed by a sentimental reversal that was likewise typical of Casanova—and of much contemporary fiction. The lantern maker's wife rushed up, with a baby at her breast and four other small children. Falling to her knees, she implored him to forgive her husband, who was the family's sole support and would be in prison indefinitely since he couldn't afford to pay a big fine. Enjoying a display of magnanimity, he wrote out a statement dropping his complaint, gave the grateful woman some money, and paid the police chief again to forget the whole thing.[19]

Much to Casanova's surprise, the reunion in Lyon with Mme. d'Urfé never happened. Passano was smarter than Casanova gave him credit for, if not the wisest being in the universe, and had managed to get through to her with the story of what had really been going on. At long last her eyes were opened, and his six-year relationship with her was over.

Casanova's account of this episode ends in August of 1763, when he claims in the *Histoire* that he received a letter from a mutual friend announcing that Mme. d'Urfé had died. But that's not true. We know that she lived on until 1775, bequeathing her possessions to the grandson already mentioned. Most probably the 1763 letter was from Mme. d'Urfé herself, breaking with him bitterly. "I learned," he says, "that my good Mme. d'Urfé had died, or had become wise, which for me would have had the same result." She did indeed become wise, and was dead to him.[20]

Conning Mme. d'Urfé was altogether different from conning Bragadin and his friends, even if Casanova claims that he was just giving all of them what they wanted. With the Venetian patricians he had a genuine relationship. They enjoyed his company and they helped him financially for the rest of their lives. His relationship with Mme. d'Urfé was simply one of exploiter and victim, and the outrage of her heirs was completely justified. His behavior can only be described as criminal.

And not only that. It wasn't just that he had systematically cheated her. Still worse must have been the cruelly humiliating blow to something she believed in so deeply. Commentators generally take for granted Casanova's cynical comments about her "madness," but Marie-Françoise Luna is surely right: "The image of the old crazy woman that he presents can't entirely conceal, in moving contrast to her guru's unscrupulous frivolity and rationalist arrogance, the purity of soul and mystical fervor of the marquise."[21]

CHAPTER 21

The End of Act I

Casanova needed to leave France not just because he was in disgrace with Mme. d'Urfé and her friends, but also because he was beginning to exhaust the loot he had extracted from her, and needed a new source of income. He picked London as a possible site to promote a lottery, which had worked so well in Paris. He would stay there for almost a year, from June 1763 to April 1764, and he devotes two hundred pages in the *Histoire* to this period of his life.

As he realized even at the time, he had reached a major turning point. Never again would he be able to pretend to great wealth, as he had when he rented the grandiose villa in Grenoble. Never again would he generate a successful income-producing scheme, as he had with the French lottery. From this time forward his existence would be increasingly random.

London was disappointing, not least because Casanova spoke no English and didn't want to. Nothing ever came of the lottery idea, either. The English already had one, and after a few desultory overtures he let his plan drop. He associated entirely with people who spoke Italian or French, and his contacts were largely confined to nobles, libertines, and gamblers, particularly a notorious rake named Lord Pembroke, which he spells *Pimbrok*. He also got to know some card sharps and other adventurers, most of them foreigners like himself. Many of these he met at the Prince of Orange coffee house, which was a favored haunt of disreputable Italians.

THE END OF ACT I

Plenty of British writers and politicians spoke French and could conceivably have been his acquaintances, but there is little mention of them in the *Histoire*. Casanova does recall spending some time with Matthew Maty, librarian of the recently founded British Museum. Late in life, not in the *Histoire* but in a pamphlet criticizing innovations in language, he mentioned that he met Samuel Johnson at the museum. He knew that Johnson was regarded as a "walking dictionary," having recently published a monumental *Dictionary of the English Language,* and they discussed possible Latin roots of a particular French word. They may well have been speaking in Latin, in which Johnson's friends said he was as fluent as English. Casanova says nothing of interest about the meeting, however. He probably didn't know what to make of that massive, myopic, and strangely awkward individual, and would have had no chance to appreciate his invigorating wit.[1]

Casanova didn't take to England any more than he had to Holland. He was shocked that the country produced no wine. Describing an excursion out of London, he comments, "Nothing is more beautiful than the English roads, and nothing more pleasing than the countryside; all it lacks is the vine. It's a peculiarity of this island's very fertile soil that it cannot yield wine." If he had reflected, he would have realized that the climate was at fault, not the soil. Large areas of France and Germany also produce no wine. As for beer—he wrote "strong beer" as *strombir*—he tried it for a week and gave it up. "The bitterness it left was intolerable."[2]

Casanova's first significant contact in London was with Teresa Imer, whom he had known in Venice when they were both young, and had encountered in Holland five years previously. She was now calling herself Mrs. Cornelys, using the name of a former lover. Over the years she had had a successful singing career and a series of lovers, usually wealthy and sometimes noble, but with middle age approaching she was ready for something more ambitious. That turned out to be establishing elegant assembly rooms for festive gatherings at which hundreds of patrons could listen to music, gamble, and dance. In Tobias Smollett's novel *Humphry Clinker* an impressionable young visitor from the country exclaims, "I have been at Mrs. Cornelys' assembly, which for the rooms, the company, the dresses, and decorations, surpasses all description."[3]

It may seem surprising that no such venue yet existed, but compared to cities on the Continent, London was still old-fashioned, dominated by finance and commerce rather than by the aristocracy. Italians were welcomed as free spirits from a less repressive culture, and Teresa seemed to embody the seductions that English travelers had enjoyed in her native Venice. A portrait

36. Teresa Cornelys (formerly Imer)

of her during her London years shows imperious confidence, although little trace of the charms that once obsessed Signor Malipiero and got Casanova thrown out of his palazzo.

With major investment from a wealthy lover, Teresa purchased Carlisle House in fashionable Soho Square, and she commissioned a huge concert room and adjacent dining hall to be added to the existing building. In the engraving (color plate 28) it's the last house on the left at the far end of the square. Like the longer building in the foreground, it has an impressive roof terrace. She assembled a staff of twenty maids and a dozen footmen.

Especially popular were Teresa's masked balls, more decorously conducted than Venetian masking but with the same allure of anonymity; moralists regularly denounced masquerades, but in vain. Tickets were expensive and eagerly snapped up by the rich and titled. A ticket for a ball ten years after Casanova

37. Masked Ball Ticket

was there shows a cheerful Venus removing a solemn mask to reveal the flirtatious reality beneath. The date of the event is indicated by a Cupid seated on an un-English bunch of grapes, while a leering mask on the ground emphasizes Dionysian liberation through alcohol.

Although Teresa's venture was popular—a poet called her "the Empress of Pleasure"—she was unfortunately a terrible businesswoman. She ran up colossal debts and was often in danger of imprisonment for not being able to pay. She also got into an acrimonious dispute with the former lover who had sunk his own fortune into the venture. He wanted to be reimbursed after they broke up, while she countered that his contribution had been a gift that he had no right to reclaim. Their lawsuit dragged on for years in the Court of Chancery that would be satirized later by Dickens in *Bleak House*.[4]

While Casanova was still in France, Teresa had written to ask that her son Joseph (or Giuseppe) be returned to her. He was sixteen by then and could easily have traveled by himself, but Casanova brought him to London. If Casanova was expecting an affectionate reunion with Teresa, however, he was disappointed. When he arrived she sent word that she was much too busy to see him, and when she eventually did, she assigned him a room in the servants' quarters.

Indignant, he asked an Italian writer he met in a tavern to recommend a furnished house to rent. He soon found one in "a great street called Pall-Mall" (he wrote it as *Pale-male*). With the house came an elderly *ausckeper* (housekeeper), and he hired a multilingual black servant called Jarba, the name of a Carthaginian king in the *Aeneid*.

As for Joseph, he had never wanted to go to London at all, or to be reunited with a demanding mother he hadn't seen for five years. As the indulged ward of the Marquise d'Urfé he was being brought up as a gentleman of leisure, but after her break with Casanova she had no more use for the so-called Count d'Aranda, and London it had to be. He was nonplussed when Teresa addressed him as "Mister Cornelys," and when she explained that that was now his name, he replied sarcastically, "I'll go and write it down so I won't forget it." From then on he sulked, and Teresa's plan to have him learn her business was doomed from the start.

For Sophie, Teresa's daughter with Casanova who was nine at this time, his paternal influence was positive, although for some reason he was reluctant to acknowledge his relationship to her. But Teresa had told her explicitly that he was her father, and people often commented on how much alike they looked. On one occasion, "Kissing me, she called me her father, her tender father, which drew tears from me."

Back in Holland he had been shocked by how abusively Teresa treated both of her children, and it was obvious now that the girl felt resentful and trapped. She had musical gifts and was being trained as a singer and dancer, as well as tutored in languages, with the obvious goal of qualifying her to be an expensive mistress or even a well-placed wife. Since she was becoming increasingly gaunt and feverish—anorexia has been suspected—Casanova stepped in and insisted that she enroll in a boarding school in the outskirts of London, paying for it himself. There she was happy for the first time in her life. Her strong intelligence was stimulated, and she formed friendships with girls her own age.

Visiting from time to time—sometimes daily—he was inevitably attracted to all of them, but didn't misbehave. Sophie was profoundly grateful to be liberated from her mother, and went on to enjoy a happy life.

Still in possession of some of Mme. d'Urfé's money, Casanova set himself up to live like a man of means, but the English were less susceptible to his act than the French had been. On the whole he found himself leading a pointless existence. He was on the prowl for women, of course, but he found even high-class prostitutes unappealing, and felt seriously handicapped by the language barrier. "Accustomed to love with all of my senses, I couldn't give myself to love without the sense of hearing."

There was also an encounter in a carriage, just the kind of thing he normally liked, that produced a humiliating sequel. A lady who spoke French offered him a lift to Whitehall (he wrote it as *Wite-ale*). After introducing himself, he got promptly to work. "I kissed her hands, then her pretty face, and then her lovely bosom. Finding sweet acquiescence and the laughter of love rather than resistance, I gave her the most powerful proof that I found her entirely to my liking."

Two weeks later he encountered the lady when calling on somebody else, and asked her to introduce him to their hostess. "She replied politely that she couldn't do that, because she didn't know me. 'But I told you my name, Madame! Do you not remember me?' 'I remember you perfectly well, but follies like that give no right to claim acquaintance.' I was staggered by this singular response." In Paris Casanova could always pass for a person of importance, but not here. Chantal Thomas comments, "Sexuality is not entitlement to acquaintance. Only a name can be that." Even if Seingalt, the name he was using in England, had been his real name, it wouldn't have counted.[5]

That was a memorable lesson in English snobbery. Casanova learned also that although a title was a valuable asset, as in France, what mattered most here was wealth. Noticing an interesting face, he asked a businessman of his acquaintance who it might be.

"That's a man who is worth a hundred thousand pounds."

"And that man over there?"

"He's not worth anything."

"But I was asking you for their names."

"I don't know them. A name means nothing. Knowing a man depends on knowing how much he's able to spend, for what is a name? Ask me for a thousand pounds and give me a receipt with the name

Attila, and that will be sufficient. You will pay me back not as Seingalt
but as Monsieur Attila, and we'll laugh."

So long as Attila the Hun can pay his debts, his value is unchallengeable. To
Casanova, accustomed to aristocratic assumptions, this was bizarre. It still
seemed bizarre to Frenchmen in the next century, when Alexis de Tocqueville
and his friend Gustave de Beaumont visited America. Beaumont recalled that
they were told, "So-and-so is worth ten thousand dollars; somebody else isn't
worth half as much."[6]

What he really needed, Casanova decided, was a live-in companion with
whom he could form a real relationship. It occurred to him to advertise for
one, and in the *Histoire* he says that he posted this notice on his door: "Furnished apartment for rent cheaply to a single young lady who speaks English
and French, and who will receive no visitors either by day or at night." Rives
Childs discovered a more elaborate notice that appeared in the *Gazetteer and
London Daily Advertiser* on July 5, 1763 (someone must have put it into English for Casanova):

> A small family or a single gentleman or lady, with or without a ser-
> vant, may be immediately accommodated with a genteel and elegantly
> furnished first floor, with all conveniences, to which belong some pe-
> culiar advantages. It is agreeably situated in Pall Mall, with boarding
> if required; it may be entered on immediately, and will be let on very
> reasonable terms, as it is no common lodging house, and more for the
> sake of company than profit. Please to inquire at Mrs. Redaw's, milli-
> ner, exactly opposite Mr. Dewar's Toy Shop in Pall Mall, near the Hay
> Market, St. James's.[7]

There were as yet no street addresses in London, so elaborate directions like
this had to be provided. Toyshops, as defined in Johnson's *Dictionary,* sold
"nice little manufactures" such as ribbons, ornamental shoe buckles, and lace.

The unspecified "peculiar advantages" meant sleeping with Casanova, and
needless to say he intended to reject any families or single gentlemen who
might apply. As it turned out, he got lucky. A modest, lovely Portuguese noblewoman turned up whom he calls Pauline. Her story, which stretches credulity but may have been true, was that to escape an unwanted marriage she
had fled Portugal by sea with her lover, a Count Al——, and that a fast naval
vessel was dispatched to intercept them. For complicated reasons they were
wearing each other's clothes, and since the officials had been told to bring back

a lady, it was the count whom they took. Pauline was now stranded in London, nearly penniless and with only a few of her own possessions, and she was very glad to take advantage of Casanova's offer.

He was immediately smitten. She was tall and pale with black hair, one of his favorite types, with an infectious laugh, and thanks to an Italian tutor in childhood she spoke that language perfectly. She was also very intelligent, and beat him at chess.

> At the third move Pauline checkmates me; my king, under attack, can neither defend himself or retreat. She laughs. We begin again, she checkmates me in five moves, and enchants me by laughing wholeheartedly. I gratify my awakening love by seeing in her laughter how perfect her teeth are, how lovely her face, and how a soul susceptible to such gaiety could be happy. I rejoice, thinking that I would contribute to that with all my might.

It's hard to believe Casanova was such a poor player that he could be checkmated in three moves, or even five. Probably he let it happen to please Pauline.

Before long they began sleeping together, and he was surprised to discover that despite the sea voyage with her lover, she was still a virgin. "This restraint on his part," she said, "as much as on mine, was precisely what the fire of love needed to be inextinguishable." But now she was restrained no longer, and it was like a reprise of the affair with Henriette, complete in itself because liberated from past and future. Casanova says they philosophized about it just as he and Henriette had done. "We laughed at philosophers who would pity us because we had no further desires. It's impossible to desire more when one has everything, and we did have everything. We couldn't have imagined being richer or happier unless we had wanted to think of the future, and we had no time to think about that. This lack of time was the true basis of our real riches."

The future, however, turned into the present, even more quickly than it had with Henriette. Word arrived from Portugal that all was forgiven, and that if Pauline would come home she could marry Count Al—— after all. Casanova claims that she hated to go, but that duty made her do it. And the comparison with Henriette wasn't lost on him. Both were extremely intelligent, and if anything Pauline was superior "in the pleasure of loving, and in the transports that follow from it." Nevertheless, "whenever I remember them I find that it was Henriette who made the stronger impression on me, and the reason is that my soul was more susceptible at twenty-two than at thirty-seven."

Actually he had been twenty-five back then, but it was true that by now he was a weary and jaded thirty-eight.

At this point in Casanova's life, a pattern was well established. An idyllic episode felt free because it was temporary, an island in the flow of time. That had happened with Lucrezia in Rome and more recently with Henriette. With Pauline it was happening for what would turn out to be the last time. There would be other women, but no more enchanted idylls.

After Pauline's departure there was one further London relationship, but it was disastrous. Marianne Charpillon, whom Casanova always refers to as "la Charpillon," was a sixteen-year-old beauty with blue eyes and light chestnut hair (like the original nun M. M.) and "skin of the purest whiteness." Altogether, she presented an image of sweet innocence, but it was only an image. "Her bosom was petite but perfect; her hands were dimpled, slender, and a bit longer than the ordinary; her feet were pretty; and her manner was assured and noble. Her sweet, open countenance indicated a soul distinguished by delicacy of feeling, and by that air of nobility that usually comes from high birth. In these two points it pleased Nature to lie. She would have done better to tell the truth only there, and lie about all the rest."

Casanova had been finding women unappealing because he "still had Pauline's image before my eyes," but now he succumbed. "I said to myself that I would no longer find her marvelous once I had slept with her, and that wouldn't take long to happen."

But the story took a very different turn. As Casanova narrates it at length, he was set up by the young woman and her corrupt family, who got a lot of money out of him before he finally tore himself away. It's far from easy to understand what was going on, let alone why he let it happen. It might be added that extracting money from a victim was exactly what he himself had done with Mme. d'Urfé.

Looking back decades later, he saw his encounter with Marianne as a tragic turning point. "It was on that fatal day, at the beginning of September in the year 1763, that I began to die and had finished living." In addition to the humiliation of being fleeced, it was his first revelation that he was no longer an irresistible lover.

Marianne's grandmother, mother, and aunt had all been kicked out of their native Berne for disreputable behavior, and had been living for ten years in Paris, where they appear in numerous police reports. According to one report, "It would be difficult to put a number to those to whom they have distributed their favors." At that time they were calling themselves Augspurgher (their real name was Brunner); they didn't adopt the Charpillon alias until they reached London. By then the older women were no longer viable sex workers, due to age and venereal disease. They now made a living as card sharps and by exploiting young Marianne's good looks.[8]

By chance, Casanova had previously encountered her in Paris when she was just thirteen. He happened to be in a shop where she was begging her aunt to buy her a pretty bracelet, and when the aunt refused, he stepped forward and grandly paid for it himself. Marianne remembered that.

The Charpillon game was to offer Marianne as a potential mistress who would take up with the right gentleman, but only for a price; they were skilled at accumulating money and gifts from suitors without ever coming to the point. Her role was to play a good girl who felt insulted by indecent treatment, and maybe it wasn't just a role. Judith Summers argues that she wasn't just playing hard to get. She hated the very idea of being gotten.

When Casanova posted his advertisement for a boarder again, it was Marianne who showed up. He asked why she would be looking for cheap lodgings, and she replied, "I needed a good laugh, and I felt like punishing the audacious person who had put up such a notice." Intrigued, Casanova asked how she expected to punish him, and she issued a provocative challenge: "By making you fall in love with me, and then by making you suffer the pains of hell from the way I would treat you."

Actually, he had already been warned about Marianne by his friend Lord Pembroke. The usual tactic of the Charpillon gang was to loiter in one of the two popular London pleasure gardens, Vauxhall or Ranelagh, and allow the girl to withdraw into the bushes with a likely mark. Pembroke had been one of those, but no sooner had he slipped Marianne twenty pounds than she vanished. There was even a warning from Ange Goudar, an accomplished card sharp who was involved in helping the Charpillons to dupe gullible men out of their money. Goudar told Casanova that even though he was their accomplice, they had cheated him too, and he offered to provide Casanova with a mechanical chair that would suddenly imprison a woman when she sat in it, leaving her at his mercy. Casanova was appalled at that. It was Goudar, incidentally, whom Casanova had specifically in mind when he told a friend that he knew all the adventurers in Europe "totally and under the skin."[9]

But how was it possible that he could be a victim? He was determined to prove that he wasn't, and he resolved to beat the Charpillons at their own game. To do so, he needed to make Marianne fall in love with him, but their encounters became a fencing match in which he could never get through her defenses. She constantly led him on and then pushed him away. At one point her mother demanded that Casanova pay one of her debts with the large sum of a hundred guineas. He did pay it, and took that as a clear invitation to sleep with Marianne, but she feigned offended virtue. As he describes their dialogue:

> "Is that amount not enough?"
>
> "Do not joke. It's not a question of bargaining. It's a matter of knowing whether you think you have the right to insult me, and believe that I'm insensible to the outrage. I've told you that you will never have me by violence or money, but only when you've made me fall in love through your attentions."

In this context Marianne's word *procédés* does mean "attentions," but it can also mean "techniques"; she knew exactly where Casanova was vulnerable. Were his techniques of seduction no longer equal to the challenge?

At this point she burst into tears, declaring that no man had ever seen her cry before. "Unhappy me! I feel that I was born for love, and I believed that you were the man sent by heaven to England to make me happy. You've done just the opposite." He recalls that in the *Histoire;* in an undated letter that has survived (and that he doesn't quote) she expresses amazement that he would criticize her conduct. "I don't know what makes you keep enraging me by saying it's my fault that you're full of bile. I'm as innocent as a newborn baby, and I would like to make you so gentle and patient that your blood would turn into veritable clarified syrup."[10]

Next, she invited Casanova to visit her house. He found himself cast as a gentleman caller who might hope that the girl's mother would encourage his interest. The mother was ready to play that role, and for two weeks he took them to theaters and showered them with presents worth four hundred guineas. Not once did he so much as kiss Marianne's hand, until one evening her mother slyly indicated that the moment had finally come. Leading him to Marianne's bed, she left the two of them there in the dark. Marianne had partly undressed, but still wore a light shift.

> As soon as I lay down, I approached her to take her in my arms, but I found her worse than fully dressed. Crouching in her long shift, with her arms crossed and her head buried in her bosom, she let me say whatever I wanted but never answered. When, tired of talking, I determined to take action, she stayed rigid in the same posture and defied

me. I believed this was a playful game, but I finally grasped that it wasn't. I could see that I had been trapped, the most contemptible of fools, and that this girl was the most abominable of whores. In a situation like that love turns easily into rage.

Casanova went on pleading with Marianne. At some point he became violent, though he doesn't say how violent. He does admit that he tried to tear off her shift and "my hands became claws." Eventually he gave up, and at three in the morning walked home. "Shame made me horrified by myself."

But the drama continued. Marianne's mother wrote to say that she was covered with bruises and running a high fever, and threatened to sue him. But soon after that a letter arrived from Marianne herself. "She said she knew she was in the wrong, so much so that she was amazed I hadn't strangled her." For two weeks he made no reply, and then she showed up at his door and insisted on coming in.

> With a modest air she sat down beside me and offered her face to be kissed, which she had never done before. I turned my head aside, but this unexpected refusal didn't bother her. She said, "What makes my face offensive is the still visible signs of the blows you gave me."
>
> "You're lying, I never struck you."
>
> "It's all the same; your tiger's claws left bruises all over my body. Take a look, there's no risk that what you see will seduce you."
>
> With that, the villainous girl got up and showed that her body was covered with bruises that were still livid even after the passage of time. Coward! Why didn't I turn my eyes away? Because she was beautiful, because I loved her charms, and because charms wouldn't deserve that name if they weren't more powerful than a man's reason. She knew that I was tasting the poison and even gulping it down.

She finished off this performance by saying, "I've come to ask for your forgiveness. May I hope for it?" She added that the only reason she had gone rigid in bed was that her mother had commanded her to do it.

Soon afterward Marianne went to bed with him again and permitted some caresses, but refused intercourse on the grounds that she was having her period. He said that that didn't matter, but she insisted. The next morning, however, he realized that she had been lying. When she awoke she got up and laughed at him, at which point he slapped her, causing a bloody nose, and she left.

By this time Casanova wasn't in love so much as addicted, and almost help-lessly he went back to courting Marianne and letting her mother coax still more money out of him. In hindsight, recounting it all in the *Histoire,* he is baffled by his own behavior. "I knew that if I didn't avoid every opportunity to see this girl, I was absolutely lost. Her countenance had a power that I was unable to resist."

Marianne's mother now made still another demand for money, and Casa-nova's patience was exhausted. Enraged, he entered their house at night and opened the door to the parlor. "There I saw, in the words of Shakespeare, the beast with two backs stretched out on the couch—Charpillon and her hair-dresser." With his poor command of English, it's unlikely that he knew the line from *Othello.* Some friend must have repeated it to him.

Casanova thrashed the man with his cane, smashed up some furniture, and left. The next day he heard that Marianne had fled screaming into the street, and her terrified family didn't locate her until the next day. She had taken refuge in a shop that happened to be open late. At that point it's likely that she was no longer play-acting.

Word now came that Marianne was ill with a dangerous fever, and even at death's door. Casanova felt responsible, but he was convinced that he had been manipulated all along. More from self-loathing than from remorse, he decided on suicide. Violence against Marianne and her boyfriend was turning into violence against himself.

After putting his affairs in order, he bought some heavy lead weights, and with those in his pockets walked out onto Westminster Bridge, intending to plunge into the Thames. At the middle of the bridge he was about to jump when a young man he knew slightly, Sir Wellbore Agar, happened along and commented that he looked distressed. Sir Wellbore insisted that they go to-gether to a tavern, where they had plenty to drink and enjoyed watching a naked prostitute dancing a hornpipe. From there they went to the Ranelagh gardens, and to Casanova's astonishment he saw Marianne dancing gaily. Far from being at the point of death, she and her family had been setting him up one more time. And just like that, the spell was broken.

No one had ever kept him on the string the way Marianne did, and he couldn't understand how it happened. What he did understand was that for the first time, his weakness had been revealed. He had become someone he couldn't recognize, and didn't like.

And what did it all mean to Marianne? She represented her family's best chance to make money, and however skillfully she played her part, it's very possible that she hated it. In Judith Summers' interpretation, Casanova was "a man for whom she felt absolutely no desire. A man whose behavior in the past had revolted her. A man who had recently beaten her black and blue."[11]

Casanova did manage a witty revenge. At a street fair he bought a young parrot that was just beginning to imitate speech, and taught it to repeat endlessly *Miss Charpillon est plus putain que sa mère*—"Miss Charpillon is more of a whore than her mother." An acquaintance warned him, however, never to admit that that it was he who had taught the parrot. A bird couldn't be prosecuted for libel, but a human could.

The joke became widely known because Casanova's servant Jarba would carry the parrot around and offer it for sale for fifty pounds, which was far more than it was worth, while it squawked out its message. At last a nobleman who was interested in Marianne bought it himself, to save her further embarrassment. In later years she became the mistress, or rather one of the mistresses, of the celebrated rake and politician John Wilkes. Afterward, as Summers says, "Marianne de Charpillon slipped quietly into obscurity."

Teresa Cornelys was less fortunate. She kept up her success as an impresario for quite a few years, but after a series of bankruptcies died in prison in 1797. Sophie, who had always hated being used by her mother, refused to pay for the funeral, saying that burial as a pauper "was good enough for a woman who had led such an improper life."

Now calling herself Sophia Williams, she became friendly with a series of noblewomen whose children she tutored, and with help from patrons she founded the Cheltenham Female Orphan Asylum in Gloucestershire in 1806, four decades after Casanova had been in London. Like a re-creation of the Ospedali in Venice, it trained girls to be governesses and schoolteachers. She followed that in 1820 with an Adult Orphan Institution in St. Pancras, London. In later years, with sponsorship from a daughter of Queen Victoria, her Cheltenham school was renamed Princess Helena College for Young Ladies, moved to Hertfordshire, and continues to thrive today.

Sophie lived until 1823. She was deeply religious, and seems to have been unlike her flagrant mother—and father!—in every way except in energy and force of will.[12]

After the Charpillon debacle, Casanova managed two more affairs, both of which were disappointing. First he became reacquainted with the Muralt family from Berne, including Sara with whom he and Mme. Dubois had once dallied in bed. She remembered him well, and they got a chance to be alone together briefly. "What charms! What shared joy in two ecstasies (*transports*) which in a single instant, upon an already unmade bed, became one! We didn't have time to say a word, or to savor the nectar that Venus was giving us, or to think about the precious gift of love, nature, and fortune." The rhetorical volume is turned up high, but the description is conventional, and so was the encounter.

That hasty ecstasy turned out to be the only one, because the family was in financial distress and Casanova generously rescued them. What happened then was unexpected. Sara said she wanted him as much as ever, but could no longer give herself freely. Since money was now involved, it would make her no better than a prostitute. He countered by suggesting marriage, but her father explained that that was impossible, since she was already promised to someone else. "At bottom this explanation did not displease me."

The Muralts soon left England, and Casanova concluded his time in London with five sisters who were effectively prostitutes, though they and their German mother put on airs. A night with each of the girls cost him twenty guineas apiece, negotiated formally beforehand. He went through the business more doggedly than enthusiastically, and so did they. If this sequence was supposed to prove to himself that he was still irresistible, it did no such thing. It was only a transaction. In London, in fact, he had experienced two extremes of desire. First there was intense mutuality with Pauline, the last he ever experienced, and then a humiliating obsession that nearly led to suicide.

Taking stock of his practical situation, Casanova grew seriously depressed. "I was nearing the exhaustion of all of my strength, both physical and moral. I was out of money, I had sold all my jewelry and diamonds and other precious stones, and all I had left was watches, snuffboxes, cases, and some trinkets that I was fond of and didn't have the heart to sell, since I wouldn't get a fifth of what they had cost me." The diamonds and jewels must have been what was still left from pillaging Mme. d'Urfé, no doubt including some of the contents of the heavy chest that he only pretended to throw into the sea at Marseille.

Still worse, he got entangled in some new mess involving forged documents, about which he is characteristically imprecise. To avoid imprisonment and possible execution he had to leave England immediately. As he comments, the lifestyle he had adopted was not without risks. "It's not difficult to get oneself hanged for trifles when one runs after adventures, if one is a bit absent-minded and not sufficiently on guard." England was the second country, Venice having been the first, where he would be ill-advised to return.

Years later he got to know Mozart's librettist Lorenzo da Ponte in Vienna, and borrowed money from him. Warning that he would probably never be able to repay it, he departed after making a comment that Da Ponte quotes in his memoirs: "I will give you three pieces of advice that will be worth more than all the treasures of this world. First, my dear Da Ponte, if you would make your fortune, do not go to Paris—go to London. Second, when you get to London, never set foot inside the Caffè degl' Italiani [i.e., the Prince of Orange coffee house]. And third, never sign your name." Da Ponte adds that he lived to regret bitterly not having followed that advice.[13]

In the years to come, financial scrapes would impel Casanova to leave one country after another under a cloud, sometimes after being formally expelled. He had enjoyed living as a citizen of the world—that was an Enlightenment ideal—but was now finding out how hard it was to be a man without a country. His charmed life was losing its charm, and a secret daemon no longer guided him toward triumphs. Anomie was overtaking his spirit, and his frank account of it is poignant.

Casanova went to Dover in March 1764 and took passage to France, along with an unexpected companion. That was a young man named Giacomo Daturi who had written to him from debtor's prison, claiming to be his own godson from Venice. At first he had no recollection of such a relationship, but the youth filled in details convincingly and produced a baptismal certificate that did indeed name Casanova as godfather. "As he was talking I remembered it all, and more even than he could have hoped for, since his mother hadn't told him everything. This young man, whom I had held at the baptismal font as the son of the actor Daturi, was very possibly my own son." Yet another child he never knew he had! But the time for feeling moved by such a discovery was past, and in the *Histoire* he makes nothing of it. Nor, after leaving London, would he ever see Sophie again. So far as we know he never even corresponded with her.

When he left England Casanova had no plans and no destination. He thought of going to Portugal, but he had promised Pauline never to do that without her permission. Not yet forty, he was no longer the person he had believed he was. As he did in the account of his escape from the Piombi, he quotes the first line of the *Divine Comedy: Nel mezzo del cammin di nostra vita,* "midway in the journey of our life," and he adds, "This marked the closure of the first act of my life." Considered as a drama, his story suffers from having reached its high point now. The thirty-four years to come will be a sustained anticlimax.

CHAPTER 22

At the Courts of Frederick and Catherine

No sooner did Casanova reach Calais than he came down with a truly awful venereal infection, very possibly syphilis this time and not the usual gonorrhea. A long journey was out of the question, even if he had had any idea where to go, and he holed up for two weeks in Calais while a doctor got him past the worst of it.

As mentioned earlier, the standard treatment for syphilis was mercury chloride, usually applied as an ointment but occasionally swallowed. Exceptionally toxic, bottles of mercury chloride nowadays are labeled "Poison." The dangers were recognized, but it did kill the bacterium, and would remain the only remedy until the discovery of penicillin in the 1940s. Casanova was well aware of the risk—he had saved Signor Bragadin's life by removing a mercury plaster from his chest—but he accepted it on this occasion.

Daturi's parents were now performing in the northern German city of Braunschweig, known in England as Brunswick (the English royal family came from nearby Hanover). Casanova agreed to accompany Daturi and drop him off there. He was still not well, but he got an introduction to an expert physician who kept him confined for five weeks until he was as near to being cured as his condition would permit. He hung about the Braunschweig court for a while—there were dozens of courts in the decentralized German states—but enjoyed himself most during a week's immersion in the library in the town of Wolfenbüttel; it was the largest library in Europe north of the Alps. He

38. The Library at Wolfenbüttel

was planning to translate the *Iliad* into Italian, and wanted to take notes on Homer commentaries.

The building that stands there today, a nineteenth-century replacement for the library Casanova knew, gives a good sense of the grandeur of the institution. "I lived in the most perfect peace," he says in the *Histoire,* "without ever thinking of the past or future; my work kept me from awareness even of the present." Maxime Rovere comments, "With books as with women, when his happiness is at its height, it excludes any other kind."[1]

FRÉDÉRIC ROI DE PRUSSE
ELECTEUR DE BRANDEBOURG

39. Frederick the Great

This was like the fantasy of seclusion that had captivated Casanova at the monastery near Zurich, when he briefly imagined becoming a monk. In the *Histoire* he declares, "I can see today that to be a true sage in this world, I would have needed only a concatenation of small circumstances, for virtue has always had more charms for me than vice. In short, I was only bad— when I *was* bad—from gaiety of heart." It wasn't always gaiety of heart, and this imagined alternative life path is preposterous.

Now it was onward to Berlin, and the Prussian royal court at nearby Potsdam. The Seven Years War had ended at last the previous year, leaving all of the participating nations financially strapped, and Casanova believed he could help.

His goal was to ingratiate himself with King Frederick II, a French-speaking intellectual and musician as well as statesman who was popularly known as "the Great," and sell him on the idea of a state lottery. It turned out, however, that Calzabigi, Casanova's old collaborator from Paris, had gotten there first. Still, he was granted a personal interview with the charismatic monarch and was invited to stroll with him in the formal gardens of his summer palace Sans Souci (color plate 29).

Frederick was notorious for changing the subject abruptly, disconcerting whomever he was talking to, and during their stroll Casanova had to mobilize all of his conversational talents. "Paying attention to his style, his sideways shifts and rapid leaps, I felt called upon to play a scene in Italian improvised comedy, where if the actor gets stalled the audience hisses him." A complicated system of waterworks was being installed in the gardens, to feed fountains in the style of Versailles, but it didn't work very well. When the conversation turned to that, Casanova did his best to impersonate a hydraulic engineer, knowing nothing about the subject, of course. For once his customary plausibility failed him; the king was not impressed.

After some more random chat it was time to go, and Casanova was startled by the monarch's parting remark. "Pausing in front of me, he looked me over from head to foot and from foot to head, and then said, after a moment's thought, 'You are a very handsome man.'" Casanova replied, "Is it possible, Sire, that after a long scientific discussion Your Majesty can see in me only the least of the qualities that shine in your grenadiers?" That was a rather daring thing to say, since Frederick was well known to be homosexual and chose his grenadiers for physical height and beauty, but the king's only response was a gentle smile. In Voltaire's *Candide* the Prussians appear as Bulgares, an allusion to buggery.

Later on in Breslau Casanova would meet an abbé who liked women but "from time to time fell in love with a young male friend, whom he sighed to conquer in the Greek manner if he encountered the obstacles that come from education, prejudice, and what are called mores." In due course, Casanova adds, this same person "went to Berlin, where the great Frederick found him worthy of his affection. It is by such paths that men often make their fortune. *Sequere deum*—follow the god."[2]

It's possible that despite the gentle smile, the king felt spurned, and disinclined to give Casanova the kind of appointment he was hoping for. When an opportunity for employment did come through, it was to serve as tutor for a group of young military cadets. That would mean living with them in a depressingly spartan dormitory, and Casanova found the offer insulting, though arguably it might have led to better things.

One further encounter with Frederick confirmed that there was nothing more for Casanova in Berlin, and he decided to try his luck next with the empress of Russia. "I saw the king at the parade, on foot. As soon as he noticed me he came over to ask when I expected to leave for St. Petersburg. 'In five or six days, Sire, if Your Majesty permits me.' 'Bon voyage. But what are you hoping for in that country?' 'What I was hoping for here, Sire, to please the ruler.'" At least Casanova didn't grovel—unless this is only what he wished he had said.

On September 1, 1764, a couple of weeks before Casanova departed, James Boswell visited a Berlin tavern and recorded in his journal that he encountered an irritating individual. "Neuhaus, an Italian, wanted to shine as a great philosopher, and accordingly doubted of his own existence and of everything else. I thought him a blockhead." The editor of Boswell's journal tried in vain to figure out who Neuhaus could be, never realizing that the answer was staring him in the face. Neuhaus, "New House," is a literal German translation of "Casanova." He sometimes gave his name in its local equivalent.[3]

A commentator remarks, "The Casanova proscenium extends by now across the whole of Europe, and we no longer know what comedy we find ourselves in." After pausing briefly in Latvia, he moved on to the Russian capital at St. Petersburg. There he fell in, as usual, with an assortment of itinerant gamblers and adventurers, as well as with the Italian dancers and musicians who seemed to be everywhere. And he got on friendly terms with the Russian aristocrats, all of whom spoke French, as indeed they would continue to do in the novels of Tolstoy a century later. Mixing with them gave him a feeling of importance, but no leads for financial gain. During a side trip to Moscow he realized that the St. Petersburg aristocrats, with their ostentatiously French ways, were very different from Russians elsewhere.[4]

Casanova didn't like Russia much—of course, he didn't like Holland or England either—and he mentions some of the reasons. He was there during both solstices, and found it highly disconcerting that winter nights were endless and that in midsummer the sun never really set. The climate was terrible, too. "In Italy we count on good weather, in Russia they count on bad." To combat the frigid winter, bedrooms were supplied with gigantic stoves that extended from floor to ceiling. They were kept smoldering round the clock, which did provide a fair amount of heat, but if servants didn't tend them properly a sleeper could die. No one yet understood what carbon monoxide is, but they were well aware of what it could do.[5]

St. Petersburg itself didn't impress. It had been created just a generation previously by Peter the Great, and still had a provisional aspect. The site was boggy, and elaborate pilings had to be sunk to prevent the buildings from toppling over. As a Venetian, Casanova knew all about that, and he found the Russian efforts amateurish.

Dinner parties were jolly but not elegant. Casanova liked to drink, but not in the quantities that Russians did. "At the big table I found myself next to the secretary of the French Embassy, who wanted to drink in the Russian style, and believing that Hungarian wine was as light as champagne, drank so much that when he got up from the table he couldn't stand. Count Orlov took care of that by making him keep on drinking until he threw up, and then had him carried away asleep."

Grigory Orlov was a favorite of the empress Catherine II, and Casanova appealed to him to make a meeting possible; he hoped to impress her with a project for calendar reform. His letter to the count—*not* quoted in the *Histoire*—is extravagantly obsequious: "My name will be obscure no longer if the great Empress of all the Russias will permit me to believe that he who bears that name would shed all of his blood to augment one single atom of the glory that surrounds her."[6]

Catherine's story is remarkable. Born a princess in Prussia, she was groomed to marry into some royal family. That was accomplished in 1745, when she was sixteen and married her second cousin, a future Czar. She then converted from Lutheranism to the Orthodox Church and became fluent in Russian as well as French, but never had a real relationship with her disagreeable spouse.

In 1762 Catherine's husband inherited the throne as Czar Peter III, proved to be utterly incompetent, and six months later was dead, probably by assassination. Determined to rule herself, Catherine had mobilized the army to depose him. Her career as empress was brilliant. Her generals won victories that extended Russian rule in large areas of Poland and Ukraine, and at home she promoted the reformist and modernizing policies of "enlightened despotism." She maintained an active correspondence with the French philosophes, and a decade after Casanova was there, Diderot spent half a year at her court. (He tried to behave with the strictest decorum, but in moments of enthusiasm couldn't refrain from slapping her legs for emphasis. "I cannot get out of my conversations with him," she complained to a friend, "without having my

40. Catherine the Great

thighs bruised black and blue.") She cultivated the arts, and had the Hermitage built to house her collection; Francesco Casanova would later create paintings for it, celebrating battles of the time.[7]

Something Casanova doesn't mention in the *Histoire,* but must have heard about, was the empress's notoriously active love life. Over the years she had many lovers, including Orlov, Grigory Potemkin, and the future king of Poland Stanislaw Poniatowski. In France she was referred to as the Messalina of Russia—after the scandalous wife of the Roman emperor Claudius—and Byron later called her "Russia's royal harlot." She was only doing, though, what was accepted as perfectly normal in male rulers.[8]

When Casanova did get to meet the empress, he found her much more congenial than Frederick had been. "Of medium height, but well built, and with a majestic manner, she had the art of making herself loved by everyone she thought was interested in knowing her. Without being beautiful, she was sure to please by her sweetness, affability, and intelligence, which she made good use of to seem free from pretentions. If she was indeed like that, her modesty must have been heroic, since she had every right to them." Casanova was struck by how much more effective this style was than Frederick's brusqueness. By listening attentively and not contradicting people, she was able to learn much more than the imperious king could.

Casanova now advanced his proposal. Russia still used the old Julian calendar, as England also had until 1752, which meant that over the centuries the dates had slipped out of alignment with the actual solar year. The Gregorian calendar rectified that in the sixteenth century, and most of Europe had adopted it. Casanova had studied the subject in some depth and was sure he could take charge of Russian calendar reform, but after hearing him out the empress said she needed time to think about it. When they next met she stunned him with a deeply technical analysis of the issues involved, having already made a thorough study of the subject. She finished by explaining that her people were not ready for such a radical change, and the promising idea evaporated. Russia wouldn't adopt the Gregorian calendar until Lenin did it in 1918.

The one relationship in St. Petersburg that Casanova describes at any length was an unusual and disturbing one, even for him: he bought a thirteen-year-old girl for sexual purposes. It suits him to describe their relationship in positive terms, but this is definitely a case in which he seems oblivious to the darker implications of his actions.

He was having difficulty making any progress with women, but one day he was strolling with an officer friend named Zinoviev in a park and commented on an extraordinarily beautiful peasant girl they happened to see. They followed her to a hut where Zinoviev engaged her parents in lengthy conversation, and reported that Casanova could have the girl "as a servant" for a hundred rubles. That was a high price because she was still a virgin, and Zinoviev assumed it was more than Casanova would care to pay, but if he did go through with it, "You'll have her in your service, and you'll have the right to sleep with her." "And what if she doesn't want to?" Casanova asked. Zinoviev replied, "Oh, that never happens! You would have the right to beat her." He could take her anywhere in Russia, he was told, but not abroad: "Although this girl will become your slave, she won't cease to be first of all the slave of the empress." Casanova replied, "I assure you that I will not treat her as a slave."

Technically the girl was not a slave but a serf; slavery had been officially abolished by Peter the Great in 1723. However, that was a distinction without a difference. Peasants were tied to the land in a particular place, and were effectively enslaved even if their masters were not legally permitted to sell them away from the land. And in practice that prohibition was ignored anyway. Owners advertised "servants" for sale and sold them freely. Although technically serfs weren't supposed to own property, many did, and some even acquired enough money to buy their freedom. It may well be that the girl's parents had hopes of doing that.[9]

Implausibly, Casanova claims that this spur-of-the-moment transaction developed immediately into a satisfying relationship. He must have been told the girl's name, but he chooses to call her Zaire, after a Christian slave in Jerusalem in a tragedy by Voltaire. No doubt the name appealed to him because Zaire falls in love with the Sultan of Jerusalem. He would have seen that role for himself as appropriate, or even as type-casting.

Normally Casanova avoided relationships where speech was useless, but according to him Zaire soon picked up enough Italian—Veneziano, actually—to communicate with him pretty well. "It was an inconceivable pleasure to hear her talk to me in Veneziano."

Casanova claims that Zaire enjoyed lovemaking immensely, and still less believably, that she was fiercely jealous if she suspected he was sleeping with anyone else. To illustrate that, he says that once after he stayed out all night at an orgy she flew into a rage. "By the merest chance I avoided a bottle that she threw at my head, which would have killed me if it had caught me on the temple. It grazed my face. I saw her throw herself furiously down on the floor and beat her head against it. I rushed to her, seized her forcibly, and asked what was the matter with her. Believing she had gone mad, I thought of calling for help. She calmed down, but burst into tears and called me an assassin and traitor."

Presently Zaire explained that she had been telling her fortune with a deck of cards, and had learned from them that Casanova had betrayed her in multiple ways. He says that he found this affecting. Still, after a night's sleep he woke up planning to get rid of her, lest she really kill him next time, "but how could I do that when I saw her on her knees before me, despairing and repentant, imploring my pardon and pity, and assuring me that in future I would find her as gentle as a lamb?"

However much Casanova may try to present this relationship in a positive light, it's an ugly nadir in his story. Plenty of women in St. Petersburg spoke

French, and might have been willing sexual partners. Instead he decided to buy a sex slave who was barely in her teens, and at first couldn't even talk to him. How could she not be upset at abruptly leaving the only life she knew, and at being forced to give up her virginity to this intimidating foreigner? By dramatizing her jealousy—if she even *was* jealous—he is seeking to normalize a relationship in which she had no power at all, and no way to protect herself. These are questions he doesn't face and maybe never perceived.

It should be added, however, that some things that shock readers today were not considered shocking in the eighteenth century. Poor families often accepted money in return for their daughters, particularly if the purchasers seemed likely to treat them well. When Rousseau was in Venice in his early twenties, he and a friend named Carrio bought a girl of eleven or twelve whom they proposed to bring up for later enjoyment. Her name was Anzoletta and she was "blonde and sweet as a lamb; it was necessary to wait until she matured, and we had to sow before we could reap." The girl had musical talent, so they got her a spinet and a singing teacher. Not long after that Rousseau had a falling-out with his employer and left Venice. He ran into Carrio in Paris later on, but doesn't mention whether he inquired what had become of Anzoletta. And although the *Confessions* is full of remorse for his misdeeds, Rousseau doesn't suggest that this might have been one of them.[10]

It appears, in fact, that this practice was quite usual in Venice. A French visitor in the previous century used an analogy similar to Rousseau's: "The patricians, selecting the best-looking eight- or nine-year-old girls, have them carefully raised like fruit to be enjoyed when it reaches perfect maturity." The girls, of course, would not come from the patrician class.[11]

As for what had happened when Casanova stayed out all night in St. Petersburg, he is circumspect but sufficiently explicit. At a dinner party he was seated next to a young army lieutenant (later a general) named Petr Mikhailovitch Lunin. "He was blond, and as pretty as a girl. He was the lover of the Cabinet secretary Teplov, and as an intelligent youth he not only defied prejudice, but made a point with his caresses of capturing the esteem and affection of all the well-placed men he frequented. . . . He showed me such coquetry during dinner that I really believed he was a girl dressed as a boy."

That would be like Bellino all over again, only this time there was no mistaking Lunin's sex. After dinner he and a French *aventureuse* sat with Casanova by the fire, and when Casanova told him his suspicion, he refuted it by exhibiting "the superiority of his sex," and offered to "bring about his happiness and mine." Casanova says there's no doubt it would have happened if the Frenchwoman hadn't indignantly pulled Lunin away, "annoyed that a lad should usurp her rights."

Casanova says that he regarded the whole thing as both agreeable and ordinary. "This conflict made me laugh, but not feeling indifferent, I didn't imagine I had to pretend to be. I told the woman that she had no right to meddle in our affairs, which Lunin took to be a declaration in his favor. He showed off all his treasures, even his white breast, and defied her to do the same. She refused, calling us buggers, we retorted that she was a whore, and she left. The young Russian and I gave each other marks of the most tender friendship, and swore that it would be eternal."

After supper "the great orgy began," with a constant changing of partners, and a Frenchwoman mocked Casanova and his young friend for refusing to join in. "Our reserve resembled the virtue of two tolerant old men who regard complacently the extravagance of unbridled youth." As on an earlier occasion in Rome, he claims that indiscriminate orgies never appealed to him.

In all of his mentions of homosexual encounters, Casanova shows neither awkwardness nor shame: they simply happened now and then. He adds that when Zaire was consulting her oracular cards, they had revealed "the boy, the bed, the combats, and even my *égarements* against nature." Having been in some social situations with him before, she probably had her suspicions. Evidently a bed was involved in the marks of tender friendship.

Égarement means going astray; a popular libertine novel by Crébillon *fils* was entitled *Les Égarements du Coeur et de l'Esprit*. Félicien Marceau's comment is convincing: "It's an *égarement,* nothing more than that, which isn't especially interesting, and although it's not in Casanova's usual trajectory, he has no objection to it in principle, much less any repulsion, and he might sometimes make a detour there." Marceau mentions other occasions in the *Histoire* when young men are described as having feminine beauty, and another commentator notes the relevance of "traditional pederasty's mimicry of heterosexual relations," difference in age taking the place of difference of gender. At any rate, as Marceau says, Casanova describes such feelings so freely that there's no reason to suspect, as with Proust, that any of the affairs with women were really with men.[12]

Michel Foucault has argued persuasively that before the nineteenth century, same-sex acts were regarded simply *as* acts, not as evidence of personality type or identity. They might be condemned as sinful or illegal, but a person who did them was not thereby "a homosexual," still less "an invert" or "a deviant." Casanova's accounts of his occasional same-sex encounters don't contradict the fact that he liked sex with women best. The Prince de Ligne, who was enthusiastically bisexual, teased him for being so little inclined that way. After reading the manuscript of the *Histoire* Ligne wrote to him, "Why did you turn down Ismail, neglect Petronio, and feel relieved when Bellino turned out to be a girl?"[13]

By the end of September 1765, Casanova was ready to leave Russia, after a stay of nine months. Making his fortune there had turned out to be no more possible than in Germany, and he acknowledged in hindsight, "In Russia they pay attention only to men who have been expressly sent for. They have no respect for those who come by their own choice. They may be right."

He says that Zaire, with whom he had spent six months, wept when she was told he was leaving and wouldn't be able to take her along. Once again he appears to be trying in the *Histoire* to normalize the relationship, as if this were a sad lovers' parting. Laurence Bergreen feels authorized to describe the relationship romantically and asks, "Who was the slave, and who the master?" The answer should be obvious.[14]

Casanova was able to transfer de facto ownership of Zaire to an Italian architect he knew (he doesn't say whether money changed hands) and he takes pride in that arrangement as a boon for all concerned. "When I left her at her father's house, I saw the whole family on their knees before me, ascribing attributes to me that belong only to the Divinity." That's remarkably similar to a scene in Laclos's *Les Liaisons Dangereuses,* and perhaps Casanova was remembering the novelistic version when he wrote the *Histoire.* The vicious Valmont, however, stages the scene merely to make a good impression on the lady he's trying to seduce.

Casanova's first destination after leaving St. Petersburg would be Warsaw. As a traveling companion, he says that he took a French actress with the stage name of Valville—she called it her *nom de guerre*—who wanted to go home. For transport they used a commodious vehicle with a comfortable mattress inside. In French he calls it a *dormeuse,* and in Germany, where he originally acquired it, it was known as a *Schlafwagen,* which after the invention of railways would be the word for a sleeping car. "I lay down with La Valville, who found this mode of traveling as comical as it was agreeable, since we were positively in a bed." There was also, of course, "an ample provision of things to eat, and good wine."

It was understood on both sides that this was a merely temporary relationship, of a kind that Casanova was very familiar with. "French girls who have sacrificed to Venus, having intelligence and some education, are all like

La Valville. They have neither passion nor temperament, and therefore they don't love. They are accommodating, and their project is always one and the same. Able to detach themselves easily, they attach themselves with the same facility, and always cheerfully. That's not from stupidity, but from a genuine system. If it's not the best, it's at least the most convenient."

At Riga in Latvia, "We parted very gaily, and our good humor was disturbed by none of the sad reflections that are usual in such separations. We had been lovers because we didn't care about love, but we had a most sincere friendship."

Diligent scholars, however, have established a surprising fact about this congenial companionship. It seems that it never happened. Records show that Valville continued to perform in St. Petersburg for four months after Casanova left. But if no one at all accompanied him, why would he bother to make this story up? A good guess would be that he did have a companion, but not Valville, and that he preferred for some reason to disguise who that was.[15]

Casanova arrived in Warsaw with letters of introduction from Russian noblemen, and he was cordially received by their Polish friends. "In less than two weeks," he says, "I was known in all the great houses, and invited therefore to all the great banquets and balls that were given almost every day in one or another of them."

Not just noblemen but the king himself, Stanislaw August Poniatowski, liked Casanova and conversed with him at banquets. The king's portrait (color plate 30), even though he is resplendent in coronation robes, shows a thoughtful and intelligent statesman. On one occasion Casanova spoke so well about the poetry of Horace that the king, knowing he was in debt, gave him afterward a purse containing two hundred ducats, "telling me to thank Horace and to mention it to no one."

It seemed that Casanova would finally get established in some responsible position, but it was not to be. This was a very tricky time to be visiting Poland, which was in the midst of intense internal conflicts, and the nobles were divided between rival factions, one pro-Russian and the other opposed. To be friendly with members of one side was automatically to be at odds with the other.

The king had been on the throne for only a year (a previous king with the same first name, Stanislaw Leszczyński, had been deposed three decades previously and was now Duke of Lorraine in France). The current Stanislaw had served as a diplomat in Russia, and while there had been the lover of the future empress Catherine. Poland had an elective monarchy, and in 1764 he was chosen. His goal was to make his nation strong and independent, but his reign was doomed to be crippled by competition among the neighboring great powers—Russia, Prussia, and Austria—to seize control. In the ensuing decades there would be three successive Partitions of Poland, and a final end of the Commonwealth in 1795.

Casanova had turned up in the middle of this fraught political situation, and although he did his best to stay out of trouble, that wasn't possible. A crisis came five months after he arrived in Warsaw, in which political allegiances played a part, as well as relationships with women. The king invited him to be his guest in his theater box to see a play, and that was an honor he couldn't refuse, though he didn't understand Polish and would never have attended otherwise.

It happened that popular support at the time was divided between two rival Italian dancers, Catarina Catai and Anna Binetti, both of whom Casanova knew. He had no wish to alienate either of them, let alone their admirers, and when he encountered them after the performance he did his best to behave tactfully toward both. It turned out, however, that Binetti had an aristocratic lover whom she encouraged to avenge what she took to be a slight, and Casanova soon found himself compelled to fight a duel with him. Thanks to the code that still governed dueling, to have backed down would have branded him as a coward and ruined the image he needed to project.

Biographers relate this episode briefly, but Casanova did not; together with the escape from the Ducal Palace, he regarded it as a defining moment of his life. Before he published the account of the escape he had published this story too, in Italian originally, with the title *The Duel, or, a Sample of the Life of G. C., Venetian.* He was beginning to think of telling his whole story someday, and like his account of the escape from the Piombi, this episode is a novella in its own right.

CHAPTER 23

The Duel

When Casanova stopped by to chat with the dancer Anna Binetti between performances at the theater, her lover turned up and took furious offense at his presumption in talking to her. The lover turned out to be someone of very high standing, Count Xavier Branicki, just returned from a diplomatic appointment in France. Casanova describes him as "Postoli to the crown, Chevalier of the White Eagle, colonel of a regiment of uhlans [cavalry], quite young, and with a handsome face." A postoli, or in French *panetier* or baker, was originally an official in charge of food production; here it meant a royal chamberlain, by this time a purely symbolic title. Casanova had already happened to be present outside the theater on a previous occasion, when people were getting into carriages in the snow and Branicki high-handedly commandeered the theater manager Tomatis's carriage, slapping Tomatis in the face when he objected to giving it up. Now it would be Casanova's turn to receive an insult.

A duel soon ensued, and years later Casanova proudly published his account of it in Italian, *Il Duello*. In this narrative he describes Branicki with respect but makes it clear that his own values were very different. "Branicki had learned to shed his enemies' blood without hating them, take revenge without anger, kill without incivility, and prefer honor, which is an imaginary good, to life, which is the only real good of mankind." Nevertheless, Casanova felt trapped in a situation that gave him only one option, and that was to play by the rules of the aristocratic code. The reason for that may be far from obvious today, but he and his contemporaries understood it very well.[1]

Accepting the duel was an opportunity for Casanova to prove himself by gambling with his life, just as he had done when he hung by his elbows from the roof of the Ducal Palace. But beyond that it represented a cultural imperative. *The Duel in European History: Honour and the Reign of Aristocracy,* by the historian Victor Kiernan, throws a flood of light on what now seems a bizarre tradition. There were already critics who argued that it was insane to give someone a chance to kill you after having first insulted you, and yet adherents of the code were impervious to argument.[2]

The tradition of dueling went back to feudal knighthood, and in the eighteenth century it was still important in aristocratic class consciousness. Not to offer a challenge in response to an insult was dishonorable, and to decline to fight after having been challenged was still worse. Even if the combatant who died was the actual injured party, that didn't matter. Either way, he would have lived or perished with honor. In the expression that was current, he would have received "satisfaction."

But an aristocrat would only fight another aristocrat; it was a way of affirming their shared status. Rousseau's father, a skilled watchmaker, was once insulted in Geneva by a patrician and demanded a duel. The patrician replied that he only used a stick on people of Rousseau's class.

In the eighteenth century dueling was technically illegal nearly everywhere, but was condoned so long as the participants were discreet and obeyed the accepted rules of conduct. The reason each combatant would be accompanied by a "second" was precisely because duels took place in secrecy. Kiernan explains, "If dueling deaths were to be easily distinguishable from murder, there would have to be witnesses, and at least a minimum of rules. And a man going to a secret rendezvous might be walking into an ambush. It became customary for each combatant to bring with him a 'second,' as an observer and as a safeguard against foul play." In Spanish and early modern French the second was known as the godfather, and he owed a duty to society, not just to his friend. "The seconds were assisting the combatants, but they were also delegates of the class to which all concerned belonged, and whose standards of conduct all of them were taking the field to vindicate."[3]

Members of the middle class might ignore this value system, and many did. An instance in seventeenth-century England became famous when the pioneer economist Sir William Petty was challenged to a duel by Sir Alan

Brodrick. Both men had been knighted, but neither one was an aristocrat. Petty was given the choice of weapons and location for the encounter. He was extremely nearsighted and had no experience with fighting, so his stipulation was: axes in a dark cellar. The duel never took place.

But for those who did adhere to the code, as Kiernan says, "A combatant's reputation, in his own little corner of the world, would depend for the rest of his life on how he had come through the ordeal." Casanova tried whenever possible to pass himself off as a nobleman, or as somehow its equivalent, and it was critical that he behave appropriately. For the noble Branicki to accept a challenge from him was in itself an honor.

In a duel, "The combatant had not merely to risk his life, but to do so with composure, an air of being as indifferent to danger as an officer in battle. Such imperturbability was part of the carriage of the superior class." Casanova passed that test triumphantly, and it didn't just confirm his status in one little corner of the world; it became known throughout Europe.[4]

His own analysis in *The Duel* agrees perfectly with Kiernan's. "Court philosophers, explicitly or tacitly, want honor to reign supreme and to be modeled on the military code. If I had acted as Plato would have recommended [by declining to fight] I would have been a good Christian and a good philosopher, but I would nevertheless have been dishonored and reviled, and perhaps expelled from court, or shut out from noble gatherings with the deepest opprobrium. Such is our century."

The duel took place because of what Count Branicki had said when he came upon Casanova talking to La Binetti at the theater. Every word counted. In the original published version, perhaps to strengthen an impression of objectivity, Casanova refers to himself in the third person as "the Venetian," and he calls Branicki by his title, "the postoli," emphasizing his high rank.

> Looking at him rudely from head to foot, as a tailor would do, the postoli demanded to know what he was doing with that woman. The Venetian, who had never spoken with this gentleman, answered in surprise that he was there to pay her a compliment. The postoli then demanded to know if he was in love with her, and he answered yes. The interrogator replied that he loved her too, and that he was not accustomed to tolerate rivals. The Venetian responded that he had not been informed of his taste. "Then," said the postoli, "you must yield her to me." The Venetian, almost bantering, replied, "Very well, Monsieur, there is no man who must not yield to such a fine cavalier as

yourself. I yield this agreeable lady entirely to you, together with any rights I might have over her."

It could well have stopped there without provoking a fight, but Branicki had no intention of allowing it to.

"That suits me well," the postoli said brusquely, "but after a poltroon yields, *il fout le camp* [he fucks off]." These words, which I write in French because he was speaking French, and because they're not easy to translate [into Italian], are a vile way of saying "go away" that a haughty person employs with superiority and uncivility toward a base person.

The word "poltroon" sounds quaint in English, but *poltron* was anything but quaint in French. He was calling Casanova a coward to his face.

Casanova's temper flared up and he almost drew his sword, but he controlled himself and began to leave with his hand on its hilt, saying simply, "That's enough." Branicki was clearly drunk, and if he would now back off, the thing might still blow over. Instead he called out loudly, "By leaving, this Venetian poltroon is taking the right course. I was going to send him *se faire foutre* [to fuck himself]." Casanova responded, without turning back, "A Venetian poltroon can dispatch a brave Pole to the other world in a moment."

The die was cast. Casanova could not ignore being called a coward, much less a Venetian coward, in the hearing of witnesses. "I believe no man can endure a term that denigrates his nation." He returned to his lodgings with a critical decision to make. He had become friends with the Prince Palatine, who held a high position directly under the king, and he went to ask what he himself would do. "I never give advice in such a situation," the prince replied, "but a gentleman should either do a great deal, or else nothing at all." It would have to be a great deal.

The next morning Casanova sent Branicki a carefully formulated challenge, and from this point forward they both behaved with the utmost courtesy. "Be so kind, my Lord, as to take me in your carriage to a place where defeating me will not make you guilty according to Polish law, and where I may enjoy the same advantage if God should assist me to kill your Excellency. I would not make this proposition, my Lord, but for the idea I have of your generosity. I have the honor to be, my Lord, your Excellency's most humble and obedient servant. G. C., this Wednesday, March 5, 1766, at the break of day."

A servant was sent off to deliver this message, and soon returned with a reply. "I accept your proposition, but you will have the goodness to let me know when I may have the honor of coming to see you. I am entirely, Monsieur, your most humble and obedient servant. Branicki P[ostoli]." It's important to note something that Casanova doesn't mention: the nobleman was willing to fight this commoner only because they were fellow Masons, and in that sense equals. The Prince de Ligne heard years later from Branicki himself that when he agreed to the duel, he demanded, "But are you a gentleman?" Casanova answered, "More than that, my Lord, I am of your society."[5]

Branicki accordingly showed up at Casanova's lodging to negotiate terms. First of all, they must not postpone the duel for a day as Casanova requested—he had some pressing correspondence to finish for the king—since if word of the intended duel got out it would certainly be prevented. If Casanova should be victorious, Branicki pointed out, he would have plenty of time to finish the correspondence, and if he should die, nobody would hold it against him.

Also to be determined was the choice of weapons. Casanova was assuming that they would fence with swords; he had probably taken lessons in Padua, and had several times engaged in rather perfunctory duels in which both parties understood that inflicting a slight scratch would suffice for honor to be upheld. Branicki, however, said that he never fought with a sword since he couldn't know how expert his opponent might be. He therefore insisted on pistols, which in theory gave each man an equal chance, and Casanova felt obliged to acquiesce. He did carry pistols as protection against robbery, but he was no practiced marksman. Branicki was famous for firing at the edge of a blade so accurately that the bullet would be split in two.

They agreed to leave together in Branicki's carriage at three in the afternoon, to a place of his choosing. His parting words were, "I will bring a perfect pair of weapons with me. You have much obliged me. I thank and esteem you. Give me your hand. You will come with me and we will fight with the most complete reciprocal satisfaction, and afterward we will be good friends." The insult at the theater had been a drunken outburst, but the two of them were now playing their roles to perfection. "Satisfaction" for both was indeed what a duel was intended to provide.

Branicki then went to make confession to a priest—Casanova wondered afterward how a priest could absolve a man in advance for a sin not yet committed—while he, characteristically, sat down to a splendid meal. He believed that it would relax him and steady his nerves. "Exquisite dishes, good wine, and the company of chosen and well-loved friends are nourishment that elevates a healthy man to the highest perfection he is capable of. . . . There is no man or woman who, after a delicate repast, will not be better looking, more eloquent, more animated, more courteous, and more present to themselves."

The carriage brought them to a secluded garden at a nobleman's estate that was technically within the area where, according to Polish law, dueling could be punished by death. Casanova pointed this out, but Branicki smiled and said he would accept full responsibility for that. He had several companions with him, including a lieutenant general who would act as his second; Casanova brought no one, declaring that he needed none because he trusted Branicki to deal with him honorably. He added that they might still settle matters amicably if Branicki would express regret for what he had said the previous evening. "Monsieur," he replied, "I didn't come here to reason, but to fight." At that his second, the lieutenant general, "lifted his eyes to heaven and took two steps backward, striking his forehead with his right hand." Branicki's friends had evidently hoped that the quarrel could still be straightened out. In any case they knew that duelists often fired to wound but not to kill.

A box containing two dueling pistols was opened. These would not have been ordinary weapons, but finely constructed for the purpose by a master gunmaker, like the superb pair that was owned by George IV when he was Prince of Wales (color plate 31). The pistols were identical, to ensure that neither combatant had an unfair advantage, and the person who supplied them would let his opponent choose first. Casanova made his choice and Branicki said, "The weapon you are holding, Monsieur, is perfect; I guarantee it." Casanova replied with some irony, "At present, Monsieur, I believe that, but I won't know it until I try it out against your head." That turned out to be a highly significant comment. Branicki was not expecting a bullet in the head.

They now retreated ten paces and prepared to fire. Casanova turned his body sideways, because that was what he was used to doing when fencing, raised his hat politely with his left hand, and told Branicki, "Your Excellency will do me the honor of firing first." It was not obligatory to fire simultaneously, and this was a generous thing to say. But Branicki, who had been facing Casanova directly, thought about the danger to his head and hesitated, turning sideways likewise in the hope of presenting a smaller target. After that slight delay they did fire simultaneously, and to the witnesses it sounded like a single explosion.

Actually Casanova had never intended to aim at the head, since it was too small a target, and they each struck the other in the body. He felt a sharp pain in his left hand, which began to bleed copiously; Branicki exclaimed, "I'm wounded," and sank to the ground. At this dramatic moment there came a truly chivalric gesture. According to Casanova, Polish officers still had a good deal of the barbarian temperament that the ancient Romans had noticed, and two of Branicki's friends rushed at him with sabers brandished. From the ground Branicki called to them furiously, "Villains, respect this *chevalier!*" To use that term was indeed to confirm that Casanova had earned the right to respect, but perhaps he was embroidering a bit in *The Duel.* In the final version in the *Histoire,* Branicki says, "*Respectez cet honnête homme,*" this gentleman.

Fearing imminent death, Branicki now offered Casanova a purse full of money and urged him to leave Poland without delay, lest he be executed for dueling on forbidden ground. Moved, Casanova replied, "I would accept your offer, Monsieur, if I had any thought of running away. I will go to Warsaw to have my wounds treated, and I hope that the wound you forced me to inflict is not dangerous. If I am guilty of your death, I will lay my head at the foot of the throne." He kissed Branicki's sweaty forehead and set off on foot, with no idea what to do next. He was in no condition to walk through the snow all the way back to the city.

Fortunately, a peasant in a sleigh came along, and after Casanova paid him, agreed to take him to the city. It was bitter cold and the horses' hooves spattered snow into the sleigh, so Casanova huddled under a mat. It was as if his secret *génie* had prompted him to do it, for just then a friend of Branicki's named Bissinski galloped by with his saber in the air and would certainly have killed him if he had realized he was in that sleigh—"so heroic does revenge still seem to the Poles."

Fearing further retribution, Casanova asked to be taken to a Franciscan monastery where he would enjoy sanctuary. His caution was appropriate, because the choleric Bissinski did indeed go looking for him at the house of the theater manager Tomatis, and when it was clear that he wasn't there, fired a pistol point blank in Tomatis' face. By mere luck it failed to go off. A Count Mosinski who was present tried to calm Bissinski down, and for that received a horrible saber slash across his face. At this point another nobleman seized Bissinski by the shoulders and forced him out of the house. After his outrageous performance became known, the king exiled him from Poland for life.

Meanwhile both combatants were receiving medical care, Branicki in an inn near the place where they had fought. It was soon clear that their wounds, though dangerous, need not be fatal. Casanova's bullet had passed cleanly through Branicki's abdomen but had not perforated the intestines, which would have caused an untreatable infection. As for Casanova, as he reports in detail, "Branicki's ball had entered my hand through the metacarpal beneath the index finger, and after breaking the first phalanx had stopped there; its force was weakened by a metal button on my jacket, and by having first grazed my belly close to the navel."

Several princes who were friends of Casanova's arrived at the monastery with a surgeon, who began to extract the flattened lump of lead. "While he was performing this painful operation, I narrated the whole story to the princes, easily concealing the anguish that the maladroit surgeon was causing me as he inserted the pincers to take hold of the ball. So much power does vanity have over the mind of man." It wasn't just vanity. Even in great pain, it was important to keep on playing the role.

Good news soon followed. A letter from the king was brought, saying that Casanova had behaved honorably and would not be punished even if Branicki should die. "I printed a respectful kiss on the letter, and showed it to the assembled nobles, who expressed admiration for a man who was truly worthy of the crown. I needed them to leave me alone, and they did."

The next day, however, the surgeons were certain that gangrene was setting in, and they prepared to amputate the hand. "You will consent then, Monsieur, to allow your hand to be cut off. We will perform it with astonishing address, and it won't take long; in just two minutes you'll be taken care of." Casanova had enough medical knowledge to doubt that there was gangrene, and he told them firmly that his arm would be no use to him without the hand; he would let them remove it only if the diagnosis became certain. It didn't, and although it was months before he had full use of the hand, he had saved it—as long ago he saved Bragadin after his stroke—by letting nature take its course. He had his own suspicions about why the surgeons were so eager to amputate—"to pay court to Count Branicki, who was doing badly, and might be helped to recover by this consolation."

All that remained was to complete the drama correctly, with admiring visitors as audience. Every day each of them sent a servant to inquire about the other's convalescence. At one point, Casanova startled Branicki's entourage by appearing in his mansion unannounced. "Branicki was wearing a dressing gown glazed in gold, lying in bed on pillows with rose-colored ribbons. Pale as a corpse, he took off his nightcap." Casanova told him, "I have come to ask your pardon for not being able to ignore a bagatelle which, if I had been wiser, I ought to have paid no attention to." In return Branicki said, "I acknowledge that I insulted you, but you will acknowledge, in turn, that I've paid for it well with my person."

He added that he would order his friends not to harm Casanova, and that

Bissinski had been deservedly banished. "As for my protection, you have no need of that. The king esteems you just as I do, and so do all those who know the laws of honor. Be seated, and from now on let us be good friends. Let Monsieur be brought a cup of chocolate." As a curious finale, Casanova presented Branicki with the pistol ball that had been extracted from his finger, and he replied wryly, "I regret not being able to return yours."

The story was at once the talk of Warsaw, and as he drank in compliments, Casanova had to believe that at last his fortune would be made. But no— unpleasant rumors began to circulate about disgraceful actions in Paris that had gotten him expelled from France. It's not clear what those might have been, or whether there was any truth to the rumors. They surfaced in anonymous letters that Casanova insisted must have come from lying rivals, but all the same, they did so much damage that he was told he must depart. An Italian who was there at the time wrote to a friend, "It's a pity that the illustrious Casanova, formerly a hero and fictitious nobleman, and above all a so-called wit, had not the ability to sustain his great role. Shortly after his brilliant feat, some unfortunate anecdotes from his past, well authenticated, faded his laurels. There, in consequence, is our glorious butterfly, transformed suddenly into the state of a worm."[6]

Once again, and far from the last time, Casanova had made a town too hot to hold him. Soon he was on the road for Breslau in Silesia, as usual with no clear plan as to what to do next. Elsewhere in Europe, numerous journalists picked up the story of the duel, and they also picked up the rumors about Casanova's departure from France. He was especially infuriated by one newsletter that was published in Cologne. When he found himself there a year later, he located the writer's house and burst in with a sword in one hand and a pistol in the other. He demanded to know where the information in the article came from, and when he was told it was in a letter from Warsaw, ordered the writer to produce it at once. "If, to your misfortune, that letter is not in this room, you are a dead man." Shaking with fright, the poor journalist did retrieve the letter, but Casanova learned nothing from it, since he didn't recognize the handwriting or the name that was signed. Thrusting it in his pocket, he stalked off.

Writing about this incident in *The Duel*, he recognized that it was a common pattern of his to fly into a murderous rage and then to calm down after reason prevailed. Also, he prided himself on generosity of spirit. "Although the Venetian vividly imagines taking vengeance, he is weak when it comes to executing it. Happily for him, he is subject to the emotion of pity."

The Duel was published in 1780, fourteen years after the event, and in 1782 there was a kind of coda. Casanova was finally living in Venice again, and he grew enraged when some noblemen insulted him. In Russia he had been asked if he would ever challenge a Venetian nobleman to a duel, and had replied that there would be no point in that since they would never fight a commoner. Now, he published in Italian a withering critique of the Venetian aristocracy, and to contrast their behavior with an example of true honor, he dedicated it "To his Excellency the Count Xavier Branicki, Grand General of the Polish crown." In the dedication he declared, "The respect inspired in me by the superiority and elevation of your mind continues to increase, mingled with gratitude, whenever I remember you."[7]

CHAPTER 24

"This Phantom Liberty"

By this time Casanova had run out of ideas, and was moving on just for the sake of moving on. In his preface he says, "A reader who likes to think will see in these memoirs that never having any fixed goal in view, the only system I've had, if it is one, has been to allow myself to go wherever the wind blew me." When Alfred de Musset reviewed the *Histoire* he understood this well, adding that there were of course intervals of intense activity as well as of passive yielding. "One class of individuals," Musset said, "timid and fearful of everything, lets its oars rest idly on the sea of this life. A second, on the contrary, strikes the waves with audacious blows, but often lets go of the helm to watch the sail fill with the breath of a propitious wind."[1]

It had been exhilarating to recreate in the *Histoire* the freshness and excitement of his earlier life, but now, with his detailed notebooks as his material, Casanova found himself recording trivial incidents and repeated disappointments. After Warsaw he stopped briefly in Breslau (Wroclaw in modern Poland), and then departed by carriage for Dresden. He had an unexpected companion. The previous day he had called on a baroness to deliver a letter from her son, whom he had met in Warsaw, and while waiting to be seen he found himself next to a pretty young woman who was seeking employment as a governess. Suggesting that such a humble position must be beneath her, he launched a little dialogue on the spur of the moment, which he captures skillfully in his narrative. He speaks first:

"If instead of being a governess for children, you would like to be the *gouvernante* [housekeeper] for a man of honor, come and stay with me, and I'll give you fifty crowns not per year but per month."

"Me as your housekeeper? For your family, I understand."

"I have no family, I'm alone, and I'm traveling. I'll be leaving for Dresden at five in the morning in my carriage, and there will be a place in it for you if you wish."

"You're joking! And anyway, I don't know you."

"I'm not joking. As for knowing me, I'll ask which of the two of us has more reason to know the other? We will know each other perfectly well in twenty-four hours. No more than that is needed."[2]

When Casanova set off the next morning he had actually forgotten about this exchange, which he never meant seriously, but to his surprise the woman showed up and climbed into his carriage. They exchanged names for the first time; hers was Maton, or at least he calls her that in the *Histoire.* Maton had attractive manners, was obviously intelligent, and must have been grateful, since she had no money and hardly any belongings. "I was surprised," he says, "at having made something turn serious that I began just to toss off a bon mot. Wanting to persuade the girl, I persuaded myself."

For once there was a good reason to head for the next destination: Casanova's mother Zanetta, his brother Giovanni Battista, and his sister Maria Maddalena were all living in Dresden. Zanetta, in her late fifties, was an actress no longer, but comfortably settled with influential friends; her daughter had become a dancer. Giovanni, whose portrait in later life shows a man comfortable with authority, was a successful painter and by now was director of the Academy of Fine Arts in Dresden. Giacomo never showed much interest in his sisters, and he doesn't even mention Maria Maddalena by name; he calls her "the wife of Peter August," a theater musician. Indirectly, however, she would play an important role, since it was her son-in-law Carlo Angiolini who, long afterward, would inherit the manuscript of the *Histoire,* and her grandson (also named Carlo) who would sell it to the Brockhaus firm.

One might expect that this family reunion was emotional. Casanova does say briefly that Zanetta "was joyous at seeing me," but that's all. Whether or not he still resented her disappearance from his life when he was a boy—it was Giovanni whom she took to Dresden back then—they had apparently had no relationship for the past thirty years. He goes on immediately to say what really mattered to him in Dresden. "Everyone made much of me, and

41. Giovanni Casanova

I had to relate the story of the duel to them all. I did it gladly, because I was proud of it." The duel had taken place months earlier, but he was still carrying his left arm in a sling.

As for Maton, they consummated their relationship the first night they were in Dresden. "At supper she pleased me very much, and I asked her tenderly and sweetly if she would like to sleep in my bed. She replied that that was what she wanted, so the nuptials took place, and in the morning we got up the best friends in the world." He was now inspired to play Pygmalion, as he had with Rosalie in Marseille seven years previously. "I spent the entire morning ordering whatever she needed—dresses, shifts, stockings, skirts, bonnets, shoes—and in short everything, because she had nothing."

But the friendship was short-lived. Casanova noticed that although he wasn't allowing Maton to go out, presumably to forestall losing her to some rival, she and a Swiss officer at a nearby window were flirting with each other. "This discovery made me laugh. I was sure they didn't see me, and I was determined, as on other occasions, not to be cuckolded. My jealousy was more from the mind than the heart." It was quite a stretch to call their new acquaintanceship "nuptials," or to regard himself as cuckolded if she were to sleep with anyone else.

That was not the worst of it. The next day, "I found myself attacked by a *galanterie* whose symptoms were truly nasty." *Galanterie* is bitterly ironic: it means a courtly expression of love. Weeping, Maton confessed that she had been infected for the past six months, but believed that if she washed scrupulously he wouldn't be at risk. It was over. He gave her fifty crowns, a generous enough sum, and told her never to see him again. She disappeared from his life as suddenly as she had entered it.

After Casanova was more or less cured (it was probably gonorrhea once again), he moved on to Vienna, where a further humiliation occurred. "A pretty girl of twelve or thirteen" appeared unexpectedly in his room and begged him for charity, after which she told him—in Latin!—"that her mother needed to come in too, because otherwise she would be put in prison if the Commissioners of Chastity should suspect that while I was alone with her, I was fucking her." That could well be true, since under the aegis of the puritanical empress Maria Teresa, the police were always on the lookout to punish vice.

"This broad expression," Casanova says, "stated in good Latin, made me burst into laughter," and he agreed to meet her later on at her own lodgings. She promised, still in Latin, "that if I joined her in bed I would find her, according to my preference, either Hebe or Ganymede." That is, he could use her either as Zeus's daughter or else, in homosexual style, as his boy cupbearer. She spoke Veneziano as well, "and I admired the singular scheme of her Venetian father in making his living by her." Casanova is impressed by the clever con man, and gives no thought at all to the plight of the girl who was evidently being prostituted for his advantage.

The following evening he set off confidently, "and I had the imprudence, at the age of forty-two, despite my wide experience, of going all alone to the address I had been given." When he arrived at an upstairs room he was confronted by someone he knew all too well as "the infamous Pocchini," together with two Slavonians armed with sabers. The girl was there too, and he realized that she had been a decoy. No doubt her father was well aware of his predilection for young girls.

Casanova had first met Antonio Pocchini in Cyprus long ago, and in later years their paths had crossed repeatedly. They were even fellow Masons. On more than one occasion Pocchini had robbed him, and in London Casanova had paid him back with a thorough caning in Hyde Park. Now it was Pocchini's turn for revenge, and "I believed my last moment was at hand." However, the men didn't beat him up, and they let him go after relieving him of his purse with two hundred ducats in it. "I went back to my place more dead than alive, not knowing what to do. I went to bed." Never, in the past, would he have allowed himself to be set up like that.

A Viennese newspaper from the previous year confirms that Adelaide Pocchini did indeed have the linguistic ability that Casanova describes. "The little daughter of a noble Paduan who arrived here recently, Antonio Pocchini [he was no nobleman, of course], was present in the house of Count Colalto; she is about nine years old. She was interrogated in French on ethics and in Latin on physical science. What is extraordinary is that the young girl, who had had only four lessons in German, responded intelligibly in that language to all questions. All those who were present rendered homage to this child by their applause." Her parents may have claimed she was only nine to make her seem more of a prodigy. And if this writer believed that she had had only four lessons in German, he was gullible indeed.[3]

What makes little Adelaide's story still more painful is that she is known to have died the following year, after having been exploited by her parents from an early age. Casanova probably never knew about that, but if he did, it's unlikely that he cared.

This humiliating episode was more than a mere setback; it was a warning that Casanova's customary good fortune was beginning to desert him. And worse was to come. The day after the confrontation with Pocchini and his Slavonian companions, a policeman showed up and told Casanova that they had accused him of cheating at cards. Accordingly, he must attend an interrogation by the Statthalter, the regional governor. There he was shown a deck of marked cards that he knew were not his, and the purse that supposedly contained his dishonest winnings. It had forty ducats in it; Pocchini and his chums had detained the rest. "There, my dear reader, was one of the terrible moments I've experienced in my life, which make me shudder whenever I remember them. Only a cowardly love of life prevented me from unsheathing my sword and running it through that fat pig of a Statthalter."

On the advice of a friend he composed a petition to the empress, which was truly abject in style. "I am sure that when V. M. I. R. A. [*Votre Majesté Impériale et Royale Apostolique,* Your Imperial and Apostolic Royal Majesty] is taking a walk, if an insect could tell you plaintively that it was about to be crushed, you would turn aside so as not to deprive the poor creature of life." The empress had no sympathy with insects of that kind, and was merciless to card sharps, whether Casanova really was one or not. Vienna was one more city from which he found himself expelled, and he doesn't conceal the depth of his humiliation.

This was not just a setback; it was a revelation of what he had become. He went to implore help from a countess who was known to be close to the empress, and she told him sarcastically that he kept his arm in a sling merely to impress people, since the wound was bound to be healed by now. As for the affair with Pocchini, she said, "I'm not going to get involved with that. You're all rascals, just like Tomatis." That was the theater manager in Warsaw when the rival dancers got Casanova into so much trouble. "I went home unable to comprehend how I could have found myself in such a crisis. Assaulted, insulted by villains and by people of quality too, powerless to crush the latter or to exterminate the former, rejected by justice, where am I? What have I done?"

By now Casanova wasn't just taking stock, he was facing an alarming emptiness.

> It's beyond question that a noble soul will never believe that it cannot be free. And yet who is free in this hell that's called the world? No one. The philosopher alone perhaps, but by making sacrifices that may not be worth it for this phantom liberty. . . . Exhausted, sick of the pleasures and misfortunes and sorrows and intrigues and pains that I had experienced in three capital cities, I felt inclined to spend four months in a free town like Augsburg.

His wish was simply to stay out of trouble for a while.

After an uneventful time in Augsburg there were short stays in several other German cities. In Stuttgart Casanova ran into his old friend Antonio Balletti, who greeted him "wild with joy. That fellow had a soul superior to that of a dancer, and great intelligence quite apart from the talent with which he had distinguished himself." In Cologne, in addition to threatening the journalist who had printed rumors about him, Casanova reconnected with the lovely Mimi, the burgomaster's wife whom he had dallied with six years previously after hiding in the chapel confessional. But that too was a dead end.

> "The confessional [she said] must serve us now only to repent of our sins in the past."
>
> "God preserve me from repentance, and from remorse whose source is nothing but prejudice. I'm leaving tomorrow."
>
> "I'm not telling you to leave."
>
> "If I can't hope, I won't stay. May I hope?
>
> "No! Absolutely not."

At Spa, a Belgian watering place that was frequented (like Aix-les-Bains) by gamblers, there was yet another rejection. The inns were full, so Casanova found lodging with a merchant and his wife, and he perked up when they mentioned that a little room adjoining his would be occupied by their niece. "At the word niece I took thought. The room had no door, and was scarcely larger than the big bed in it."

Sure enough, the girl was pretty. Making inquiries, he learned that she was known to be pious and prudish, and took that as a challenge. Disturbingly, he was beginning to resemble Valmont, the seducer in *Les Liaisons Dangereuses*, who targets the pious Mme. de Tourvel for no other reason than a desire to overcome her piety. But Valmont manages his campaign carefully and manipulates Tourvel into yielding of her own free will. With a crude aggressiveness that was new in him, Casanova didn't bother with preliminaries.

"She was enveloped in her sheet," he says, "since it was very cold, but her bed was so narrow that she couldn't prevent me from putting my arms around her. Embracing her, I begged her to let me kiss her, which she brusquely refused. Her tone annoyed me. I reached my hand under the sheet from the bottom, and moved rapidly up her legs to the most important place. She immediately pulled out an arm, and a fist struck my nose, hard enough to make me feel tender no longer. I started bleeding copiously." If he had once been irresistible, he wasn't now, least of all after making this unsubtle move. "After I stanched the blood I had a contusion that made my face frightful."

Indignantly, Casanova left for new lodgings. He claims that the girl showed up there to ask his pardon, which is hard to believe after what had just happened, but perhaps her relatives made her do it. At any rate, he fails completely to recognize how appalling his behavior was. That fist to the face had been a long time coming.

Also at Spa was Antonio della Croce, an adventurer Casanova had first met in Venice nineteen years previously, together with his beautiful mistress Charlotte. She was in an advanced stage of pregnancy. Croce, who was now calling himself Crosin, had run up enormous gambling debts and decided to skip town, abandoning Charlotte and palming her off on Casanova. "'Adieu,' Croce said, 'I commend Charlotte to you, who would have been happy if I had never known her.' After these words he embraced me, shedding tears, and went off without an overcoat, without a spare shirt in his pocket, wearing silk stockings, with a cane in his hand, leaving me immobile and petrified, in despair at having to give the terrible news to a pregnant young woman who adored this unfortunate man who likewise loved her."

There went a typical adventurer, remembered in a freeze-frame vignette, striding away unencumbered into the unknown (he would pay Casanova a visit in Bohemia thirty years later). As for Casanova, he felt genuinely moved at finding himself responsible for Charlotte. Her identity has been discovered: Charlotte Lamothe or Lamotte from Brussels. He treated her with great consideration, making clear that he had no erotic designs, and they agreed to go together to Paris.[4]

There Casanova secured a midwife. When it was time for the birth Charlotte began to run a high fever, and it got worse after the delivery. A competent doctor was called in but couldn't help. At Charlotte's direction, the baby was registered at the Hôpital des Enfants Trouvés, as one of Casanova's own offspring had been long before. The midwife took the infant to be baptized in a church, and he was named Jacques Charles, after Giacomo and Charlotte.

Casanova remained by Charlotte's bed all day and all night, until the end came.

> She expired in my presence on the twenty-sixth of October, at five in the morning. Before closing her beautiful eyes she told me adieu, saying that it was the final one, and before letting go of my hand she raised it to her lips in the presence of a priest who had heard her confession at midnight. The tears that I'm shedding at this moment while I'm writing will no doubt be the last with which I will honor the memory of this charming creature, a victim of love and of a man who is still alive, and whose cruel destiny seems to have been impelled to make people miserable. Still bathed in tears, I sat by the bed of Charlotte, who was now a corpse, not listening to the midwife who tried to persuade me to go downstairs.

At least Casanova shed tears for Charlotte, though as we have seen, he always did weep easily.

He concludes this story by transcribing the official record of Charlotte's burial:

> Extract from the register of burials in the church of St. Laurent in Paris, October 27, 1767. Charlotte, aged seventeen, spinster, died yesterday in the Rue du Faubourg St. Denis in this parish, and was interred in the cemetery of this church with the attendance of three priests and in the presence of Claude Louis Ambezar [a magistrate] who has signed this. Collated with the original and delivered by myself, the undersigned priest, Besombet.

Guillaume Simiand, in *Casanova dans l'Europe des Aventuriers,* comments that such circumstantial—and verifiable—details are most unusual in the *Histoire.* "Is it a desire to give meaning to an episode that deeply impressed him, notwithstanding his vast experience? A concern for authenticity? A wish to forestall, by means of documentary testimony, any accusation of making it all up in an especially grave moment? Or is it a cathartic gesture toward the child of a friend, a child who bears his first name?"[5]

There were more blows to come. At this very moment, word came from Signor Dandolo that their friend Matteo Bragadin was dead, with legal commitments that had made it impossible for him to bequeath anything to Casanova. Foreseeing this, Bragadin had already given Casanova all that he could over the years—"he was a man who for twenty-two years had been as a father to me." Dandolo added a generous contribution of his own.

Still in Paris, Casanova hoped to resume his old life there, but that was impossible too. At the intermission during a concert a young relative of the Marquise d'Urfé accused him of having robbed her of at least a million. Casanova retorted, "You are nothing but an impudent fellow, and if we were outside I would teach you how to talk with kicks in the rear end." Casanova went out, expecting to be followed and challenged to a duel, but this was not Warsaw and the young aristocrat would not dignify him with a response. Instead, he was served the next day with a document signed simply "Louis," a *lettre de cachet* from Louis XV himself, ordering him to leave Paris within twenty-four hours and France within three weeks. That was the same monarch whose splendid style he had admired so much at Fontainebleau, and would later celebrate in the *Histoire.*

Venice, London, Warsaw, Vienna, and now Paris—the list was growing

longer of the cities from which Casanova had been exiled. No doubt this punishment had been instigated by Mme. d'Urfé herself, though he persists in
pretending that she was no longer alive.

In quick succession, he had lost a woman who was in his care, his adoptive
father, and a city he deeply loved. What next? He decided to go to Madrid.

CHAPTER 25

Spain

Casanova traveled as far as the Pyrenees in a one-person carriage, and then sold it and crossed the mountains by mule. When he stopped for the night in a small town he asked its name and was surprised to hear that it was Ágreda, the home of the nun whose pious treatise had fascinated and appalled him in the Piombi. "It was a prodigy of ugliness and gloom, a place where someone with no employment must become crazy, bad tempered, and visionary. Sister María de Ágreda did go crazy, to the point where she wrote the life of the Blessed Virgin dictated by herself."[1]

By the end of 1767 Casanova was in Madrid. His hope was to finagle some sort of employment at the court, but that turned out no better than it had at previous courts. The chief obstacle this time was that he could only be considered if the Venetian ambassador approved of him. The ambassador, Alvise Mocenigo, was friendly enough, but well aware that Casanova was still considered an outlaw at home.

In addition, Casanova couldn't speak Spanish, and French was less widely understood here than in other European capitals. He engaged a Spanish tutor and made quick progress—Italians generally find the language easy to learn—and was impressed by its eloquence. He says in the *Histoire*, "The Spanish language is, beyond contradiction, one of the most beautiful in the world—sonorous, energetic, and majestic, pronounced *ore rotundo* [with rounded mouth], and capable of the harmony of the most sublime poetry." He was now calling himself Casanova again, not Seingalt; he probably thought it sounded better in Spanish. People addressed him as Don Jaime.

In a way he may have thought of Spain as an ancestral homeland, if we recall his claim at the beginning of the *Histoire* that he was descended from the illegitimate son of a Spanish nobleman. In the same way he liked to believe that his real father was the Venetian nobleman Michele Grimani; but in that case, of course, he wouldn't have been descended from the Casanovas at all.

He found lodgings with a *zapatero,* which he translates into French as *savetier,* meaning a cobbler. This man was known as Don Diego, a title indicating that despite his humble employment he was an hidalgo, a member of the minor nobility. (So was Cervantes' impoverished gentleman farmer Alonso Quejana, who renamed himself Don Quixote.)

Don Diego declined, however, to make Casanova a pair of boots, because it would necessitate touching his feet. An hidalgo would never do that. This hierarchy of prestige would have seemed bizarre elsewhere in Europe. In England, for example, shoemakers practiced a skilled trade (they were known as cordwainers, as in French *cordonnier*) whereas cobblers who merely mended shoes were considered inferior, as in the expression "to cobble something together." Why was it demeaning in Spain to touch someone's feet? Casanova was often amused by arbitrary distinctions that varied from one culture to another.

He was struck, also, by a strange new way of using tobacco rolled into what was known as a *cigarro,* and was both fascinated and revolted by bullfighting, "that magnificent and cruel festival that gives delight to the nation."

Soon Casanova made a new friend who was well placed to help ingratiate him with Ambassador Mocenigo. This was a charming young Venetian named Antonio Niccoló Manuzzi, who was well known to be the ambassador's lover. "He said that he knew me by reputation, having heard his father and mother deplore my misfortune a hundred times." His father was in fact the police informant in Venice who got Casanova condemned to the Piombi, but Antonio may not have known that. Whether he did or not, Casanova chose to overlook it—for the time being, anyway.

It occurred to him also to write to Bragadin's friend Marco Dandolo, and beg him to assure the ambassador that he was no longer considered a criminal in Venice. Dandolo promptly did so, and although this didn't necessarily mean that it would be safe for him to return, it dispelled Mocenigo's doubts. Soon Casanova was being received by Spanish government officials, and they encouraged him to develop a plan to found new settlements in the barren

Sierra Morena range in southern Spain. He was always in his element devising projects, and worked hard at this one. There were even hints that if it succeeded he might be appointed governor. Foreigners did begin to settle there at this time, but Casanova's plan wasn't adopted, and it's not clear why he ever imagined it would be. He was very different by now from the man who glibly talked his way into establishing a state lottery in France, and who made it a huge success.

Someone else he got to know was Anton Raphael Mengs, German by origin, who had been his brother Giovanni's mentor in Rome and was now the court painter in Madrid. In the *Histoire* Casanova says, "Great painter though he was where coloring and design are concerned, he didn't have the most important quality of a great painter, invention. He was extremely ignorant and wanted to pass for learned; he was a drunkard, lascivious, choleric, jealous, and miserly, and wanted to pass for virtuous. He spoke four languages, all of them badly."

Mengs did make one remark that struck Casanova as profound. For a couple of weeks he kept saying that a painting of Mary Magdalene—the repentant prostitute who became a saint—would be finished the next day, and it never was. "You should learn," Mengs told him, "that no painting in the world is more than relatively finished. This Magdalene won't ever be, even when I stop working on it, for it's certain that if I did work on it one day more, it would be still more finished. You should know that even in your Petrarch there is not a single sonnet that could be called really finished." In the same way, Casanova's *Histoire de Ma Vie* is a work of art that he rethought and rewrote throughout the last decade of his life.

Suddenly he found himself under arrest, allegedly for possessing concealed weapons. His servant, probably in anticipation of a reward, had turned him in. He did keep pistols in case of need, and it's not certain anyway that that was illegal. He had evidently been set up, though it wasn't clear by whom, and he found himself in a truly appalling prison that was infested with fleas, bedbugs, and lice. It was like the Piombi all over again, but worse, since the floor stank with urine. As soon as he was allowed paper and ink he sent off urgent pleas to Mocenigo and to some Spanish grandees he had met, and after they intervened he was allowed to leave. "Let's forget everything," he said to the police chief, "but admit that if I hadn't known how to write, you would have sent me to the galleys." "Alas, that's very possible," was the reply.

It struck Casanova that his life was a classic illustration of the wheel of Fortune. "She amused herself to make me see constantly that she is not blind, as people say. She never threw me into an abyss without raising me up again just as far, and she evidently made me rise up high only for the pleasure of watching me fall. She forced me to act, and also to understand that far from making me free, my will was nothing but an instrument that she used to make me do whatever she wanted." During Casanova's hopeful days in Paris, Fortune had been a blind goddess who might unexpectedly shower him with riches. Now she knew exactly who he was, and amused herself by tormenting him. This was a much darker concept than the Stoic maxim "follow the god" that he had learned from Signor Malipiero, or the benevolent prompting of an interior *génie*.

Casanova was on the lookout for women, but that had become an increasing challenge. Partly it was due to advancing age. "Apart from the not yet healed wound that Charlotte had made in my heart, I got discouraged when I saw that women didn't give me the welcome they used to give."

Religion was an obstacle, too. Most Spanish women were sincerely pious, made their confessions weekly, and dreaded the disapproval of their confessors. Even courtesans were careful, before getting down to business, to cover their crucifix with a handkerchief and turn pictures of saints to face the wall. Casanova was told, "If a man should laugh at that and call this ceremony absurd and superstitious, he would be taken for an atheist, and the courtesan might well go to denounce him."

He got into trouble with the church when he fell seriously ill on Easter Sunday and didn't attend Mass, which was obligatory. His absence was reported, and to escape punishment he had to show proof that the illness was real, and also that he had made his confession the day before. He had only bothered to do that, Félicien Marceau comments, "because for him confession was a pure formality, a visa not for eternal salvation but for tranquility in society."[2]

Casanova decided to undertake a gradual and tactful seduction. Don Diego, his landlord, had a tall, lovely daughter named Ignacia—Casanova refers to her as Doña Ignacia—who was hoping to marry a young man who couldn't afford to get married. Casanova said he would be glad to supply the necessary funds, but claimed he couldn't yet manage it. He understood that he had to proceed with caution, since the pious Ignacia must not be hurried. Meanwhile her parents were very willing to see their lodger take an interest. They began to think that maybe he was the one who should marry her.

Casanova had been told by friends that the best way to court a girl was to take her to a ball, with the understanding that her mother or some other chaperone would wait in a carriage outside. He had already witnessed the fandango dance and had found it thrilling, much like the furlana that he once performed so passionately in Constantinople. "The partners dance face to face," he says, "taking only three steps, striking castanets that they hold between their fingers, and accompanying the music with attitudes that are the most lascivious one could ever see. The man's portray the action of successful love, the woman's of consent, ravishment, and ecstasy of pleasure. It seemed to me that no woman whatever could refuse anything to a man with whom she has danced the fandango." He started taking lessons. "According even to Spaniards, there was no one in Madrid who could boast of dancing the fandango better than myself."

Ignacia turned out to be a fine dancer, and they both enjoyed the ball. "This girl, who I was sure intended to give herself to me, danced the fandango so voluptuously that she couldn't have promised it more eloquently in words. What a dance! It burns, it inflames, it carries one away." Still, Casanova was careful not to force the pace.

An immediate obstacle was that Holy Week was approaching. "She told me that she wanted it as much as I did, but that during those days she must reject any thoughts of that kind, since God had died for us, and we must think not of criminal pleasures but of penitence. After Easter we could think about our love." That seemed like obvious casuistry, and it became evident that what Ignacia really feared was not so much sin itself as having to admit it to her confessor. Yet she was certain that it would be a mortal sin *not* to confess. The challenge was to help her talk herself out of this conviction, and an exchange they had convinced Casanova that he would succeed.

> "What need is there for you to go to confession so often?"
>
> "What need? Would to God I didn't need to! But I only go there once a week."
>
> "That's too often."
>
> "It's not too often, because when I am in mortal sin I can't sleep—I'm afraid I'll die while I'm asleep."
>
> "I feel sorry for you, my dear friend, because this fear must make you miserable. I have a privilege that you don't. I count much more than you do on the mercy of God."

Presumably they were speaking Spanish. If so, Casanova had made good progress in the language.

As time went on Ignacia permitted increasing liberties, even if she felt flustered and guilty. When she told her confessor that she refused to stop loving Casanova, he in turn refused her absolution, and she was defiant. "For the first time in my life," she told Casanova, "I bore that affront with a strength of mind I didn't believe I was capable of. Placing myself in God's hands I said, 'Lord, thy will be done.' While hearing Mass I made my decision. So long as you go on loving me I will belong to you, and when you leave Spain I'll find another confessor."

About the consummation Casanova is characteristically discreet. "After this declaration, which showed me all the beauty of her soul, I took her in my arms and led her to my bed, where I kept her, entirely free from scruples, until the first rays of dawn. She left me more in love than ever." He doesn't mention that she must have been twenty-five years younger than he was, or explain how he could be so sure that she was free from scruples. He always wanted to believe that after a young woman's sexual initiation, all previous scruples would disappear.

Fortune's wheel continued to revolve, and suddenly his happiness evaporated. An adventurer turned up who called himself the Baron de Fraiture. Casanova had met him at Spa in Belgium, and knew him to be "a roué and a rascally gamester." Nonetheless, he started hanging out with this shady character, and was incautious enough to tell him what he knew about the Venetian Antonio Manuzzi—not his relationship to the ambassador, which was public knowledge, but the fact that although he claimed to be a count he was just the son of a Venetian tradesman.

Fraiture immediately reported this to Manuzzi himself, who was enraged. His alleged noble status was essential to his role. And although Casanova doesn't say so, it's probable that he also told Fraiture that Manuzzi's father was the spy who got him imprisoned in Venice.

If Casanova was seeking revenge, it backfired. Manuzzi had plenty of influence in Madrid, and now every door was closed to Casanova. Within a few weeks he saw no alternative but to leave town, as he had left so many other towns over the years. He had been there for eight months.

He claims that he felt grief at giving up Ignacia, but it was probably time for that to end too. "We spent our final days together in pleasures that were always followed by sadness, and by tears that seemed to relieve it." A year later he heard that Ignacia had married a rich shoemaker, "submitting through self-interest to the mortification that a misalliance caused her father." Rich or not, the shoemaker wasn't an hidalgo.

Now it was on to Saragossa and Valencia, where Casanova admired Roman ruins but was becoming increasingly hard to please. "One is badly lodged, eats badly, and can't drink; there's no one worth conversing with or to argue with, since despite its university one can't find a single individual who could be called a man of letters."

In Valencia he got acquainted with a Venetian dancer named Nina Bergonzi, the mistress of the captain-general of Catalonia. Casanova was appalled by her willful behavior, and yet he allowed her to treat him imperiously. She was wealthy, and it's a good guess that he was getting support from her. During his first visit to her big country house she required him to watch while she undressed a doltish attendant "and performed experiments on him that were too dirty and disgusting to write down." Afterward Casanova asked how she could allow someone to enjoy her "whose only merit was that of a donkey."

> "You're mistaken. He didn't enjoy it, I made him work. If I could believe he loved me, I would die rather than satisfy him, because I abhor him."
>
> "How is it that you don't love him, and still use him to procure the pleasure of love for yourself?"
>
> "The same way I would use a dildo."

That didn't stop Casanova from accepting the role of the donkey, or dildo, for himself. "After supper I performed with her all the amorous follies that she wanted—or all that I was capable of, for my days as a prodigy were over." In the *Histoire* he avoids acknowledging more explicitly how degrading this was.

Before long Nina had created enough public scandal to be advised to leave Valencia, and she and Casanova proceeded together to Barcelona. There yet another person from his past turned up, someone he really did not want to see. It was Giacomo Passano, otherwise Ascanio Pogomas, who had played Querelinth in the mystical ceremony with Mme. d'Urfé in Marseille. Their partnership had ended when Casanova high-handedly refused to share the loot, in return for which Passano had convinced Mme. d'Urfé that Casanova had been deceiving and swindling her all along. There were definitely old scores to settle.

In Barcelona, Passano informed on Casanova—it's not clear how or to whom—and one dark night he was jumped by two men. Drawing his sword, he ran it deep into one attacker and escaped up the street, barely avoiding injury from two pistol shots that left holes in his overcoat. The next thing he knew he was in prison once more, though he wasn't told what became of the mugger he had wounded or possibly killed. He was charged instead with carrying invalid passports, which wasn't true, and was incarcerated in the tower of San Juan.

Fortunately his cell was decently furnished, unlike the holding tank in the Madrid jail, and he was allowed to have writing materials. He spent his time there drafting a long treatise in Italian entitled *Refutation of the History of the Venetian Government by Amelot de la Houssaie.* The history in question was a highly tendentious book by a French historian. Casanova was coming to the conclusion that after years as a man without a country, he needed the security of his own country again, and this *Refutation* might please the Venetian authorities. He did publish the book in the following year, and it was a step in the right direction.

After six weeks he was released, his sword and overcoat were returned along with his passports, and he was told that he was free to go. He never got a clear explanation of why he had been imprisoned in the first place, but strongly suspected that it wasn't due to Passano alone. Very likely Nina had amused herself by exciting jealousy in her lover, the captain-general, who in turn had commissioned the street attack and the arrest. "She had brought me to the brink of a precipice, and plunged me into an abyss that could have cost me my life."

As for the charge of carrying invalid passports, that was never more than a cover story. Nor did the officials care that Casanova had stabbed, if not killed, one of his attackers. To protect the captain-general, they dismissed the whole thing as if it had never happened. "They say," he was told, "that the pistol shots that were heard were fired by yourself, and it's you who must have bloodied your own sword, for no corpse or wounded person has been found."

On the last day of 1768, Casanova left Spain and headed for Provence. To be sure, the king's *lettre de cachet* had ordered him to leave France, but probably no fixed term of exile was specified, and he surmised correctly that a brief stay in the south might not be known in Paris in time to do anything about it. Paris itself was probably still off limits, though eventually that prohibition would be relaxed.

Casanova concludes this stage in his narrative by saying, "That, my dear reader, is the whole of the strange story of what happened to me in Barcelona. You have never read anything truer or more faithfully detailed, and with all of its circumstances it's known to many people still alive in that city, all of whom are worthy of credit." This emphasis that he has told the whole truth would seem to imply that other unpleasant rumors had gotten around. Long afterward, recounting the story in the *Histoire,* he was still determined to quash them.

CHAPTER 26

Whiling Away the Years in Italy

Casanova was just forty-four in 1769, but it was an old forty-four. He had accumulated a lot of mileage by this time, literally as well as figuratively, and his optimism was gone. He still had another thirty years to live, but they would be increasingly depressing, and after pushing the *Histoire* forward to cover just five of those years he would give it up. From then on his efforts would be devoted to rewriting and deepening the story of his earlier life.

The journey from Barcelona nearly ended right after it started. Casanova's coachman detected three brutal-looking toughs following them on the road. Deducing that one or more of his enemies had sent them to murder him, Casanova got the coachman to take an unusual route, and they shook off the pursuers.

Leaving Spain was a huge relief, and although legally Casanova had no right to be in France, Provence was evidently far enough away from Paris to be safe. The climate was serene, he says in the *Histoire*, the women were beautiful, and the food was excellent. "I breathed again, finding myself in France, after all the misfortunes that had tormented me in Spain. It seemed to me that I was born again, and indeed I felt rejuvenated." The feeling would be temporary.[1]

He stayed for a while in Aix-en-Provence—that was the occasion described earlier when he was sick with pleurisy and never suspected that the woman who nursed him had been sent by Henriette—and then moved on to Marseille. These were familiar scenes. In Marseille he happened to meet the older sister of Nina, who had gotten him into such trouble in Barcelona. The sister agreed wholeheartedly with Casanova that Nina was a monster, and added a revelation that staggered even him.

> "I myself am unhappy because of her, and God is justly punishing me for bringing her into the world."
>
> "What do you mean, bringing her into the world?"
>
> "Yes, Nina is my daughter."
>
> "How is that possible? Everyone believes she's your sister."
>
> "She is my sister too, since she's my father's daughter."
>
> "What are you saying! Your father made love to you?"
>
> "Yes, I was sixteen when he got me pregnant with her. She is the daughter of crime, and a just God intends to punish me through her. My father died to escape her vengeance; maybe I'll cut her throat before she cuts mine. I should have strangled her in the cradle."

Casanova liked to play with the idea that the incest taboo was nothing more than an arbitrary convention, but this lurid tale was going too far. "I was overwhelmed with horror."

After Marseille he went on to Turin, another familiar town. There he bought books with which to finish the defense of Venice that he had begun in the Barcelona prison, and went to Lugano in Switzerland, just north of the Italian lakes, where it could be published beyond the reach of Italian censorship.

Though Casanova doesn't mention it in the *Histoire,* we know that he spent some time next in Florence, from which a newspaper item survives. It's clear that he himself had urged the editors to print it:

> There remains in Florence that gentleman whom we described in the last *Gazetta* as Signor Giacomo Casanova di San Gallo [that would be "Seingalt"], a Venetian nobleman. We must state that the person mentioned has come in person to tell us that he is a Venetian, but not noble, declaring that he has never attributed this quality to himself, which greatly exceeds his qualifications, and that he is restricted to being a good subject of that nation but not a noble.[2]

Well might Casanova hasten to make it clear that he was no aristocrat. Years before, putting on airs as if he actually was noble had been one of the offenses that got him into the Piombi. If he hoped to receive amnesty in Venice, he had to make clear that he now knew his place as a "good subject."

In Siena, he had a conversation with a marchesa that revealed deep weariness with the libertine ethos, the old pattern of leaving each high point of pleasure to seek for the next. He would offer her sincere homage, he said, but "only of the mind," for otherwise he was sure to end up with disappointment. That seems to mean that conversation with an intelligent woman offered his best hope for satisfaction. By now, sexual affairs were not only hard to initiate, but likely to end badly.

The marchesa protested, just as he once would have, that intense pleasure is an end in itself. To that he replied soberly, "The good that one desires is often limited to the pleasure of desiring. It's a fiction of the mind, and during my life I've come to know its vanity all too well." That was precisely the wisdom that Yusuf, in Constantinople, had told him he would arrive at if he lived long enough.

Heading next for Rome, Casanova had an encounter that was both romantic and generous. A young couple asked if they could share his carriage, and because the woman was very pretty he agreed. The man was a cocky Frenchman in an officer's uniform who spoke hardly a word of Italian; the woman was a slender blonde who spoke both Italian and French well. She was English and her name was Betty.

After they set off, it became evident that her companion was not her husband and that he was completely broke. He called himself the Count de l'Étoile, but far from being a count or even an officer, he was only an itinerant actor, as Casanova ascertained when he looked into his suitcase and found it stuffed with play scripts. This man's practice was to ride ahead on a horse, leaving Casanova to pay the bills for their meals and lodging and to follow in the carriage with Betty. This was a type Casanova was very familiar with. The man would play the complaisant husband, and expect Betty to sleep with their dupe while they siphoned money out of him. She, however, had no idea that that was the game, while Casanova felt insulted at being taken for a dupe.

Soon he got her story out of her. He was touched to find that at school in London her best friend had been his own daughter Sophie. Now she was engaged to an Englishman whom he calls Sir B. M., but while he was away on a trip she had been seduced by the so-called count and had run away with him. She claimed to love this fellow deeply, but it was obvious to Casanova that he was a rascal just in it for her money, and he soon found a way to enlighten her.

After drinking a lot at dinner her companion declared that people who truly loved each other would not object if their partners slept with someone else, at which Casanova challenged him to a wager.

"I'll bet you twenty-five zecchini—here they are—that you won't let me go to bed with your wife."

"Permit me to laugh. I'll bet you fifty that I have the strength to be present throughout the performance. Meanwhile I accept your bet. Betty, my dear Betty, let us punish this disbeliever. I beg you to go to bed with him."

"You must be joking."

"Not at all, I beg you. I will love you all the more."

"I believe you're crazy! I will never sleep with anyone but you!"

When it became clear that she really meant it, the man saw that he wasn't going to get his fifty zecchini, and he really did go crazy. Casanova says, "He called her *foutue bête* [fucking idiot], hurled the most atrocious insults at her for a quarter of an hour, and ended by saying that her resistance was pure hypocrisy, since during the past three days she must have given me everything that a whore like herself had to give."

So now poor Betty knew the truth, and was miserably humiliated. She sobbed all night, and in the morning the Frenchman decamped by himself for Rome. She did sleep with Casanova, but he understood that what she needed was not a temporary relationship with him, but reconciliation with the Englishman. Accordingly the two of them wrote to him—he was now back from his trip—and he promptly showed up in a state of fury. Bursting in, he assumed that Casanova must be the vile seducer and rushed at him with a pistol, while Betty screamed, "You're wrong, this is my savior!" Fortunately Casanova succeeded in wrestling the man to the floor, while his pistol fell away.

After Betty got him to calm down he heard the whole story and was truly grateful. "I couldn't have guessed," he said, "that the man I found with her would be her liberator. Be my friend, Monsieur, and forgive my mistake." Casanova embraced him cordially and said that in his place he would have done exactly the same thing. Everyone wept.

This is another of those episodes in the *Histoire* that reads like contemporary sentimental fiction, which doesn't mean it couldn't have happened like that. People often interpret their lives through fictional categories, and Casanova, writing a quarter century later, couldn't avoid being novelistic any more than Rousseau could in his *Confessions*.

Sir B. M. wanted to travel on to Rome with them in order to avenge himself on his rival, but here Casanova's knowledge of the world was invaluable. He knew that if that happened, there would be severe penalties under Roman law, and he advised the Englishman to leave it to him to take care of. When they got to Rome he went to the chief of police, "a personage who can do a lot, who takes a great many matters into his own hands, and is most expeditious when he understands them clearly and when those who solicit him spare no expense. Accordingly he is rich, living with a certain ceremony, and has prompt access to the Cardinal Vicar, to the governor of Rome, and even to the Holy Father." No doubt money changed hands. The Frenchman was thrown into jail, and released only after he promised to leave Rome.

Also visiting Rome was Lord Baltimore, an Englishman Casanova had known in London when they were both entangled with the infuriating Charpillon. He was the proprietor of the colony of Maryland, to whose major city his family had given their name, though it never occurred to him to go there. Casanova doesn't mention, but must have known, that he had fled England after being accused of abduction and rape.

Baltimore and some friends were on their way to Naples, a city Casanova loved, and he joined them. "We are in the month of June," Félicien Marceau says. "In Naples the weather is radiant. In the sky, not a single cloud. On the sea, no waves. Far off, emerging from the heat haze, Capri and Ischia. All, of course, things that Casanova doesn't tell us. The first object to strike his sight in Naples is 'the too well known Chevalier Goudar.'" That was the professional card sharp who had been Charpillon's pimp; in this book we first noticed him as author of a treatise on how to cheat at cards.[3]

Long afterward, when Goudar was in Austria, Casanova gave a friend this sketch of what he had been like in those Naples days. "He's a native of Montpellier, a man of intelligence, a pimp, a thief at gambling, police spy, false witness, and deceiver, bold and ugly. In London he found a very beautiful Irish girl in a beer hall. He had brought her with him [to Naples] and told me he had married her; that's possible, but I wouldn't bet on it." The woman, Sarah, had indeed been a sixteen-year-old barmaid when Casanova knew her in London (and was disappointed at the time that Goudar refused to share her).[4]

Trained in music since then, Sarah now "sang like a nightingale." She had also become a talented *aventureuse*. "She dressed with all the elegance that a French or Italian woman could have achieved, carrying herself well, receiving guests still better with manners that were both noble and easy, speaking Italian with the eloquence of a Neapolitan, and ravishingly pretty. Unable to forget how I had last seen her in London, I was stunned. She could see that I was, and laughed heartily." With a nice theatrical touch she had impressed people in Naples by converting to Catholicism and receiving baptism. That was hardly necessary, since she had been a Catholic all her life.[5]

Casanova always claimed that he would never stoop to cheating at cards, but if he was collaborating with Goudar he must now have been doing so. Whatever fortune he had extracted from Mme. d'Urfé was gone, and Bragadin's death had deprived him of his last reliable income. "Goudar told me that he supported himself by games of chance. Faro and biribi supplied his entire income, and it must have been considerable, since everything *chez lui* was magnificent. When he invited me to join in I took care not to refuse. My purse was emptying fast, and I might not have had any other way to support my style of living."

As so often happened, other people from Casanova's earlier life also turned up. One was a woman named Agata, with whom he had had a brief affair in Turin seven years previously before surrendering her to a wealthy Englishman. Another was Teresa Cornelys' son Giuseppe or Joseph, making a grand tour on his own. His days of discontent in London seemed forgotten, not to mention his role as the Count d'Aranda in the attempted reincarnation of Mme. d'Urfé.

Casanova enjoyed several weeks of unabated high living in sophisticated circles, which included the English envoy to Naples Sir William Hamilton (best known today for later marrying the notorious Emma, whom he shared with Admiral Nelson). Casanova remembered with special delight a party hosted by a Spanish grandee, the Prince de Montena y Francavilla; at that time Spain controlled the Kingdom of Naples. It was at a cliffside estate in Piano di Sorrento, reached by a jolly day-long journey in a felucca, a small galley that could be rowed if there wasn't enough wind for sailing. The setting was the opulent gardens and palace of the Villa Maresca Sopramare, which still exists today as a hotel.

The Marquis de Sade places a scene in *Juliette* at the villa, calling Francavilla "the richest lord in Naples, and at the same time the greatest bugger." That novel, however, is an unremitting sequence of elaborate tortures and murder ("'Fuck!' replied that woman of character. 'Do you think one ever tires of the sight of death?'") Casanova didn't witness even a conventional orgy, though he was present at an entertainment when the prince commanded his pages to swim naked in a seaside pool. "Charming boys of fifteen, sixteen, and seventeen, they were all minions of this amiable prince, whose nature preferred the masculine sex to the feminine." Some English visitors asked if they might see girls perform as well, and were told that that could be arranged the following day. Casanova remarks gloomily, "This party at Sorrento was the last true pleasure I have tasted in my life."[6]

Still, he was able to complete his pursuit of a fourteen-year-old beauty whom he calls Callimena (he was getting older, but the girls were not). This happened in another garden, much as with Lucrezia in Rome long ago. "Callimena went with me along the covered walks, where the already dazzling sun couldn't penetrate with the slightest of its rays. It was there that she crowned my flame, after having fought against her own desires for the past two days. At five in the morning, in the presence of Apollo as he rose above the horizon, seated together on the grass, we abandoned ourselves to our desires."

Couronna ma flamme is the language of classic French romance, but it was frankly a business transaction. The girl's aunt, "whose character was excellent," gratefully received six hundred ducats from Casanova that would pay for music lessons, and also for appropriate outfits when Callimena launched a career. "It seemed to me that I had purchased my happiness very cheaply." Not all that cheaply. It was equivalent to 2,500 modern euros, eight times more than the annual wages of an ordinary worker at the time.

As for the Goudars, their glamorous life in Naples came to an abrupt end, and it was Sarah's fault: she was having an affair with the young King Ferdinand IV and the queen found out.

Now it was back to Rome for Casanova, stopping off on the way for the remarkable reunion with Lucrezia, and with the daughter Leonilda whom he didn't know he had, that has been recounted earlier. In Rome there were quite a few old acquaintances, including the abbé Gama who had been his first mentor there and afterward a friend in Florence, and also his two youngest brothers. Giovanni was about to go home to Dresden; Gaetano, who begged for money, was coldly turned down. Giacomo did agree to give him a small stipend so long as he accepted a humble appointment at a church in Palestrina, twenty-five miles away. In the *Histoire* he adds coolly, "After my departure he entered a monastery where he died suddenly thirteen or fourteen years later. He may have been poisoned."

The reason for Giovanni's departure is notable. He had sold a purportedly ancient art work to the famous specialist Winckelmann, who then discovered that it was a forgery. A commentator remarks, "The Casanova blood runs true." Giovanni left Rome in a hurry.[7]

Also in Rome was the painter Mengs, with whom Casanova had spent time in Madrid, taking a year of absence from the Spanish court. It may have been at this time that Mengs painted the portrait reproduced here (color plate 32), though it's not universally accepted that it's of Casanova, or even that it's by Mengs. Some authorities attribute it to the Genoese painter Francesco Narici. If it does indeed show Casanova, it's not to best advantage, since the expression is supercilious and off-putting, with none of his charisma and wit. But in other respects the symbolism is appropriate. The velvet suit, opulent waistcoat, gilt buttons, and flourishing ruffles were Casanova's preferred costume whenever he could afford it. To convey his intellectual interests, which were genuine if amateurish, he is holding a big folio volume open, with several more books at his elbow. That's certainly appropriate, since he was always a voracious reader. A cherub looks down at him affectionately, holding a silver vase of flowers and fluttering on insect wings. Casanova's gaze is direct and cool, as if sizing the viewer up. The prominent nose is definitely true to life.

It's unlikely that any portrait could have done justice to Casanova's vitality and charm. Something Diderot wrote, reviewing the Salon exhibition of 1767, would apply well to him. On view was a portrait of Diderot himself by Michel Van Loo, and he complained that it was a terrible likeness. Besides, he said, no portrait can ever capture the expressions that give a person his individuality. "In a single day I've had a hundred different physiognomies. I've been serene, sad, dreamy, tender, violent, passionate, enthusiastic; but I've never been as you see me there."[8]

Someone Casanova was happy to see in Rome was his old friend Bernis, who had been named a cardinal in 1758, and although still in disgrace at Versailles was now the French ambassador in Rome. They hit it off well, as always. "I told him that I was determined to behave myself, without the least luxury. He said he would write to M. M. to tell her about this novelty, and I entertained him greatly with the story of the nun in Chambéry." One would have thought that that story was more poignant than entertaining.

Bernis was fifty-five by now and fat, no longer the active ladies' man of old. Instead he had established a decorous relationship with a beautiful young Princess Santa Croce. Her husband was jealous, which Casanova thought inappropriate, since he acquiesced willingly in the steady supply of income Bernis provided. Bernis was tactful enough to disguise his support by pretending to lose to the princess at cards every day—always the same amount.

Casanova says, "In the princess, the prince, and the cardinal, I saw three beautiful souls, innocent and without malice, who went their own way without harming anyone or disturbing the peace and good rules of society." Naturally he himself found the princess attractive, but he knew better than to attempt anything. He does remark wryly that at his first visit she received him informally, which was "the privilege of being a man of no consequence."

There were, in fact, no affairs of the heart for Casanova any more, and hardly any of the flesh. He slept with his landlady's daughter a few times, but was more interested when he watched her and a female friend perform together with a heroically endowed young tailor named Marcuccio. That youth was hoping to marry a different girl once he could afford it, which presented Casanova with another opportunity for a good deed.

Marcuccio's girlfriend Emilia was confined in a sort of convent called the Institutio di Santa Caterina dei Funari, a charitable refuge for girls with no money who would be lodged there until they found husbands. They were permitted to see visitors only through two thick gratings while standing in the dark, and in addition, any visitor had to be accompanied by one of a girl's relatives.

Marcuccio's sister Armellina was also an inmate there, and Casanova went along with him for a visit. He was immediately smitten with Armellina, and because he seemed wealthy and impressive, the supervisor permitted him to take her and Emilia to the theater. He found an opportunity for some erotic teasing as well, but he had to admit that he was getting too old to appeal as a lover. After a handsome young Florentine saw Armellina at the theater and proposed marriage, Casanova willingly surrendered her. In addition he provided funding for Marcuccio to marry Emilia.

The good deed went still further. Casanova figured out why the inmates were restricted to receiving visits in darkness and behind bars: they were being shielded from ever meeting potential spouses. If they did leave to get married they would receive substantial dowries. The governors of the institute had been appropriating this money for themselves, over many years if not centuries. Casanova explained the situation to Bernis, who told the pope, and the entire place was shaken up and put on a proper footing.

At this point Casanova went out into the countryside to visit a woman named Mariuccia, whose own marriage he had made possible—after sleeping with her himself—a decade previously. Her eldest daughter looked exactly like him. Mariuccia acknowledged that she was indeed his daughter, yet another child he never knew he had. She had been named Giacomina after him; her husband knew all about that and had no hard feelings. The girl had a friend, Guglielmina, who turned out to be Casanova's niece, since she was the illegitimate daughter of his brother Giovanni.

Sexual dalliance with Guglielmina ensued, but what Casanova especially appreciated was yet another episode of voyeurism, the last of its kind in the *Histoire,* and one with a new depth of awareness. After the girls went to sleep Mariuccia led him to their room, and intending to please him, stealthily pulled the covers back.

"I viewed the two innocents, each with an arm extended down her stomach and a slightly curved hand on the evidence of her puberty that was beginning to appear. The middle finger rested motionless on a tiny and almost imperceptible piece of flesh. I felt a delicious horror. This new emotion compelled me to cover up their nakedness myself, with trembling hands. In good faith Mariuccia had betrayed the great secret of these two innocent souls, at a time of their greatest security. They would have died of grief if they had awakened when I was gazing at their beautiful pose."

The "horror" was indeed something new. Mariuccia thought she was giving Casanova a treat, but he suddenly felt that he had no right to spy on the girls like that. If they should happen to wake up, they would be mortified to realize that he had seen them touching themselves, even if unconsciously in their sleep.

It was time to move on yet again. As usual, Casanova had shown no interest in knowing more about his daughter Giacomina. He headed north to Florence, where he settled down and began translating the *Iliad* into Italian ottava rima stanzas, a project he had had in mind for some years (he would eventually publish it, but without making much of an impression). He was in Florence for seven months, taking a break now and then to socialize with adventurers, but only to avoid boredom. Then things went sour. He was accused of involvement in a gambling scheme—unjustly, he insists—and his old expulsion from Florence was remembered, when he had cashed a forged bill of exchange. Once again he was kicked out. "It was the twenty-eighth of December, the same day on which I was ordered to leave Barcelona within three days, exactly three years before."

Casanova moved still further north, to Bologna this time, and at last his longed-for goal seemed within reach. There were encouraging signals from Venice that he might finally be allowed to return, and his friends there encouraged him to take up residence nearby while awaiting that outcome. He decided to go to Trieste, close to the Venetian holdings in Istria. As shown on a contemporary map (color plate 8) that was a region, divided today between Croatia and Slovenia, that lay directly across the Adriatic Sea.

CHAPTER 27

Trieste, and Venice at Last

On a whim, Casanova chose to begin his journey to Trieste from Ancona, though that wasn't the nearest port for crossing the Adriatic. He wanted to go full circle, revisiting the place from which he had started out on his travels twenty-eight years before, but he would be returning to Venice filled with self-reproach and chagrin. "Despite myself I knew, and had to admit, that I had wasted all my time, which meant I had wasted my life. . . . I was seeking to return as a free man to my *patrie,* which meant confining my desires to retracing my steps and undoing what I had done, good or bad. I considered it was a question of making less disagreeable a descent whose end point must be death."[1]

Part of Italy today, Trieste has changed hands many times over the years, and at that time was ruled by Austria. A print made a few years earlier shows an active and impressively protected port, an upper town with a wall of its own, and flourishing orchards on the hills. He soon acquired friends there, including the genial Venetian consul, who was happy to help in his campaign for reinstatement at home.

In Trieste Casanova settled down to complete a multivolume *History of the Troubles in Poland.* That much-disputed nation was repeatedly partitioned among neighboring powers, and when he was there he had begun to collect materials for such a project. This book would be a bid for literary distinction,

42. Trieste

harvesting something lasting from the years of wandering. His *History* has been described as "full of high erudition and penetrating in its observations," but it attracted little notice. One drawback was that he wrote it in Italian, whereas French would have found a much larger audience. Another was that he had a falling-out with his publisher in Gorizia (also known as Goritz) in northern Italy, and only three of four volumes ever got into print.[2]

By now Casanova was desperate to go home. "I was attacked by the malady which the Germans call *Heimweh,* homesickness. The Greeks called it *nostalgia.*" He was receiving encouragement from friends in Venice, and at this point he stopped claiming that the Inquisitors had been justified in imprisoning him. "Having absented myself from my fatherland (*patrie*) only to save myself from an illegal prison, the government—not one of whose laws I had violated—could not consider me to be guilty." Actually he knew perfectly well that although Venice did have a written code of laws, the Inquisitors had complete authority to imprison anyone for reasons of their own, with no obligation to prove that any law had been broken. Also, "absenting himself" was a highly euphemistic description of what he had done.

With the consul's help, Casanova now concentrated on carrying out various minor tasks that might gratify the Venetian authorities. He lobbied to get a commercial sea route from Trieste changed for the benefit of Venice, and passed along information he had acquired about an impending decision on customs charges. He seems to have received some modest financial recompense for these efforts.

"As for the pleasure of love," Casanova says, "I procured it with young girls who were wholly without consequence, spending little and exposing my health to no risk." They may have been servants or shop girls rather than prostitutes. He also intervened on behalf of a beautiful Slavonian servant who was resisting her lover's demand that she move with him to Vienna; she wanted to return home. Casanova persuaded him to let her go, and was rewarded with a couple of nights in bed, but he seems to have regarded this more as a good deed than as an erotic adventure. "Everyone in Trieste thought I had acted well."

There was also an infatuation with a married woman who interested Casanova as a cross-dressing Harlequin during Carnival. "I fell in love with her, but being thirty years older than she, and having started out by showing only the tenderness of a father, a feeling of shame that was altogether new in my character prevented me from doing anything to convince her that I felt the affection of a lover."

One further anecdote in the *Histoire,* just before it abruptly stops, concerns a different humiliation. An eccentric young Count Torriano struck up a friendship with Casanova and urged him to come for a visit at his country estate. When he got there he was lodged in a dark, badly furnished room, with a single candle of poor quality to read and write by. At meals, his host was withdrawn and irascible by turns, and the rest of the time was nowhere to be seen. He even left on a week-long trip without warning, leaving Casanova to fend for himself. Yet he stayed on. Perhaps he was putting up with this treatment in return for free room and board.

Eventually there was a showdown. Casanova had seen the count brutally beating the peasants who farmed his lands and vineyards, and soon he witnessed that brutality in a more personal way. He had induced a pretty peasant girl named Sgualda (a diminutive for Osvalda) to sneak into his room at night, and one morning the count saw her leaving and began to thrash her with his cane.

To see this and to jump on him was the work of an instant. We both fell, he beneath and me on top, and Sgualda ran away. In a nightshirt as I was, with one hand I took hold of his arm with the stick, and with the other I tried to strangle him. Meanwhile he held me by the hair with his free hand and tried to break free. He didn't release his grip until he felt that I was strangling him, and I instantly seized his cane. Standing up, I bloodied his head with blows that he was fortunate to parry with his hands while taking flight, picking up stones that I didn't wait to receive. I went back inside and locked myself in.

The next day Torriano challenged Casanova to a duel, which he viewed with equanimity. He had no doubt that the count was a coward, and if they did fight, "I felt certain that I would lay him flat in a moment with my infallible direct thrust, and then wound him in the knee if he wanted to keep going."

Solemnly, they got into a carriage to ride together, just as he and Branicki had done, to a secluded wood where the encounter could take place. However, the carriage kept right on until it came to Gorizia. There it stopped at an inn, they went inside, and the count admitted that he had been in the wrong. He asked only that Casanova keep quiet about what had happened. "I promised, and we embraced." Casanova remained at the inn while the count went home. Researchers have established that some years after this, Torriano was officially declared insane.

Bragadin's old friends Barbaro and Dandolo in Venice had been working behind the scenes for years to win permission for Casanova's return, and now the consul in Trieste was helping too. Casanova gives no details about how they managed it, or why it took so long, but in the fall of 1773 his eighteen-year exile was over at last. A safe conduct document arrived for him in Trieste, and we know from other sources that the consul then wrote to the Inquisitors to describe Casanova's reaction: "He read it, he reread it, he kissed it repeatedly, and after a moment of concentration he released a torrent of tears of joy and gratitude for such an exceptional and precious act of mercy." Of course that was framed to gratify the Inquisitors. Casanova himself says nothing about it in the *Histoire,* though he easily could have. But when he was writing the *Histoire* he was in exile yet again.[3]

Before leaving Trieste, Casanova encountered yet another character from his past, an actress named Irene whom he had known in Augsburg and who was now an accomplished card sharp. Her career change amused him, and he liked her nine-year-old daughter—a disturbingly familiar story—who was training to be a dancer. "At the beginning of Lent she departed with her troupe, and three years later I would see her in Padua, where I formed a more tender relationship with the girl." At this exact point the *Histoire* stops, right in mid-air, just as he was about to turn fifty.

Chantal Thomas observes that the ending is appropriate in its way. "It brings together a number of elements that had a decisive role in Casanova's life: the theater, little girls, and the city of Padua which was the first 'foreign' city where he lived as a child, learning there among other things Latin and the sufferings of love." In his original French, the very last word in this enormous narrative is *tendre*.[4]

But why does the story suddenly stop now? Every reader must feel shock when, right on the verge of reentering Venice, the great storyteller falls silent. In some notes about his life that he gave to a friend later on, he did recall his arrival there as "the most beautiful moment of my life." But that moment would be short-lived, and it's no wonder that he couldn't bear to continue the *Histoire* past this point. He had received a decisive comeuppance not from an individual but from life itself.[5]

Shakespeare gave Macbeth language that might have resonated with Casanova:

> My way of life
> Is fall'n into the sere, the yellow leaf,
> And that which should accompany old age,
> As honor, love, obedience, troops of friends,
> I must not look to have, but, in their stead,
> Curses, not loud but deep, mouth-honor, breath
> Which the poor heart would fain deny, and dare not.

For Casanova there would not even be mouth-honor. He was no longer someone who mattered.[6]

With the *Histoire* finished, or rather discontinued, we lose the wealth of stories and reflections that have formed the heart of this biography. As a result, most biographers have unfortunately said little about Casanova's final quarter-century, fully one-third of his life beyond this point in the story. But a great many letters and documents do survive, and some recent writers have drawn upon them effectively, notably Angelo Mainardi in *Casanova: L'Ultimo Mistero*. The "final mystery" is how to think about those years of Casanova's life.[7]

In Venice Casanova found modest lodgings in the Calle delle Balote, midway between San Marco and the Rialto. It was a far cry from the Palazzo Bragadin, though he did sometimes have the use of a casino belonging to Bragadin's old friend, Marco Dandolo. Barbaro, his other friend, had died a few years before Casanova's return. When Dandolo also died in 1779, Casanova lost the casino, as well as a relationship that had been so important for thirty-three years. Dandolo's will has recently been discovered; he directs his family to take good care of Giacomo Casanova, "who has long been close to my heart," and bequeaths to him the furnishings in the room where he used to sleep, as well as books, clothing, and a gold watch.[8]

At one point Casanova went out to the village of Valle San Giorgio, in the Euganean Hills near Padua, to visit his old mentor Antonio Gozzi, who was now an archpriest, a title denoting an assistant to a bishop. Living with him was his sister Bettina, Casanova's very first love, who had feigned demonic possession so long ago, had nearly died from smallpox, and had then run away with a rascal whom she soon left. Casanova mentions this reunion with Bettina at the very beginning of the *Histoire:* "I found her old, sick, and dying. She expired before my eyes in 1776, twenty-four hours after my arrival. I will speak of her death in the proper place." But his narrative never reached the proper place.[9]

Hoping to make money by writing, he finished the Italian verse translation of the *Iliad* that he had been working on for years; we saw him doing serious research for it in the great library at Wolfenbüttel. Three volumes were published, but sales were disappointing and a projected fourth volume never appeared. He organized a troupe of French actors and began a weekly journal of theater criticism to boost its productions, but those ventures petered out too. That wasn't surprising; plays in the French manner had never been popular in Venice. As for ordinary employment, Casanova made repeated attempts, but without success. Although he had official permission to be in Venice, he was still *non grata* to most of the aristocracy, though he did resume some old friendships among them. Even after he left Venice for good, two of them, Pietro Zaguri and Andrea Memmo, would be faithful correspondents.

Casanova had fallen far, but now there was a new low. His old expedients for acquiring money, the gambling and the scams, were probably failing him. Unbelievable as it may seem, he now offered to become a secret informant for the Inquisitors, spying on the nobility in return for a salary of fifteen ducats per month, equivalent to 600 euros today. No doubt they thought that the longtime bad boy would know what to look for. He was now performing exactly the same ignoble role as Giovanni Battista Manuzzi, whose evidence had sent him to the Piombi. We only know about this because his reports survived in the government archives, and were brought to light in the nineteenth century. Stefan Zweig emphasizes the depth of his humiliation: "Casanova, Chevalier de Seingalt, the darling of women, the victorious seducer, has become Antonio Pratolini, informer and nark." Possibly he meant his pseudonym ironically. *Pratoline*—the noun would have a feminine ending—means "daisies."[10]

Casanova's reports are notable for a sententiously moralizing tone that he evidently felt obliged to adopt. Thus he writes, "The excess of luxury, and of women without restraint, with entire freedom to dispose of themselves, contrary to the indispensable duties of the family—these are the causes by which corruption gains in strength day by day." In another report he expresses outrage at an art school where boys "sketch, in various poses, on certain nights a naked man, and on other nights a naked woman."[11]

Especially shocking, he reports, is the clandestine sale of libertine books, including the "postures" of Aretino and *La Religieuse en Chemise*—both of which he had of course owned and enjoyed himself. After providing a long list of scandalous titles, including serious works by Voltaire and Rousseau, he names names: "The greater part of the books mentioned in my humble report are in the quarters of N. H. [*Nobile Homine*] Ser Angelo Querini; N. H. the chevalier Giustinian has many of them; N. H. Carlo Grimani and N. H. the cavalier Emo have them also, as do many others for whom this page is too small to contain the names." "Informer and nark" is right.

All of this seems so absurd that Casanova may have been privately chuckling at his latest feat of impersonation, playing the role of a high-minded moralist shocked by offenses far milder than the ones he himself used to commit. One commentator makes the plausible suggestion that he enjoyed an opportunity to avenge himself on the arrogant patrician class that undervalued him all his life; another notes that the very triviality of the offenses may have been the point—he offered no evidence that would get someone in serious trouble. The authorities obviously grasped that; they stopped his salary and thereafter paid him only when they thought the information useful.[12]

In any event, the degradation must have been wounding. When Casanova addresses the Inquisitors directly his style is downright abject: "I, Giacomo Casanova, a subject of Your Excellencies, come to supplicate and implore the beneficent rays of your inviolable justice, prostrating myself before the August Tribunal in whose presence I would think myself deserving of death if I were to declare anything but the purest truth." It's hard not to believe that he despised himself for writing like that.[13]

At this time Casanova formed a long-term relationship with a woman, though nothing is known about it apart from the fact that in 1779 he began living with a dressmaker named Francesca Bruschini, twenty years younger than himself, together with her mother and brother. Their modest house was on the Calle Barbaria delle Tolle, close to the church of San Zanipolo where he once had his assignations with M. M. He evidently helped with expenses. This was the first and last time in his life that he ever lived with a woman. Ian Kelly thinks that she gave him "the warm domesticity he had never really known," but that's only a guess. She might have been someone convenient to sleep with, at a time when women no longer wanted him. Another writer suggests that "he considered her as a species of servant."[14]

We do have some letters that Francesca wrote to Casanova (in Italian mingled with Veneziano) later on, after he was forced to leave Venice. The biographer Rives Childs says that these are valuable "for the sympathetic light they throw on her unreserved devotion to him," but that's definitely a sentimental misrepresentation. Francesca does say things like "I am grateful to you and will be until I die, because I have no one else in the world but you," but she is talking about financial gratitude, and her letters are all pleas for money. In return she sends him the Venetian gossip of the day, including news of the death of his old enemy Pocchini.[15]

Casanova apparently wrote back regularly and sent modest sums when he could, but it was never enough. Francesca and her family were reduced to pawning most of their possessions; in 1787 they were evicted for nonpayment of rent and had to move in with friends. Always indistinct, she fades away entirely.

At one point in the *Histoire* Casanova says ruefully, "At my age, my independence is a kind of slavery. If I had married and had submitted to a woman skillful enough to direct me so that I wouldn't perceive my subjection, I would have looked after my fortune and had children, and I would not be as I am now, alone in the world and with nothing." But he must have known really that he could never have done that.[16]

After eight discouraging years in Venice, it all came crashing down. Once again Casanova brought it on himself. He had finally gotten a job as secretary to an eccentric nobleman, but was soon entangled in some obscure quarrel about money that made him a public laughingstock. That he couldn't bear, and he rashly took revenge not just on his employer but on the entire aristocracy that he felt was shaming him.

He now published a satirical pamphlet denouncing the aristocracy, *Né Amori né Donne, Ovvero la Stalla Ripulta*—"neither loves nor ladies, or the stable newly cleansed." The allusion in the title is to the Augean Stables, which were so foul that Hercules could clean them only by diverting a river through them. Casanova, then, was performing a labor of Hercules by exposing the corruption of the Venetian aristocrats. That could hardly be more insulting; as a commentator says, he was calling Venice "a swamp full of shit."[17]

Specifically, he suggested that Carlo Grimani, who had gotten involved in the financial mess, should not be regarded as noble at all, since his real father was probably not his mother's husband. And he went further. As was mentioned earlier, a 1755 novel by the Abate Chiari had publicly described Casanova, under a thin disguise, as "of unknown origin, and by many said to be not of legitimate extraction." Now he himself announced publicly that he was probably the illegitimate son of Michele Grimani, who had owned the San Samuele theater when his mother was the star there. Thus, as Ian Kelly says, "he and Grimani were brothers of sorts, and Casanova had a twisted claim to nobility: he was the son of Grimani's supposed father Michele, but doomed to walk on the wrong side of the road for having been born to an actress. Carlo Grimani, born in a palazzo to an adulterous mother, was no son of Michele."[18]

This wasn't just an insult, it was an attack on Venice itself. The hereditary transmission of rank was a fundamental principle of the ruling aristocracy. What mattered was legal paternity as acknowledged by both spouses, not compromised by speculation about who someone's "real" father might be.

All his life Casanova had struggled against the status system that excluded him despite his gifts. He felt himself to be a natural aristocrat, and the eminent senator Bragadin had loved him as a son. But not even Bragadin could legally adopt a commoner, or bequeath his fortune and palazzo to him. This was a quarrel that Casanova couldn't help reviving again and again, self-destructive though it was to do so. He saw through the hypocrisy and unearned privilege of the Venetian establishment. While he knew himself to be a con man, he saw the hierarchy that lorded it over him as a con on a far bigger scale.

On January 13, 1783, Casanova fled Venice under threat of being imprisoned. It was not banishment this time, strictly speaking, but it might as well have been. He knew he could never live there again, and he returned only briefly to retrieve his belongings. Even then he remained in a gondola and never set foot on the pavement. He told a friend later on, "In 1782 I got embroiled with the entire body of the Venetian nobility. At the beginning of 1783 I voluntarily quitted my ungrateful country and went to Vienna." Only technically could his departure be called voluntary.[19]

CHAPTER 28

The Gathering Gloom

Casanova now had no idea what to do with himself, in Vienna or anywhere else. He wrote to a friend, "I'm fifty-eight years old, I can't travel on foot any more, winter is coming on, and if I have any thoughts of becoming an adventurer again, I look in the mirror and burst out laughing."[1]

After leaving Venice he resumed his old itinerant way of life. From Francesca Bruschini's letters we know that he spent time in Vienna, Innsbruck, Frankfurt, Spa, and Brussels. When he reported that he had once kept going for twenty-eight hours without a pause, she replied, "Great man that you are for traveling! I'm glad to know you're in perfect health."[2]

After that he went to Paris, where his brother Francesco was completing a set of battle scenes for the monarchy. Evidently Giacomo's banishment by Louis XV (who had died in 1774) was forgotten by now, but he knew hardly anyone and soon gave up. He mentions that he had been looking forward to reestablishing contact with d'Alembert, but the great philosophe died just two weeks after his arrival. We do know that he met Benjamin Franklin in Paris and attended a lecture on ballooning with him, but no details of their conversation survive.

In 1784 he and Francesco traveled together to Dresden, where they spent some time with their sister Maria Maddalena. Their mother Zanetta had died in 1776 at the age of sixty-nine; that happened two years after the narrative in the *Histoire* breaks off, so he says nothing there about what he felt. Maria

Maddalena's husband, Peter August, was harpsichord master at the Dresden court; their son-in-law Carlo Angiolini was likewise a court musician.

The city where Giacomo stayed longest was Vienna, which he found more hospitable now, since the puritanical empress Maria Teresa had died in 1780. Her son, Emperor Joseph II, was a far more liberal ruler, and among other policies gave encouragement to the previously distrusted Masons. For a time Casanova actually held a job, one of the rare times he had done so, writing dispatches for the Italian ambassador. That ended, however, when the ambassador died.

Suzanne Roth, in her valuable study of eighteenth-century adventurers, evokes the grief with which Casanova experienced his shrinking world. "While the cities changed, countries were closed to him one by one as he accumulated distressing adventures. That was why he had to leave Poland and then Vienna; a *lettre de cachet* expelled him from France; he was compelled to leave Barcelona, and he preferred to leave Spain altogether. . . . The world was no longer a vast realm to conquer, tempting and open everywhere. If he didn't watch out there would soon be no place for him at all on this *peau de chagrin*." The allusion is to a famous novel by Balzac, sometimes translated as *The Skin of Sorrow*. That was a piece of rawhide that granted magical wishes but shrank ever smaller each time.[3]

Stefan Zweig concludes, "Casanova is unwanted, as unwelcome as a louse."[4]

Well aware that he was aging, Casanova wrote in an unpublished essay, "During my fine adolescence, that charming season in life which it's useless to regret since it can't be recovered, it made me impatient to see that the world was full of nothing but oldsters. Today it seems to me that it's peopled only by the young. I was wrong then, and I'm wrong now."[5]

A remarkable portrait of Casanova was made in 1788, one year before he started writing the *Histoire*. Appearing as the frontispiece by Jan Berka in a book Casanova published in Prague, it is the only authentic image we have from Casanova's final decades. His self-presentation now is as a thinker, altogether different from the complacent ladies' man in the Rome portrait—if that one is indeed of him. The Latin text within the circle describes him as "Jacobus Hieron[imus] Chassanaeus Venetus, sixty-three years of age." Below it is a rueful admission: "Now comes another face of things. I am seeking myself, but I am not here. I am not what I was, nor what I think I am. I was." The final word seems to mean that the real Casanova existed now only in the past.

The phrase *non sum qui fueram* comes from a poem by Sextus Propertius, and the full context is relevant: "I am not what I was. A distant journey can

Altera nunc rerum facies, me quero, nec adsum:
Non sum qui fueram non putor esse: fui.

43. Casanova at 63

change a girl's heart! How mighty was that love, and in how brief a space is it fled! Now for the first time I am forced to face the long, long hours of night alone, and to vex my own ears with my complaining."[6]

Casanova must have approved of this portrait, and yet its effect is disquieting. A biographer once offered this analysis: "The countenance is lined by tribulations and wrinkled deeply. The neck is thin, the shoulders have fallen under the weight of his destiny. A disenchanting grin tortures the mouth. Under the denuded forehead, the arched nose, the lips now so thin, and the hollow cheeks, appear the skull bones as if the skeleton had begun to put off its useless covering of flesh as death called still more loudly. But if he is haunted by the knowledge of his decline, this man does not try the less to keep up appearances. His head is still held in a combative attitude, his eye shines with arrogance and pride." When the portrait was made Casanova still had ten years to live.[7]

By now he had finally settled down, for the first time in his life, in a small Bohemian town called Dux (modern Duchkov in the Czech Republic). That came about because he had become friends with Count Joseph Karl Emmanuel von Waldstein, thirty years his junior, who owned a castle there. Waldstein belonged to a highly distinguished family. One of his relatives was Ferdinand Ernst Gabriel von Waldstein, to whom Beethoven dedicated the Waldstein Sonata, and a celebrated ancestor was Albrecht von Wallenstein, the great Habsburg general during the Thirty Years War in the previous century.

The Dux castle, in the modern Palladian style (color plate 33), contained no fewer than a hundred rooms, as well as an armory that was like an armaments museum and an impressive library. Waldstein found Casanova's wit and storytelling amusing, and as an act of kindness invited him to become the castle librarian with an annual salary of 450 florins, equivalent to 11,000 modern euros. He was also provided with a pleasant apartment, a personal servant, and the use of horses and carriages whenever he wanted to travel.[8]

Casanova says that the library held forty thousand books, but that may be an exaggeration, and Waldstein's brother said that he would fling most of them into the fire. Still, it was an impressive collection, including for example a seventy-volume edition of the complete works of Voltaire. Neither Count Waldstein nor Casanova expected the position of librarian to entail much work; it was frankly a sinecure. His nominal task was to compile a catalogue of the books, but he never got very far with that. At first, in fact, he declined the appointment, but eventually he decided it was the best he could do. He would spend the last thirteen years of his life there.[9]

Rives Childs calls Dux a "final haven," but from Casanova's point of view it was more like a minimum security prison. The town was dull and the company duller. Waldstein, who lived elsewhere most of the time, was seldom there except to go hunting. The local people spoke only Czech and Casanova essentially ignored them. In an aside in the *Histoire* he mentions "the ignoramuses in the country where I'm now living, who are quite rightly my enemies, since the donkey can never be a friend of the horse." In the same way he had called the people of the village of Martirano "animals" when he went there to work for Bishop Bernardis.[10]

A view of the town made early in the next century (color plate 34) confirms how small and remote it was. The castle and church dominate, and the foreground is occupied by farm laborers and by a woman praying fervently at a wayside shrine. From Casanova's point of view the only encouraging feature would be the nobleman's carriage, with a gilt coat of arms on its side, arriving for a visit.

The best thing about Dux was its relative proximity to places Casanova did enjoy. As the map shows, Vienna was two hundred miles away but reachable, and other destinations were much closer: Prague at sixty miles, Dresden at forty-five, and the fashionable watering place Teplice (or Toeplitz) just six miles from Dux, as is indicated in the original caption to plate 34. Visitors went there only during the warmer months, however, from May through September, and in winter travel anywhere was almost impossible. Still, it has been calculated that during the thirteen years at Dux, Casanova spent the equivalent of four years elsewhere.[11]

In Prague, he passed some time with his fellow Venetian Lorenzo Da Ponte, Mozart's librettist, and he may have met Mozart himself. All three of them were Masons. A writer on Da Ponte comments that it was that poet's unlucky fate to have his name linked forever to Mozart and Casanova—one an infinitely greater artist, and the other "a gigantic personality."[12]

In the 1770s Casanova had known Da Ponte in Venice, where he acted as secretary for a while to Casanova's patrician friends Pietro Zaguri and Andrea Memmo, until he was banished on account of his scandalous way of living. Unlike Casanova, Da Ponte had been ordained as a priest, but he never pretended to practice religion. Writing to Casanova at a later time, Zaguri called Da Ponte "a strange man, well known to be a rascal with a mediocre mind but a great talent for writing, and good-looking enough to be loved."[13]

In 1782 Da Ponte became the official poet of the imperial theater in Vienna; he specialized in libretti for operas, working first with Antonio Salieri.

In a biography of Mozart, Marcia Davenport conjures up an engaging scene:

> Prague saw the three roisterers parading the tiny cobbled streets—huge, toothless Lorenzo, with his booming laugh, senile Casanova with sparks of old fire in his eyes; between them Wolfgang, trotting along in a vacuum of bliss and ideas, a quiet little man, looking up at each in turn to catch the last outrageous remark and cap it with some *Salzburger dreckiger Witz* [dirty Salzburg wit] that made them pound his slight back and bellow with joy. They drank rivers of wine and punch and beer.

That's wholly imaginary, however. If it did happen, it left no trace. It might be added that Casanova was far from senile, and he hated beer.[14]

44. Casanova's Central Europe

There have been strenuous efforts to prove that Casanova contributed directly to *Don Giovanni*, which premiered in Prague in 1787. It's certainly true that Da Ponte knew about his history with women, and might well have discussed the libretto with him when it was in progress. There are a couple of pages among Casanova's papers that sketch an alternative version of Leporello's escape in the second act, after he and his employer have been detected exchanging clothes and identities. It's not known if Da Ponte ever saw this; certainly he didn't use it. The author of an authoritative recent study of *Don Giovanni* says firmly, "The question of Casanova's involvement in the libretto of this scene can be quickly dismissed."[15]

It's true that an *opera buffa* treatment of the Don Juan legend might have appealed to Casanova (Da Ponte himself called it a *drama giocoso*) but he is hardly likely to have approved of the final chorus:

> *Questo è il fin di chi fa mal!*
> *E de' perfidi la morte*
> *Alla vita è sempre ugual!*

"This is the fate of all who do wrong! And the death of evildoers is always like their life!" More appropriate for Casanova, perhaps, are the lines Da Ponte wrote about Cherubino in *The Marriage of Figaro*:

> *Non più andrai, farfallone amoroso,*
> *Notte e giorno d'intorno girando,*

"You won't go around any more, amorous butterfly, night and day fluttering about indoors."

In *Casanova, or the Anti-Don Juan*, Félicien Marceau notes some important differences between Casanova and the fictional libertine. Don Juan (or Giovanni) doesn't drink, gamble, or relish the pleasures of the table; he lives only for conquest. Even sexual pleasure is just a means to that end. In contrast, Casanova drinks and gambles and loves good food; he is eager to share pleasure with his partners; and he remembers each one for her individuality, not as items in a catalogue. Still, these are differences in degree, not in kind. Casanova was unquestionably a libertine, self-proclaimed in fact, and most of his seductions were indeed conquests.[16]

While Casanova was at Dux he corresponded regularly with Da Ponte, who addressed him affectionately as *Carissimo e dolce amico*, "most dear and sweet friend"; Da Ponte's companion Nancy added in one letter, "Most kind Signor Casanova, I assure you of all my esteem, kindness, and friendship." They had much in common, including a love of poetry, a history of libertinism, and an endless scramble for money. In one letter Da Ponte writes, "Right now I am *padrone* of nothing; I'm like a man who has fallen into the water and is struggling with hands and feet not to drown."[17]

Da Ponte lived long enough to read the *Histoire de Ma Vie* when it was finally published in 1826; by then he was a professor of Italian at Columbia University in New York City. He wrote to a friend, *Casanova disse tutto, forse troppo, e qualche volte il non vero,* "Casanova tells everything, maybe too much, and sometimes what isn't true." To that Casanova might have responded with the Italian saying *Se non è vero, è ben trovato,* "If it's not true, it's well found"— that is to say, well invented.[18]

During visits to Dresden Casanova stayed in touch with Giovanni and Maria Maddalena. A letter he wrote in 1791 to Giovanni's son Carlo was discovered in the library of Trinity College, Cambridge just before this book went to press. Addressed in French style to "Charles Casanova," the letter begins with righteous outrage. Carlo had written for money to settle a debt Giacomo had contracted with a merchant, but in fact his uncle had already paid it—"So as usual you lied."

This letter gives a fascinating glimpse of Casanova's manner when asserting familial authority, and since it has never appeared in print, it deserves to be quoted at some length. *Signore Nipote Carlo,* the letter begins, "Mr. Nephew Carlo":

> You've written me the letter of a reckless madman, impertinent, inso-lent, and dishonest, such as no creditor ever wrote to a debtor and no nephew to an uncle. Whatever did your empty and ignorant head ex-pect to accomplish with the insults in that letter? You, who have told me a hundred times that you're sensitive only to words and who once said that compared to words a beating would seem like caresses to you; you who begged my "divine forgiveness" in Venice after you stole; you who told me once to beat you rather than reproach you. And I didn't reproach you, or beat you, or have you locked up, as your father wrote to tell me I should, but I forgave you; and I'm not reproaching you now for that disgraceful action, since the audacity in your letter shows that you've forgotten all about it. Tell me, were you drunk when you wrote that letter?

Giacomo goes on to admit, however, that he may actually owe Carlo himself an unpaid debt, though it would only have been through oversight. In any case,

It can never be, my poor nephew, that money I owe you should be the reason you flee from Dresden again. Before you go to that extreme, throw yourself once more at your father's feet, beg him for *his* "divine forgiveness," and refrain from giving him greater affliction. Be prepared, however, to receive paternal correction with a contrite mind, and lastly, be ashamed to say you would rather be beaten. That's the language of a galley slave. . . . Do not believe that I'm angry at you for your strange behavior. No, I hope you've already regretted it, and I want to end my letter by giving you some good advice. Here it is: alter your conduct before your father pays the great inevitable debt to nature, or I foresee that you will be wretched until your own death. Meanwhile prepare to reveal to him all the imbroglios you've gotten into, which are well known to me. God bless you.

I am always truly your most affectionate uncle,

Giacomo[19]

Actually Giacomo and his brother Giovanni were never on good terms; it's not clear whether this was an attempt to make peace by siding with Carlo's father, or an assertion of his own authority as family patriarch. If it was the latter, Giovanni undoubtedly resented it. Giacomo was the eldest, but he was a notorious con man and spendthrift, whereas Giovanni had successfully pursued a distinguished career.

Giacomo's relations with Maria Maddalena and her children were much happier. Her son-in-law Carlo Angiolini—not to be confused with Giovanni's son Carlo—would be present at Giacomo's deathbed and become his executor, and her daughter Teresa was his special favorite. In a letter she called him *molto amabile, molto caro zio,* her much loved and dear uncle.[20]

The most interesting of Casanova's friends during these years was Waldstein's uncle. Charles Joseph Lamoral, Prince de Ligne, was an Austrian field marshal (known in German as Karl-Josef Lamoral, Fürst von Ligne) who had retired to Vienna and devoted himself to writing.

Born in Brussels, he was fluent in French, and indeed, as quoted earlier, was somewhat critical of Casanova's eccentric use of that language. His own collected works filled three dozen volumes on a variety of subjects; among them is *Mélanges Militaires, Littéraires, Sentimentaires,* which includes extended reminiscences of Casanova that have been frequently quoted in this book.

Many of Ligne's letters to Casanova survive, filled with warm friendship. He loved Casanova's agile mind and his tales of adventures past. "When Casanova has something to relate," he wrote, "his adventures for example, he brings to it such originality, naturalness, rapidity, and such a dramatic gift for putting everything into action, that one can't admire him enough." Ligne eagerly read installments of the *Histoire* in manuscript, said it was even better than Montaigne, and urged its publication. He added that one third of it made him laugh, one third made him think, and one third gave him an erection.[21]

Ligne was also aware of Casanova's "hypersensitivity, anxiety, and resentment, which give him a rather ferocious air." Those were indeed qualities that often got him into trouble. And although Ligne enjoyed his storytelling, he commented, "You must never tell him that you already know the story he's about to tell. Act as if you're hearing it for the first time." His grandson noticed the same thing. "At dinner Casanova recounted one of his quarrels for at least the tenth time."[22]

Samuel Johnson once said, "Old men are generally narrative, and fall easily into recitals of past transactions and accounts of persons known to them in their youth." The *Histoire de Ma Vie* would turn out to be the right place for Casanova to satisfy that impulse.[23]

In his portrait the Prince de Ligne adopts a haughty demeanor, but he was widely admired for good humor and congeniality. He had had an active love life with both sexes, and sympathized with his friend's grief at his declining sexual powers. "Women, little girls especially, are in his head, but they can no longer emerge from there. This makes him angry with the fair sex, with himself, with heaven, with nature, and with the year 1724 [i.e., his birth so long ago, though actually it was 1725]. He takes his revenge for all of that on everything eatable and drinkable. No longer able to be a god in the gardens or a satyr in the woods, he is a wolf at the table."

At about the same time a Russian diplomat, Prince Belosselski, characterized Casanova in a brisk epigram:

> *Favori d'Apollon, amant aimé du Diable,*
> *Il boit, il mange, il rit, et conte l'incroyable.*

"Favorite of Apollo, well-beloved of the Devil, he drinks, he eats, he laughs, and he tells incredible things."[24]

Another correspondent whom Casanova valued greatly was Count Maximilien Lamberg, an old friend whom he had first known in Paris thirty years previously. After a somewhat desultory government career Lamberg had retired to Brünn in his native Moravia (Brno today in the Czech Republic), two hundred miles southeast of Dux. His portrait presents him in profile in clas-

45. The Prince de Ligne

sical style, with a caption indicating that he was "sweeter than Democritus." The Greek thinker was known as the laughing philosopher, but there was a sarcastic edge to his laughter.

Lamberg and Casanova hailed each other as kindred spirits and exchanged letters regularly, though only Lamberg's have been preserved. Like Casanova, he had had a university education, and was passionately interested in science and languages. Perhaps surprisingly, his voluminous letters aren't especially interesting to read today; they're filled with details about current publications, gossip about people he knew, and the troubled politics and wars of the late eighteenth century, all seasoned with endless Latin quotations. But the affection is obvious, especially in the extravagant salutations: *Mon indulgent et chérissime maître! Homme rare! Flambeau de ma pensée! Médecin de l'âme!*—"My indulgent and most cherished master! Rare man! Flame of my thought! Physician of the soul!"[25]

46. Maximilien Lamberg

The end came abruptly for Lamberg in 1792. Like Casanova, he had had recurring venereal infections. "A dozen *chaude-pisses* unfortunately provided me with a code of instruction that the devil seemed to have traced with his malevolent claws. I was seldom without a rhapsody of that kind going on in my trousers." Now he had developed a swollen gland on his groin and was sure it was the same affliction, though it probably wasn't. He wrote to Casanova that his doctor had applied no fewer than thirty-six mercury plasters, which was the very treatment that would have killed Bragadin if Casanova hadn't intervened. Casanova replied at once to warn of the danger, but it was too late, as he told Lamberg's grieving brother: "He would be living still if he had consulted me about this little indisposition, which he should never have

47. Johann Ferdinand Opiz

attempted to cure with mercury. The surgeon Feuchter was his executioner."
Casanova also asked the brother to burn his letters to Lamberg, which is why
they no longer exist.[26]

Less satisfactory was a protracted correspondence with Johann Ferdinand
Opiz or Opitz, a tax collector in the town of Čáslav fifty miles east of Prague,

and editor of a miscellaneous literary journal (it was in German, so Casanova never read it). Opitz's rather severe portrait celebrates his distinctions, and indicates an important point of connection with Casanova: the oval emblem contains Masonic symbols, together with a motto in English, TRUTH MANS ARTS ("mans" should be "man's," but the apostrophe isn't used in German possessives and it got left out).

Their mutual friend Lamberg had encouraged Opitz to get to know Casanova, and his initial letters were full of hearty admiration. They also exchanged detailed mathematical and geometric proofs, as well as endless discussions of philosophy. Casanova found those pedantic and boring, and he was exasperated by Opitz's pushy assertions of deep friendship. They had both loved Lamberg, "but between him and me," Casanova told Opitz, "there was neither mine nor thine; we shared everything, including our pleasures and afflictions. His death has left a great void in my heart and you want to fill it, but is that possible? Do we have the same dispositions toward each other? That's what remains to be seen."

Casanova was especially annoyed that Opitz said he had "chosen" him as a friend. "That's strange, because friendship isn't a matter of choice. A friend is a gift from heaven. I have had three; they are dead. They were all Italians, altogether different from me in birth, wealth, penchant, and character, but *amicitia nos fecit pares*—friendship made us equal." Casanova doesn't name them, but he must have meant Bragadin, Barbaro, and Dandolo.[27]

Indeed, with the exception of the three Venetian patrons, it's remarkable how few friends Casanova accumulated over the years. It's not clear that he kept in touch even with Antonio Balletti unless their paths happened to cross. And we know nothing about how Balletti may have felt about the way his sister Manon had been treated. Casanova took friendship as it came, enjoyed it in the moment, and let it go easily when the moment had passed. In that respect he was more of a loner than the hermit Rousseau, who avoided society but did have a strong lifelong relationship with his partner Thérèse, and for many years was very close to Diderot.

Opitz, a former Jesuit priest, kept harping on philanthropy in its root meaning, "love of mankind." Casanova was having none of it. He himself was a misanthrope, he said, and proud of it. "I tell you not only that I detest the human race, but I despise it." That was said at least partly to goad Opitz, and if Casanova actually was a misanthrope, he was never the sour kind. He could and did love individuals. What he rejected was the religious mandate to love all of humanity collectively.[28]

Finally Casanova had had enough, and in 1794 he told Opitz that their relationship was over. Opitz wrote a note to himself: "I don't hate Monsieur de Casanova and never will. I only pity him for his bad humor and his outrageous character, which makes him very inconsistent and which strikes me as due to a highly atrabilious temperament." There was some truth to that. "Atrabilious" means domination by black bile or melancholy, and Casanova always acknowledged that that was his prevailing mood in these final years. Opitz added piously, "I feel sorry for him with all my heart."[29]

Also among Casanova's correspondents were several young women who looked up to him as a mentor. His letters haven't survived, but their replies, which he kept, express warm admiration. The most interesting of them was Cécile de Roggendorff, who was just twenty-one, fifty years younger than he. They never met face to face, but her brother had seen him at Dux and had led her to hope that he could be a wise counselor and guide. Their mother had died when Cécile was eight and their father a few years after that, leaving her to be tyrannized by a hated aunt; her fiancé had died in battle against the French just one year before. She was now enduring an unhappy existence in Cassovie in Slovakia (modern Košice), close to the Hungarian border.

Cécile obviously knew nothing about Casanova's earlier life and flagrant reputation, but he was clearly touched, and responded regularly in the way that she needed. At one point she quotes him as declaring, "True love is that to which *jouissance* is foreign." Probably he was talking the way a wise mentor is supposed to talk. He also took pains to find her a position as a maid of honor with the family of Ligne's grandson, thus liberating her from her abusive relatives.[30]

Soon Cécile was addressing her mentor as *mon cher Casanova,* and he was calling her Zénobie, after a third-century Syrian queen who was celebrated for strength of mind and chastity. "Be assured," Cécile told him, "that you have all the rights of a father, a friend, and a lover over the heart of Zénobie." Her own self-portrait was playfully modest. "I'm pretty without being extremely pretty, amiable without being very amiable, sometimes witty, always frank." Her final letters are full of anxiety at Casanova's impending death. We know that she did take up the maid of honor position and afterward got married in Vienna, bore four children, and died in 1814 at the age of thirty-eight.[31]

As for everyday life at Dux, Casanova found it alternately tedious and upsetting. A constant source of exasperation for several years was the behavior of Waldstein's steward or majordomo, a retired Austrian army officer named Georg Feldkirchner, who continued to wear his dragoon's uniform and in-

sisted on being addressed as "Lieutenant." Feldkirchner made it his project to
harass Casanova as much as possible, especially after Casanova went into debt
and had to discharge his personal cook. Thereafter he dined at the common
table with the rest of the staff, who conversed in German which he couldn't
understand. His servant Caumont, who came from Alsace, did speak French
and was loyal to him, but otherwise his usual enjoyment of conversation was
completely neutralized.

Smoldering with resentment, Casanova wrote out in French nineteen letters, accumulated over a period of time, which he kept in a folder labeled
*Nineteen Letters Addressed to Faulkurcher, Maître d'Hôtel of the Count de Wald-
stein, Seigneur of Dux, by Jacques Casanova de Seingalt, Venetian.* Calling the
man "Faulkurcher" was a deliberate insult: the German word *faul* means both
"lazy" and "foul." Since he wrote in French, he advised his tormentor to get
someone to translate. These prolix documents are filled with obsessive details,
and despite their tone of outrage are tedious to read.

The spite and pettiness of this quarrel are depressing. In the old days Casanova would probably have laughed at the self-important majordomo. It seems
likely, though, that he never actually sent the letters, and kept adding to them
just to relieve his feelings. Sebastiano Vassalli, in an account of the years at
Dux, says that they "erupted from the depths of his soul in moments when
his rage had no other way to manifest itself, and his pride sought compensation, if not in the real world, then at least in writing."[32]

Feldkirchner had a pair of accomplices who also detested Casanova. One
was a courier who carried mail for the castle, Karl Wiederholt (Casanova spells
it *Viderol*), and the other was a beautiful young woman named Caroline
Werthmüller, in charge of the wardrobe and also Waldstein's mistress when he
happened to be in residence.

Mostly these people annoyed him with minor slights: he wasn't treated
properly when distinguished visitors were present, he was given soup that was
intentionally too hot or too cold, dogs were encouraged to wake him up by
barking. Two incidents, however, really got under Casanova's skin. His servant discovered his portrait pasted to a privy wall, but not with actual paste.
"You had me hung up in effigy with shit in the castle latrine. Your executioner
of a valet [Wiederholt] stole one of my books, tore out my portrait, wrote the
epithet you taught him under my name [it's not clear what that was], and
attached it there either with his shit or yours." When charged with the deed,
Wiederholt replied cheerfully that if he did do that, it was only to give the
portrait an appropriate place of honor.

As for the other offense, "Finally, Monsieur Faulkurcher, you deployed your masterstroke. You ordered your executioner valet to beat me with a stick in the public street of Dux, at ten in the morning, Sunday, October eleventh, 1791. That was easy to do, old as I am, unarmed, and even without my cane."

In the past Casanova had wielded his cane energetically, as when he thrashed Pocchini in Hyde Park in London. Now he had been publicly shamed. And still worse, he could get no redress. He composed a formal complaint in Latin, had it translated into German, and presented it to the town burgomaster. That official advised him to calm down, and still worse, said that he had already learned from Wiederholt that Casanova had started it all by shouting "Executioner!" when they met in the street. Besides, the burgomaster had no authority to discipline anyone in the castle.[33]

At this time Waldstein was away on travels for the better part of three years, and unable to intervene. We now know that he was involved in highly secretive negotiations, which undoubtedly included fellow Masons, in the hope of uniting to overthrow the revolutionary government in France. His countess mother told Casanova, "Nobody knows where my son is living." She visited Dux herself to investigate, sympathized with Casanova, and referred to Caroline as a whore. Still, she advised Casanova to calm down and promised that her son would sort things out.[34]

When the count eventually returned the situation did get resolved. Feldkirchner was fired and joined a body of reserve troops anticipating a French invasion. But as for Wiederholt, he and Casanova were reconciled, and Casanova was on good terms also with Caroline. He seems even to have talked about taking her with him to Venice, though that never happened.[35]

In these last years, indeed, Casanova dreamed increasingly of returning to Venice, for a visit or even to stay. Angelo Mainardi evokes the contrast between the city of his birth and the dull, chilly land where he was living now: "The babble of voices in the streets and little *campi,* the extraordinary light, the architecture reflected in the water, the masks and the gambling, the erotic intrigues, the political plots, the storied noble families, the obscurity and austerity of power—this unique world that he had missed during his eighteen-year exile was returning again to disturb his imagination in the severe Bohemian landscape.[36]

In Constantinople half a century earlier, when Casanova turned down Yusuf's offer of his daughter in marriage, he declared his hope "of becoming celebrated among the cultivated nations, whether in the fine arts, in literature, or in some other way." By now his brothers Francesco and Giovanni were indeed celebrated in the arts. As for himself, Giacomo had always imagined that literature was his proper field. Thus far, however, he was celebrated for deeds, not writings.[37]

For the first time in his life Casanova now devoted his days to writing, which he did almost nonstop. He filled thousands of manuscript pages with essays on various topics, almost none of which got published. He also conducted a large correspondence, creating a virtual social life with people who enjoyed his originality and verve. His one remarkable piece of writing from this period was the story of the escape from the Ducal Palace that he would later retell in the *Histoire de Ma Vie*. That narrative, *Histoire de Ma Fuite*, was published in Leipzig in 1787 with "Written at Dux in Bohemia" on the title page. It was his second experiment in autobiography, after *Il Duello* seven years previously.

When scholars began long afterward to study his manuscripts, efforts were naturally made to show that he was an accomplished thinker, but none of his essays would still be read if we didn't know that Casanova wrote them. In fact they are not read by anyone who isn't a Casanova specialist.

The Prince de Ligne identified an interesting paradox: "It's only in Casanova's writings on philosophy that there's no philosophy. His other writings are filled with it; there's always something distinctive, new, piquant, and profound. They are a well of knowledge, though he does quote Horace so much that one gets sick of it." Ligne also remarked, "There's nothing that he doesn't claim to know: the rules of dance, the French language, taste, the usages of the social world, and the art of *savoir-vivre*."[38]

Ligne's point about philosophical thinking is convincing. Again and again in the *Histoire,* an aphoristic formulation emerges from the narrative to crystallize its meaning. A commentator calls these "flashes of illumination from a libertine moralist." That might seem oxymoronic, but "moralist" is used in the Italian and French sense to mean a philosophical commentator on human life.[39]

Casanova's book with the portrait that Feldkirchner defiled was a novel entitled *Icosameron,* published in Prague in 1788. It ought to be more interesting than it is. This bloated five-volume tale, or fable, is not really a novel at all, but a philosophical critique of religion and politics. After a shipwreck Édouard and his sister Elisabeth find that they are the only human beings in the subterranean world of the Mégamicres ("Macromicros"), an allusion to the title of Voltaire's *Micromégas.* These beings, tiny whereas Voltaire's were gigantic, are androgynous or maybe hermaphroditic, combining male and female in each individual. As the sole humans in this new world, the brother and sister are effectively an Adam and Eve, and can propagate their race only by an incestuous union—the survival of humanity being a more fundamental principle than any incest taboo. As we have seen, Casanova never thought that that taboo made sense, except as a guard against social disorder. Curiously, the Mégamicres themselves have no sexual organs at all, and it's never clear how they reproduce. Androgyny always did fascinate Casanova.

Once the couple have children they institute a version of Enlightenment "natural religion," based not on dogma but on simple moral precepts that are supposedly self-evident. However, they are threatened by an outside force, a republic called Quatre-Vingt ("Eighty") that seems a lot like Venice, and by the time they escape from the subterranean world its peculiar utopia is about to be destroyed.

The moral seems to be that high-minded philosophical reforms are always thwarted by the intractable facts of human nature. Casanova told a correspondent that he had set out to invent an altogether new kind of narrative, with new topics and phenomena, "but not new as to character, since from a moral perspective man cannot be other than he is." He added virtuously that the book would have sold much better if he had filled it with obscenity, "but I had no wish to shine in that kind of genre."[40]

Icosameron barely sold at all. An early reviewer commented that it is not only too long but boring. To this Casanova returned a furious and characteristically prolix reply. His self-defense took two parts. One was that the title, fabricated from Greek, means "twenty parts," and each part needed to be savored in detail, not speed-read. The other was that he was writing for educated and sophisticated readers, which the reviewer clearly was not. He never took criticism well.[41]

The commercial failure of the novel was a financial disaster. Following a common practice, Casanova had paid the full costs of publication himself, expecting to recover his investment from advance subscriptions paid for by readers, but there were few of them and he ended up owing the shocking sum of 2,000 florins, equivalent to 50,000 euros today. Very possibly the publisher cheated him. It appears that Waldstein generously bailed him out.

Casanova's unpublished papers include essays on philosophy and religion, but as Ligne said, they make tiresome reading. They are also utterly conventional, recycling ideas that the Enlightenment philosophes had already expressed much better. Quite possibly Casanova never intended to publish them; they may have represented an ongoing debate within his own mind.

More deeply personal are two earlier essays on suicide, one published in Italian in 1769 and the other written in French in 1782 but never published. The view of the philosophes was that although suicide was forbidden by the Church, it had to be permissible under certain circumstances; they admired ancient Romans for choosing to die instead of submitting to tyranny or enduring an incurable disease. At various times, however, Casanova declared that he personally would never do it. He loved life too much, and besides, he feared that even if there is an afterlife, it might be merely a disembodied existence with no physical delight. He felt profoundly that his body was himself. "What will the soul of the person who commits suicide do without the body? What will be the happiness of this soul when it finds itself reduced to possessing nothing more than the power of thinking? That is a true hell, and it makes a philosopher tremble more than the one that is threatened by religion."[42]

Something else Casanova took very seriously in his last years was mathematics, at which he had always been gifted. This was no mere dabbling, but intense and well-informed study; he wrote up notes on the work of the latest thinkers. He even drafted essays with such titles as *Solution to the Delos Problem* and *Geometrical Demonstration of the Duplication of the Cube*. That was a challenge first conceived in ancient times, which was eventually proved impossible: given one edge of a cube, a second cube was to be constructed with twice the volume of the first, using only the compass and straight-edge of classical geometry.

What Casanova loved about mathematics was that unlike all other disciplines, philosophy and religion included, only this one could claim to rest on a bedrock of absolute certainty. As he wrote in another essay, "This science is the proudest of all those that depend on reason; it dares not affirm a truth if it isn't demonstrated. Whatever can't be demonstrated is not within its competence. Its axioms are infallible, and not even God himself could make them false." That was a shrewd dig at theologians, many of whom insisted that God could have made two plus two equal five if he had felt like it.[43]

The cumulative effect of all that writing is discouraging, but unexpectedly, Casanova still had a great book in him. Grumbling and frustrated in exile, he was driven to create an enduring classic of world literature, which he began to do in 1789 and continued to work on throughout his final decade. If he had been happier he would never have written the *Histoire de Ma Vie*. Kierkegaard famously said that life can only be understood backward, but has to be lived forward. Casanova had lived forward always, and he was now ready to try to understand backward.

It seems clear also that he began the *Histoire* as therapy against depression. The Prince de Ligne, who found his reminiscences so fascinating, actively encouraged him to write them down. A letter also survives that a doctor named James O'Reilly wrote to him early in 1789: "My dear friend, you must refrain for several months from gloomy studies that fatigue the brain, and also from sex. To soothe your feelings, you need only recapitulate the fine days you passed in Venice and in other parts of the world." That was good advice, but Casanova, always skeptical of doctors, characterized O'Reilly three years later as "barbarous, illiterate, crazy, rambling, a physician of scant reputation, often too unsure of himself, more often too certain, still more often a danger to the sick, contemptuous of practical experience, libidinous, choleric, violent, unfriendly, superstitious, an astrologer, lewd, indiscreet, suspicious, malicious, ignorant, and erratic."[44]

Surveying his past life, Casanova saw it as taking the form of a drama in three acts. The first act ended during his stay in London, the second in his final expulsion from Venice in 1783, "and the third is evidently arriving here, where I amuse myself by writing these memoirs." He understood that this act would be the final one. "The comedy will then be finished."[45]

Casanova was never really introspective, and the contrast with Rousseau's *Confessions* is stark. The two autobiographies are complementary, a double helix of lifestyles and of ways of understanding.

Rousseau was a classic introvert who found social interaction painful. He was eloquent only in writing, which he achieved slowly and with great care. In addition to the *Confessions* he produced books on a wide range of subjects—politics, education, music—that became lastingly influential. Casanova was a classic extrovert. He hated isolation, drew energy from social interaction, and charmed many of the people who met him—men as well as women—with his conversation and wit. Those gifts couldn't be truly captured in writing, and his essays fell flat; his real subject was his lived experience. Rousseau withdrew from society to reflect and to probe his own psyche. Casanova immersed himself in society and brought scores of personalities to life in the *Histoire,* which he wrote rapidly and with delight.

Casanova's narration has often been called novelistic, and as quoted earlier, he himself pauses at one point to say, "Here, my dear reader, is an altogether novelistic event, but for all that it's no less true. If you believe it's fantastic, you're mistaken." But the word translated here as "novelistic" is *romanesque,* and that has a double meaning in French. The word for novel, *roman,* descended from the old romances of chivalry, whether in tales of Arthur's knights or in Casanova's beloved *Orlando Furioso.*[46]

As the critic Northrop Frye argued, novels usually follow what he calls a "hence" pattern of cause and effect, with a plot that arrives at a convincing dénouement (the word literally means "untying the knot"). Romances, in contrast, tell an episodic story, a series of events connected by "and then" rather than "hence." Many autobiographers seek to identify a coherent plot in their life stories; Casanova didn't. All his life he rejoiced in escaping from plot, starting over again as chance happened to lead him. He didn't untie the knot, he just cut through it.[47]

There's a memorable anecdote in Plato's *Republic.* Socrates says, "I remember someone asking Sophocles, the poet, whether he was still capable of enjoying a woman. 'Don't talk in that way,' he answered; 'I am only too glad to be free of all that. It's like escaping from bondage to a raging madman.'" Socrates adds, "I thought that a good answer at the time, and I still think so, for certainly a great peace comes when age sets us free from passions of that sort."[48]

Casanova never stopped being tormented. He never wanted "great peace" of that kind. The *Histoire* served as compensation, and escape. Aldo Toffoli offers a memorable analogy: no longer able to make love in reality, Casanova was now "the voyeur of his own memories."[49]

When he was finishing the first draft he told Opitz, "I write thirteen hours a day, which go by like thirteen minutes." He added, "I write from morning to night, and I can assure you I write even when I'm asleep, since I always dream of writing." That is a familiar experience for some writers—to wake up with sentences or even paragraphs ready to set down.[50]

The old humor theory of psychology was still respected in Casanova's era, according to which each person has a fixed temperament from birth onward. Casanova, the shapeshifter, thought he had experienced all of them in succession. "I have had all four of the temperaments: the phlegmatic in childhood, the sanguine in youth, after that the bilious, and finally the melancholic, which will evidently never leave me."[51]

And yet, what is amazing about the *Histoire de Ma Vie* is its freedom from bitterness and its celebration of life. "It is astonishing," Marie-Françoise Luna says, "that the unhappiness of growing old, the farewell to the passion for living, the deep malaise of Dux, should have brought forth the hymn to joyfulness and gratitude that is the *Histoire de Ma Vie.*"[52]

$\mathcal{A}$ Pink Louis XV Armchair

Casanova lived to see the end of an era, which was decisively overthrown by the French Revolution in 1789, followed by wars and threats of revolution thereafter throughout Europe. In 1797 he published a document in French that is ostensibly a critique of linguistic changes, but whose real theme is a furious denunciation of the Revolution. The formidable title is *My Neighbor, Posterity: To Léonard Snetlage, Doctor of Laws at the University of Göttingen, by Jacques Casanova, Doctor of Laws at the University of Padua.* Casanova did indeed have a law degree; this was a proud assertion of his academic qualifications.

Snetlage had published *A New French Dictionary, Containing the Newly Created Expressions of the French People.* Casanova thought that languages can and should evolve—he didn't approve of the rigid attempts of the Académie Française to prevent change—but that the evolution should be natural and organic, not a drastic rejection of an entire culture. And like George Orwell long afterward, he deplored the ideological use of terms like "equality" and "the people" to mask a new despotism that was more vicious than the one it replaced.

Edmund Burke, in *Reflections on the Revolution in France,* had foretold brilliantly in 1790 how even the best-intentioned revolution was likely to lead to a bloodbath and then to the emergence of a charismatic dictator: "Some popular general, who understands the art of conciliating the soldiery, and who possesses the true spirit of command, shall draw the eyes of all men upon himself. At the moment in which that event shall happen, the person who really commands the army is your master." The Terror had been the bloodbath, during which people Casanova knew must have died on the guillotine. And in the very year when *My Neighbor, Posterity* came out, Napoleon was proclaimed First Consul and in effect dictator of the new France.[1]

In the *Histoire* Casanova exclaims at one point, "Alas! Happy days of the *lettres de cachet,* you are no more!" Those were the orders, sealed with the *cachet* of the king, that committed individuals to prison without charges or sentence. Just such an order had commanded him to leave France, yet even so he wished the Ancien Régime had never ended.[2]

As for "the people," they were a nation of sheep, easily led and all too willing to shed their blood in Napoleon's wars. They had been seduced into thinking of themselves as a collectivity, but as Casanova says in an essay entitled *The French People,* "It is an enormous monster, ferocious, atrocious, bloodthirsty, and appalling." So much for "equality." The old absolutism, he believed, was vastly preferable to anarchy.[3]

Casanova's correspondent Lamberg, the retired government bureaucrat, was equally appalled by the Revolution. Lamberg wrote to him in November 1789, just four months after the storming of the Bastille: "The king imprisoned, the Duc d'Orléans in flight, Mirabeau more than ever leader of the pack—barbarous citizens, thieves, executioners and cannibals—doesn't all of this announce the destruction of an empire delivered to tyrants and threatened by traitors? Poor France!"[4]

After his initial blunders in French when he was first in Paris, Casanova had made himself at home in the cultivated language of the Ancien Régime, with its infinite nuances. Now that world was abolished, and even its language was being mutilated. "One feels that each word is a combat," Chantal Thomas says. "His thinking, even though it's addressed to ideas, evokes an image of the adventurer at bay in his final den, defending himself savagely. He will not let go."[5]

The boy born on the wrong side of the canal had lived among aristocrats and like an aristocrat; he had always needed the old order to remain secure so that he could exploit it for his own advantage. Even now, when he could exploit it no longer, he respected the social system that had yielded him so many rewards.

A loss that was equally bitter, or maybe even worse, was the end of Venice as he had known it. In 1797, after fifteen hundred years as an independent republic, the city and its territories surrendered to Napoleon. On his way to attack Austria from the south, he stopped off to conquer Venice. *Io sarò un Attila per lo stato Veneto,* he declared grimly—"I will be an Attila to the Venetian state." The wearing of masks was forbidden, and even the Bucintoro was demolished, that elegant vessel from which the doges used to cast an annual wedding ring into the sea. The Golden Book, the roster of the oldest noble families, was ceremonially burned in the Piazza San Marco.

On the façade of a majestic building in the Campo San Zanipolo, where Casanova once had his assignation with the nun M. M., the winged lion of St. Mark holds in his paws a book inscribed *Pax tibi, Marce, evangelista meus*—"Peace be unto thee, Mark, my Evangelist." That inscription was replaced in 1797 by the French slogan *Droits de l'Homme et du Citoyen,* "Rights of Man and of the Citizen." A gondolier commented that the lion had finally turned the page.[6]

Soon afterward, Napoleon signed a peace treaty with Austria, and Venice became an Austrian province. Casanova added a note in the manuscript of the *Histoire:* "Venice exists today only to its eternal shame."[7]

By now his mood was much like the one that Robert Browning, who rented the Ca' Rezzonico palazzo in Venice, evokes in his melancholy poem *A Toccata of Galuppi's.* Baldassare Galuppi had been a popular composer and choir director at San Marco and the Ospedale dei Mendicanti, and later in St. Petersburg where Casanova met him. Browning imagines Galuppi's voice creaking "like a ghostly cricket" as one of his pieces is played:

> As for Venice and her people, merely born to bloom and drop,
> Here on earth they bore their fruitage, mirth and folly were the crop:
> What of soul was left, I wonder, when the kissing had to stop?
> Dust and ashes! So you creak it, and I want the heart to scold.
> Dear dead women, with such hair, too—what's become of all the gold
> Used to hang and brush their bosoms? I feel chilly and grown old.[8]

The fall of Venice appeared to have one positive outcome for Casanova. Now that it was ruled by Austria, it would be possible for him to return, especially since his enemy Carlo Grimani had died in 1792. His friend Pietro Zaguri wrote to him, "Poor Carlo Grimani died September 28 in Padua, all alone with one lackey, a valet de chambre, and Rivetta." That was one of his wife's lovers. Casanova did make some tentative plans for a trip, but his health was continuing to decline and nothing came of that.[9]

The indignities of age were constantly increasing. In the *Histoire de Ma*

Fuite he explained why, after telling the tale of his escape from the Piombi orally for many years, he was now writing it down: "To narrate one must be able to pronounce well. It's not enough to have a nimble tongue, one must also have teeth, since they're needed for the dental consonants that compose more than a third of the alphabet; but I've had the misfortune to lose mine." That misfortune was all too common. Voltaire was fluent in English but told Boswell he refused to use it: "To speak English one must place the tongue between the teeth, and I have lost my teeth."[10]

Casanova commented that getting old means losing not only one's teeth but almost everything; yet even so it could be worse, "since if they've taken away all our furniture, they've at least left us the house. *Debilem facito manu— debilem pede, coxa—lubricos quate dentes—vita dum superset bene.*" The Latin is adapted from the Stoic philosopher Seneca: "Fashion me with a palsied hand, weak of foot, and a cripple; build upon me a crook-backed hump, shake my teeth till they rattle—all is well, if my life remains." Casanova added, "Life is like a mischievous girl whom we love, and to whom we permit everything she demands right up to the end, so long as she won't leave us. Loving life, I love myself, and I hate death because it's the executioner."[11]

Despite his poor health, Casanova wrote to Zaguri that he still had his love of life. "I'm old, but all is not lost. I still have curiosity, born of my intellect, to remain connected to the things that strike me. When I find myself in a state of indifference, then I'll know that it's the eve of my death."[12]

Having cheated death on so many occasions, Casanova had to acknowledge now that the end must be near. "The whole of our lifetime," Augustine says in *The City of God*, "is nothing but a race towards death, in which no one is allowed the slightest pause or any slackening of the pace." Early in 1798 Casanova began to suffer from an intractable urinary infection, probably a consequence of his lifetime of venereal infections.[13]

A touching message from his brother Francesco survives, written from Vienna: "Your letter distresses me more than you can imagine, loving you so sincerely, and if I were to lose you, no one on earth could fill your place in my heart." That would never have been said by the other brother, Giovanni. Opitz's son Georg Emmanuel was being apprenticed to Giovanni in Dresden, but when Opitz asked Giacomo to put in a good word, he got this bitter reply: "My brother is my enemy. He has given me convincing evidence of that, and to all appearances his hate will end only when he knows that I've ceased to exist." As it turned out Giovanni died three years before Giacomo, in Dresden in 1795. Francesco lived on in Vienna until his own death in 1804.[14]

At some point during these last years Casanova wrote down a remarkable note that survives in his papers, entitled *Dream. God. Me.* "I saw an immense and dazzling mass of light, filled with globes, eyes, ears, feet, hands, noses, mouths, and the genitals of both sexes, which circulated in a continual but irregular movement. . . . Transported with the pleasure this spectacle gave to my hearing and sight, I cried out in admiration, 'God! My God! What joy! What am I seeing?' The mass replied, 'You are seeing God.'"[15]

Casanova doesn't mention this dream in the *Histoire,* which isn't surprising, since he wanted to conceal the extent of his religious skepticism. As we know from his unpublished writings, his actual beliefs were much closer to this pantheist vision, in which God is at one with a nature that teems with energy and body parts, than to orthodox faith. For him the only certainty was the epicurean philosophy of living in the moment. "I have loved, I've been loved, I felt well, I had plenty of money and spent it; I was happy and I said to myself that I was, laughing at the stupid moralists who claim that there's no true happiness on earth. It's the expression 'on earth' that makes me laugh, as if one could seek it anywhere else. *Mors ultima linea rerum est.*" We have often seen him quoting Horace's line, "death is the end of all things." And if the moments of happiness are fleeting, that makes them all the more precious. "This happiness passes, but its ending doesn't mean that it didn't exist, or that someone who enjoyed it can't bear witness to it."[16]

In the *Histoire* Casanova includes an imaginary conversation with Catherine the Great, who had died of a stroke in 1796 at the age of sixty-seven. A journalist had commented that it was a happy death, since it overtook her suddenly with no previous suffering. On the contrary, Casanova imagines her spirit telling him, she would have been grateful for a warning to accomplish what she could before it was too late. "But that's enough," she concludes; "the pain I'm condemned to doesn't permit me to say any more." "Please tell me what that pain is," he begs, and she replies, "To be bored. Adieu." That was a true dread of Casanova's. What if there is indeed an afterlife *but you have nothing to do?*[17]

When he was known to be close to death, one of his young admirers, Élise de la Recke (or von der Recke), wrote earnestly that she hoped he believed in eternal salvation: "As a lovely butterfly emerges from the gloomy covering of the caterpillar, our thinking self will reappear in other forms, leaving behind this body that was given for a short time to a being capable of eternal happiness." Casanova's reply was surely tinged with irony. "Yesterday they administered the sacraments to me, providing me with the spiritual passport that a

Christian must have to enter, after this earthly life, the kingdom of the happy immortals." Alain Jaubert comments that this was a man who had traveled with passports all his life, and was now going through "a simple formality" to please those who wanted him to.[18]

At the beginning of June in 1798, he began a letter thanking Élise for a present, but broke off abruptly. His nephew Carlo Angiolini, son of his sister Maria Maddalena, had come from Dresden to be with him. Carlo sent the letter to Élise after adding these words: "I take the liberty, venerable lady, of telling you that my poor uncle is dying. He wanted to finish, but no longer had the strength." Indications in Zaguri's correspondence suggest that Casanova had been suffering from hydropsy—fluid retention now known as edema— and he was finally overtaken by complications from the urinary infection.[19]

On June 4 the end came, as he was sitting in the pink Louis XV armchair in which he had written the *Histoire*. He was seventy-three. The Prince de Ligne, who wasn't there, heard that his last words were "Great God, and you who are witnessing my death, I have lived as a philosopher and I die as a Christian." If he did say that, he was a Christian by cultural allegiance only, certainly not with respect to beliefs.[20]

There was a simple funeral. His young correspondents, Élise de la Recke and Cécile de Roggendorff, lived close enough to join Carlo Angiolini at the ceremony. The location of Casanova's burial site is unknown, and Mainardi comments that like Mozart, he left "a nonexistent tomb." He conjectures further that that may have been deliberate. As fear of revolution spread across Europe, Masons were once again held in deep suspicion, and there may have been fears that his remains would be dug up and mutilated.[21]

He was laid to rest in the churchyard of the little chapel of St. Barbara, and a simple plaque was mounted on the wall outside:

✝

JAKOB CASANOVA
VENEDIG, 1725
DUX 1798

When Philippe Sollers went to Duchkov he was struck by the irony that the plaque is in German, a language that Casanova detested.[22]

In his preface to the *Histoire* Gérard Lahouati quotes an ancient Roman inscription preserved on a tomb in Lyon: "During my lifetime I carved this epitaph, so that when my soul is reposing among the shades, it will survive as a witness to my existence, and my voice, preserved in these lines entrusted to

48. The Santa Barbara Chapel

marble, will live again in your voice, whoever you may be, passing by to read them. Here rests Raffio, once filled with vigor and youth." Lahouati adds that Casanova's tomb is lost, and it is in the *Histoire* that his voice still speaks.[23]

The *Histoire* is the saga not just of a seducer but of a libertine in the largest sense, skeptical of conventional rules and dogmas, forever on the move through the world. A quintessential outsider, Casanova never settled down in a profession or a stable relationship, but he contrived to fit in for a while wherever he went. A man without a country, expelled from many countries over the years, he remained a Venetian through and through, performative, a man of masks.

Casanova relates his many cons and scams with remarkable frankness, suggesting that organized society is itself a kind of con, and that he is simply beating it at its own game. Depending on circumstances, his schemes and games could have positive effects. His magic and numerology gave great pleasure to Signor Bragadin, who loved him like a son. But they broke the heart of Mme. d'Urfé.

An inspired improvisor, Casanova faced each new challenge with eagerness, and he needed challenges. At his best, he was the ingenious problem-solver who achieved an unprecedented escape from the Ducal Palace, and the inexperienced duelist who defeated a crack marksman in Poland even though he despised the ethos of dueling. It's no wonder that those were the two stories he published during his lifetime. In them, risk-taking rises to the level of an existential act.

It was also a life filled increasingly with frustrations and disappointments, and Casanova fully acknowledges that. All the same, the *Histoire* is a book bursting with vitality. As he says in his preface, "By recalling the pleasures I've had, I renew them." It was an artistic achievement to narrate his early life without letting the final depression darken the story at all.[24]

If, in telling that story, Casanova did invent as much as recreate, that's really what every autobiographer does. Rousseau, the great apostle of sincerity, boasted in the *Confessions* that he was telling only the truth, but some years later admitted, "I loved to expand on the happy periods of my life, and at times I embellished them with such ornaments as my tender regrets provided. I described things that I had forgotten as it seemed to me they must have been, and as they may indeed have been, but never in contradiction to the way I remembered them." Rousseau found a perfect expression for what he was doing: "Instead of describing them *j'y retombais*—I fell back into them." Casanova's *Histoire de Ma Vie,* so different from the *Confessions* in many ways, shares that vivid presentness.[25]

In any case, good biography, like good history, is more than its verifiable details. Its goal is to recover what past experience felt like to those who lived it. This is how Richard Holmes describes gifted storytellers: "Much of what they said was to do with what *might* have happened to them, what they wanted to happen rather than what actually happened. . . . This world of possibilities was no less part of them, part of their truth as personalities, than the more normal grammar of reality and the everyday recorded fact. We are what we dream, in the same way that we are what we eat."[26]

It's the power of Casanova's story *as* a story—the seductions and affairs, the scams, the impersonations, the joie de vivre, the enormous risks and hair-raising escapes, the lifelong struggle to invent and reinvent himself, and the shocking discovery of what it feels like to wear the mask of aging—that remains unforgettable. We know more about Casanova, and in more depth, than we do about almost anyone who lived long ago. The *Histoire de Ma Vie* conjures a world that was once as alive as ours is now, and we travel through it with a storyteller who opens that world to our minds, senses, and feelings. It is a book of life.

Chronology

1725   Giacomo Casanova born in Venice, April 2, to the actress Zanetta Casanova and her husband Gaetano.

1727   Brother Francesco born (rumored to have been sired by the Prince of Wales while Zanetta was performing in London); four more siblings born by 1734.

1733   "Cure" by a witch on the island of Murano; vision of the lady in the night. Death of Gaetano; the children live with their grandmother Marzia while Zanetta is working abroad, and the Grimani brothers become their guardians.

1734   Giacomo is sent to board in Padua, first with a landlady and then with his kindly tutor Antonio Gozzi.

1737   First tentative erotic experiments, with Gozzi's young sister Bettina. Matriculation at the University of Padua. Zanetta leaves Venice for good, moving to Dresden.

1738   Return to Venice in the expectation of launching an ecclesiastical career.

1740   Becomes a protégé of the patrician Gasparo Malipiero; delivers a successful sermon and then a failed one; playful sexual relationship with the sisters Nanetta and Marta.

1741   First voyage to Constantinople, where he is befriended by Turkish gentlemen and by a French convert to Islam; brief period of military service in Corfu. (In the *Histoire* Casanova conflates this episode with a return to Constantinople four years later.)

1742   Doctorate in law awarded by the University of Padua. Kicked out by Mali-
        piero for fooling around with his young neighbor Teresa Imer.

1743   Death of Marzia. Zanetta writes to say she has secured an appointment for
        him with Bernardino de Bernadis, soon to be named bishop of Martirano in
        Calabria. While waiting, unsatisfactory episode as a seminarian; after expul-
        sion for sexual misbehavior, is sent to the island fortress of Sant'Andrea,
        where he contracts his first case of venereal disease. Sails to Ancona, on his
        way to take up his position with Bernardis. Stays briefly in Rome.

1744   Returns to Venice and then back to Ancona, where he has a memorable
        encounter with the faux castrato "Bellino," who is actually Teresa. In June,
        joins Bernardis in Martirano but is disgusted by its rusticity; quits his ap-
        pointment and returns to Rome. Is taken up by Cardinal Acquaviva, learns
        to speak French, has a brief affair with the married Donna Lucrezia. Is forced
        to leave Rome after involvement in a scandal (he says not his own fault), and
        returns to Venice, on the way to a sea voyage to Constantinople.

1745   Constantinople and Corfu again; inconclusive affair with Andriana Foscarini.
        Return to Venice. Twentieth birthday this year.

1746   Brief stint as violinist at the San Samuele theater where his parents once
        worked. Happens to encounter Matteo Bragadin just before that senator
        suffers a stroke; supervises his recovery, impresses Bragadin and his friends
        with alleged cabbalistic knowledge, and begins a new life as an adopted son
        in the Palazzo Bragadin.

1747   Begins a lifelong addiction to gambling. Generously arranges a marriage for
        a young woman, Cristina.

1748   Continued life as a playboy. Forced to leave Venice after an alleged rape,
        which he strongly denies, and an outrageous prank with the arm of a corpse.

1749   Milan and Mantua. Invents a ceremony at Cesena to recover a buried trea-
        sure by magic. Encounters Henriette, who had run away from an abusive
        marriage in Provence; falls deeply in love, and lives with her in Parma until
        her family negotiates her return. They part in Geneva: "You will also forget
        Henriette." He does not.

1750   Travels to Paris with a new friend, a dancer named Antonio Balletti, and in
        Lyon is initiated as a Mason. In Paris is warmly welcomed by Balletti's the-
        atrical family, especially his mother, whose stage name is Sylvia. Begins im-
        proving his French with coaching from the distinguished writer Crébillon
        père. Meets Mme. de Pompadour.

1751   Brother Francesco arrives to pursue a career as a painter.

1752   Meets the young Louise Murphy and helps her to become a mistress of

Louis XV. In the autumn, goes with Francesco to Dresden for a reunion with their mother.

1753 Moves on to Prague and Vienna, then back to Venice. Falls in love with young C. C. (Caterina Capretta); her father forbids marriage and consigns her to a convent on Murano. She begins to correspond secretly with Casanova.

1754 Passionate affair with the nun M. M., who is the lover of the French ambassador Bernis (and also of C. C.). Meetings in private casini, which turn into performances à trois while Bernis watches through a spyhole. Brief affair with Teresa Imer.

1755 Arrested for irreligious talk, practice of magic, and extracting money from patrician patrons. Committed without trial or charges to the Piombi, "the Leads," cells beneath the roof of the Ducal Palace.

1756 Spectacular escape through the roof, accompanied by a fellow prisoner Balbi, after fifteen months' incarceration. Reaches the mainland by gondola, sets off northward.

1757 In Paris once again, reconnects with Bernis, who recruits him for one or more spying missions. Comes up with a hugely successful plan for a national lottery, making him temporarily rich. Becomes engaged to Manon Balletti, but unenthusiastically; her poignant letters have survived.

1758 Meets Mme. d'Urfé, a deep student of the occult. In Amsterdam, conducts financial negotiations for her and for the French government. Becomes involved with Esther, the young daughter of a banker. Encounters Teresa Imer, who convinces him that he is the father of her young daughter, and permits him to place her son under the care of Mme. d'Urfé.

1759 Rents a country villa in the Little Poland district. Failed attempt to establish a factory to produce painted silk. Return trip to Amsterdam, where he encounters Lucia, now a prostitute, who had flirted with him when they were young. Accused of involvement in some financial irregularity, feels obliged to leave Paris.

1760 In February, Manon Balletti writes unexpectedly to say that she is marrying someone else. Casanova sets off on his travels: gambling and quarrels in Cologne and Bonn, and a brief covert affair with Mme. X. Hasty escape from Stuttgart after being bilked by card sharps. In Switzerland, briefly considers entering the monastery of Einsiedeln, but is deflected by the sight of the attractive Mme. = . Follows her to Soleure, where he is victimized by her jealous rival, Mme. F. Begins calling himself the Chevalier de Seingalt. In Berne, romantic relationship with the widow Mme. Dubois, but willingly yields her to a worthy suitor who can give her a stable life. Spends several days in intense conversation with Voltaire, near Geneva. Goes to Aix-les-Bains to gamble and has a brief but intense relationship with a nun, a second M. M. who strikingly resembles the first one. Sojourns in Grenoble, Avignon (chiefly to visit a town that Petrarch made famous), and Marseille. New relationship with the young Rosalie, whom he accompanies to Genoa; there she is re-united with a former suitor and Casanova once again withdraws. In Florence in December, encounters Teresa ("Bellino"), who introduces him to a son he never knew he had. Expelled from Florence due to suspicious involvement with a dishonest adventurer, he goes to Rome and then to Naples. There he encounters Donna Lucrezia, who tells him that he is the father of her daughter Leonilda; sexual relations with both women.

1761 In Rome again, arranges a marriage for Mariuccia, one of Casanova's acts of generosity that includes sexual favors for himself. Back in Florence, brief involvement with a young dancer, Marianna Corticelli, and encounter with the abbé Gama, an old acquaintance who promises him a diplomatic role in the Portuguese delegation at a peace conference in Augsburg. In Chambéry visits M. M. at her convent. The peace conference is canceled.

1762 Moonlight ceremony at Mme. d'Urfé's château at Pontcarré near Paris, which Casanova declares a failure so that there can be a repeat performance later. At Aix-la-Chapelle, another ceremony with Mme. d'Urfé and Mari-anna Corticelli, who however refuses to keep up the game without proper pay and is sent packing. Mme. d'Urfé returns to Paris, agreeing to meet again the next year in Marseille. Casanova goes to Geneva and has a brief relationship with two young women, Hedwige and Hélène; spends the rest of the year in Italy.

1763 In Milan, heavy gambling and various sexual involvements. Encounters his despised youngest brother Gaetano, from whom he detaches the young Marcolina to play a role in the next magical session; quarrels with Gaetano and sends him away. Marcolina plays a water nymph and the adventurer Giacomo Passano impersonates a supernatural being called Querelinth; this time it's he who quarrels over dividing the spoils, and Casanova tells Mme. d'Urfé the event must be postponed yet again. Before she leaves they cast a heavy casket into the sea, which she believes to contain priceless jewels, but in actuality a substitute that Casanova has replaced it with. She departs for Lyon; Casanova stops unknowingly at Henriette's country estate near Aix-en-Provence, where Marcolina spends the night in her bed; he afterward re-ceives a farewell letter. Passano contacts Mme. d'Urfé again and this time she believes his story; at some point in this year she breaks bitterly with Casanova, who moves on to London. Reconnects with Teresa Imer (now "Mrs. Cornelys") and develops a paternal relationship with their daughter Sophie. After hu-miliating mistreatment by Marianne Charpillon, nearly commits suicide.

1764   Accused of cashing a forged bill of exchange, Casanova leaves England in a
        hurry in March, accompanied by a recently encountered godson (or possi-
        bly son) named Daturi, who goes on to join his family in Germany. After
        being cured of a bad case of venereal disease, proceeds to Berlin, but is un-
        able to interest King Frederick II in any lucrative project, and by the end of
        the year is in St. Petersburg.

1765   Meets the empress Catherine II and is highly impressed, but once again fails
        to generate employment. Associates with gamblers, adventurers, and army
        officers; acquires a young peasant girl whom he names Zaire. In October
        moves on to Warsaw, where he forms friendships with influential noblemen
        and has a cordial relationship with the recently crowned king, Stanislaw Au-
        gust Poniatowski.

1766   A quarrel at the theater leads to a public insult by a prominent noble, Count
        Xavier Branicki; Casanova challenges him to a duel in which both are wounded
        by pistols, Branicki more seriously. Having conducted themselves with honor,
        they are thereafter good friends. Some of his colleagues are angry with Casa-
        nova, however, and when stories about his misbehavior in Paris begin to cir-
        culate, the king commands him to leave. In July goes to Breslau in Silesia, and
        then to Dresden where he reconnects with his mother and two of his sib-
        lings. Ends the year in Vienna.

1767   Expelled from Vienna after being framed by an old enemy, Antonio Poc-
        chini. Augsburg, then Spa, where he accepts responsibility for Charlotte, the
        pregnant lover of an old friend who has to leave town in a hurry. They travel
        to Paris where she gives birth and then dies from an infection. Learns that
        his adoptive father Matteo Bragadin has died. Expelled from France by a
        lettre de cachet instigated by Mme. d'Urfé and her relatives; sets out for
        Spain.

1768   Madrid; protracted seduction of Doña Ignacia. Failed attempts to get em-
        ployment at the court. A quarrel with "Count" Manuzzi, son of the informer
        who had caused Casanova's imprisonment in Venice, results in rejection by
        the Venetian ambassador and expulsion from Madrid. Valencia and Barce-
        lona; equivocal involvement with a dancer, Nina, and then lengthy impris-
        onment. After being freed, leaves Spain on the last day of the year.

1769   Aix-en-Provence, Marseille, Turin. Publication in Lugano of *Confutazione
        della Storia del Governo Veneto d'Amelot de la Houssaie,* begun in the Barce-
        lona prison, as a bid for clemency from Venice.

1770   Sienna and then Rome; a memorable episode along the way with a young
        Englishwoman, Betty, whom he restores to her lover. Naples, where he part-
        ners with the card sharp Ange Goudar and encounters his old love Lucrezia

and their daughter Leonilda. Rome again; renewed friendship with Bernis, now a cardinal.

1771   Literary efforts of various kinds. Helps two young convent girls, Emilia and Armellina, to emerge from semi-captivity and find husbands. Discovers another daughter he never knew he had, Giacomina. Then on to Florence, where he works on his *Iliad* translation until he is expelled under suspicion of cheating at cards.

1772   Bologna for eight months; publishes *Lana Caprina,* a treatise disputing claims that female thinking is controlled by the uterus. Sails to Trieste from Ancona, in order to be near Venice in anticipation of permission to return.

1773   In Trieste, makes friends with Venetians and Austrians (whose empire then governed that city); carries out various tasks calculated to ingratiate himself with the authorities in Venice.

1774   Publishes several volumes of an ambitious *History of the Troubles in Poland.* Further behind the scenes efforts on behalf of Venice. Official permission to return arrives in September; he goes home at last, and is invited to dinner by the current Inquisitors to tell the story of his escape from the Piombi.

1775   Publishes first installment of Italian translation of the *Iliad,* and final volume of the history of Poland. Death of Michele Grimani, owner of the San Samuele theater and rumored to be Casanova's biological father.

1776   Begins working as an informant for the Inquisitors, under the name of Antonio Pratolini. Controversy with Ange Goudar, his old gambling acquaintance, about the translation of Homer. Death of his mother Zanetta.

1777   Revisits his old teacher Gozzi, now an archpriest, and his sister Bettina, who dies in his presence. (Casanova remembered it as 1776).

1779   Begins relationship with his last female companion, Francesca Bruschini. Death of his longtime friend and patron Marco Dandolo.

1780   Short-lived attempt to publish a literary journal. Publishes *Il Duello,* the account of his duel with Count Branicki. Starts a theater company to produce French plays. Continues to work as an informant.

1781   Theater company folds.

1782   Several minor publications. Takes a position as secretary to a nobleman. After a falling-out, publishes a satire on the Venetian nobility entitled *Né Amori, Né Donne, ovvero la Stalla Ripulita,* which provokes his final departure from Venice. Goes to Trieste.

1783   Brief visit to Venice to settle his affairs, then Vienna. Travels throughout Europe, meets Benjamin Franklin in Paris, returns to Vienna.

1784   Dresden, then Vienna, where he forms friendships with the counts Lamberg
        and Waldstein, and becomes secretary to the Venetian ambassador. Miscel-
        laneous publications.

1785   Death of the ambassador and loss of employment. More publications. Moves
        to Dux (modern Duchkov) in Bohemia as librarian in the château of the
        Count de Waldstein.

1786   More publications.

1787   Spends time in Prague where he publishes *L'Histoire de Ma Fuite* and possi-
        bly collaborates with Lorenzo da Ponte on the libretto for *Don Giovanni.*

1788   Publishes his novel, *Icosameron.* Returns to Dux. Writes a number of unpub-
        lished essays.

1789   Begins work on *L'Histoire de Ma Vie.*

1791   Continues work on the *Histoire.* Increasingly unhappy at Dux, especially
        after a mugging in the street engineered by his enemies in the château.

1792   More essays. Occasional visits to Prague, Dresden, and Vienna.

1793   Returns to Dux after his enemies are punished. More unpublished essays.

1794   Meets the Prince de Ligne, who becomes his favorite correspondent and reads
        the *Histoire* in manuscript.

1795   Continues revising the *Histoire.*

1797   More writings. Fall of the Venetian Republic, and an unrealized plan to move
        back there.

1798   June 4, death of Casanova, burial in an unmarked grave in the cemetery of
        the neighboring chapel.

Short Titles

Three authoritative editions of the *Histoire* are cited with short titles:

Histoire   Giacomo Casanova, *Histoire de Ma Vie,* ed. Gérard Lahouati and Marie-Françoise Luna (Paris: Gallimard, Bibliothèque de la Pléiade, 3 vols., 2013–2015).

Bouquins (1993)   *Histoire de Ma Vie,* ed. Francis Lacassin (Paris: Robert Laffont, Éditions Bouquins, 1993).

Bouquins (2013)   *Histoire de Ma Vie,* ed. Jean-Christophe Igalens and Érik Leborgne (Paris: Robert Laffont, Éditions Bouquins, 2013–18).

Notes

INTRODUCTION

1. Judith Summers, *Casanova's Women: The Great Seducer and the Women He Loved* (London: Bloomsbury, 2006), 21–22.

2. Lydia Flem, *The Man Who Really Loved Women,* trans. Catherine Temerson (New York: Farrar, Straus and Giroux, 1997), 76, 72.

3. François Roustang, *The Quadrille of Gender: Casanova's Memoirs,* trans. Anne C. Vila (Stanford: Stanford University Press, 1988), 84; Angelo Mainardi, *Casanova: L'Ultimo Mistero* (Rome: Tre Editori, 2010), 187.

4. Casanova, *Lana Caprina,* ed. Paul Mengal (Paris: Honoré Champion, 1999), 190.

5. On methods of birth control, see Margaret R. Hunt, *Women in Eighteenth-Century Europe* (London: Routledge, 2014), ch. 3.

6. *Lana Caprina,* 175–78.

7. The classic study is Thomas W. Laqueur, *Making Sex: Body and Gender from the Greeks to Freud* (Cambridge MA: Harvard University Press, 1990). See also Londa Schiebinger, *Nature's Body: Gender in the Making of Modern Science* (Boston: Beacon, 1993), and Anthony Fletcher, *Gender, Sex and Subordination in England, 1500–1800* (New Haven: Yale University Press, 1995).

8. *Boswell's London Journal 1762–1763,* ed. Frederick A. Pottle (New York: McGraw-Hill, 1950), 139.

9. Peggy J. Kleinplatz et al., "The Components of Optimal Sexuality: A Portrait of 'Great Sex,'" *Canadian Journal of Human Sexuality* 18 (2009), 1–13.

10. *Histoire* 1: 212.

11. Marine Riva-Ganofsky, "*L'Histoire de Ma Vie* de Casanova: Le Libertinage comme Rencontre entre le Profane et le Sacré," in *Amour Divin, Amour Mondain,* ed. Maurice Daumas (Pau: Cairn, 2011), 118.

12. Laurence Bergreen, *Casanova: The World of a Seductive Genius* (New York: Simon & Schuster, 2016), xix.

13. Frédéric Manfrin, "Casanova ou l'Appétit en Lisant," in *Casanova: La Passion de la Liberté,* ed. Marie-Laure Prévost and Chantal Thomas (Paris: Seuil, 2011), 184; Gino Benzoni, "In Viaggio per l'Europa," in *Giacomo Casanova tra Venezia e l'Europa,* ed. Gilberto Pizzamiglio (Venice: Leo S. Olschki, 2001), 38.

14. *Moniteur Universel,* Jan. 28, 1830, quoted by Marie-Françoise Luna, *Casanova Mémorialiste* (Paris: Honoré Champion, 1998), 452.

15. Federico Montecuccoli degli Erri, *Cammei Casanoviani* (Geneva: L'Intermédiare des Casanovistes, 2006), 5; on Casanova's travels, see Alexandre Stroev, *Les Aventuriers des Lumières* (Paris: Presses Universitaires de France, 1997).

16. Angelo Mainardi, *Il Demone di Casanova* (Rome: Tre Editori, 1998), 31; Ligne in *Histoire* 3: 933.

17. Stefan Zweig, *Adepts in Self-Portraiture: Casanova, Stendhal, Tolstoy,* trans. Eden and Cedar Paul (New York: Viking, 1928), 97–98.

18. Cynthia C. Craig, "Casanova at the Bicentenary: Familiar Questions, New Directions," *Eighteenth-Century Studies* 33 (2000), 580.

19. *Boswell's London Journal,* 40.

20. Préface, *Histoire* 1: 6; letter of Dec. 13, 1793, *Correspondance avec J. F. Opiz* (Leipzig: Kurt Wolff, 1913), 1: 201.

21. Casanova to J. F. Opiz, Feb. 20, 1792, *Correspondance avec J. F. Opiz,* 1: 88; Béatrice Didier, "Plaisir et Autobiographie: Réflexions sur un Préface," *Europe* 697 (May 1987), 50; Marie-Françoise Luna, *Casanova Mémorialiste,* 217.

22. See Arthur M. Schlesinger, "The Lost Meaning of 'The Pursuit of Happiness,'" *William and Mary Quarterly* 21 (1964), 325–27.

23. Friedrich Wilhelm Barthold, *Die Geschichtlichen Persönlichkeiten in Jacob Casanovas Memoiren* (Berlin, 1746), quoted by J. Rives Childs, *Casanova: A New Perspective* (New York: Paragon House, 1988), 2.

24. Zweig quoted in *Histoire* 1: xii.

25. Casanova, *History of My Life,* trans. Willard R. Trask (New York: Harcourt Brace, 1966).

26. Sophie Rothé, *Casanova en Mouvement: Des Attraits de la Raison aux Plaisirs de la Croyance* (Paris: Éditions Le Manuscrit, 2016), 9.

27. Bergreen, *Casanova,* 497. Bergreen's notes indicate page references to the Pléiade edition, but it's not clear why, since it's the Trask translation that he's following.

CHAPTER 1. CITY OF MASKS AND MIRRORS

1. *Histoire* 1: 18–19.

2. Quoted by Maurice Andrieux, *Daily Life in Venice in the Time of Casanova,* trans. Mary Fitton (New York: Prager, 1972), 165. On attempts to identify the Casanovas' house,

see Jacques Marsan's comments in *Sui Passi di Casanova a Venezia* (Milan: Idealibri, 1993), 46–47.

3. Lydia Flem, *The Man Who Really Loved Women*, trans. Catherine Temerson (New York: Farrar, Straus and Giroux, 1997), 90.

4. Andrieux, *Daily Life in Venice in the Time of Casanova*, 13–14.

5. Emilio Ravel, *L'Uomo Che Inventò Se Stesso: Vita e Commedia di Giacomo Casanova* (Rome: La Lepre Edizioni, 2010), 20.

6. Shakespeare, *The Merchant of Venice* II.ii.

7. *Histoire* 2: 495–96.

8. George Gordon, Lord Byron, *Beppo*, stanza 44.

9. *Memoirs of Carlo Goldoni*, trans. John Black (New York: Knopf, 1926), 154.

10. *Histoire* 2: 399; Goldoni, *Memoirs* 4.

11. There is a full account of the commedia dell' arte tradition in Pierre Louis Duchartre, *The Italian Comedy*, trans. Randolph T. Weaver (1929, reprinted New York: Dover, 1966).

12. Cicero, *De Oratore* II.239, *denique corpore ridetur ipso*.

13. Johann Wolfgang von Goethe, *Italian Journey 1786–1788*, trans. W. H. Auden and Elizabeth Mayer (New York: Pantheon, 1962), 75; Norbert Jonard, *La Vie Quotidienne à Venise au XVIIIe Siècle* (Paris: Hachette, 1965), 141, 243n.

14. Quoted by Duchartre, 17.

15. Goldoni quoted by Duchartre, 46; James H. Johnson, *Venice Incognito: Masks in the Serene Republic* (Berkeley: University of California Press, 2011), 154.

16. Pierre Jean Grosley, *New Observations on Italy and Its Inhabitants*, trans. Thomas Nugent (London: 1769), 1: 237.

17. Charles Burney, *The Present State of Music in France and Italy* (London, 1771), 138–39, 150–51.

18. Jean-Jacques Rousseau, *Dictionnaire de Musique, Oeuvres Complètes*, ed. Marcel Raymond et al. (Paris: Gallimard, Bibliothèque de la Pléiade, 1959–1995), 5: 650; Goethe, *Italian Journey*, 77.

19. Richard Symanski, *The Immoral Landscape: Female Prostitution in Western Societies* (Toronto: Butterworth, 1981), 3. See Anne McCants, *Civic Charity in a Golden Age: Orphan Care in Early Modern Amsterdam* (Urbana: University of Illinois Press, 1997), and Eugenio Sonnino, "Between the Home and the Hospice: The Plight and Fate of Girl Orphans in Seventeenth and Eighteenth-Century Rome," in *Poor Women and Children in the European Past*, ed. John Henderson and Richard Wall (London: Routledge, 1994), 94–116.

20. Rousseau, *Confessions*, Book VII, *Oeuvres Complètes*, 1: 315; Patrick Barbier, *La Venise de Vivaldi: Musique et Fêtes Baroques* (Paris: Bernard Grasset, 2002), 123.

21. Rousseau, "Fragment d'une Épitre à M. Bordes," *Oeuvres Complètes* 2: 1145.

22. Grosley, 1: 257.

23. *Histoire* 1: 987.

24. *Histoire* 1: 690.

25. Philippe Monnier, *Venise au XVIIIe Siècle* (Brussels: Complexe, 1907, reprint 1981), 34. See also Johnson, *Venice Incognito*.

26. Francis Maximilien Mission, *A New Voyage to Italy,* 2nd ed. (London, 1699), 1: 198.

27. Voltaire, *Candide,* trans. Theo Cuffe (London: Penguin, 2005), ch. 24, p. 72; I have slightly altered the translation.

28. See Jonathan Walker, "Gambling and Venetian Noblemen c. 1500–1700," *Past and Present* 162 (1999), 32–33, 60.

29. Guillaume Simiand, *Casanova dans l'Europe des Aventuriers* (Paris: Classiques Garnier, 2016), 167.

30. Carlo Goldoni, *La Scuola di Ballo,* I.iii.

31. Ian Kelly, *Casanova: Actor Lover Priest Spy* (New York: Tarcher/Penguin, 2008), 18. The complicated rules of the many card games mentioned in the *Histoire* are explained in an appendix in Bouquins (2013) 1: 1549–57.

32. Stefan Zweig, *Adepts in Self-Portraiture: Casanova, Stendhal, Tolstoy,* trans. Eden and Cedar Paul (New York: Viking, 1928), 48; *Histoire* 1: 437; Roger Caillois, *Man, Play and Games,* trans. Meyer Barash (New York: Free Press, 1961), 5–7.

33. Thomas M. Kavanagh, *Dice, Cards, Wheels: A Different History of French Culture* (Philadelphia: University of Pennsylvania Press, 2005), 185.

34. See Thomas Madden, *Venice: A New History* (New York: Penguin, 2012), ch. 12.

35. Andrieux, *Daily Life in Venice,* 68–69.

36. See John Julius Norwich, *A History of Venice* (New York: Vintage, 1989), 595–96, and Johnson, *Venice Incognito,* 148.

37. Mission, 1: 211; Jan Morris, *Venice* (London: Faber, 1993), 36.

38. Andrieux, 55; Morris, 162.

39. *Mémoires du Cardinal de Bernis,* ed. Philippe Bonnet (Paris: Mercure de France, 1980), 123.

40. Mary McCarthy, *Venice Observed* (New York: Harcourt, 1963), 48.

41. Charles-Louis de Secondat, baron de La Brède et de Montesquieu, *The Spirit of the Laws,* trans. Anne M. Cohler et al. (Cambridge: Cambridge University Press, 1989), 16, 54 (I.iii and viii).

42. Goldoni, *Memoirs,* 101–3.

CHAPTER 2. AWAKENINGS

1. Quotations in this chapter are from *Histoire* 1: 19–73. To avoid a distracting overload of notes, references henceforth will be given in this collective way when appropriate.

2. Angelo Mainardi, *Il Demone di Casanova* (Rome: Tre Editori, 1998), 2; Bartolo Anglani, "Il 'Premier Souvenir': Nascita di Uno Scrittore," in *L'Histoire de Ma Vie de Giacomo Casanova,* ed. Michele Mari (Milan: Cisalpino, 2008), 129.

3. John Ruskin, *The Stones of Venice* (London: Smith, Ellis and Co., 1873), 1: 344.

4. Rodney Bolt, *Lorenzo da Ponte* (London: Bloomsbury, 2006), 14; Félicien Marceau, *Une Insolente Liberté: Les Aventures de Casanova* (Paris: Gallimard, 1983), 12.

5. Casanova, *Examen des Études de la Nature* (Utrecht, 1985), 34–35.

6. Casanova to the daughter of Maximilien Lamberg, Feb. 25, 1791, *"Mon Cher Casanova": Lettres du Conte Maximilien Lamberg et de Pietro Zaguri à Giacomo Casanova,* ed. Marco Leeflang et al. (Paris: Champion, 2008), 290.

7. *Histoire* 1: 532.

8. Prince de Ligne, *Mélanges, Histoire* 3: 921.

9. "Abatino": Virgilia Boccardi, *Casanova: La Venezia Segreta* (Venice: Filippi Editore, 2000), 7.

10. Chantal Thomas, *Casanova: Un Voyage Libertin* (Paris: Denoël, 1985), 104; Voltaire, *Dictionnaire Philosophique* (1764), article *abbé*.

11. Virgil, *Aeneid* X.113.

12. *Histoire* 1: 114; see Ivo Cerman, "Casanova's Observations on Moral Philosophy," in *Casanova: Enlightenment Philosopher*, ed. Cerman et al. (Oxford: Voltaire Foundation, 2016), 39–40.

CHAPTER 3. AN EROTIC EDUCATION

1. Quotations in this chapter are from *Histoire* 1: 77–112.

2. Casanova, *Confutazione della Storia del Governo Veneto d'Amelot de la Houssaie*, Bouquins (2013) 1: 1350.

3. Laurence Bergreen, *Casanova: The World of a Seductive Genius* (New York: Simon & Schuster, 2016), 35, 106.

4. Félicien Marceau, *Une Insolente Liberté: Les Aventures de Casanova* (Paris: Gallimard, 1983), 57.

5. Jean-Jacques Rousseau, *Julie, ou La Nouvelle Héloïse*, I.xxxviii, *Oeuvres Complètes*, ed. Marcel Raymond et al. (Paris: Gallimard, Bibliothèque de la Pléiade, 1959–1995), 2: 115.

6. Chantal Thomas, "The Role of Female Homosexuality in Casanova's *Memoirs*," *Yale French Studies* 94 (1998), 181.

7. *Histoire* 2: 1079–80.

8. *Histoire* 1: 394.

9. François Roustang, *The Quadrille of Gender: Casanova's Memoirs*, trans. Anne C. Vila (Stanford: Stanford University Press, 1988), 3.

10. Lydia Flem, *The Man Who Really Loved Women*, trans. Catherine Temerson (New York: Farrar, Straus and Giroux, 1997), 90; Maxime Rovere, *Casanova* (Paris: Gallimard, 2011), 46.

CHAPTER 4. A CAREER IN THE CHURCH

1. Quotations in this chapter are from *Histoire* 1: 112–216.

2. See Federico Montecuccoli degli Erri, *Cammei Casanoviani* (Geneva: L'Intermédiare des Casanovistes, 2006), 17–20.

3. Félicien Marceau, *Une Insolente Liberté: Les Aventures de Casanova* (Paris: Gallimard, 1983), 65.

4. *Histoire* 1: 17–18.

5. Emilio Ravel, *L'Uomo Che Inventò Se Stesso: Vita e Commedia di Giacomo Casanova* (Rome: La Lepre Edizioni, 2010), 28.

6. *Le Président de Brosses en Italie*, ed. Hubert Juin (Paris: Club des Libraires de France, 1958), 229.

7. Ibid., 291.

8. Georges Cucuel, "La Musique et les Musiciens dans les *Mémoires* de Casanova," *Revue du Dix-huitième Siècle* 1 (1913), 44.

9. Manuscript note quoted by Federico di Trocchio, "The Philosophy of the Adventurer," in *Casanova: Enlightenment Philosopher*, ed. Ivo Cerman et al. (Oxford: Voltaire Foundation, 2016), 77n.

10. François Roustang, *The Quadrille of Gender: Casanova's Memoirs*, trans. Anne C. Vila (Stanford: Stanford University Press, 1988), 46.

11. *Histoire* 3: 923.

12. *Histoire* 1: 216, 244–46; see J. Rives Childs, *Casanova: A New Perspective* (New York: Paragon House, 1988), 33.

13. *Histoire* 1: 196, 198.

CHAPTER 5. THE MYSTERIOUS CASTRATO

1. Quotations in this chapter are from *Histoire* 1: 247–76.

2. Historical details are from J. S. Jenkins, "The Voice of the Castrato," *The Lancet* 351 (1998), 1877–80.

3. *An Eighteenth-Century Musical Tour in France and Italy; Being Dr. Charles Burney's Account of His Musical Experiences*, ed. Percy Scholes (Oxford: Oxford University Press, 1959), 1: 247.

4. Anonymous, *Eunuchism Displayed* (London, 1718), quoted by Jenkins.

5. Roger Pickering, *Reflections on Theatrical Expression in Tragedy* (1755), 63.

6. *Histoire* 3: 835–36.

7. An invaluable table of equivalents for eighteenth-century and modern currencies is available in Bouquins (2013) 1: 1545–47.

8. See "Age of Consent Laws," Roy Rosenzweig Center for History and New Media, https://chnm.gmu.edu/cyh/primary-sources/24.

9. See Larry Wolff, "'Depraved Inclinations': Libertines and Children in Casanova's Venice," *Eighteenth-Century Studies* 38 (2005), 417–40.

10. Chantal Thomas, *Casanova: Un Voyage Libertin* (Paris: Denoël, 1985), 135.

11. *Histoire* 2: 558.

12. It's often assumed that she was a singer called Teresa Lanti, but that has never been proved, and she may have been a different woman, Angiola Calori. A quite spectacular portrait of Teresa Lanti is often reproduced as "Bellino," but not in this book, since even if Casanova's lover was Teresa Lanti, it's not at all certain she's the person in the picture.

13. Horace Walpole to Sir Thomas Mann (quoting Lady Townshend), Nov. 17, 1748, *Correspondence*, ed. W. S. Lewis (New Haven: Yale University Press, 1954–1971), vol. 26.

14. Courtney E. Thompson, "Picturing the Hermaphrodite in Eighteenth-Century France and England," *Eighteenth-Century Studies* 49 (2016), 404, 406.

15. François Roustang, *The Quadrille of Gender: Casanova's Memoirs*, trans. Anne C. Vila (Stanford: Stanford University Press, 1988), 62.

16. *Histoire* 2: 639–40.

CHAPTER 6. CASANOVA'S CHILDREN

1. Quotations in this section are from *Histoire* 2: 556–66.
2. Michel Delon, *Album Casanova* (Paris: Gallimard, 2015), 42.
3. This episode appears in *Histoire* 2: 611–25.
4. Delon, 128.
5. *Histoire* 3: 703.
6. *Histoire* 3: 708–9.
7. François Roustang, *The Quadrille of Gender: Casanova's Memoirs,* trans. Anne C. Vila (Stanford: Stanford University Press, 1988), 160–61.
8. *Histoire* 3: 780.
9. *Histoire* 2: 622.
10. *Histoire* 2: 668.

CHAPTER 7. CORFU AND CONSTANTINOPLE

1. Quotations in this section are from *Histoire* 1: 287–301.
2. *Histoire* 1: 282–83; see Michel Delon, "Uniformes de Caprice," in *Casanova: La Passion de la Liberté,* ed. Marie-Laure Prévost and Chantal Thomas (Paris: Seuil, 2011), 28.
3. Guillaume Simiand, *Casanova dans l'Europe des Aventuriers* (Paris: Classiques Garnier, 2016), 116.
4. *Histoire* 1: 1233.
5. See Guy David Toubiana, "Casanova: Magicien ou la Fabrication d'un Mythe?," *Romance Quarterly* 56 (2009), 217–25.
6. See Marie-Françoise Luna, "Casanova à Constantinople: Turquie ou Turquerie?," in *L'Histoire de Ma Vie de Giacomo Casanova,* ed. Michele Mari (Milan: Cisalpino, 2008), 271–72. In the twentieth century the Pera name was changed to Beyoglu.
7. See Séverine Denieul, "Du Beau Parleur Occasionel au Conteur Professionel: La Conversation dans l'*Histoire de Ma Vie* de Casanova," *Largesse de Casanova,* ed. Michel Delon (Bergamo and Paris, 2011), 55–73.
8. Emilio Ravel, *L'Uomo Che Inventò Se Stesso: Vita e Commedia di Giacomo Casanova* (Rome: La Lepre Edizioni, 2010), 81.
9. Quotations in this section are from *Histoire* 1: 310–29.
10. *Le Philosophe et le Théologien,* Bouquins (1993) 1: 1186; see Wolfgang Rother, "Italian Enlightenment Debates on Religion and Church: Casanova's Philosophy and Its Background," in *Casanova: Enlightenment Philosopher,* ed. Ivo Cerman et al. (Oxford: Voltaire Foundation, 2016), 95–117.
11. Carlo Blasis, *Manuel Complet de la Danse* (Paris: Manuel-Rorel, 1830), 15.
12. *Histoire* 1: 1142, 182.
13. Gemelli Careri, *Giro del Mondo,* quoted by Luna, "Casanova à Constantinople," 277.
14. J. Rives Childs, *Casanova: A New Perspective* (New York: Paragon House, 1988), 36; Mary Wortley Montagu, *Letters from the Levant During the Embassy to Constantinople, 1716–18* (London: Joseph Rickerby, 1838), 127; Ian Kelly, *Casanova: Actor Lover Priest Spy* (New York: Tarcher/Penguin, 2008), 99.

15. Gérard Lahouati, "Le Spectateur Immobile: Esthétique Littéraire et Mise en Scène des Souvenirs dans l'*Histoire de ma Vie*," *Europe* 697 (May 1987), 72.

16. *Histoire* 1: 393; on these vessels see the note at 1: 1237–38.

17. Quotations in this section are from *Histoire* 1: 349–82.

CHAPTER 8. METAMORPHOSIS

1. Quotations in this section are from *Histoire* 1: 395–410.

2. "Gang rape": Judith Summers, *Casanova's Women: The Great Seducer and the Women He Loved* (London: Bloomsbury, 2006), 137.

3. Casanova, *Lana Caprina,* ed. Paul Mengal (Paris: Honoré Champion, 1999), 200, adapting Pliny, *Natural History* XXIX.i.8.

4. *Histoire* 1: 175.

5. John Maynard Keynes, "Newton, The Man," *Proceedings of the Royal Society, Newton Tercentenary Celebrations, 15–19 July 1946* (Cambridge: Cambridge University Press, 1947); see Michael White, *Isaac Newton: The Last Sorcerer* (Reading, MA: Addison-Wesley, 1997) and Jason Josephson-Storm, *The Myth of Disenchantment: Magic, Modernity, and the Birth of the Human Sciences* (Chicago: University of Chicago Press, 2017), esp. ch. 2.

6. *Histoire* 2: 357, 373.

7. See Alexandre Stroev, *Les Aventuriers des Lumières* (Paris: Presses Universitaires de France, 1997), 14.

8. See B. Dompnier, "Les Hommes d'Église et la Superstition entre XVIIe et XVIIIe Siècles," *La Superstition à l'Âge des Lumières* (Paris: Champion, 1998), 46–47; and Sophie Rothé, *Casanova en Mouvement: Des Attraits de la Raison aux Plaisirs de la Croyance* (Paris: Éditions Le Manuscrit, 2016), 85.

9. Denis Diderot, *Paradoxe sur le Comédien.*

10. Jean-Didier Vincent, *Casanova: La Contagion du Plaisir* (Paris: Odile Jacob, 1990), 177–78; Guillaume Simiand, *Casanova dans l'Europe des Aventuriers* (Paris: Classiques Garnier, 2016), 547; and see also Guy David Toubiana, "Magicien ou la Fabrication d'un Mythe?," *Romance Quarterly* 56 (2009), 217–25.

11. This hypothesis is advanced by Ian Kelly, *Casanova: Actor Lover Priest Spy* (New York: Tarcher/Penguin, 2008), 106–8.

12. Félicien Marceau, *Une Insolente Liberté: Les Aventures de Casanova* (Paris: Gallimard, 1983), 101.

13. See Piero Del Negro, "Giacomo Casanova e il Patriziato Venetiano nell' *Histoire de Ma Vie*," in *L'Histoire de Ma Vie de Giacomo Casanova,* ed. Michele Mari (Milan: Cisalpino, 2008), 3–32.

CHAPTER 9. PLAYBOY

1. Quotations in this section are from *Histoire* 1: 411–15.

2. *Histoire* 3: 921. On portraits of Casanova see Corinne Le Bitouzé, "Ce serait un bien bel homme, s'il n'était pas laid," in *Casanova: La Passion de la Liberté,* ed. Marie-Laure Prévost and Chantal Thomas (Paris: Seuil, 2011), 68–69.

3. *Histoire* 1: 904, 1321.

4. Pietro Chiari, *La Commediante in Fortuna* (1755), quoted by Federico Montecuccoli degli Erri, *Cammei Casanoviani* (Geneva: L'Intermédiare des Casanovistes, 2006), 101–2.

5. As before, I follow the table of currency equivalents in Bouquins (2013) 1: 1545–47.

6. *Histoire* 1: 718–19.

7. *Histoire* 1: 413–36.

8. *Histoire* 1: 438–60.

9. Didier Kihli-Sagols, *La Comédie Médicale de Giacomo Casanova* (Paris: Éditions Thélès, 2005), 57.

10. See Maxime Rovere, *Casanova* (Paris: Gallimard, 2011), 79.

11. Quoted by Guillaume Simiand, *Casanova dans l'Europe des Aventuriers* (Paris: Classiques Garnier, 2016), 335.

12. *Histoire* 1: 466–70.

CHAPTER 10. LIBERTINISM

1. *Histoire* 1: 898.

2. James G. Turner, "The Properties of Libertinism," in *'Tis Nature's Fault: Unauthorized Sexuality During the Enlightenment,* ed. Robert P. MacCubbin (Cambridge: Cambridge University Press, 1987), 77–78.

3. Genesis 1: 31; *Histoire* 1: 1115.

4. Jean Starobinski, *The Invention of Liberty,* trans. Bernard C. Swift (Geneva: Skira, 1964), 10; Robert Darnton, *The Forbidden Best-Sellers of Pre-Revolutionary France* (New York: Norton, 1995), xix.

5. *Histoire* 1: 9, 1113.

6. Horace, *Epistles* I.iv.15–16; *The Works of Horace Translated into English Prose* (London, 1753), 2: 229.

7. Marie-Françoise Luna, *Casanova Mémorialiste* (Paris: Honoré Champion, 1998), 324.

8. *Histoire* 2: 809, quoting Horace *Epistles* I.x.79 and *Odes* I.xi.8, III.xxix.34.

9. *Histoire* 1: 768 (a fragment intended for insertion in the *Histoire*).

10. Denis Diderot, *Sequel to the Conversation,* in *Rameau's Nephew and D'Alembert's Dream,* trans. Leonard Tancock (London: Penguin, 1966), 230–31.

11. Catherine Cusset, "The Lesson of Libertinage," *Yale French Studies* 94 (1998), 2.

12. *Histoire* 1: 718, 2: 739.

13. Bouquins (2013), 1: 1327.

14. References in the *Histoire* are listed by Luna, *Casanova Mémorialiste,* 335.

15. *Histoire* 1: 672.

16. On cubebs and copaiba, see J. L. Milton, *On the Pathology and Treatment of Gonorrhoea* (New York: W. Wood & Co., 1884), 73–82.

17. *Examen des Études de la Nature et de Paul et Virginie,* Bouquins (1993) 2: 1130; I have abridged this long passage somewhat.

18. *Histoire* 1: 450, 265; *The Complete Poetry and Prose of William Blake,* ed. David V. Erdman (New York: Doubleday, 1988), 474.

19. John Wilmot, Earl of Rochester, *The Imperfect Enjoyment,* lines 62–67.

20. See Donald Posner, "The Swinging Women of Watteau and Fragonard," *Art Bulletin* 64 (1982), 75–88, and Jennifer Milam, "Playful Constructions and Fragonard's Swinging Scenes," *Eighteenth-Century Studies* 33 (2000), 543–59.

21. Michel Delon, *Le Savoir-Vivre Libertin* (Paris: Hachette, 2000), 12, 318–19.

CHAPTER 11. "YOU WILL ALSO FORGET HENRIETTE"

1. *Histoire* 1: 471–75.

2. Jean-Didier Vincent, *Casanova: La Contagion du Plaisir* (Paris: Odile Jacob, 1990).

3. John 18: 11.

4. Guillaume Simiand, *Casanova dans l'Europe des Aventuriers* (Paris: Classiques Garnier, 2016), 127.

5. Quotations in this section are from *Histoire* 1: 505–56.

6. *Histoire* 3: 604.

7. See Jean-Christophe Igalens, "'Un Mixte si Beau': Le Discours d'Henriette, ou le Bonheur selon Casanova," *Le Bonheur au XVIIIe Siècle,* ed. Guilhem Farrugia and Michel Delon (Rennes: La Licorne, 2015), 172–73.

8. Georges Poulet, *Études sur le Temps Humain* (Paris: Presses Pocket, 1990), 4: 108 (not in the standard abridged English edition).

9. Choderlos de Laclos, *Dangerous Liaisons,* trans. Helen Constantine (London: Penguin, 2007), 19 (Part I, Letter 5).

10. Angelo Mainardi, *Casanova: L'Ultimo Mistero* (Rome: Tre Editori, 2010), 56.

11. *Histoire* 2: 385.

12. *Histoire* 2: 874.

13. Nicolas Faret, *L'Honnête Homme, ou l'Art de Plaire à la Cour* (1630), quoted in *Le Robert Dictionnaire Historique de la Langue Française* (Paris: Dictionnaires le Robert, 1998), 2: 1734.

14. *Histoire* 3: 600.

15. Lydia Flem, *The Man Who Really Loved Women,* trans. Catherine Temerson (New York: Farrar, Straus and Giroux, 1997), 112; Judith Summers, *Casanova's Women: The Great Seducer and the Women He Loved* (London: Bloomsbury, 2006), 148.

16. Michel Delon, *Album Casanova* (Paris: Gallimard, 2015), 46.

CHAPTER 12. PARIS AT LAST

1. *Histoire* 1: 566.

2. Joan DeJean, *How Paris Became Paris: The Invention of the Modern City* (New York: Bloomsbury, 2014), p. 1.

3. *Histoire* 1: 581–86.

4. Casanova to Maximilien Lamberg, July 28, 1787, *"Mon Cher Casanova": Lettres du Conte Maximilien Lamberg et de Pietro Zaguri à Giacomo Casanova,* ed. Marco Leeflang et al. (Paris: Champion, 2008), 101. Guillaume Simiand lists nearly sixty adventurers, with detailed accounts of many of them, in *Casanova dans l'Europe des Aventuriers* (Paris: Classiques Garnier, 2016).

5. Simiand, 11; Charles-Augustin Sainte-Beuve, *Premiers Lundis* (Paris: Michel Lévy, 1874), 2: 211, "Mémoires de Casanova de Seingalt."

6. *Histoire* 1: 590; see Charles Porset, "Casanova Franc-Maçon," *Chroniques d'Histoire Maçonnique* 49 (1998), 9.

7. See P.-Y. Beaurepaire, "Naissance d'un Microcosme Européen: La Franc Maçonnerie," in *Le Mythe de l'Europe Française au XVIIIe Siècle* (Paris: Autrement, 2007), 53, and Norbert Jonard, *La Vie Quotidienne à Venise au XVIIIe Siècle* (Paris: Hachette, 1965), 116–17.

8. The Lyon ritual is quoted in full by Daniel Tougne, *Casanova: Un Franc-Maçon en Europe au XVIII Siècle* (Paris: Éditions Trajectoire, 2013), 251–63; two pages of the manuscript are reproduced on p. 69.

9. Jorge Luis Borges, *Collected Fictions,* trans. Andrew Hurley (New York: Penguin, 1998), 504–7.

10. Helmut Watzlawick, "Casanova et la Vienne de Joseph II à Franz II," in *Casanova Fin de Siècle,* ed. Marie-Françoise Luna (Paris: Honoré Champion, 2002), 52; on Masonic lodges in countries Casanova visited, see Porset.

11. *Histoire* 1: 595–98.

12. *Histoire* 1: 482–83.

13. *Histoire* 1: 624.

14. Jean-François Marmontel, *Éléments de Littérature, Oeuvres Complètes* (Paris, 1787), 7: 404–5; *Histoire* 1: 678.

15. *Histoire* 1: 1037–38, 607.

16. *Histoire* 1: 1178, 1156.

17. Stefan Zweig, *Adepts in Self-Portraiture: Casanova, Stendhal, Tolstoy,* trans. Eden and Cedar Paul (New York: Viking, 1928), 12.

18. *Histoire* 1: 1043–45; Casanova's wisecrack is quoted from Sara Goudar's *Supplément aux Remarques sur la Musique et la Danse* (1773) by J. Rives Childs, *Casanova: A New Perspective* (New York: Paragon House, 1988), 52.

19. *Histoire* 1: 618–22; the quotation is from *Aeneid* 1.71.

20. Nina Kushner, *Erotic Exchanges: The World of Elite Prostitution in Eighteenth-Century Paris* (Ithaca: Cornell University Press, 2013), 17, 118.

21. *Histoire* 1: 637–40; on the Enfants Trouvés see Camille Bloch, *L'Assistance et l'État en France à la Veille de la Révolution* (Paris: Picard, 1908), 57–120.

22. *Histoire* 1: 670.

23. Quotations in this section are from *Histoire* 1: 646–57.

24. Kushner, 1.

25. *Histoire* 1: 659–61, and notes on 1290; also C. D. Dickerson, "The Art of Display," in *Casanova: The Seduction of Europe,* ed. Frederick Ilchman et al. (Boston: Museum of Fine Arts Publications, 2017), 32–34.

26. *Histoire* 1: 1054; Laforgue's addition is quoted by Chantal Thomas, *Casanova: Un Voyage Libertin* (Paris: Denoël, 1985), 172.

27. *Histoire* 1: 628.

28. Charles-Maurice de Talleyrand-Périgord, *Mémoires du Prince de Talleyrand: La Confession de Talleyrand* (Paris: Calmann Lévy, 1891), 1: 5.

29. Angelo Mainardi, *Il Demone di Casanova* (Rome: Tre Editori, 1998), 60.

CHAPTER 13. NUNS AND LOVERS

1. Jean Laforgue, quoted by Philippe Sollers, *Casanova the Irresistible,* trans. Armine Kotin Mortimer (Urbana: University of Illinois Press, 2016), 8; quotations in this section are from *Histoire* 1: 689–722.

2. Chantal Thomas, *Casanova: Un Voyage Libertin* (Paris: Denoël, 1985), 46.

3. On the earlier connection with Capretta, see Federico Montecuccoli degli Erri, *Cammei Casanoviani* (Geneva: L'Intermédiare des Casanovistes, 2006), 47–52.

4. See Margaret R. Hunt, *Women in Eighteenth-Century Europe* (London: Routledge, 2014), ch. 3.

5. Remaining quotations in this chapter are from *Histoire* 1: 722–880.

6. See Pompeo Molmenti, *Venice: Its Individual Growth,* trans. Horatio E. Brown (Chicago: McClurg, 1908), 2: 84–86.

7. Alexander Pope, *The Rape of the Lock* (1714), III.160; on lapdogs and rings, see Rolf Bagemihl, "Pietro Longhi and Venetian Life," *Metropolitan Museum Journal* 23 (1988), 236.

8. *Histoire* 1: xxiii.

9. See the biographical note in *Histoire* 1: 1306.

10. Gunter Passavant, *Verrochio: Sculptures, Paintings and Drawings* (London: Phaidon, 1969), 64.

11. *Histoire* 2: 798, 1: 382.

12. *Histoire* 1: 141; Lydia Flem, *The Man Who Really Loved Women,* trans. Catherine Temerson (New York: Farrar, Straus and Giroux, 1997), 196.

13. Friedrich Nietzsche, *Beyond Good and Evil,* in *The Philosophy of Nietzsche,* trans. Helen Zimmern (New York: Modern Library, 1954), aphorism 168, p. 470.

14. *Venus in the Cloister,* in *When Word Becomes Flesh: An Anthology of Early Eighteenth-Century Libertine Literature,* ed. Bradford K. Mudge (Oxford: Oxford University Press, 2004), 199.

15. Félicien Marceau, *Une Insolente Liberté: Les Aventures de Casanova* (Paris: Gallimard, 1983), 77–78.

16. Marine Riva-Ganofsky, "*L'Histoire de Ma Vie* de Casanova: Le Libertinage comme Rencontre entre le Profane et le Sacré," in *Amour Divin, Amour Mondain,* ed. Maurice Daumas (Pau: Cairn, 2011), 118.

17. Ian Kelly, *Casanova: Actor Lover Priest Spy* (New York: Tarcher/Penguin, 2008), 131.

18. Vladimir Nabokov, *Lolita* (New York: Vintage, 1997), afterword, 313.

19. Flem, 72.

20. *Histoire* 2: 6–7, 1: 887.

21. See Riccardo Selvatico, *Cento Note per Casanova a Venezia* (Venice: Neri Pozza, 1997), 155–57.

22. Patrick Barbier, *La Venise de Vivaldi: Musique et Fêtes Baroques* (Paris: Bernard Grasset, 2002), 156.

23. The Prince de Ligne to Casanova, *Histoire* 3: 940; James Joyce, *Ulysses,* ed. Hans Gabler (New York: Random House, 1986), 34.

24. Marceau, 136–44.

25. Angelo Mainardi, *Il Demone di Casanova* (Rome: Tre Editori, 1998), 89.

26. Pierre Gruet, "M. M. et les Anges de Murano," Bouquins (1993) 1: 1069.

CHAPTER 14. THE GREAT ESCAPE

1. *Histoire de Ma Fuite des Prisons de la République de Vénise, qu'on Appelle les Plombs,* reprinted as an appendix in Bouquins (2013), 1: 1354; Dante, *Divine Comedy, Inferno,* trans. Charles S. Singleton (Princeton: Princeton University Press, 1970), 1: 3. Subsequent quotations in this chapter, unless otherwise noted, are from the version of the story in *Histoire* 1: 892–999.

2. Laurence Bergreen makes the claim that Casanova was devout: *Casanova: The World of a Seductive Genius* (New York: Simon & Schuster, 2016), 19.

3. Most of Manuzzi's reports are given in French translation in *Histoire* 1: 1129–36. The Italian originals are collected, together with reports by forty-three other informants from 1705 to 1797, by Giovanni Comisso, *Agenti Segreti di Venezia* (Milan: Longanesi, 1963).

4. This quote, not in the selection in the *Histoire,* is in *Agenti Segreti,* 187.

5. *Histoire* 1: 827.

6. Varutti's report is quoted in Bouquins (2013) 1: 1170n.

7. Ian Kelly, *Casanova: Actor Lover Priest Spy* (New York: Tarcher/ Penguin, 2008), 182.

8. Maurice Andrieux, *Daily Life in Venice in the Time of Casanova,* trans. Mary Fitton (New York: Prager, 1972), 58.

9. See Jacques Marsan's comments in *Sui Passi di Casanova a Venezia* (Milan: Idealibri, 1993), 70–71.

10. "Des Rats dans les Catacombes de l'Esprit," in *Le Mythe en Littérature,* ed. Yves Chevrel and Camille Dumoulié (Paris: Presses Universitaires de France, 2000), 332; see also Jacques Berchtold, "La Peur des Rats dans les Récits d'Emprisonnement de Cyrano de Bergerac à Casanova," in *La Peur au XVIIIe Siècle,* ed. Berchtold and Michel Porret (Geneva: Droz, 1994), 99–119.

11. Horace, *Odes* I.xxxvii.29; Emilio Ravel, *L'Uomo Che Inventò Se Stesso: Vita e Commedia di Giacomo Casanova* (Rome: La Lepre Edizioni, 2010), 21.

12. William Spaggiari, "Pauline, o la Seduzione delle Lettere," in *L'Histoire de Ma Vie de Giacomo Casanova,* ed. Michele Mari (Milan: Cisalpino, 2008), 314.

13. The 1723 definition of *amadou* is quoted in *Le Robert Dictionnaire Historique de la Langue Française* (Paris: Dictionnaires le Robert, 1998), 1: 102.

14. Bouquins (2013) 1: 1405.

15. We're told by modern editors of the *Histoire* that when Casanova mentions "macaroni," he usually means what today is called gnocchi.

16. Ludovico Ariosto, *Orlando Furioso,* trans. Guido Waldman (Oxford: Oxford University Press, 1998), 82.

17. Psalm 117: 17; *Histoire de Ma Fuite,* Bouquins (2013) 1: 1452.

18. Bouquins (2013) 1: 1486; *Histoire* 1: 1322n.

19. *Histoire* 2: 243; Bouquins (2013) 1: 1487.

20. *Histoire* 1: 893.

21. Casanova to an actor named Soulé, *Pages Casanoviennes: Correspondance Inédite de Jacques Casanova, 1760–1766* (Paris: Société Casanovienne, Jean Fort, 1925), 39, 42.

CHAPTER 15. IN SEARCH OF THE BLIND GODDESS

1. Alexandre Stroev, *Les Aventuriers des Lumières* (Paris: Presses Universitaires de France, 1997), 18.
2. Bouquins (2013), 1: 1325.
3. Quotations in this chapter are from *Histoire* 1: 1004–14 and 2: 5–20.
4. Maxime Rovere, *Casanova* (Paris: Gallimard, 2011), 126.
5. Stroev, *Les Aventuriers des Lumières,* 14; Bouquins (1993) 2: 291n.
6. *Histoire* 2: 718; Marie de Nairne, quoted by Sophie Rothé, *Casanova en Mouvement: Des Attraits de la Raison aux Plaisirs de la Croyance* (Paris: Éditions Le Manuscrit, 2016), 176; Chantal Thomas, *Casanova: Un Voyage Libertin* (Paris: Denoël, 1985), 251.
7. Corinne Le Bitouze, "Toujours Soigné comme un Narcisse," in *Casanova: La Passion de la Liberté,* ed. Marie-Laure Prévost and Chantal Thomas (Paris: Seuil, 2011), 52.
8. A full account of the lottery scheme is given by Guillaume Simiand, *Casanova dans l'Europe des Aventuriers* (Paris: Classiques Garnier, 2016), 481–502.
9. Denis Diderot, *Salons de 1759, 1761, 1763,* ed. Gita May (Paris: Hermann, 1984), 162–64, 247.
10. Diderot to Mme. de Maux, autumn 1769, *Correspondance,* ed. Laurent Versini (Paris: Robert Laffont, 1997), 985.
11. On the deletions see *Histoire* 3: 1082.
12. *Histoire* 2: 107. See J. Rives Childs, *Casanova: A New Perspective* (New York: Paragon House, 1988), 86–87.
13. Mme. du Rumain to Casanova, Jan. 8, 1760, Bouquins (1993) 1: 1101.
14. *Histoire* 2: 95.
15. Félicien Marceau, *Casanova, ou l'Anti-Don Juan* (Paris: Gallimard, 1985), 132.
16. Ian Kelly, *Casanova: Actor Lover Priest Spy* (New York: Tarcher/Penguin, 2008), 295–300; Jean-Bernard Naudin, *Casanova: Un Vénitien Gourmand* (Paris: Éditions du Chêne, 1998).

CHAPTER 16. MANON

1. *Histoire* 2: 48.
2. *Histoire* 3: 47.
3. The complete set of forty-one letters was collected by Aldo Ravà and reproduced in a French edition by Édouard Maynial, *Lettres de Femmes à Jacques Casanova* (Paris: Louis-Michaud, 1912). My quotations come from a selection in the Pléiade *Histoire* 2: 1112–32, with one exception as noted below, and they are supplemented by another selection in Bouquins (2013) 2: 1395–1415.
4. *Histoire* 2: 133; Robert Herrick, "To the Virgins, to Make Much of Time."
5. *Histoire* 2: 229.
6. *Lettres de Femmes,* 103.
7. Ian Kelly, *Casanova: Actor Lover Priest Spy* (New York: Tarcher/Penguin, 2008), 195;

Judith Summers, *Casanova's Women: The Great Seducer and the Women He Loved* (London: Bloomsbury, 2006), 214–15.

8. Chantal Thomas, *Casanova: Un Voyage Libertin* (Paris: Denoël, 1985), 19, 209.

CHAPTER 17. ROLLING STONE

1. See J. Rives Childs, *Casanova: A New Perspective* (New York: Paragon House, 1988), 112.

2. See Guillaume Simiand, "Casanova et le Nom 'Seingalt,'" *Dix-Huitième Siècle* 44 (2012), 564.

3. *Histoire* 1: 465.

4. *Histoire* 2: 963.

5. Bernard de Muralt to Albrecht Haller, June 21, 1760, *Histoire* 2: 1110–11. (I have somewhat abridged this letter.)

6. Quotations in this section are from *Histoire* 2: 240–58.

7. Rives Childs, 109.

8. *Orlando Furioso* XI.67–69, trans. Guido Waldman (Oxford: Oxford University Press, 1983), 114.

9. Quotations in this section are from *Histoire* 2: 279–349.

10. The receipt is given in Bouquins (1993) 2: 291.

11. See *Histoire* 2: 1193n.

12. Quotations in this section are from *Histoire* 2: 365–85.

13. Details about "Sara" and her father are in *Histoire* 2: 1204–5n.

CHAPTER 18. JOUSTING WITH VOLTAIRE

1. Quotations in this chapter are from *Histoire* 2: 387–405.

2. Marie-Françoise Luna, "Un Cas de Voltairomanie: Giacomo Casanova," *Voltaire et ses Combats* (Oxford: Voltaire Foundation, 1997), 837; Alexandre Stroev, *Les Aventuriers des Lumières* (Paris: Presses Universitaires de France, 1997), 76.

3. Stroev, 2–3, 26.

4. Emilio Ravel, *L'Uomo Che Inventò Se Stesso: Vita e Commedia di Giacomo Casanova* (Rome: La Lepre Edizioni, 2010), 280.

5. Mitterrand quoted by Luna, 847.

6. Voltaire, *Candide, or Optimism*, trans. Theo Cuffe (London: Penguin, 2005), ch. 3, p. 8.

7. https://www.voltaire.ox.ac.uk/news/blog/public-figures-invention-celebrity-eighteenth -century.

8. Voltaire, *Épître 5, À Monsieur l'Abbé de *** qui Pleurait la Mort de sa Maîtresse* (1715), final lines.

CHAPTER 19. STILL ROLLING

1. Quotations in this section are from *Histoire* 2: 411–48.

2. *Histoire* 3: 499; Luke 11: 27.

3. Angelo Mainardi, *Il Demone di Casanova* (Rome: Tre Editori, 1998), 94.

4. *Histoire* 2: 385.

5. Quotations in this section are from *Histoire* 2: 451–93.

6. Marie-Françoise Luna, "La Maison de Casanova à Grenoble et la Société Dauphinoise en 1760," *Casanova Fin de Siècle,* ed. Luna (Paris: Honoré Champion, 2002), 13–26. I am grateful to Professor Luna for helping me to obtain the picture.

7. Jean-François Regnard, *Le Joueur* (1696) IV.x.

8. Georges Cucuel (1918), quoted by J. Rives Childs, *Casanova: A New Perspective* (New York: Paragon House, 1988), 131.

9. Petrarch, *Canzoniere* CXXVI; quotations in this section are from *Histoire* 2: 481–551.

10. *Sur Pétrarque et l'Amour Platonique,* Bouquins (2013) 2: 1385.

11. Quotations in this section are from *Histoire* 2: 499–583.

12. *Boswell on the Grand Tour: Italy, Corsica, and France 1765–1766,* ed. Frank Brady and Frederick A. Pottle (New York: McGraw-Hill, 1955), 84, 55.

CHAPTER 20. MAGUS

1. The aphorism is quoted by Guillaume Simiand, "Casanova et le nom 'Seingalt,'" *Dix-Huitième Siècle* 44 (2012), 562; Ian Kelly, *Casanova: Actor Lover Priest Spy* (New York: Tarcher/ Penguin, 2008), 206.

2. Casanova, *Soliloque d'un Penseur* (1786), ed. Raoul Vèze (Paris: Jean Fort, 1926), 14–15.

3. *Histoire* 2: 84; *Soliloque d'un Penseur,* 35, 13.

4. Félicien Marceau, *Une Insolente Liberté: Les Aventures de Casanova* (Paris: Gallimard, 1983), 223.

5. *Souvenirs de la Marquise de Créquy* (Paris: Garnier, 1842), 3: 60. This "memoir" was put together from the Marquise's papers by her grandson, with comments of his own.

6. François Roustang, *The Quadrille of Gender: Casanova's Memoirs,* trans. Anne C. Vila (Stanford: Stanford University Press, 1988), 130. (I have changed the translator's "its favors" to "her favors," which reflects the original French and is more appropriate for the goddess Fortune.)

7. *Histoire* 2: 463.

8. Quotations in this section are from *Histoire* 2: 669–79.

9. J. Rives Childs, *Casanova: A New Perspective* (New York: Paragon House, 1988), 150.

10. Marceau, 240.

11. *Histoire* 2: 718.

12. Angelo Mainardi, *Casanova: L'Ultimo Mistero* (Rome: Tre Editori, 2010), 31.

13. *Histoire* 2: 688–89.

14. *Histoire* 2: 789.

15. Chantal Thomas, *Casanova: Un Voyage Libertin* (Paris: Denoël, 1985), 357.

16. *Histoire* 2: 737–43.

17. Quotations in this section are from *Histoire* 2: 853–65, supplemented from the Laforgue and German versions of now-lost chapters that are reprinted in this volume.

18. Judith Summers, *Casanova's Women: The Great Seducer and the Women He Loved* (London: Bloomsbury, 2006), 260.

19. *Histoire* 2: 912.

20. *Histoire* 2: 1018.
21. Marie-Françoise Luna, *Casanova Mémorialiste* (Paris: Honoré Champion, 1998), 245.

CHAPTER 21. THE END OF ACT I

1. Casanova, *Ma Voisine, la Posterité, À Leonard Snetlage* (Paris: Éditions Allia, 1998), 69. This work was first published in 1797.
2. Quotations in this chapter are from *Histoire* 3: 5–204.
3. Tobias Smollett, *The Expedition of Humphry Clinker* (1771), Lydia Melford to Laetitia Willis, May 31.
4. Teresa's London career is very fully described by Judith Summers, *Empress of Pleasure: The Life and Adventures of Teresa Cornelys* (London: Penguin, 2004).
5. Chantal Thomas, *Casanova: Un Voyage Libertin* (Paris: Denoël, 1985), 123.
6. The quotation is from a novel published after their American journey by Tocqueville's companion Gustave de Beaumont: *Marie, ou l'Esclavage aux États-Unis, Tableau de Moeurs Américaines* (Paris: Gosselin, 1835), 1: 386.
7. J. Rives Childs, *Casanova: A New Perspective* (New York: Paragon House, 1988), 180. In the *Histoire* Casanova quotes the advertisement inaccurately from memory and says it was in the *St. James's Chronicle,* but Rives Childs was able to track it down.
8. The police report is quoted by Judith Summers, *Casanova's Women: The Great Seducer and the Women He Loved* (London: Bloomsbury, 2006), 273.
9. See above, p. 144.
10. *Lettres de Femmes à Jacques Casanova,* ed. Aldo Ravà and Édouard Maynial (Paris: Louis-Michaud, 1912), 137.
11. Summers, *Casanova's Women,* 290.
12. Sophie's later story is related by Summers, *Casanova's Women,* 331–32.
13. *Memoirs of Lorenzo Da Ponte,* trans. Elizabeth Abbott (Philadelphia: Lippincott, 1929), 232–33.

CHAPTER 22. AT THE COURTS OF FREDERICK AND CATHERINE

1. Maxime Rovere, *Casanova* (Paris: Gallimard, 2011), 198. Except when otherwise noted, quotations in this section are from *Histoire* 3: 217–31.
2. *Histoire* 3: 350.
3. *Boswell on the Grand Tour: Germany and Switzerland 1764,* ed. Frederick A. Pottle (New York: Mc-Graw-Hill, 1953), 78; see J. Rives Childs, *Casanova: A New Perspective* (New York: Paragon House, 1988), 177.
4. Emilio Ravel, *L'Uomo Che Inventò Se Stesso: Vita e Commedia di Giacomo Casanova* (Rome: La Lepre Edizioni, 2010), 207.
5. Quotations in this section are from *Histoire* 3: 276–318.
6. Casanova to Count Orlov, Sept. 1765, *Pages Casanoviennes: Correspondance Inédite de Jacques Casanova, 1760–1766* (Paris: Société Casanovienne, Jean Fort, 1925), 33.
7. Catherine's comment about Diderot is quoted by Arthur M. Wilson, *Diderot* (New York: Oxford University Press, 1972), 632.
8. George Gordon, Lord Byron, *Don Juan* X.26.

9. See Peter Kolchin, *Unfree Labor: American Slavery and Russian Serfdom* (Cambridge: Harvard University Press, 1987), 41–42.

10. Jean-Jacques Rousseau, *Confessions, Oeuvres Complètes,* ed. Marcel Raymond et al. (5 volumes, Paris: Gallimard, Bibliothèque de la Pléiade, 1959–95), 1: 323.

11. A. T. Limojon de Saint-Didier, *La Ville et la République de Venise au XVIIe Siècle,* quoted by Ravel, *L'Uomo Che Inventò Se Stesso,* 34.

12. Félicien Marceau, *Une Insolente Liberté: Les Aventures de Casanova* (Paris: Gallimard, 1983), 85; Ted Emery, "Queer Casanova: Subversive Sexuality and the (Dis)embodied Subject in *History of My Life*," *Italian Culture* 24–25 (2006–2007), 32.

13. Prince de Ligne to Casanova, Sept. 25, 1794, *Histoire* 3: 939; Michel Foucault, *History of Sexuality,* 3 vols. (London: Penguin, 1976–84).

14. Laurence Bergreen, *Casanova: The World of a Seductive Genius* (New York: Simon & Schuster, 2016), 363.

15. On evidence showing that Valville couldn't have traveled with Casanova, see *Histoire* 3: 1032n.

CHAPTER 23. THE DUEL

1. Quotations in this chapter are from the original published version of the story, *Le Duel, ou Aperçu de la Vie de G. C., Vénitien,* as reprinted in French translation in Bouquins 3: 1133–80. Occasional supplementary details are taken from *Histoire* 3: 319–27.

2. V. K. Kiernan, *The Duel in European History: Honour and the Reign of Aristocracy* (Oxford: Oxford University Press, 1988).

3. Kiernan, 63, 138.

4. Kiernan, 138, 148.

5. Prince de Ligne, *Mélanges, Histoire* 3: 932.

6. The Abate Tartuffi to Melchiore Cesarotti, quoted by Ian Kelly, *Casanova: Actor Lover Priest Spy* (New York: Tarcher/Penguin, 2008), 294.

7. Casanova, *Né Amori né Donne, Ovvero la Stalla Ripulta, traduction Française,* ed. Jean Fort (Paris: Librairie de la Société Casanovienne, 1926), 3–4.

CHAPTER 24. "THIS PHANTOM LIBERTY"

1. Préface, *Histoire* 1: 4; Alfred de Musset in *Le Temps,* March 20, 1831, quoted by Annarosa Poli, "Les Amants de Venise et Casanova," *Revue d'Histoire Littéraire de la France,* 59: 1 (1959), 1.

2. Quotations in this chapter are from *Histoire* 3: 350–427.

3. J. Rives Childs, *Casanova: A New Perspective* (New York: Paragon House, 1988), 217.

4. On Charlotte's identity and Croce's later visit, see *Histoire* 3: 1056–57.

5. Guillaume Simiand, *Casanova dans l'Europe des Aventuriers* (Paris: Garnier, 2016), 549.

CHAPTER 25. SPAIN

1. Quotations in this chapter are from *Histoire* 3: 434–570.

2. Félicien Marceau, *Une Insolente Liberté: Les Aventures de Casanova* (Paris: Gallimard, 1983), 287.

CHAPTER 26. WHILING AWAY THE YEARS IN ITALY

1. Quotations in this section are from *Histoire* 3: 575–647.
2. *Gazetta Toscana,* April 21, 1770, quoted by J. Rives Childs, *Casanova: A New Perspective* (New York: Paragon House, 1988), 242.
3. Félicien Marceau, *Une Insolente Liberté: Les Aventures de Casanova* (Paris: Gallimard, 1983), 302.
4. Casanova to Maximilien Lamberg, July 28, 1787, *"Mon Cher Casanova": Lettres du Conte Maximilien Lamberg et de Pietro Zaguri à Giacomo Casanova,* ed. Marco Leeflang et al. (Paris: Champion, 2008), 101.
5. Quotations in this section are from *Histoire* 3: 665–826.
6. Marquis de Sade, *Juliette,* trans. Austryn Wainhouse (New York: Grove, 1968), 963, 978.
7. *Casanova,* ed. Giampaolo Zagonel, *Lettere di Lorenzo Da Ponte a Giacomo* (Vittorio Veneto, 1988), 51.
8. Denis Diderot, *Salon de 1767, Oeuvres: Salons* 2 (Paris: Brière, 1821), 2: 34.

CHAPTER 27. TRIESTE, AND VENICE AT LAST

1. Quotations in this chapter are from *Histoire* 3: 853–918.
2. J. Rives Childs, *Casanova: A New Perspective* (New York: Paragon House, 1988), 260.
3. The consul's letter is quoted in the notes to *Histoire* 3: 1136.
4. Chantal Thomas, *Casanova: Un Voyage Libertin* (Paris: Denoël, 1985), 138.
5. *Précis de Ma Vie,* Bouquins (2013) 3: 1199.
6. Shakespeare, *Macbeth* V.iii.
7. Angelo Mainardi, *Casanova: L'Ultimo Mistero* (Rome: Tre Editori, 2010).
8. See Piero Del Negro, "Giacomo Casanova e il Patriziato Venetiano nell' *Histoire de Ma Vie,"* in *L'Histoire de Ma Vie de Giacomo Casanova,* ed. Michele Mari (Milan: Cisalpino, 2008), 29n.
9. *Histoire* 1: 58.
10. Stefan Zweig, *Adepts in Self-Portraiture: Casanova, Stendhal, Tolstoy,* trans. Eden and Cedar Paul (New York: Viking, 1928), 76.
11. The full set of Casanova's reports is collected in Giovanni Comisso, *Agenti Segreti di Venezia* (Milan: Longanesi, 1963).
12. Maxime Rovere, *Casanova* (Paris: Gallimard, 2011), 239; Emilio Ravel, *L'Uomo Che Inventò Se Stesso: Vita e Commedia di Giacomo Casanova* (Rome: La Lepre Edizioni, 2010), 285.
13. Quoted by Rovere, 239.
14. Ian Kelly, *Casanova: Actor Lover Priest Spy* (New York: Tarcher/Penguin, 2008), 327; Sebastiano Vassalli, *Dux: Casanova in Boemia* (Turin: Einaudi, 2002), 9.
15. J. Rives Childs, *Casanova: A New Perspective* (New York: Paragon House, 1988), 274; Bouquins (2013) 3: 1125. The full set of letters was edited by Aldo Ravà and reproduced in a French edition by Édouard Maynial, *Lettres de Femmes à Jacques Casanova* (Paris: Louis-Michaud, 1912).
16. *Histoire* 2: 1069.
17. Ravel, 290.

18. Pietro Chiari, *La Commediante in Fortuna* (1755), quoted by Federico Montecuccoli degli Erri, *Cammei Casanoviani* (Geneva: L'Intermédiare des Casanovistes, 2006), 101–2; Kelly, 330.

19. *Précis de Ma Vie,* 1199.

CHAPTER 28. THE GATHERING GLOOM

1. Casanova to Francesco Lorenzo Morosini, Sept. 22, 1782, *Correspondance Inédit de Jacques Casanova* (Paris: Jean Fort, 1926), 116.

2. Francesca Bruschini to Casanova, July 11, 1783, *Lettres de Femmes à Jacques Casanova,* ed. Aldo Ravà and Édouard Maynial (Paris: Louis-Michaud, 1912), 170.

3. Suzanne Roth, *Les Aventuriers au XVIIIe Siècle* (Paris: Éditions Galilée, 1980), 69.

4. Stefan Zweig, *Adepts in Self-Portraiture: Casanova, Stendhal, Tolstoy,* trans. Eden and Cedar Paul (New York: Viking, 1928), 73.

5. *Essai de Critique sur les Moeurs, sur les Sciences, et sur les Arts,* ed. Gérard Lahouati (Université de Pau, 2001), 27.

6. Propertius, *Elegy* I.xii.11–14, trans. H. E. Butler (Cambridge, MA: Harvard University Press, Loeb Classical Library, 1912), 33.

7. Joseph Le Gras, *Casanova: Adventurer and Lover,* trans. A. Francis Steuart (London: John Lane the Bodley Head, 1923), 100.

8. Details of Casanova's life at Dux are provided by Helmut Watzlawick, "Les Tristesses de Dux: Critique d'un Mythe," in *Giacomo Casanova tra Venezia e l'Europa,* ed. Gilberto Pizzamiglio (Venice: Leo S. Olschki, 2001), 67–77.

9. Waldstein's brother is quoted from the Duchkov archives by Ian Kelly, *Casanova: Actor Lover Priest Spy* (New York: Tarcher/Penguin, 2008), 339.

10. J. Rives Childs, *Casanova: A New Perspective* (New York: Paragon House, 1988), 279; *Histoire* 3: 389.

11. Watzlawick, 73.

12. Aldo Toffoli, preface to *Lettere di Lorenzo Da Ponte a Giacomo Casanova,* ed. Giampaolo Zagonel (Vittorio Veneto, 1988), 8.

13. *"Mon Cher Casanova": Lettres du Conte Maximilien Lamberg et de Pietro Zaguri à Giacomo Casanova,* ed. Marco Leeflang et al. (Paris: Champion, 2008), Oct. 4, 1792, 548.

14. Marcia Davenport, *Mozart* (New York: Avon, 1979, first pub. 1932), 289. On Casanova's off-and-on friendship with Da Ponte, see Rodney Bolt, *Lorenzo da Ponte* (London: Bloomsbury, 2006), esp. 171–74.

15. Julian Rushton, *W. A. Mozart: Don Giovanni* (Cambridge: Cambridge University Press, 1981), 142. On Casanova's draft, see Francis-L. Mars, "Casanova et Don Giovanni," Bouquins (1993), 1152–56.

16. Félicien Marceau, *Casanova, ou l'Anti-Don Juan* (Paris: Gallimard, 1985), 115, 146–57.

17. *Lettere di Lorenzo Da Ponte a Giacomo Casanova,* 47, 44, 47.

18. Da Ponte's letter to Filippo Pananti, Nov. 29, 1828, is quoted by Jean-Claude Hauc, *Miscellanées Casanoviennes* (Paris: Hippocampe Éditions, 2017), 222.

19. For providing a transcript of this letter, I am grateful to Maria Giovanna De Simone of the Wren Library, Trinity College, Cambridge.

20. Letter of 1796, quoted by Angelo Mainardi, *Casanova: L'Ultimo Mistero* (Rome: Tre Editori, 2010), 245.

21. Prince de Ligne, *Mélanges,* in *Histoire* 3: 921–22, 952; Ligne to Casanova, Sept. 25, 1794, *Histoire* 3: 939. Further quotations from Ligne are in this section of the Pléiade *Histoire;* they are also printed in Bouquins (2013) 3: 1211–33.

22. Journal du Comte de Clary [Ligne's grandson], 3: 952.

23. Samuel Johnson, *Rambler* 41 (Aug. 7, 1750).

24. Quoted by Alexandre Stroev, "Les Frères Casanova et le Prince Alexandre Belosselski," in *Casanova Fin de Siècle,* ed. Marie-Françoise Luna (Paris: Honoré Champion, 2002), 64.

25. *"Mon Cher Casanova,"* 185–93.

26. Ibid., 366, 371.

27. *Correspondance avec J. F. Opiz* (Leipzig: Kurt Wolff, 1913), 1: 133–34, 165–66.

28. Ibid., 1: 182.

29. Ibid., 2: 84.

30. *Pages Casanoviennes: La Dernière Amie de Jacques Casanova,* ed. Jean Fort (Paris: Librairie de la Société Casanovienne, 1926), 97.

31. Ibid., 75, 104.

32. Sebastiano Vassalli, *Dux: Casanova in Boemia* (Turin: Einaudi, 2002), 29–30.

33. *Dix-neuf Lettres Adressées à Faulkurcher, Histoire* 3: 963, 971.

34. Quoted by Mainardi, 181.

35. See Vassalli, 53–54, drawing on archival material at Dux (Duchkov); the countess is quoted by Mainardi, 126.

36. Mainardi, 169.

37. *Histoire* 1: 320.

38. Prince de Ligne, *Mélanges, Histoire* 3: 921.

39. Gino Ruozzi, "'Il ne Faut pas Nourrir les Serpents': Fulminanti Illuminazioni di un Moralista Libertino," in *L'Histoire de Ma Vie de Giacomo Casanova,* ed. Michele Mari (Milan: Cisalpino, 2008), 323.

40. *L'Esprit de l'Icosameron,* in a letter to the countess of Lichtenau, Bouquins (1993) 2: 1079, 1088.

41. *Confutation de Deux Articles Diffamatoires,* Bouquins (1993), 2: 1049–76.

42. See Paolo Bernardini and Diego Lucci, "Casanova on Suicide," in *Casanova: Enlightenment Philosopher,* ed. Ivo Cerman et al. (Oxford: Voltaire Foundation, 2016), 135–55. Casanova is quoted in the same book at p. 87.

43. *Essai de Critique sur les Moeurs, sur les Sciences, et sur les Arts,* ed. Gérard Lahouati (Université de Pau, 2001), 66.

44. James Columb O'Reilly, quoted in Bouquins (1993) 1: xvii; Casanova quoted by Mainardi, 207.

45. *Histoire* 3: 128.

46. *Histoire* 2: 411.

47. See Northrop Frye, *The Secular Scripture: A Study of the Structure of Romance* (Cambridge: Harvard University Press, 1976).

48. *The Republic of Plato,* trans. Francis MacDonald Cornford (Oxford: Oxford University Press, 1941), 4–5.
49. Preface to *Lettere di Lorenzo Da Ponte a Giacomo Casanova,* 12.
50. *Correspondance avec J. F. Opiz,* 71; *Histoire* 1: 6; Casanova is quoted by Opitz in a letter to Lamberg, *"Mon Cher Casanova,"* 114.
51. *Histoire* 1: 7.
52. Marie-Françoise Luna, *Casanova Mémorialiste* (Paris: Honoré Champion, 1998), 497.

CHAPTER 29. A PINK LOUIS XV ARMCHAIR

1. Edmund Burke, *Reflections on the Revolution in France,* ed. Conor Cruise O'Brien (London: Penguin, 1969), 342.
2. *Histoire* 3: 120.
3. *Le Peuple Français,* Bouquins (1993), 1: 1368.
4. Lamberg to Casanova, Nov. 7, 1789, *"Mon Cher Casanova": Lettres du Conte Maximilien Lamberg et de Pietro Zaguri à Giacomo Casanova,* ed. Marco Leeflang et al. (Paris: Champion, 2008), 194.
5. Chantal Thomas, *Casanova: Un Voyage Libertin* (Paris: Denoël, 1985), 141–42.
6. See Norbert Jonard, *La Vie Quotidienne à Venise au XVIIIe Siècle* (Paris: Hachette, 1965), 238.
7. *Histoire* 3: 877.
8. Robert Browning, *A Toccata of Galuppi's* (1855), final lines.
9. *"Mon Cher Casanova,"* Oct. 4, 1792, 548.
10. *Boswell on the Grand Tour: Germany and Switzerland, 1764,* ed. Frederick A. Pottle (New York: McGraw-Hill, 1953), 280.
11. *Histoire de Ma Fuite,* Bouquins (2013) 1: 1355; Seneca, *Ad Lucilium,* trans. Richard M. Gummere (Cambridge, MA: Harvard University Press, Loeb Classical Library, 1917), No. 101, par. 11.
12. Casanova to Pietro Zaguri, Dec. 2, 1797, quoted by Angelo Mainardi, *Casanova: L'Ultimo Mistero* (Rome: Tre Editori, 2010), 14.
13. Augustine, *The City of God,* trans. Henry Bettenson (Harmondsworth: Penguin, 1972), XIII.x, 518.
14. Francesco to Giacomo, early 1798, *Pages Casanoviennes: La Dernière Amie de Jacques Casanova,* ed. Jean Fort (Paris: Librairie de la Société Casanovienne, 1926); *Correspondance avec J. F. Opiz* (Leipzig: Kurt Wolff, 1913), 1: 120.
15. *Rêve. Dieu. Moi,* Bouquins (1993) 1: 1278.
16. *Histoire* 2: 809, quoting Horace *Epistles* I.x.
17. *Histoire* 3: 297.
18. Élise de la Recke to Casanova, April 29, 1798, Bouquins (1993) 3: 1159; Casanova's reply is quoted by Alain Jaubert, "Une Horreur Délicieuse," in *Casanova: La Passion de la Liberté,* ed. Marie-Laure Prévost and Chantal Thomas (Paris: Seuil, 2011), 67.
19. Letter to Élise de la Recke, quoted by Emilio Ravel, *L'Uomo Che Inventò Se Stesso: Vita e Commedia di Giacomo Casanova* (Rome: La Lepre Edizioni, 2010), 341–42.
20. Ligne, *Mélanges, Histoire* 3: 936.

21. Mainardi, 276–79.

22. Philippe Sollers, *Casanova the Irresistible,* trans. Armine Kotin Mortimer (Urbana: University of Illinois Press, 2016), 14, 17.

23. *Histoire* 1: xxvii–xxviii.

24. *Histoire* 1: 6.

25. Jean-Jacques Rousseau, *Rêveries du Promeneur Solitaire,* in *Oeuvres Complètes,* ed. Marcel Raymond et al. (Paris: Gallimard, Bibliothèque de la Pléiade, 1959–1995), 1: 1035, 1003.

26. Richard Holmes, *Footsteps: Adventures of a Romantic Biographer* (London: HarperCollins, 2005), 168–69.

Illustration Credits

14. The Palazzo Bragadin. Photo by Angelo Feletto.
15. Windows on the Rio San Lo. Photo by Angelo Feletto.
16. Henriette's Farewell. Bibliothèque Nationale de France.
17. The Tuileries Gardens. *Le Roi et la Famille Royale au Jardin Des Thuileries.* Musée Carnavalet, Paris.
18. Jean-Honoré Fragonard, *L'Allée Ombreuse* (ca. 1773). Petit Palais, Musée des Beaux-Arts de la Ville de Paris.
19. A Murano Convent. *Veduta di S. Mattia di Murano.* The Metropolitan Museum of Art, New York.
20. Andrea del Verrochio, *Bartolomeo Colleoni.* Photo by Leo Damrosch.
21. A Casanova Illustration. *Amours et Aventures de Jacques Casanova de Seingalt* (1885). New York Public Library.
22. An Aretino Illustration. J. J. Coigny, *L'Aretin par Agostino Carracci.* Private Collection. Erich Lessing / Art Resource, New York.
23. The Hall of the Great Council. *Sala del Maggior Consiglio* (1766). Rijksmuseum, Amsterdam.
24. The Dungeons in the Ducal Palace. Photo by Angelo Feletto.
25. Casanova's Escape. *L'Histoire de Ma Fuite des Prisons de la République de Venise, qu'on Appelle les Plombs.* (1787). Houghton Library, Harvard University.
26. The Giants' Staircase, Ducal Palace. Photo by Leo Damrosch.
27. The Piazzetta. Photo by Leo Damrosch.
28. The Giudecca Canal. Photo by Leo Damrosch.
29. Francesco Casanova, *Cavalry Charge.* The Metropolitan Museum of Art, New York.
30. Monastery at Einsiedeln. *Closter Einsiedeln* (1700). Harvard University Map Collection.
31. Jean-Baptiste Michel, *Voltaire, Écrivain et Philosophe.* Musée Carnavalet, Paris.
32. Jean-Jacques Lequeu, *Et Nous Aussi Nous Serons Mères, Car . . .* (1794). Bibliothèque Nationale de France.
33. The La Tronche Estate. Pierre Alexandre Parisot, *Vue du Site de La Tronche.* © Collection Musée Dauphinois, Grenoble—Département de l'Isère.
34. *Joseph Balsamo, dit Alessandro Comte de Cagliostro.* Musée Carnavalet, Paris.
35. *The Count de St. Germain.* The History Collection/Alamy Stock Photo.
36. Teresa Cornelys (formerly Imer). *Teresa Cornelys.* Chronicle/Alamy Stock Photo.
37. Francesco Bartolozzi, *Ticket to the Masqued Ball, New Club, Soho* (1775). Yale Center for British Art, Paul Mellon Collection.
38. The Library at Wolfenbüttel. Olaf Mahlstedt/Alamy Stock Photo.
39. Frederick the Great. The Metropolitan Museum of Art, New York.
40. Catherine the Great. *Catherine II, Impératrice de Russie.* Musée Carnavalet, Paris.
41. Jacob Seydelmann, *Giovanni Giacomo Casanova* (ca. 1795). ©Bildarchiv Foto Marburg / Art Resource, NY.
42. Trieste. Albrecht Carl Seutter, *Prospetto Vero del Porto e della Città di Trieste* (ca. 1755). Harvard University Map Collection.
43. Casanova at 63. Giacomo Casanova, *Icosameron* (Prague, 1787), frontispiece. Houghton Library, Harvard University.
44. Casanova's Central Europe. Map by Bill Nelson.

45. Prince de Ligne. HIP/Art Resource, NY.
46. *Count Maximilien Lamberg.* [Casanova's] *Correspondance avec J. F. Opiz* (Leipzig: Kurt Wolff, 1913).
47. *Johann Ferdinand Opiz.* [Casanova's] *Correspondance avec J. F. Opiz* (Leipzig: Kurt Wolff, 1913).
48. Santa Barbara Chapel, Duchkov. Muzeum města Duchkova.

COLOR PLATES

1. First page of the *Histoire de Ma Vie.* Bibliothèque Nationale de France.
2. Venice from the South. John Bowles, *A Perspective View of Venice.* Yale Center for British Art, Paul Mellon Collection.
3. Arlecchino and Arlecchina. Franz Anton Bustelli, *Harlequin and Harlequina,* Nymphenburg Porcelain Manufactory (1760). The Metropolitan Museum of Art, New York.
4. Gabriele Bella, *The San Samuele Theater.* Fondazione Querini Stampalia, Venice. Bridgeman Images.
5. Carnival Costumes. J. David, *Masques Vénétiens.* New York Public Library.
6. Francesco Guardi, *The Ridotto.* The Picture Art Collection/Alamy Stock Photo.
7. Caravaggio, *The Card Sharps.* Kimbell Art Museum, Fort Worth, Texas.
8. Italy in 1730. Herman Moll, *A New Map of Italy* (1830). Harvard Map Collection, Harvard University.
9. Francesco Guardi, *Venice from the Bacino di San Marco* (ca. 1765–75). The Metropolitan Museum of Art, New York.
10. Domenico Tiepolo, *Il Burchiello.* Kunsthistorisches Museum, Vienna. Heritage Image Partnership Ltd./Alamy Stock Photo.
11. Pierre Hubert Subleyras, *Pope Benedict XIV* (1746). The Metropolitan Museum of Art, New York.
12. Jacopo Amigoni, *Farinelli.* CCo Paris Musées / Musée Carnavalet—Histoire de Paris.
13. Francesco Casanova, *Audience Given to the Count of Saint-Priest by the Grand Vizier Aimali Carac* (1779). Châteaux de Versailles et de Trianon. Erich Lessing / Art Resource, NY.
14. Pietro Longhi, *The Alchemists* (1757). Ca' Rezzonico, Museo del Settecento, Venice. Bridgeman Images.
15. The Palazzo Bragadin. Photo by Angelo Feletto.
16. Francesco Casanova, *Giacomo Casanova.* State Historical Museum, Moscow. Photo ©Fine Art Images/Bridgeman Images.
17. Jean-Honoré Fragonard, *The Happy Accidents of the Swing. Les Hasards Heureux de l'Escarpolette.* Wallace Collection, London. Bridgeman Images.
18. François Boucher, *Madame de Pompadour.* Private Collection. Bridgeman Images.
19. François Boucher, *Reclining Nude (Louise Murphy),* Wallraf Richartz Museum, Cologne. Bridgeman Images.
20. Francesco Guardi, *The Parlor of the San Zaccaria Convent.* Ca' Rezzonico, Museo del Settecento, Venice. Bridgeman Images.
21. Jean-Baptiste Greuze, *Cardinal Bernis.* Private Collection. Bridgeman Images.

22. Henry Robert Morland, *The Fair Nun Unmasked.* Private Collection / © Photo Philip Mould Ltd., London. Bridgeman Images.
23. The Hall of the Great Council. lowefoto/Alamy Stock Photo.
24. Nathaniel Parr, *A View of the Doge's Palace at Venice with the Grand Landing Place Before It.* Yale Center for British Art, Paul Mellon Collection.
25. Jean François de Troy, *The Oyster Lunch.* Musée Condé, Chantilly. Bridgeman Images.
26. Jean-Marc Nattier, *Manon Balletti.* Photo ©Josse. Bridgeman Images.
27. Jean Huber, *Le Lever de Voltaire* (ca. 1772). Musée Carnavalet, Paris.
28. Unknown artist, *King's Square in Soho.* Yale Center for British Art, Paul Mellon Collection.
29. Palace and Gardens of Sans Souci. Photo Nicolas Sapieha. Art Resource New York.
30. Marcello Bacciarelli, *Stanislaw Poniatowski in Coronation Robes.* World History Archive/Alamy Stock Photo.
31. Durs Egg, gunmaker, *Pair of Flintlock Dueling Pistols of George IV, Prince of Wales* (1788). The Metropolitan Museum of Art, New York.
32. Anton Raphael Mengs (or Francesco Narice?), *Giacomo Casanova* (1767–70). Private Collection. Bridgeman Images.
33. Dux (Duchkov) Castle. imageBROKER/Alamy Stock Photo.
34. View of Dux (Duchkov). Muzeum města Duchkova.

Index

Note: Page numbers in italics indicate illustrations.